CONFUCIUS

ANALECTS

CONFUCIUS

ANALECTS

WITH SELECTIONS FROM TRADITIONAL COMMENTARIES

TRANSLATED BY

EDWARD SLINGERLAND

Hackett Publishing Company, Inc.
Indianapolis/Cambridge

20 19 18 17   4 5 6 7 8

For further information, please address
    Hackett Publishing Company, Inc.
    P.O. Box 44937
    Indianapolis, IN 46244-0937

    www.hackettpublishing.com

Cover design by Abigail Coyle
Text design by Jennifer Plumley
Composition by SNP Best-set Typesetter Ltd., Hong Kong

Library of Congress Cataloging-in-Publication Data
Confucius.
        [Lun yu. English]
        Confucius analects / translated by Edward Slingerland.
            p.   cm.
        Includes bibliographical references.
        ISBN 0-87220-636-X—ISBN 0-87220-635-1 (paper)
        I. Slingerland, Edward G. (Edward Gilman)   II. Title.
    PL2478.L8 2003
    181'.112—dc21

                                                        2003047772

ISBN-13: 978-0-87220-636-6 (cloth)
ISBN-13: 978-0-87220-635-9 (pbk.)

TABLE OF CONTENTS

PREFACE

The *Analects* is not a "book" in the sense that most modern Westerners usually understand a book—that is, a coherent argument or story presented by a single author, to be digested alone in the quiet of one's study. It is instead a record—somewhat haphazardly collected and edited together at an unknown point in history—of a dynamic process of teaching, and most likely was only committed to writing many years after the primary touchstone of the process, the Master Confucius, had passed away. It probably represents an attempt by later students and followers to keep alive the memory of his teaching, which had been conveyed both verbally and by personal example. Many, if not most, of the passages are quite cryptic, and this may be at least partially intentional. In 7.16, the Master is reported as saying, "I will not open the door for a mind that is not already striving to understand, nor will I provide words to a tongue that is not already struggling to speak. If I hold up one corner of a problem, and the student cannot come back to me with the other three, I will not attempt to instruct him again." As we see throughout the text, Confucius' comments are often intended to elicit responses from his disciples, which are then corrected or commented upon by the Master. Therefore, these "ordered sayings" of Confucius were originally embedded in a conversational context within which their meaning could be gradually extracted.

By the late fourth century B.C.E., with the Master gone, direct conversation was no longer possible, but this merely forced the dialogue to take a different form. It is at this point that we get the beginning of what came to be an over two thousand year old tradition of commentary on the words of Confucius. The tradition begins with such Warring States texts as the *Mencius*, *Xunzi*, and the *Record of Ritual*, and continues up to the present-day—carried on for most of this time in classical Chinese, branching out into the various vernaculars of East Asian nations in the Chinese cultural sphere, and finally expanding in the 18th century into a wide variety of Indo-European languages. For the most part, this commentarial tradition represents an attempt by later followers or admirers of the Master to find "the other three corners," no longer in dialogue with the Master himself, but rather by embracing extant clues about the Master's possible intention, the views of previous students of the text, and the opinions of contemporaries. For later students of the *Analects*, this written commentarial tradition serves as a proxy for the original conversational environment, providing context, making connections, and teasing out implications.

Since at least the Han Dynasty (202 B.C.E.–220 C.E.), no Chinese student of the text has attempted to approach the *Analects* outside of the context of this written commentarial tradition. Most modern Chinese people, of course, read the text—originally written in classical Chinese, a purely literary language—with a translation into modern Chinese as well as extensive commentaries, but even traditionally educated Chinese conversant with the classical language find it necessary to base their understanding of the text upon the foundation of earlier commentaries. Indeed, the text of the *Analects* itself is arguably so concise as to be incomprehensible without some sort of interpretative apparatus imposed upon it. As John Makeham has noted, "Unless a reader is provided with a commentarial 'context' in which flesh is added to the very spare bones of the text, [the *Analects*] frequently reads as a cryptic mixture of parochial injunctions and snatches of dry conversation. It is the commentaries which bring the text to life and lend it definition" (1997: 261). I have therefore always found it astounding that Western readers of the *Analects* have, for the most part, been left to their own devices in understanding this exceedingly difficult text, being presented with simply the bare, original passages with usually no more than a translator's introduction and occasional textual notes to rely on. Small wonder that so many have come away from the *Analects* with their impression of cryptic, mysterious Eastern "fortune cookie" wisdom reinforced. This, however, is not how the text is read in China, and is not at all how the text itself was originally meant. The passages that make up our received *Analects* were probably originally intended to be recited aloud, with teachers and students together discussing their meaning and subtleties. The commentarial tradition that has accreted around the text merely represents a written substitute for this original verbal interaction.

What this edition attempts to do is give the English-language reader a hint of the richness of this context, a glimpse of the living text in its natural habitat, by presenting it with extensive running commentary. Perhaps the best way to characterize the experience I am trying to create is to imagine reading the *Analects* with a friend by your side who knows classical Chinese, and already has some definite opinions about how to read the text, who then proceeds to skim through vast quantities of commentaries, sub-commentaries, textual notes, and other arcana surrounding the text and occasionally shout out things he or she thinks are helpful or illuminating, as well as providing recommendations for further exploration in the English-language scholarship. Not ideal, of course, but still a far sight better than being set adrift with only a translator's introduction and the text itself, in all its cryptic glory. Of course, that actual situation is usually worse than that, for much of the cryptic quality of the original is already hidden in the translation by virtue of the choices the translator has to make in rendering the passages into intelligible English. As Alice Cheang has noted,

> The first thing to disappear in a translation of the *Analects*—its most distinctive formal characteristic—is the opacity of the text. Much that in the original is dense and abstruse becomes clear, comprehensible, and pellucidly simple. The translator, constrained by the limits of the grammatically feasible, usually has to choose among several interpretations . . . so that most of the latent ambiguity in the original is suppressed in the converted text . . . What has been added is necessary in order to render the words of Confucius intelligible in another language, but the result is a text in which the balance of power is shifted towards the author (in this case the translator) and away from the reader. (Cheang 2000: 568–569).

Another way to describe what I am trying to do, then, is that by providing alternative interpretations of individual passages and identifying where various understandings are coming from, as well as by pointing the reader in the direction of works that contain more detailed discussions of the issues at hand, I am trying to give back at least a measure of this power to the English-language reader. Not *too* much, of course, because a certain measure of control has to be exerted to avoid producing utter nonsense, but something approaching the maximum amount of power someone cut off from the text in its original language can reasonably hope. I myself have ceded a great deal of power to the editor of the four-volume critical edition of the *Analects* which this translation is based, Cheng Shude 程樹德, one of the most important of 20th-century Chinese students of the text. The reader may be reassured to know that, at the very least, the hands holding the hands into which you have put yourself are trustworthy.

ACKNOWLEDGMENTS

The task of translating the primary text of the *Analects* was eased considerably by the labor of previous translators, whose work I have built on, and whose well-turned phrases I have, in many cases, been entirely helpless to improve on. Uffe Bergeton and Ho Su-mei provided invaluable assistance in my translation of traditional commentaries by checking my work, catching many errors and infelicitous translations, and Uffe did much of the initial biographical research for Appendix 4.

Ivan Perkins was a great help in preparing the appendices, and an anonymous reader solicited by Hackett Publishing provided very helpful comments on the Introduction. Daniel Gardner, whom I initially contacted for assistance in solving a Song question of identity, very graciously agreed to read the entire manuscript, and provided extremely useful feedback that has made this a much more readable book. Jennifer Plumley and her production team at Hackett Publishing did a wonderful job of copyediting, helped me to clean up my sometimes turgid prose, and have generally made the publication process smooth and painless, which is by no means the norm in academic publishing. The completion of this work was facilitated by a USC Individual Zumberge Research Grant for the summer of 2002.

My biggest debts, however, are owed to Deborah Wilkes and Joel Sahleen. Deborah, my editor at Hackett Publishing, has been a source of constant encouragement and lucid advice, and has managed to skillfully balance our desire for academic integrity with the demands of common sense. Sensitive to the sometimes rather finicky needs of the author and yet thoroughly professional and efficient, Deborah has been a sheer pleasure to work with, and one could not hope for a better editor. Joel Sahleen, my longtime friend and colleague, generously agreed—despite the demands of new fatherhood and dissertation-writing—to watch my sinological back, commenting extensively on the first draft of this translation and saving me from innumerable embarrassing gaffs and stylistic crimes. I have only explicitly noted Joel's contributions where lack of attribution would constitute egregious intellectual theft, but as a result of his consistent firm guidance—urging me toward clarity of expression, grammatical responsibility, and historical accuracy—his voice in fact permeates this entire translation. In keeping with Confucius' dictum on friendship, Joel would remonstrate with me gently, desisting when I was too stubborn to listen (12.23), and was unable to save me from all of the sinological and stylistic errors no doubt still to be found in this translation. For these, of course, I take full responsibility.

CONVENTIONS

The *pinyin* system of romanization is used throughout. In order to avoid confusion, Chinese words appearing in quotations from Western scholars have also been converted into *pinyin*, with the exception of titles of articles or books.

References to *Analects* passages will be in the form x.x, where the first number refers to the "book" and the second to the passage number within the book.

Due to the fact that this classroom edition is oriented primarily toward readers with little or no knowledge of Chinese, references for traditional Chinese texts cited by Cheng Shude or other commentators are only provided in cases where a complete English translation is easily available. All translations from Chinese are my own unless otherwise indicated.

Traditional Chinese commentators often make direct or oblique references to classical texts, and these I will note with brackets.

To avoid cluttering the text and commentary with Chinese characters, the characters for proper names will be omitted unless immediately relevant, but will be included in the entries in Appendix 3 ("Historical Personages").

The disciples of Confucius are often referred to by a variety of names. Their more formal style-name (*zi* 字) is usually used in third-person narrative, whereas in first person speech or when they are usually addressed by Confucius their personal name (*ming* 名) is generally used. The benefits of reflecting these differences in level of formality in the translation seem to be outweighed by the confusion they will create for the English reader, so throughout the translation I have kept to one form of reference—usually the style-name, but sometimes the full name when the style-name is not used or is only rarely used in the text. I have followed the same practice with other potentially confusing proper names, such as the Shang Dynasty, which is also referred to as the Yin.

In order to avoid confusion, I have adopted nonstandard romanizations of certain proper names:

> Zhow 紂, for the evil last king of Shang, to distinguish him from the Zhou 周 Dynasty;
>
> Qii 杞, for a minor state mentioned in the text, to distinguish it from the much more prominent state of Qi 齊;
>
> Jii 姬, for the Zhou clan name, to distinguish it from the Ji 季 of the Ji Family that ruled the state of Lu in Confucius' time.

I have exclusively used the male third-person pronoun when referring to the Confucian practitioner because, as far as we can tell, the *Analects* was composed by and for men, and the idea that women might have any place in the Confucian worldview—other than as temptations to immorality, or (from the Han

Dynasty on) subsidiary helpmates toward morality—has no place in an account of traditional Confucianism (refer to the commentary to 17.25). I am not at all unsympathetic toward certain modern Western attempts to make Confucianism more gender-neutral, but feel it is a scholarly disservice to obscure the gender attitudes of traditional Confucians.

INTRODUCTION

The *Analects*, or *Lunyu* 論語 (lit. "ordered sayings"), purports to be a record of the teachings of Kongzi 孔子 and his disciples. Kongzi is more commonly known in the West by the latinization "Confucius," bestowed upon him by Jesuit missionaries in the 18th century; his traditional dates are 551–479 B.C.E. The *Analects* has been traditionally viewed as a coherent and accurate record of the teachings of the Master, recorded during his lifetime or perhaps shortly after his death, but this view of the text began to be called into question by the philologists of the Qing Dynasty, and modern textual critics have argued convincingly that the text actually consists of different chronological strata, assembled by an editor or series of editors, probably considerably after the death of Confucius.

The earliest explicit quotation from the *Analects* in another early text is found in the *Record of Ritual*,[1] which most scholars agree is of pre-Han Dynasty provenance. Unattributed quotations of the *Analects* found in other pre-Han texts suggest that something like our received version was circulating during the Warring States period. According to the first discussion of the *Analects* as a text, that of Pan Gu (32–92) in the *History of the Han*, there were three different versions circulating in his day: the Lu 魯 version (of twenty books), the Qi 齊 version (of twenty-two books), and the "Ancient text" (*gu* 古) version (of twenty-one books), the last of which was supposedly found in the walls of Confucius' house, hidden there and therefore saved from the infamous burning of the books carried out by the first emperor of Qin in 213 B.C.E. From the comments of early textual critics we know that these versions—none of which have survived in their entirety—apparently varied not only in number of books, but also in the content of the individual books. In the early Han Dynasty, scholars specialized in mastering any one of the three versions, and the imperial academy instituted by Emperor Wu (r. 141–87 B.C.E.) trained and tested students on all three. This situation began to change during the reign of Chu Yuan (48–44 B.C.E.), who appointed a scholar by the name of Zhang Yu (d. 5 B.C.E.) as tutor to the crown prince. Zhang Yu was trained in both the Lu and Qi *Analects*, and edited them together to create his own eclectic version, since referred to as the Marquis Zhang version. Zhang Yu's student became Emperor Cheng in 32 B.C.E., and Zhang himself was appointed Prime Minister in 25 B.C.E., at which point his eclectic version of the *Analects* began to eclipse the other "original" versions. Another prominent eclectic edition of the text circulating at the time was that of Zheng Xuan (127–200), which consisted of the Lu version amended with

---

[1] Chapter 30 ("Record of the Dykes"); Legge 1967, vol. 2: 290. For brief accounts of traditional texts mentioned in the translation and commentary, the reader is referred to Appendix 5.

textual variants from the Qi and Ancient versions, with Zheng Xuan's commentary appended. Neither the Marquis Zhang nor the Zheng Xuan version survived intact, and what we will be referring to as the "received" version is a doubly eclectic version assembled by He Yan (190–249), which drew on the Marquis Zhang and Zheng Xuan versions.

It is that received version on which this translation is based, although occasional reference will be made to textual variants—points where the Lu, Qi, or Ancient versions differed from the received version—that were recorded by early textual critics and that managed to survive the demise of these original versions. Reference will also be made to textual variations found in various "extant" versions of the text—copies of the text that have survived in stone carvings or handwritten manuscripts, usually in very fragmentary form. Until recently, the earliest of these extant versions was the Xiping stone text, which dates to approximately 178 C.E., but an additional twist was added to *Analects* textual scholarship by the discovery in 1973 of the so-called Dingzhou 定州 version, written on bamboo strips and found in a Han Dynasty tomb that was sealed in 55 B.C.E. The Dingzhou *Analects* appears to be a variant of the Lu version and reflects slightly less than half of the received text. Due to difficulties involved in reconstructing the order of the bamboo strips, which were originally strung together by cords that have long since rotten away, the Dingzhou text was not published until 1997. Although it contains many textual variations from the received text, most of them are not conceptually significant; the few that are will be noted in the translation.

As for the received version of the text, there is no doubt among contemporary scholars that it is a somewhat heterogeneous collection of material from different time periods, although scholars differ in their identification of the different strata, as well as in the significance they attribute to these differences. At one end of the spectrum of opinion are scholars such as D.C. Lau 1979, who—drawing upon the work of the Qing scholar Cui Shu (1740–1816)—separates the book into two strata (the first 15 books and the last 5) of different ages, but treats the work as more or less thematically homogenous. Steven Van Zoeren 1991 represents what was until recently the other end of the spectrum. He uses a form-critical approach to divide the work into four strata—from earliest to latest, the "core books" 3–7, books 1–2 and 8–9, books 10–15, and books 16–20—which he sees as representing not only different time periods, but also substantially different viewpoints. This end of the spectrum has recently been pushed to a new extreme by Brooks and Brooks 1998, who see each individual book as representing a discrete stratum, identify vast numbers of "later interpolations" within each stratum, and claim that the work was composed over a much longer period of time than has been generally accepted—the later strata being put together as late as the third century B.C.E. Brooks and Brooks radically reorganize the structure of the *Analects* and regard it as an extremely heterogeneous collection of different (and in many cases competing) viewpoints. Their view is quite speculative, however, and it is the D.C. Lau-Cui Shu's approach that seems most plausible. Though no doubt representing different time periods and somewhat different concerns, the various strata of the *Analects* display enough consistency in terminological use, conceptual repertoire, and general religious viewpoint to allow us to treat the text as a whole. The probable late date of the last books in the *Analects* (especially books 15–20) should always be kept in mind. Nonetheless, the fact remains that nowhere in the *Analects* do we find even a hint of the sophisticated new conception of the heart-mind (*xin* 心)[2] debates about human nature and inter-school rivalries that so permeate Warring States texts such as the *Mencius, Zhuangzi,* and *Xunzi*. It is highly unlikely that any stratum of the *Analects* was composed after the early fourth century B.C.E., which means that we can safely view the text as a genuine representation of the state of the "School of Confucius" before the innovations of Mencius and Xunzi.

The primary distinguishing characteristic of this edition of the *Analects* is the inclusion of traditional Chinese commentary on the text. For a translator wishing to include such commentary, several approaches are possible. One strategy would be to choose a single traditional commentator—preferably someone widely read and respected—and follow his commentary throughout. This is the explicit approach of William Soothill, and the implicit approach of scholars such as D.C. Lau, who fairly consistently follows Zhu Xi's commentary in his translation, although he rarely mentions Zhu Xi explicitly. The problem with this approach is that it chains us to the interpretative vision of one person, however brilliant or influential, and confines us to their hermeneutic assumptions. In the case of a neo-Confucian commentator, such as Zhu Xi, who read quite a bit of anachronistic Buddhist metaphysics into the *Analects*, this is at times undesirable. I therefore provide a selection of commentaries, in order to afford the reader choices and give a sense of the variety of the commentarial tradition, as well as the sorts of debates that it has engendered. This decision, however, creates the problem of choosing from the hundreds of extant traditional commentaries that fill the 408-volume edition of the *Analects* edited by Yan Lingfeng (Yan Lingfeng et al. 1966). Since scholarship works by building upon the contributions of others, the solution was to confine myself to the commentaries already culled by the eminent 20th century scholar Cheng Shude in his exhaustive, four-volume critical edition of the *Analects* that serves as the standard in the field. Cheng reviewed more than 140 commentaries, as well as references to the *Analects* in other early texts, and his selection seems ideal to me because he also made a conscious effort to include many sides of various debates (although he usually ends up weighing in on one side or the other), as well as unusual or unorthodox readings.

The commentators cited are all listed in Appendix 4, which includes their dates and brief biographical sketches. This is intended to give the reader some impression (however vague) of the interpretative standpoints that might inform their views of the text. The overarching interpretative standpoint adopted in the translation—the standpoint that has determined which commentators will be cited, and when—is that of a modern, historically and philologically responsible

---

[2] For the early Chinese, the *xin* 心 (originally a pictogram of the heart organ) was the seat of both emotions and reason, thus encompassing both "heart" and "mind" in English. Depending upon the context, it will be variously translated below as "heart," "mind" or "heart-mind."

student of the text (whether a Qing Dynasty Chinese philologist or a contemporary Asian or Western scholar), fluent in reading classical Chinese and interested in the thought of "Confucius." This standpoint assumes that the text of the *Analects* is a relatively coherent whole, edited together at one time by an editor or group of editors (the "early Confucian school") in accordance with a vision they had of what their Master, Confucius, was trying to teach. In attempting to understand this vision, modern readers of the text should try to be as historically and philologically responsible as possible—that is, they should avoid imputing to the editor(s) of the text views that would have been unrecognizable to them, and whenever possible should refrain from introducing anachronistic terms or ideas. In practice, this means that our knowledge of late Spring and Autumn and Warring States language usage, society, history, and thought should delimit the parameters of possible interpretations of the text. While this set of assumptions is by no means the only angle from which one might approach the text of the *Analects*, ultimately it seems the most rewarding and historically responsible standpoint for someone interested in understanding the text in something resembling its original religious and cultural milieu.

Pre-Confucian Background

Traditional Chinese historiography presents the Xia Dynasty as the first of the legendary dynasties of the Golden Age, supposedly founded by the legendary sage-king Yu. Yu is also credited with taming the floods of the Yellow River, thereby making what we now think of as north-central China habitable for the Chinese people. The earliest Chinese civilization for which we have archeological and written evidence, however, is the Shang Dynasty (sometimes alternately referred to as the Yin Dynasty), the traditional dates of which are 1751–1122 B.C.E. It is from the Shang that we have the first written records from China, in the form of so-called "oracle bones." These oracle bones are pieces of ox scapula or tortoise shells used in divination. Questions concerning the proper course of action or requests for things such a rain, directed to the spirits of the Shang ancestors, were written upon them, and heat was then applied. The answer from the ancestors—yes, this military campaign will be successful or no, rain will not be forthcoming—were revealed in the resulting pattern of cracks decoded by the diviner, who was often the Shang king himself.

Often the ancestors were asked to intercede with the being who wielded the greatest power of all over the Shang people, the ur-ancestor known as the "Lord on High" (*shangdi* 上帝). The Lord on High seems originally to have been a nonhuman god who gradually came to be viewed as the first human ancestor of the Shang people, and therefore—by virtue of seniority—the most powerful of the ancestor spirits. The Lord on High and the other ancestor spirits of the Shang were viewed as dwelling in a kind of netherworld somewhere above the human realm (hence the Lord "on High"), from which vantage point they continued to monitor the behavior of their descendents, receive sacrificial offerings, hear questions and requests, and control all the phenomena seen as lying beyond human control (weather, health and sickness, success or failure in battle, etc.). Establishing and maintaining a good relationship with these spirits—especially the most powerful of them, the Lord on High—was one of the primary concerns of the Shang ruler. In the oracle bones we find a special term, *de* 德, referring to the power accrued by a ruler who, through timely and appropriate sacrifices, successfully established and preserved such a relationship with the ancestors. We will translate this term as "Virtue,"[3] with the caveat that the reader should keep in mind the original sense of the Latin *virtus*—the particular "power" residing in a person or thing, preserved in modern English in such expressions as, "By virtue of his great intelligence, he was able to solve the problem." Virtue in the early Shang context refers to a kind of attractive, charismatic power residing in a ruler who had won the endorsement of the ancestral spirits. This power could be perceived by others, serving as a visible mark of the spirits' favor, and its attractive qualities allowed the ruler to both win and retain supporters.

Sometime near the end of the second millennium B.C.E., a people known as the Zhou invaded the Shang realm and deposed the last of the Shang kings. The traditional date of the conquest is 1122 B.C.E., but this has been the subject of great dispute and the conquest may in fact have occurred over a period of time rather than in one fell swoop. In any case, what is clear is that the Zhou people were very eager to identify with the religious and political systems of their predecessors. We have much more in the way of written material from the Zhou Dynasty that helps us to understand their religious worldview. The most reliable source is the set of inscriptions that have been found on bronze ritual vessels discovered in tombs, intended as commemorations on the occasion of the making of the vessel, which reveal much about early Zhou history and thought. Less reliable—because subject to scribal changes, both intentional and unintentional—but far more rich in content are the received texts that purport to date from the Zhou Dynasty. The most helpful of these are the *Book of Documents* (*shangshu* 尚書 or *shujing* 書經) and the *Book of Odes* (*shijing* 詩經), the former a collection of historical documents and governmental proclamations supposedly dating back to earliest years of Chinese history, and the latter a collection of folk songs and official state hymns. The current belief in scholarly circles is that at least half of the *Book of Documents* is a fourth century C.E. forgery, whereas much of the *Book of Odes* represents genuinely pre-Confucian material, probably dating between 1000–600 B.C.E.

The traditional account of the Zhou conquest credits King Wu ("The Martial King") with defeating the last of the Shang kings, the infamous Zhow 紂, and posthumously declaring his father to be the first of the Zhou kings, King Wen ("The Cultured King"). When King Wu died, his designated heir, the future King Cheng ("The Perfected King"), was not yet old enough to assume the throne. For the duration of his minority, China was ruled by King Wu's brother,

---

[3] *De* as a particular power derived from Heaven will be translated as "Virtue" in order to distinguish it from "virtue" in a more general sense, although in the *Analects* and later writings it sometimes does possess the latter sense.

the famous Duke of Zhou, a wise and strong regent who promptly ceded his position once King Cheng came of age. This triumvirate who established the early Zhou—King Wen, King Wu, and the Duke of Zhou—became bywords for virtue and wisdom.

The religious worldview of the Zhou borrowed heavily from the dynasty that they replaced. One reflection of the Zhou eagerness to identify with the Shang was their adoption of the Shang high god, the Lord on High, who was conflated with and eventually replaced by their own tribal god, *tian* 天. Early graphic forms of *tian* seem to picture a massive, striding, anthropomorphic figure, who is from the earliest times associated with the sky. Hence "Heaven" is a fairly good rendering of *tian*, as long as the reader keeps in mind that "Heaven" refers to an anthropomorphic figure—someone who can be communicated with, angered, or pleased—rather than a physical place. Heaven possessed all of the powers of the Lord on High and in addition had the ability to charge a human representative on earth with the "Mandate" (*ming* 命) to rule. *Ming* refers literally to a command issued by a political superior to an inferior or a decree issued by a ruler; in a metaphorical and religious sense, it refers to Heaven's command to its proxy on earth, the king, to rule the human world. Just as the Lord on High sent blessings down to those of his descendents who performed the sacrifices correctly, Heaven was believed to grant the Mandate to the ruler who maintained ritual correctness. The *Book of Odes* and *Book of Documents* claim that the Shang lost the Mandate because of gross ritual improprieties and general immorality, which motivated the Lord on High/Heaven to withdraw the Mandate and give it to the Zhou. In this way, the Zhou rulers presented their motivation for conquering the Shang as merely the desire to enact Heaven's will, rather than any selfish desire for power on their part.[4] Similarly, since the holder of the Mandate was believed to also receive Virtue from Heaven as a sign of its favor, early texts present the conquest as relatively effortless—King Wu simply arrived on the battlefield with his troops and the awesome power of his Virtue caused most of the opposing armies to immediately submit to him.[5] This is the origin of two themes in Chinese religious thought that were inherited by Confucius: only someone who is selfless and sincere will receive Virtue from Heaven, and political order is properly brought about only through the charismatic, noncoercive power of Virtue—the need to exert force viewed as evidence that a ruler does not truly enjoy Heaven's favor.

Another important development seen in early Zhou texts is what might be described as the increasingly impartial nature of their supreme deity. The Lord on High was the blood ancestor of the Shang royal line and thus had a special loyalty to the Shang kings. Heaven, on the other hand, is a supreme deity who has chosen to bestow the Mandate upon the Zhou because of their ritual pro-

---

[4] See, for instance, the *Book of Documents*-like fragment reproduced in 20.1, where Tang, mythical founder of the Shang Dynasty, humbly declares to Heaven that his vanquishing of Jie, the evil last king of the Xia, is intended merely as punishment for Jie's transgressions against Heaven's order.

[5] See, for instance, the account of the conquest given in Chapter 31 ("The Successful Completion of the War") of the *Book of Documents* (Legge 1991b: 306–316).

priety. In this case, what has been given can also be taken away. Ancestors still play a crucial role, and the Zhou were eager to claim for their ancestral line the same sort of privileged access to the supreme deity that the Shang line enjoyed, but there is no longer any guarantee that the ancestors can protect their descendents from the wrath of Heaven if they go against its will. This accounts for a constant refrain seen throughout the *Book of Odes* and the *Book of History*: the Zhou kings must be extremely careful about preserving their Virtue, lest they suffer the same fate as the Shang. As in Shang times, the manner in which to assure the favor of the supreme being was through the proper observance of a set of practices collected referred to as "ritual" (*li* 禮), but in the Zhou conception both the scope and nature of ritual practice was understood differently. Shang ritual consisted primarily of sacrificial offerings to the spirits of the ancestors, and the main concern was that the sacrifices were performed properly—that the food and drink offered were of sufficient quality, that the proper words were intoned, etc. By Zhou times, the scope of ritual had grown significantly, encompassing not only sacrificial offerings to the spirits, but also aspects of the Zhou kings' daily lives that we might be tempted to label as "etiquette," the manner in which one dressed, took one's meal, approached one's ministers, etc. In addition, proper performance of ritual duties became more than a matter of simply observing external forms because in order for ritual practice to be acceptable to Heaven, it was necessary that the king perform it with *sincerity*. We thus see in the Zhou beginnings of a concern with internal state of mind—a demand that one's emotions and thoughts match one's external behavior—that becomes a primary theme in the thought of Confucius.

Related to the perceived need for sincerity in ritual practice are the hints in early Zhou texts of a religious ideal that will come to be known as "wu-wei" (*wuwei* 無為). Meaning literally "no-doing" or "non-doing," wu-wei might be best translated as "effortless action," because it refers not to what is or is not being done, but to the *manner* in which something is done. An action is wu-wei if it is spontaneous, unselfconscious, and perfectly efficacious. Wu-wei action represents a perfect harmony between one's inner dispositions and external movements, and is perceived by the subject to be "effortless" and free of strain.

In early Zhou texts, a sort of unselfconscious skill and sincerity is associated with ideal exemplars, both the aristocratic lord or gentleman (*junzi* 君子)—who throughout the *Book of Odes* is described as embodying the martial and social virtues that become his station with an effortless ease—and the more explicitly moral sage-ruler of old, such as Shun or Yao. Throughout early Zhou texts, the effortless moral skill of these aristocratic warriors or virtuous sage-kings is portrayed as a result of a special relationship to Heaven. Virtue is understood in these texts as accruing to those who are ritually correct in an wu-wei fashion—that is, those who accord with Heaven's Mandate in a completely sincere, spontaneous, unselfconscious fashion. Attaining a state of wu-wei harmony with Heaven, they are thus rewarded with a power that not only brings them personal benefit, but that also allows them to more effectively realize Heaven's will in the world. We will see this theme elaborated in the *Analects* where Confucius' wu-wei gentleman combines both the physical mastery of the martial aristocrat in the *Odes*—although his mastery shows itself in ritual performance rather than in war—and the unselfconscious ease and selflessness of the virtuous kings of the Zhou, also sharing with them a special relationship to Heaven.

The Age of Confucius

The Zhou system resembled that of feudal Europe, where the king enjoyed the fealty of the local feudal lords—usually relatives of the royal family or favored retainers—to whom he had granted hereditary fiefdoms. Although these fiefdoms were governed independently, all of the feudal lords were bound to obey the Zhou king in times of war and to submit periodic tribute to the Zhou royal court. The beginning of the decline of the Zhou can be traced to the sack of the Zhou capital in 770 B.C.E. by barbarian tribes allied with rebellious Chinese principalities. The Zhou court was forced to flee and a new capital was established farther east. The movement of the capital marks the beginning of the so-called "Eastern Zhou" period (770–221 B.C.E.), the latter part of which is often subdivided into the "Spring and Autumn" (722–481 B.C.E.) and "Warring States" (403–221 B.C.E.) periods. The Eastern Zhou period was characterized by a gradual decline in the power of the Zhou kings, with local feudal lords and ministers gradually usurping the traditional Zhou kingly prerogatives, and more and more openly running their fiefdoms as independent states. By the time of Confucius' birth in 551 B.C.E., the Zhou kings had been reduced to mere figureheads, and even many of the feudal lords had seen their power usurped by upstart ministers. This was the case in Confucius' native state of Lu 魯, where the authority of the dukes—who could trace their ancestry back to the Duke of Zhou himself—had been usurped by a group of powerful clans, collectively known as the "Three Families": the Ji-sun family, Meng-sun family, and the Shu-sun family.[6]

Not very much is known about the life of Confucius. Most of the traditional details are derived from a biography in the *Record of the Historian*, compiled around 100 B.C.E. by the Grand Historian Sima Qian, much of which clearly consists of legend and literary invention. Some modern scholars have attempted to construct coherent chronologies of Confucius' life from a variety of early sources and to separate potential facts from clear fiction, but so little can be known for sure that it seems best to stick to whatever facts we might glean from the *Analects* itself. Confucius was clearly a native of Lu (18.2), of humble economic background (9.6), and seems to have been a member of the scholar-official (*shi* 土) class, the lowest of the three classes of public office holders.

---

[6]The designation Ji-sun 季孫 (Ji Descendents) was derived from the fact that the ancestor of this family was the *ji* 季 son (youngest son) of Duke Huan of Lu (711–694 B.C.E.), who in 626 B.C.E. granted each of his three sons sizeable, independent domains within the state of Lu. Similarly, the other families that make up the "Three Families"—the "Meng-sun" 孟孫 (Meng descendents) and Shu-sun 叔孫 (Shu descendents)—were descendents of, respectively, the *meng* 孟 son (eldest after the heir) and the *shu* 叔 son (second to youngest) of this Duke, which is why these families are often alternately referred to as the *sanhuan* 三桓, or "Three [Families descended from Duke] Huan."]

Originally referring to an aristocratic warrior, *shi* had, by the time of Confucius, come to refer to a class of people who filled the middle and lower ranks of state governments, primarily in civil posts. Like Confucius, it seems that a subset of these scholar-officials were also *ru* 儒. This term, which later came to mean "Confucian," appears only once in the *Analects* (6.13) and referred in Confucius' time to a class of specialists concerned with transmitting and preserving the traditional rituals and texts of the Zhou Dynasty. Mastery of the Zhou classics and traditional ritual etiquette was a valued skill in public officials and led many aspiring scholar-officials to seek out *ru*-like training for the sake of acquiring public office and—most importantly—the salary and public prestige that went along with it. As we shall see, this was only one of many contemporary phenomena that troubled Confucius, who felt that training in traditional Zhou cultural forms should be pursued as an end in itself.

"Would that I did not have to speak!" Confucius sighs in 17.19. His stubbornly obtuse disciple Zigong is puzzled. "If the Master did not speak," he asks, "then how would we little ones receive guidance?" Confucius' response is brief, poetic and perhaps tinged with a trace of bitterness: "What does Heaven ever say? Yet the four seasons go round and find their impetus there, and the myriad creatures are born from it. What does Heaven ever say?" Heaven governs the natural world in an wu-wei fashion, without having to resort to words. The seasons go round, the myriad creatures are born and grow to maturity, and all these phenomena find their source in Heaven. The counterpart to Heaven in the human world is the sage-king of old, someone like Shun: "Was not Shun one who ruled by means of wu-wei? What did he do? He made himself reverent and took his [ritual] position facing South, that is all" (15.5). In the ideal state of harmony between Heaven and humans that prevailed in ancient times, the ruler had no need to act or to speak. He simply rectified his person and took up the ritual position fitting for a ruler, and the world became ordered of its own accord.

In Confucius' view, this sort of natural, spontaneous, unselfconscious harmony had once prevailed during the reigns of the ancients sage-kings Yao and Shun, as well as during the Golden Age of the "Three Dynasties"—the Xia, the Shang, and the Zhou. This idealized vision of the past serves as Confucius' moral and religious benchmark, which is why he finds the need to "speak"— that is, to teach, cajole, admonish—so distasteful, and is so contemptuous of "glibness" and those who speak too much. The social world should function in the same effortless, wu-wei fashion as the natural world, and Confucius has been summoned to speak, to bring the world back into the state of wordless harmony, only because the Way has been lost in his own age. Confucius' own speech—the "categorized conversations" that constitute the *Analects*—is thus a necessary evil, a wake-up call sent from Heaven to a fallen world. Such is the opinion of the border official of Yi in 3.24, who clearly perceives the sacred nature of Confucius' mission. After being presented to Confucius, he has some comforting and prophetic words for the disciples: "Why should you be concerned about your Master's loss of office? The world has been without the Way for a long time now, and Heaven intends to use your Master like the wooden clapper for a bell."

This mention of "the Way" (*dao* 道) should be noted because Confucius seems to have been the first to use this term in its full metaphysical sense. Referring literally to a physical path or road, *dao* also refers to a "way" of doing things, and in the *Analects* refers to *the* Way—the unique moral path that should be walked by any true human being, endorsed by Heaven and revealed to the early sage-kings. More concretely, this "Way" is manifested in the ritual practices, music, and literature passed down from the Golden Age of the Zhou, which were still preserved in the state of Lu by a few high-minded, uncompromising *ru* (6.13, 19.22).[7] The fact that "the Way of Kings Wen and Wu has not yet fallen to the ground" (19.22) serves for Confucius as a glimmer of hope in an otherwise bleak landscape. He saw his mission to be serving Heaven by helping to reinvigorate this "Way" in his otherwise fallen and corrupt age, and to thereby bring about a restoration of the lost Golden Age—a "second Zhou in the East," as he puts it in 17.5. Below we shall briefly explore the various elements of Confucius' religious vision: his diagnosis of the causes of the fallenness of his age; the path of self-cultivation that he proposes to remedy this state of fallenness; and the characteristics of the ideal state which lies at the end of this path—the state of wu-wei or "effortless action."

Contemplating his own age, Confucius was appalled by the sorry state of his contemporaries. In 8.20, he reflects wistfully upon the relative wealth of talented officials who served the ancient sage-kings Yao and Shun, and notes that this flourishing of Virtue reached its peak in the Zhou Dynasty. Infused with this powerful Virtue, the ritual practice of the Zhou was of the highest efficacy and brought order throughout the world. Asked in 3.11 about the *di* sacrifice—the performance of which was the prerogative of the Zhou kings—Confucius answers: "I do not understand it; one who understood it could handle the world as if he had it right here," pointing to his palm. By his time, however, the performance of the *di*—continued by the nominal successors of the Zhou in his own native state of Lu—had degenerated to the point where Confucius could no longer bear to look upon it (3.10). This degeneration in ritual performance was accompanied by a similar decline in the quality of men participating in public life. After explaining the various grades of worthiness in 13.20, Confucius is asked, "What about the men who are in public service today?" He answers dismissively: "Oh! Those petty functionaries are not even worth considering." Even in their faults and excesses, the men of ancient times were superior to those of Confucius' own day (17.16), and the general state of decline that followed the demise of the Zhou is summed up by the disciple Master Zeng in 19.19: "For a

---

[7] One might wonder why Confucius so venerated the culture of the Zhou, and not that of the even more ancient Shang or Xia. In 3.14, Confucius suggests that the Zhou represents the culmination of ancient culture, combining the best features of the cultures that preceded it: "The Zhou gazes down upon the two dynasties that preceded it. How brilliant in culture it is! I follow the Zhou" (cf. 8.20). He also, however, seemed to have a more pragmatic rationale: there simply was not very much extant information about the cultures of the Shang or the Xia that one could follow (3.9), whereas the great advantage of the state of Lu was that, as the fiefdom of the descendents of the Duke of Zhou, it preserved Zhou culture more or less intact (commentary to 3.17, 6.24).

long time those above have lost the Way and the common people have therefore become confused."

What, in Confucius' view, are the causes of this degeneration? It would seem
that two factors can be distinguished. The first is the panoply of basic human
weaknesses: lust, greed, sloth, etc. These seem to be barriers that all people aspiring to the moral life must learn to overcome. The second factor—of relatively
more timely concern to Confucius—is the quality of the tradition into which
one is acculturated. This tradition is the system of ritual practice, music, and language use that, in Confucius' opinion, plays a primary role in shaping human
character. It is clear that by the time of Confucius the Zhou ritual tradition had
been severely corrupted, and that this corrupted tradition was in turn responsible for leading the vast majority of people astray. What *caused* the Zhou tradition to decline is never adequately explained in the *Analects*, but it is quite clear
that natural weaknesses of human beings are only magnified under the rule of
a corrupted tradition, making the re-establishment of harmony between humans
and the cosmos difficult indeed. In his only recorded comment on human nature
in the *Analects*, Confucius seems to emphasize the importance of the practice
of traditional forms over that of inborn human nature: "By nature people are
similar; they diverge as the result of practice" (17.2). The view that prevails in
the *Analects* seems to be that the imperfections inherent in human beings are
not too great a problem for a tradition in good order—one which has the
resources to trim, guide and reform one's raw nature in such a way that a state
of harmony between both the individual and society and the social order and
the cosmos can be attained. The Way of the Zhou in its heyday was such a tradition. It is only in the absence of such a tradition—or in the presence of a
corrupted or decadent tradition—that these unsavory qualities of human nature
are allowed to run amok.

Such a situation of moral chaos is what Confucius saw around him in a society
that had lost the true Way because of its obsession with externalities (5.27, 14.24).
In ancient times, people focused on the internal goods of the Confucian practice,[8] such as their own moral qualities, their level of self-cultivation, and their
love for the Way. Although Confucius believed that such devotion to the Way
of Heaven would ideally result in external rewards—good reputation, social
honor, wealth, etc.—the correlation was not perfect. The actions of the Heaven
are mysterious, and inner Virtue is not always immediately rewarded with external goods, which means that the true servant of Heaven should focus solely upon
his Virtue and leave its recompense to fate (4.9, 4.14, 4.16, 11.18, 12.4–12.5,
14.36, 15.32). The problem with his contemporary world, in Confucius' view, is
that it has lost sight of the goods internal to Confucian moral self-cultivation.

---

[8]The use of the terms "internal" and "external" to categorize goods begins in the commentarial
tradition with Mencius, for whom "internal" goods are the Confucian virtues, which have moral
value and can be sought after and attained through human effort, as opposed to "external" goods
(such as wealth, fame, or longevity) that have no moral value, and the attainment of which is ultimately outside of human control (see especially *Mencius* 7:A:3).

People of his day mechanically fulfill the outward forms of the rites and engage in study as if they were true seekers after the Way, but their activities amount to nothing more than empty show. Even the most intimate and personally significant of the rites—one's filial duties toward one's parents—have in Confucius' view been rendered hollow and meaningless: "These days 'filial' means simply being able to provide one's parents with nourishment. But even dogs and horses are provided with nourishment. If you are not respectful, wherein lies the difference?" (2.7).

For Confucius, the emptiness and superficiality of his age is personified in the figure of the "village worthy" (*xiangyuan* 鄉愿), who carefully observes all of the outward practices dictated by convention, and in this way attains a measure of social respect and material comfort, but who lacks the inward commitment to the Way that characterizes the true Confucian gentleman. Confucius refers to the village worthy as the "thief of Virtue" (17.13), for from the outside he *seems* to be a gentleman and so lays a false claim to virtue. This is no doubt the sentiment informing 17.18: "I hate it that purple is usurping the place of vermilion, that the tunes of Zheng are being confused with classical music, and that the clever of tongue are undermining both state and clan." Just as the debased people of his time use the mixed color of purple in place of pure vermilion and confuse the decadent music of Zheng with true music, they mistake village worthies and "clever talkers" for true gentlemen. The prevalence of these counterfeiters of virtue and the popularity of decadent music are not the only signs of the fallenness of Confucius' age. The most prominent and egregious reflection of the sorry state of his contemporaries is the corruption of ritual practice among the political and social elite. It has already been noted that in Confucius' native state of Lu, the practice of the *di* sacrifice had degenerated to the point that Confucius could not bear to look on it. Similarly, the overweening pride of the Three Families who ruled Lu in Confucius' time caused them to usurp the ritual privileges properly accorded only to the Zhou kings—a transgression against the very structure of the cosmos that appalled and saddened Confucius (3.1–3.2, 3.6).

Confucius himself probably never held anything more than minor posts in his lifetime, failing to realize his ambition of being employed at a high level, under a virtuous ruler, so that he could put his vision into practice. He did, however, gather around himself a fairly sizeable group of disciples, some of whom managed to obtain high governmental posts after the Master's death. His vision was picked up by two prominent Warring States followers, Mencius and Xunzi, the latter of whom was an extremely influential intellectual and teacher of Hanfeizi and Li Si, the two Legalists thinkers who helped the first Emperor of Qin unify China in 221 B.C.E. The Qin finally put an end to the Zhou Dynasty once and for all, and laid the groundwork for two thousand years of Chinese imperial rule by, for the first time, unifying China under a single, centrally-administered government. It was not until well into the Han Dynasty, however, that Confucius was finally officially recognized as a great sage by the rulers of China, at which time the book that purports to be the record of his teachings, the *Analects*, became required reading for any educated Chinese person. Although Confucianism was eclipsed during the Sui and Tang Dynasties by Buddhism, it continued during this period to exert a powerful influence on the Chinese mind, and it was officially revived in the Song Dynasty by the so-called "neo-Confucian" school. During the Ming Dynasty the so-called "Four Books" assembled by Zhu Xi (1130–1200) as the core of Confucian teachings—the *Analects* and the *Mencius*, along with two chapters from the *Record of Ritual* called the "Great Learning" and the "Doctrine of the Mean," all accompanied by Zhu Xi's commentary—became the basis of China's civil service examination, and were therefore memorized by every educated Chinese person from 1313 until the last nationwide exam in 1910. Similar national exams in Korea, Japan, and Vietnam assured the hold of the *Analects* on the minds of the educated classes in those nations as well. Therefore, although the Master had little influence during his own lifetime, the cultural legacy he left to East Asia is difficult to overestimate. As Simon Leys has observed, "no book in the entire history of the world has exerted, over a longer period of time, a greater influence on a larger number of people than this slim little volume" (1997: xvi).

Hopefully the background information provided above and the commentary provided in the translation that follows will give the reader some sense of *why* the *Analects* has been so influential, and allow her to see the text as more than merely a historical curiosity or collection of quaint homilies, but as an expression of a powerful religious and moral vision—one still capable of both speaking to and instructing us today.

Note to Readers

This edition is designed primarily for nonspecialists. Scholarly notes, including technical textual notes, references to the secondary literature, and an extensive annotated bibliography on Analects scholarship are available online at www.hackettpublishing.com.

TRADITIONAL CHRONOLOGY

To give the reader some orientation, below is a list of the traditional dates of major figures (some of the earliest of whom are no doubt legendary) and a rough chronology of early Chinese history.

Sage-king Yao 堯 r. 2357 B.C.E.–2257 B.C.E.

Sage-king Shun 舜 r. 2255 B.C.E.–2205 B.C.E.

Hou Ji 后稷 ("Lord Millet"). Supposedly Minister of Agriculture under Shun, progenitor of what became the Zhou royal line.

Xia 夏 Dynasty 2205–1766 B.C.E.
There is, as yet, no archeological evidence for the existence of this dynasty.

Sage-king Yu 禹 2205–2197 B.C.E. Supposed founder of the Xia, also credited with taming the floods of the Yellow River, thereby making what we now think of as north-central China habitable for the Chinese people.

King Jie 桀. 1818–1766 B.C.E. Evil tyrant, last of the Xia rulers.

Shang 商 Dynasty 1751–1122 B.C.E.
Alternately referred to as the Yin 殷 Dynasty, source of the first written records from China, in the form of so-called "oracle bones, and also amply attested to in the archeological record.

King Tang 湯 1766–1753 B.C.E. Defeated the evil Jie to found the Shang Dynasty.

King Zhow 紂 1154–1122 B.C.E. Evil last king of the Shang, infamous tyrant.

(Western) Zhou 周 Dynasty 1122 B.C.E.–770 B.C.E.
The Golden Age of China, in the view of Confucius.

King Wen 文 ("The Cultured King"). Remained loyal to the evil King Zhow, last ruler of the Shang Dynasty, hoping to reform him through virtuous example.

King Wu 武 ("The Martial King") r. 1122–1115 B.C.E. Son of King Wen, militarily defeated the evil Zhow, who showed himself incapable of reform, to found the Zhou Dynasty.

Duke of Zhou 周公. Brother of King Wu, who, after King Wu's death, served as regent for Wu's son, the future King Cheng, until the son was old enough to take office.

(Eastern) Zhou Dynasty 770 B.C.E.–221 B.C.E.

A period of decline following the sacking of the Zhou capital. Usually subdivided into two periods:

Spring and Autumn Period 722–481 B.C.E.

The period covered by the court history of the state of Lu, the *Annals* (*chunqiu* 春秋; lit. "Spring and Autumn").

Confucius 551–479 B.C.E.

Warring States Period 403–221 B.C.E.

This period begins when the Zhou kings officially recognize the partitioning of the state of Jin 晉, which inspires the rulers of former vassal state of the Zhou to assert increasing levels of autonomy, eventually usurping the title of "king" for themselves. Time of intense inter-state warfare, social chaos, and intellectual innovation.

Laozi (legendary figure, but text bearing name composed in latter part of 5th c. B.C.E.)

Mozi c. 480–390 B.C.E.

Mencius 4th c. B.C.E.

Zhuangzi 4th c. B.C.E.

Xunzi fl. 298–238 B.C.E.

Hanfeizi c. 280–233 B.C.E.

Qin 秦 Dynasty (221–206 B.C.E.)

Founded by the self-declared First Emperor of Qin (*qinshi huangdi* 秦始皇帝) along Legalist lines, this marks the real beginning of China's imperial period, the first time it was unified under a central government. Great Wall constructed, monetary system, weights and measures, and writing system standardized. Origin of the word "China" ("Qin" is pronounced with an initial "ch" sound) in Western languages.

Former Han 漢 Dynasty (206 B.C.E.–9)

After a brief power struggle, the Han Dynasty is founded in 206 B.C.E. By the first century B.C.E., a syncretic form of Confucianism becomes the state religion, and Confucian classics are made basis of a nationwide civil service examination.

Later Han (25–220)

Buddhism introduced to China, Han imperial power begins to degenerate.

Three Kingdoms Period (220–280)

China divided in three kingdoms, each struggling for dominance.

Jin Dynasty 晉 (266–316)

China briefly united under weak central government.

Northern and Southern Dynasties Period (316–589)

China divided along north-south lines (demarcated by the Yangzi River), and ruled by a series of short-lived dynasties. Buddhism grows in importance in Chinese religious and political life.

Sui 隋 (581–618)

China once again unified; various forms of Buddhism, Daoism, and Confucianism all enjoy offical patronage.

Tang 唐 (618–907)

Although Buddhism is dominant religion in China, near end of the dynasty Confucianism begins to grow in importance as a revived civil service examination system grows in importance.

Song 宋 (906–1279)

The so-called "neo-Confucian" movement successfully puts Confucianism back at the center of elite Chinese cultural and religious life. Although it sees itself as merely a reestablishment of the thought of Confucius and Mencius, neo-Confucianism in fact incorporates a great deal of Buddhist metaphysics and other nonclassical Confucian influences.

Yuan 元 (1279–1368)

China is ruled by a series of Mongol rulers, who gradually become sinified.

Ming 明 (1368–1644)

Reestablishment of "native" Chinese rule.

Qing Dynasty 清 (1644–1912)

China again conquered by northern "barbarians," the Manchus, who also quickly adopt Chinese culture and Confucianism. Civil service examination system finally abolished in 1905.

BOOK ONE

One of the central themes of this Book is that learning (xue 學) *has more to do with actual behavior than academic theory, and that virtuous public behavior as an adult is rooted in such basic familial virtues as filial piety* (xiao 孝) *and respect for elders* (ti 弟) *(lit. "being a good younger brother").*[1]

1.1 The Master said, "To learn and then have occasion to practice what you have learned—is this not satisfying? To have friends arrive from afar—is this not a joy? To be patient even when others do not understand—is this not the mark of the gentleman?"

As Cheng Shude (following Mao Qiling) notes, "People today think of 'learning' as the pursuit of knowledge, whereas the ancients thought of 'learning' as cultivating the self." For evidence, he points to 6.3, where Confucius cites Yan Hui as the only one of his disciples that truly loved learning because he "never misdirected his anger and never repeated a mistake twice," and 2.18, where learning is described in terms of seldom erring in one's speech and seldom having cause for regret in one's behavior. This is an important point: we will see throughout the text that the sort of learning Confucius is interested in is a practical kind of "know-how" rather than abstract theoretical knowledge (see 1.7). Li Chong explains that the three activities mentioned in 1.1 refer to the stages of learning: mastering the basics, discussing them with fellow students and working hard at mastering them, and finally becoming a teacher of others.

1.2 Master You said, "A young person who is filial and respectful of his elders rarely becomes the kind of person who is inclined to defy his superiors, and there has never been a case of one who is disinclined to defy his superiors stirring up rebellion.

"The gentleman applies himself to the roots. 'Once the roots are firmly established, the Way will grow.' Might we not say that filial piety and respect for elders constitute the root of Goodness?"

The line enclosed in quotation marks is probably a traditional saying. A comment upon this passage found in the *Garden of Persuasions* reads, "If the roots are not straight then the branches will necessarily be crooked, and if the beginning does not flourish then the end will necessarily wither. An ode says, 'The highlands and lowlands have been pacified/ The springs and streams have been made clear/ Once the roots are firmly established, the Way will grow.'" The quoted ode is a variant of the extant Ode

---

[1] Although the literal meaning of the term is something like "being a good younger brother," *ti* often refers more generally to showing respect and being obedient to one's elders, and the more general rendering will be used throughout to maintain consistency.

227. We see from the common Confucian theme that political order grows naturally out of the moral character formed within the context of family life. As Chen Tianxiang notes, we find a similar theme in *Mencius* 4:A:11: "If everyone simply loved their parents and respected their elders, the world would be at peace."

1.3 The Master said, "A clever tongue and fine appearance are rarely signs of Goodness."

This suspicion of glib speech and superficial appearance is found throughout the *Analects*. This saying is repeated in 17.7 below (cf. 5.5, 11.25, 12.3, 16.4), and in 15.11 the danger presented by "glib people" (*ningren* 佞人) is compared to the derangement of morals brought about by the music of Zheng. David Nivison (1999: 751) has made a very interesting observation that may explain Confucius' hatred for these clever, ingratiating people: in archaic Chinese, *ning* was pronounced **nieng*[2] and is actually a graphic modification of its cognate *ren* 仁 (AC **nien*). The original meaning of *ren* was something like "noble in form," and it would appear that *ning* was its counterpart in the verbal realm: "attractive or noble in speech." In giving *ning* a negative meaning in the *Analects*, Confucius drives a wedge between the two qualities: *ren* now becomes "true" (i.e., inner) nobleness or Virtue, whereas *ning* represents the false, external counterfeit of *ren*. This is no doubt the sentiment behind such passages as 12.3, "The Good person is sparing of speech," and 13.27, "reticence is close to Goodness," as well as Confucius' general suspicion of language and outward show.

1.4 Master Zeng said, "Every day I examine myself on three counts: in my dealings with others, have I in any way failed to be dutiful? In my interactions with friends and associates, have I in any way failed to be trustworthy? Finally, have I in any way failed to repeatedly put into practice what I teach?"

Here again we find the emphasis on practice—actual social behavior—as opposed to academic, theoretical knowledge. The sort of incessant self-examination practiced by Master Zeng no doubt informs his observation in 8.7 that "the burden is heavy and the Way is long." For the importance of introspection, cf. 5.27.

1.5 The Master said, "To guide a state of one thousand chariots, be respectful in your handing of affairs and display trustworthiness; be frugal in your expenditures and cherish others; and employ the common people only at the proper times."

A great deal of commentarial ink has been spilled over the question of exactly how large a state of one thousand chariots is, but for our purposes, it suffices to note that it is not small. Employing the common people refers to the use of peasant farmers in public work projects, which should be timed so as to not interfere with their agricultural activities. Early texts suggest that the levy should not exceed three days in a year. As Brooks and

---

[2] Generally the modern Mandarin pronunciation of Chinese characters will be given, the Mandarin dialect being the standard form of modern spoken Chinese. When relevant, however, the postulated archaic pronunciation—reconstructed indirectly by historians of phonetics, and denoted with an asterisks—will also be provided.

Brooks note, "The description does not imply a minister 'leading' [a] state, but a middle administrator: dutiful toward his superiors, thoughtful of his junior colleagues, and appropriate in his demands on the subject population" (1998: 170).

1.6 The Master said, "A young person should be filial when at home and respectful of his elders when in public. Conscientious and trustworthy, he should display a general care for the masses but feel a particular affection for those who are Good. If he has any strength left over after manifesting these virtues in practice, let him devote it to learning the cultural arts (*wen* 文)."

There is some debate about how to understand the term *wen* ("writing," "culture") here, but it most likely refers to a set of cultural practices such as those later formalized as the so-called "six arts" of ritual, music, archery, charioteering, calligraphy, and mathematics in which any cultured person was trained (see 7.6). Liu Baonan notes that the purpose of this passage is to emphasize that "manifesting filial piety and respect for elders in one's behavior is the primary concern, while the study of the cultural arts is secondary"; as Yin Tun puts it, "Virtuous behavior is the root, while the cultural arts are the branches; only by exhausting both root and branches, and knowing which is primary and which secondary, can one enter into virtue." This theme is reinforced in 1.7 below.

1.7 Zixia said, "Imagine someone who recognizes and admires worthiness and therefore changes his lustful nature, who is able to fully exhaust his strength in serving his parents and extend himself to the utmost in serving his lord, and who is trustworthy in speech when interacting with friends and associates. Even if you said of such a person, 'Oh, but he is not learned (*xue*),' I would still insist that it is precisely such qualities that make one worthy of being called 'learned.'"

Many commentators believe the first line to be a reference to proper relations between the sexes, which makes the four qualities mentioned map nicely to the "four great human relationships": husband-wife, child-parent, minister-lord, and friend-friend. As You Zuo explains, "During the Three Dynasties, 'learning' had solely to do with illuminating human relations. One able to master the four relationships (mentioned in this passage) can be said to have a deep understanding of human relations. In learning this as the Way, can anything be added to it? Zixia was famous for his culture and learning, so to have him speaking like this gives us a good sense of what the ancients meant when they spoke of 'learning.'" Alternately, *yise* 易色 (rendered above as "changing one's lustful nature") could also be understood as "thinking lightly of sex/physical appearance."

1.8 The Master said, "If a gentleman is not serious, he will not inspire awe, and what he learns will be grasped only superficially.

Let your actions be governed by dutifulness and trustworthiness, and do not accept as a friend one who is not your equal. If you have committed a transgression, do not be afraid to change your ways."[3]

---

[3] The second paragraph is repeated in 9.25.

"Seriousness" (*zhong* 重; lit. "heaviness") seems here to refer to a kind of genuine emotional commitment to the Confucian Way. Kong Anguo reports the opinion that "what this means is that if one is not able to be sincere and serious, one will lack a demeanor that would inspire respect in others, and will also be unable to firmly grasp the underlying ethical principles of what one is taught." In the second half, we see again the emphasis upon improving one's actual behavior in one's interactions with others. The sentiment that one should not accept a friend who is not one's equal might seem a bit puzzling (or even offensive) to someone not acquainted with the idea of "character-friendship" in the Aristotelian sense, but what Confucius means by a "friend" (*you* 友) here is a person who shares one's moral aspirations (cf. 9.30, 16.4, 16.5). One is to compare oneself with other people in general in order to evaluate one's moral progress (4.17, 7.22, 16.11), but the fellowship provided by a friend in virtue combines a powerful spur to further moral development with a deeply felt solidarity of purpose—an important solace during the long and arduous process of self-cultivation. As Confucius explains in 15.10, the practice of Goodness is like learning a craft, and one "sharpens one's tools" by seeking out the company of like-minded souls. Similarly, a true friend in virtue serves as a support and comfort—the gentleman "relies upon his friends for support in becoming Good" (12.24).

1.9 Master Zeng said, "Take great care in seeing off the deceased and sedulously maintain the sacrifices to your distant ancestors, and the common people will sincerely return to Virtue."

The target audience for this saying seems to be rulers or potential rulers, the message being that the key to ordering the state is paying attention to one's own behavior (a theme often repeated in Books Twelve and Thirteen below). As Cheng Shude observes,

> By the time of the Spring and Autumn Period, education in ritual had sadly declined, and cruelty to one's parents had become prevalent among the common people. Therefore, Master Zeng rebuked those in power by noting that if they would merely take care in seeing off their deceased and sedulously maintain the sacrifices to their distant ancestors, the common people would naturally become aware of their own meanness and be moved to return to kindness. As the *Record of Ritual* says, "Cultivate the ancestral temples, respectfully perform the ancestral sacrifices, and thereby teach the common people to maintain filial piety."[4]

1.10 Ziqin asked Zigong, "When our Master arrives in a state, he invariably finds out about its government. Does he actively seek out this information? Surely it is not simply offered to him!"

Zigong answered, "Our Master obtains it through being courteous, refined, respectful, restrained and deferential. The Master's way of seeking it is entirely different from other people's way of seeking it, is it not?"

Huang Kan believes the point of this passage to be that the quality of rulership in a state is revealed in the sentiment of the common people, to which Confucius was particularly sensitive because of his virtuous nature. Rulers thus "give away" this

---

[4] From Chapter 27, the "Record of the Dykes"; Legge 1967, vol. 2: 291.

information inadvertently to one as attuned as Confucius, who therefore does not have to make inquiries in the ordinary fashion. Zhu Xi believes that it is the rulers who, drawn by the power of the Master's virtue, actively seek Confucius out to discuss the problems of governance. In any case, the point seems to be that Confucius "sought it in himself, not in others" (15.21), or that (as Lu Longqi puts it) "the sage seeks things by means of virtue, unlike ordinary people who seek things with their minds." That is, while ordinary people consciously and deliberately pursue external goals, the sage focuses his attention upon his own inner virtue and allows external things to come to him naturally. Confucius does not actively pry or seek out information, but is so perfected in virtue that what he seeks comes to him unbidden, in a wu-wei fashion.

1.11 The Master said, "When someone's father is still alive, observe his intentions; after his father has passed away, observe his conduct. If for three years he does not alter the ways of his father, he may be called a filial son."

Three years (usually understood as into the third year, or twenty five months) is the standard mourning period for a parent. As Kong Anguo explains, "When his father is still alive, the son is not able to act as he wants [because he must obey the father's commands], so one can only observe his intentions in order to judge his character. It is only once his father has passed away that the son can learn about his character by observing his own actions. As long as the filial son is in mourning, his sorrow and longing is such that it is as if the father were still present, and this is why he does not alter the ways of his father." Yin Tun clarifies, "If the ways of his father are in accordance with the Way, it would be perfectly acceptable to go his entire life without changing them. If they are not in accordance with the Way, though, why does he wait three years to change them? Even in the latter case, the filial son goes three years without making any changes because his heart is blocked by a certain reluctance." In this passage, we see hints of the priority given to familial affection and loyalty over considerations of what is more abstractly "right" that is expressed more starkly in 13.18.

1.12 Master You said, "When it comes to the practice of ritual, it is harmonious ease (*he* 和) that is to be valued. It is precisely such harmony that makes the Way of the Former Kings so beautiful. If you merely stick rigidly to ritual in all matters, great and small, there will remain that which you cannot accomplish. Yet if you know enough to value harmonious ease but try to attain it without being regulated by the rites, this will not work either."

What it means to practice ritual with "harmonious ease" (i.e., in an wu-wei fashion) is illustrated in the description of Confucius' ritual behavior in Book Ten. Ritual behavior must be accompanied by such easy joy and harmony if it is to be truly valued. On the other hand, such "ease" involves more than simply indulging one's innate emotions: the innate emotions must be properly shaped by ritual forms before they can become truly "harmonious." The message here is related to the theme of possessing both "native substance" (*zhi* 質) and "cultural refinement" (*wen* 文) in their proper balance (cf. 3.8, 6.18).

1.13 Master You said, "Trustworthiness comes close to rightness, in that your word can be counted upon. Reverence comes close to ritual propriety, in that it allows you to keep shame and public disgrace at a distance. Simply following these virtues, never letting them out of your sight—one cannot deny that this is worthy of respect."

> Described here are secondary virtues that allow one to live a respectable life, but that lack the flexibility and subtlety of the primary virtues. In explaining why trustworthiness (*xin*) is only "close" to rightness, Liu Baonan cites *Mencius* 4:B:11 "The great person is not always necessarily true to his word (*xin*), because he is concerned only with rightness," explaining that "trustworthiness must always be practiced with an eye toward what is right." Huang Kan illustrates the potential tension between trustworthiness and rightness with the story of the legendary paragon of trustworthiness, Wei Sheng, who once promised to meet a girl under a river bridge, come hell or high water. Unfortunately there was a great storm the next day, and the high water did come: the girl stayed at home, but Wei Sheng obstinately refused to abandon the appointed meeting place and so was drowned. "This is an example of trustworthiness not according with what is appropriate to the situation (*yi* 宜), where in fact it would be best if one did not keep one's word," Huang Kan concludes. Similarly, the feeling of reverence—although the root of ritual propriety—can in its raw form motivate actions that do not accord with the subtly-tuned dictates of ritual propriety.

1.14 The Master said, "The gentleman is not motivated by the desire for a full belly or a comfortable abode. He is simply scrupulous in behavior and careful in speech, drawing near to those who possess the Way in order to be set straight by them. Surely this and nothing else is what it means to love learning."

> We see here the first expression of a theme that will be repeated throughout the *Analects* (cf. 4.16, 7.12, 8.12, 14.1, 14.24, 15.32): the true lover of the Way is not concerned with externalities such as fine, abundant food or other material comforts. The general theme of Book One—that learning pertains to one's actual deportment rather than to theoretical knowledge—is also reinforced. As Wang Shu comments: "The primary focus of students in ancient times was to cultivate themselves by being meticulous in speech and careful in action, rather than merely memorizing, reciting, and composing texts . . . Students nowadays, on the other hand, devote themselves exclusively to memorizing, reciting, and composing texts with the sole purpose of passing the civil service exams and obtaining official positions. Very few of them ever get around to paying careful attention to their actual behavior or speech. Perhaps this is why they pale in comparison to the ancients." For the importance of being careful with regard to one's speech, cf. 2.13, 4.22, 4.24, 12.3, 14.20, and 14.27.

1.15 Zigong said, "Poor without being obsequious, rich without being arrogant—what would you say about someone like that?"

The Master answered, "That is acceptable, but it is still not as good as being poor and yet joyful, rich and yet loving ritual."

Zigong said, "An ode says,

> 'As if cut, as if polished;
> As if carved, as if ground.'

Is this not what you have in mind?"

The Master said, "Zigong, you are precisely the kind of person with whom one can begin to discuss the *Odes*. Informed as to what has gone before, you know what is to come."

"Cutting and polishing" refer to the working of bone and ivory, while "carving and grinding" refer to jade work: cutting and carving being the initial rough stages, and polishing and grinding the finishing touches. Here the task of self-cultivation is understood metaphorically in terms of the arduous process of roughly shaping and then laboriously finishing recalcitrant materials. Zigong's quotation of this ode shows that he has instantly grasped Confucius' point, explained quite nicely by Zhu Xi:

> Ordinary people become mired in poverty or wealth, not knowing how to be self-possessed in such circumstances, necessarily leading to the two faults of obsequiousness or arrogance. A person who is able to be free of both knows how to be self-possessed, but has still not reached the point of completely transcending poverty and wealth . . . When a person is joyful he is relaxed in his mind and physically at ease, and therefore forgets about poverty; when he loves ritual, he is at peace wherever he goes and follows principles in a cheerful, good-natured fashion, being equally unconscious of wealth. Zigong was a businessman, probably starting out poor and then becoming rich, and therefore had to exert effort to remain self-possessed. This is why he asked this particular question. The Master's answer was probably intended to acknowledge what Zigong had already achieved while at the same time encouraging him to continue striving after that which he had yet to attain.

Zhu Xi also notes that Zigong's quotation reveals not only that he has grasped Confucius' specific point—that he, Zigong, still has quite a bit of "finishing" work to do—but also serves as a general statement of the Confucian view of self-cultivation: that one "should not be so satisfied with small achievements that one fails to urge oneself on" (5.8). This instant grasping of the larger point to be taught is an excellent example of a student "being given three corners of a square and coming up with the fourth" (7.8).

1.16 The Master said, "Do not be concerned about whether or not others know you; be concerned about whether or not you know others."

The first half of this saying refers to the need to be unconcerned about public opinion or fame: the gentleman studies for his own sake, not in order to impress others (14.24), and seeks for it in himself, not in others (15.21). Commentators generally explain the second half as having to do with the ability to morally judge others (cf. 1.3, 4.3). Also compare this passage with 12.20, 14.30.

BOOK TWO

In this book, we see elaborations of a theme suggested in 1.2: political order is not obtained by means of force or government regulations, but rather by the non-coercive influence of the morally perfected person. Several descriptions of such wu-wei perfection appear in this book (including Confucius' famous spiritual autobiography in 2.4), and we also find an extended discussion of the "root" virtue of filial piety that emphasizes the importance of having the proper internal dispositions.

2.1 The Master said, "One who rules through the power of Virtue is analogous to the Pole Star: it simply remains in its place and receives the homage of the myriad lesser stars."

The point of this passage is that the spontaneous harmony brought about by Heaven in the natural world is to be a model for the human ruler, who—in a wu-wei fashion— will bring the world to order silently, inevitably, and unselfconsciously through the power of his perfected moral Virtue. As Bao Xian notes, "One who possesses Virtue is wu-wei, and—like the Pole Star—does not move yet receives the homage of the myriad lesser stars." Cf. 2.3, 2.21, 12.17, 12.19, and especially 15.5.

2.2 The Master said, "The *Odes* number several hundred, and yet can be judged with a single phrase: 'Oh, they will not lead you astray.'"

The quoted phrase is from Ode 297. The original reference is to powerful war horses bred to pull chariots and trained not to swerve from the desired path. The metaphorical meaning is that one committed through study to the *Odes*—"yoked" to them, as it were—will not be lead astray from the Confucian Way.

2.3 The Master said, "If you try to guide the common people with coercive regulations (*zheng* 政) and keep them in line with punishments, the common people will become evasive and will have no sense of shame. If, however, you guide them with Virtue, and keep them in line by means of ritual, the people will have a sense of shame and will rectify themselves."

This passage represents another expression of the theme of ruling through the power of Virtue (wu-wei) rather than force. As Guo Xiang notes, "If you employ governmental regulations you may correct people's outer behavior, but in their hearts, they will not have submitted. Concerned only with expediency and evasion, they will behave shamelessly toward things. Is this not a superficial way of transforming people?" Zhu Xi adds, "Although they will probably not dare to do anything bad, the tendency to do bad will never leave them." Cf. 8.9.

2.4 The Master said, "At fifteen, I set my mind upon learning; at thirty, I took my place in society;[1] at forty, I became free of doubts;[2] at fifty, I understood Heaven's Mandate;[3] at sixty, my ear was attuned; and at seventy, I could follow my heart's desires without overstepping the bounds of propriety."

We have here Confucius' spiritual autobiography. We can see his evolution as encompassing three pairs of stages. In the first pair (stages one and two), the aspiring gentleman commits himself to the Confucian Way, submitting to the rigors of study and ritual practice until these traditional forms have been internalized to the point that he is able to "take his place" among others. In the second pair, the practitioner begins to feel truly at ease with this new manner of being, and is able to understand how the Confucian Way fits into the order of things and complies with the will of Heaven.[4] The clarity and sense of ease this brings with it leads to the final two stages, where one's dispositions have been so thoroughly harmonized with the dictates of normative culture that one accords with them spontaneously—that is, the state of wu-wei. Some interpretations take the ear being "attuned" to mean that Confucius at this point immediately apprehends the subtle content of the teachings he hears (Zheng Xuan), some that there is no conflict between his inner dispositions and the teachings of the sages (Wang Bi), and some both of these things. As Li Chong explains, "'Having an attuned ear' means that, upon hearing the exemplary teachings of the Former Kings, one immediately apprehended their virtuous conduct, and 'following the models of the Lord' (a reference to King Wen in Ode 241), nothing goes against the tendencies of one's heart." As Huang Kan explains, "By age seventy, Confucius reached a point where training and inborn nature were perfectly meshed, 'like a raspberry vine growing among hemp, naturally standing upright without the need for support.'[5] Therefore he could then give free rein to his heart's intentions without overstepping the exemplary standards." Or, as Zhu Xi explains it, "Being able to follow one's heart's desires without transgressing exemplary standards means that one acts with ease, hitting the mean without forcing it."

2.5 Meng Yizi asked about filial piety. The Master replied, "Do not disobey."

Later, Fan Chi was driving the Master's chariot. The Master said to him, "Just now Meng Yizi asked me about filial piety, and I answered, 'Do not disobey.'"

Fan Chi said, "What did you mean by that?"

The Master replied, "When your parents are alive, serve them in accordance with the rites; when they pass away, bury them in accordance with the rites and sacrifice to them in accordance with the rites."

---

[1] That is, through mastery of the rites; cf. 8.8, 16.13 and 20.3.

[2] Cf. 9.29, 14.28.

[3] Cf. 16.8, 20.3.

[4] The link between these two stages—being without doubts and understanding the Mandate of Heaven—is also suggested by the line from 9.29, "One who understands does not doubt."

[5] A common saying emphasizing the transformative effect of environment upon one's character; see, for instance, Chapter 1 "Encouraging Learning" of the *Xunzi*: "When a raspberry vine grows among hemp, it naturally stands upright without the need for support; when white sand is mixed with mud, both of them become infused with blackness" (Knoblock 1988: 137). The idea, of course, is that the tall, straight hemp acts as a natural stake guiding the growth of the raspberry vine, which otherwise would grow into a tangled bramble.

Confucius' initial response is ambiguous; the most natural way to take it would be "do not disobey your parents," and this is presumably how Meng Yizi understood it. In his elaboration to Fan Chi, however, Confucius reveals that he had something else in mind: the locus of obedience should be the rites. There are differing interpretations concerning the identity of Meng Yizi,[6] with the most coherent identifying him as an official in Confucius' native state of Lu, the head of the Meng[-sun] clan of the infamous Three Families—*de facto* rulers of Lu—criticized in Book Three for their ritual excesses. Confucius' elaboration of his answer to Meng Yizi is thus intended as a rebuke of the Three Families in general, and Meng Yizi in particular: ritual propriety takes precedence over obedience to one's parents' unethical customs.[7] The ritual excesses of the Three Families thus give Confucius' injunction to "bury them in accordance with the rites and sacrifice to them in accordance with the rites" added bite. Wei Guan notes that one may ask why Confucius did not give the full explanation to Meng Yizi himself, and instead reserved it for Fan Chi. The answer, he says, is that Meng Yizi wished to employ Confucius, "and Confucius wished to use this encounter to demonstrate to Fan Chi that this was not the type of person worthy of compromising oneself for." The exchange is thus an educational opportunity for Fan Chi rather than Meng Yizi, who is presumably beyond hope at this point.

2.6 Meng Wubo asked about filial piety. The Master replied, "Give your parents no cause for anxiety other than the possibility that they might fall ill."

Meng Wubo[8] is the son of Meng Yizi from 2.5. The grammar of this passage is ambiguous, and many commentators and translators have taken it to mean, "when it comes to one's parents, one is worried only that they may fall ill," but it is more convincing to see the focus as being upon the son's behavior. As Huang Kan explains, "The point is that a son should constantly be respectful, careful, and self-possessed, and should not engage in illicit behavior that would cause his parents undue worry. It is only the state of physical health that is something beyond one's ability to control or predict, and therefore worth worrying about."

2.7 Ziyou asked about filial piety. The Master said, "Nowadays 'filial' means simply being able to provide one's parents with nourishment. But even dogs and horses are provided with nourishment. If you are not respectful, wherein lies the difference?"

The focus here is upon the importance of internal involvement when it comes to virtuous behavior, "respect" (*jing* 敬) encompassing both a manner of behaving and an emotional attitude.

2.8 Zixia asked about filial piety. The Master said, "It is the demeanor that is difficult. If there is work to be done, disciples shoulder the burden, and when wine and food are served, elders are given precedence, but surely filial piety consists of more than this."

---

[6] His name means literally, "Yi, eldest son and leader of the Meng Family."
[7] At least after the three-year mourning period is finished; see 1.11 above.
[8] Literally, "Wu, the eldest son and heir of the Meng Family."

A convincing way of understanding this passage is to see it as building upon and clarifying 2.7, in which case "demeanor" (*se* 色) should be understood as referring to one's internal emotional state as revealed in one's features. As Zhai Hao puts it, "The point of this passage is that even respect does not constitute filial piety unless it is accompanied by affection. Taking upon the burden of work to be done and offering sustenance are the sorts of things disciples or students do to show reverence for their elders. Serving one's parents, on the other hand, involves in addition deep affection, a harmonious disposition, and a willing heart." Qian Dian gives an historical example, "When King Wen was the crown prince and participated in the court audiences of Wang Ji [his father], he would ask the eunuchs three times every day whether or not the Prime Minister was feeling well that day. When they replied that he was well, King Wen's demeanor became suffused with joy; when they replied that he was unwell, King Wen's demeanor became filled with anxiety—he would be so shaken that even his gait became unsteady. This is what is meant by 'it is the demeanor that is difficult.'" True filial piety involves not only the respect due to any elder family member, but in addition a kind of spontaneous, profoundly affectionate bond.

2.9 The Master said, "I can talk all day long with Yan Hui without him once disagreeing with me. In this way, he seems a bit stupid. And yet when we retire and I observe his private behavior, I see that it is in fact worthy to serve as an illustration of what I have taught. Hui is not stupid at all."

Here, in our first mention of Confucius' favorite disciples, Yan Hui, in the text, we get a clear indication that there is something special about him. Some commentaries (particularly the early ones) assume that the "private behavior" that Confucius observes is Yan Hui engaged in informal conversation with other disciples, while other commentaries believe that Confucius is observing Yan Hui's behavior when he is alone, in solitary repose. Line three of the following passage ("discover where it is that he feels at ease") suggests that latter reading. In any case, the point is that Hui does not disagree or ask questions because he immediately comprehends everything that he is taught (cf. 9.20, 11.4), suggesting that he might be one of those superior few who are "born knowing it" (16.9), unlike those such as Confucius who must learn in order to know the Way (7.20). Cf. 5.9, 6.1, and 6.7.

Confucius is a learner

2.10 The Master said, "Look at the means a man employs, observe the basis from which he acts, and discover where it is that he feels at ease. Where can he hide? Where can he hide?"

That is, how can his true character remain hidden? A person's character is not properly judged by his words or his public reputation, but is rather revealed to one who carefully observes his actual behavior, comes to know something about his motivations, and discovers what he is like in private. It is in the details of one's daily behavior that true virtue is manifested. Cf. 4.2, "The Good person feels at home in Goodness."

2.11 The Master said, "Both keeping past teachings alive and understanding the present—someone able to do this is worthy of being a teacher."

There is commentarial disagreement over whether this passage refers to keeping ancient teachings alive, or to keeping what one has previously learned in a lifetime current in one's mind so that one knows what to expect in the future. The role of the teacher would suggest the former. Li Ao points out, however, that passages such as 1.15 ("Informed as to what has gone before, you know what is to come") seem congruent with the latter interpretation.

2.12 The Master said, "The gentleman is not a vessel."

Qi 器, literally a ritual vessel or implement designed to serve a particular function, is also used metaphorically to refer to people who are specialized in one particular task. Although some commentators take this passage to mean that the gentleman is universally—rather than narrowly—skilled, the point seems rather that the gentleman is not a specialist (cf. 6.13, 9.2, 9.6, 13.4 and 19.7). As Li Guangdi explains,

> We call a "vessel" someone who establishes a name for himself on the basis of a single ability. Consider Zilu's ability to collect taxes, Ran You's ability to serve as a steward, Gong Xihua's ability to regulate the etiquette of host and guest [5.8], and even Zigong's ability to serve as a "precious jade vessel" [5.4]—these are all cases of being a "vessel" in this sense. The learning of the gentleman emphasizes the perfection of Virtue over attainment in the arts, and perfection in behavior over the mere accomplishment of tasks. Somewhere in Yan Hui's manner of seeing and hearing, speaking and moving, or Zengzi's appearance, attitude, and demeanor . . . we can discern the working of Virtue—this is what it means to "not serve as a vessel." Taking this passage to mean that there is nothing the gentleman does not know or nothing that he cannot do is simply to fall back into the trap of "vessel"-thinking.

2.13 Zigong asked about the gentleman.
The Master said, "He first expresses his views, and then acts in accordance with them."

We see here again the suspicion of glibness—the tendency of people to "talk the talk" without "walking the walk" (Cf. 1.14, 4.20, 4.24, 12.3, 14.20, and 14.27). The gentleman is trustworthy and consistent.

2.14 The Master said, "The gentleman is broad and not partial; the petty person is partial and not broad."

Early commentaries tend to take this passage as referring to social associations: the gentleman comes together openly with others in accordance with general principles of trustworthiness and role-specific dutifulness, whereas the petty person relies upon secret, partisan connections. Alternately, one might see this as a reference to the scope of one's social circle: the gentleman associates widely with others (the literal sense of *zhou* 周), and thus is broad-minded, while the petty person falls into narrow cliques that restrict his vision (cf. 4.10). Later commentaries often understand it in terms of learning: the gentleman understands the broad, overarching principles of the Way, whereas the petty person becomes stuck in biases, trivialities, and details. The latter interpretation seems to resonate better with other passages in this Book, such as the idea that the gentleman is not a specialist (2.12) and that he does not become mired in heterodox teachings (2.16).

2.15 The Master said, "If you learn without thinking about what you have learned, you will be lost. If you think without learning, however, you will fall into danger."

As Bao Xian notes, "If one learns but does not reflectively seek out the meaning of what is being taught, one will be lost and will have gained nothing from it." Some commentators, such as He Yan, take *dai* 殆 ("danger") in its alternate sense of exhaustion: "If one thinks without studying, one will achieve nothing in the end, and will have merely exhausted one's intellectual energy for nothing." Learning requires the active participation of the student (cf. 1.16, 5.27, 7.8, 15.16), but also imposes essential structure upon the student's activities (17.10 and especially 15.31).

2.16 The Master said, "Working from the wrong starting point will lead to nothing but harm."

Later commentators take "wrong starting point" (*yiduan* 異端) as "heterodox teachings," arguing that Confucius had in mind Daoism, Yang Zhuism, or Mohism, but this seems anachronistic. Cheng Shude notes that there are hints of proto-Mohist teachings in 17.21 and primitivist ideas in 13.4, and it is possible that these are the targets of this passage, but that it is more likely that the "wrong starting points" mentioned are something like the "minor ways-teachings" (*xiaodao* 小道) mentioned in 19.4 that threaten to "bog down" the aspiring gentleman.

2.17 The Master said, "Zilu, remark well what I am about to teach you! This is wisdom: to recognize what you know as what you know, and recognize what you do not know as what you do not know."

An elaborated version of this story, which also links it to 2.18 below, is found in the *Xunzi*. Zilu appears to Confucius dressed in what the Master deems to be a pretentious manner, and is therefore scolded. After hurrying out to change into more humble clothing, Zilu reappears and is lectured to by the Master:

> "Remark well what I am about to tell you. One who is not careful about[9] his words becomes pompous, and one who is not careful about his behavior becomes a show-off. One who puts on the appearance of knowledge and ability is a petty person. Therefore, when the gentleman knows something, he says, 'I know it,' and when he doesn't know something, he says, 'I do not know it.' This is the essence of speech. When the gentleman is able to do something, he says, 'I am able to do it,' and when he is not able to do something, he says, 'I am not able to do it.' This is the perfection of behavior."[10]

We also read in the *Xunzi* the helpful comment, "Knowing when it is appropriate to speak is wisdom; knowing when it is appropriate to remain silent is also wisdom."[11]

2.18 Zizhang asked about obtaining official position.

Confucius said, "If you first learn as much as you can, then guard against that which is dubious and speak carefully about the rest, you will seldom speak in

---

[9] Following the emendations of Yu Yue based upon a parallel passage in the *Exoteric Commentary*, which also echoes *Analects* 2.18.

[10] Chapter 29 ("On the Way of the Son"); Knoblock 1994: 254.

[11] Chapter 6 ("Refuting the Twelve Philosophers"); Knoblock 1988: 225.

error. If you first observe as much as you can, then guard against that which is perilous and carefully put the rest into action, you will seldom have cause for regret. If in your speech you seldom err, and in your behavior you seldom have cause for regret, an official position will follow naturally."

> If the gentleman can concentrate on the internal goods of the Confucian practice, the whole panoply of external goods—official position, material wealth, renown—will likely follow naturally, in an wu-wei fashion. There is no guarantee that this happen, though, since such external goods are subject to the vagaries of fate (cf. 11.18, 12.14–12.15). Therefore, the sole proper attitude of the gentleman is to focus on what is within his control: becoming a good person. As we read in *Mencius* 6:A:16,
>
>> There are Heavenly official honors and human official honors. The Heavenly honors are such things as benevolence (*ren*), rightness, dutifulness, and trustworthiness, and an unflagging joy in goodness; the human honors are such things as being declared a Duke, Minister, or Counselor. The ancients cultivated the Heavenly honors, and the human honors followed naturally. People nowadays cultivate the Heavenly honors only as a means to obtaining the human honors, and once they get the latter, they abandon the former. This is the ultimate in delusion and, in the end, can only lead to disaster.
>
> Confucius' response to Zizhang is thus no doubt intended to correct what he sees as an excessive focus on external goods.

2.19 Duke Ai asked, "What can I do to induce the common people to be obedient?"

Confucius replied, "Raise up the straight and apply them to the crooked, and the people will submit to you. If you raise up the crooked and apply them to the straight, the people will never submit."

> The metaphor for the virtuous influence of superiors found here and in 12.22 below recalls the image of the "press-frame" for straightening out crooked wood that became a favorite of Xunzi's for describing the process of self-cultivation. The reference is to the salutary effect of moral officials upon the Virtue of the common people; cf. the "wind and grass" metaphor in 12.19. Duke Ai was the nominal ruler of Confucius' native state of Lu. As Jiang Xi comments:
>
>> Duke Ai was presented with a once-in-a-lifetime opportunity, and sagely worthies filled his state. If he had simply raised them up and employed them, he could have become the true King of Lu. Unfortunately, he cared only for sensual pleasures and left control of the administration to a flock of evil-doers. As a result, the hearts of the people were filled with resentment. Duke Ai was troubled by this state of affairs, and so asked this question of Confucius.

2.20 Ji Kangzi asked, "How can I cause the common people to be respectful, dutiful, and industrious?"

The Master said, "Oversee them with dignity, and the people will be respectful; oversee them with filiality and kindness, and the people will be dutiful; oversee them by raising up the accomplished and instructing those who are unable, and the people will be industrious."

> Here Confucius is speaking to someone who wields real power in the state of Lu: Ji Kangzi, head of the most powerful of the infamous Three Families who were the *de facto* but illegitimate rulers of Lu. He receives similar advice about ruling from Confucius in 12.17–12.19 below: essentially, make yourself virtuous and the people will follow.

2.21 Some people said of Confucius, "Why is it that he is not participating in government?"[12]

[Upon being informed of this,] the Master remarked, "The *Book of Documents* says,

> 'Filial, oh so filial,
> Friendly to one's elders and juniors;
> [In this way] exerting an influence upon those who govern.'

Thus, in being a filial son and good brother one is already taking part in government. What need is there, then, to speak of 'participating in government'?"

There are probably two layers of meaning here. The more general point is that one should "do government" through "not doing" (wu-wei): that is, by perfecting oneself—as Master You puts it in 1.2, establishing the "root" of virtue—and letting the rest follow naturally through the power of one's personal example and Virtue. Some commentators also see here an indirect criticism of the Ji Family, whose usurpation of power in Lu involved shocking mistreatment of parents and brothers. Cf. 12.11, 13.3.

2.22 The Master said, "I cannot see how a person devoid of trustworthiness could possibly get along in the world. Imagine a large ox-drawn cart without a linchpin for its yolk, or a small horse drawn cart without a linchpin for its collar: how could they possibly be driven?"

Most commentators understand this as a comment upon an individual's character—the "linchpin" of trustworthiness linking together one's words and one's actions—as in Zhu Xi's comment that "the words of a person devoid of trustworthiness have no substance," or Ames and Rosemont's observation that "like the carriage pins, making good on one's word (*xin* 信) is the link between saying and doing" (1998: 234). It may also, however, be a comment on society as a whole—requiring as it does the mutual trust inspired by trustworthiness in order to function—as in Dai Zhen's comment that "among people, trustworthiness is the linchpin of social relations and mutual support." The portrayal of trustworthiness as a metaphorical "linchpin" here contrasts with passages such as 1.13, where the importance of trustworthiness is downplayed.

2.23 Zizhang asked, "Can we know what it will be like ten generations from now?"

The Master responded, "The Yin followed the rituals of the Xia, altering them only in ways that we know. The Zhou followed the rituals of the Yin, altering them only in ways that we know. If some dynasty succeeds the Zhou, we can know what it will be like even a hundred generations from now."

Although the object of knowledge in Zizhang's question is not specified, we can imagine that it is something like "way of life," which of course is defined by ritual observance. Zhu Xi's commentary here is helpful:

---

[12] Lit., "Doing government" (*weizheng* 為政). The reference is to Confucius' lack of an official position.

The Three Dynasties [Xia, Yin, Zhou] succeeded one another, each following its predecessor and unable to change its predecessors ways. The only sorts of alternations made involved such [minor matters as standards for ritual emblems. . . .], and all of their past traces can be fully observed today. Thus, if in the future some king arises to succeed the Zhou, the manner in which he will follow or make alterations to ritual will not exceed what we have seen in the past. This will be true even one hundred generations hence, let alone only ten generations. This is the manner in which the sage [Confucius] judged the future—unlike those students of prophetic and occult arts who arose in later generations. As Hu Anguo notes, "Zizhang probably asked his question wanting to know about the future, but the sage enlightened him by directing his attention toward the past."

As far as we can tell, fortune telling was as prevalent in Confucius' age as in present-day China. Confucius was not interested in such occult practices, and wished to focus his disciple's attention on something more morally useful: the practices of the ancients.

2.24 The Master said, "To sacrifice to spirits that are not one's own is to be presumptuous. To see what is right, but to fail to do it, is to be lacking in courage."

As Huang Gan observes, "The former refers to doing that which one is not supposed to do, and the latter to not doing what one is supposed to do." *Gui* 鬼 can refer to either previously human, ancestral spirits or nonhuman spirits dwelling in the landscape; the latter reading allows us to connect this passage to 3.6 below, where the head of the Ji Family sacrifices to Mt. Tai—a spirit that is not "his own." Liu Baonan records an anonymous observation that attempts to map both halves of 2.24 onto 3.6: "The head of the Ji Family making an offering to Mt. Tai is a case of sacrificing to a spirit that is not one's own . . . while Ran Qiu's failure to prevent the Ji Family from doing so, even though he was serving under them in an official position, is a case of seeing what is right to do, but failing to do it."

BOOK THREE

Much of this book consists of criticisms (direct or indirect) of the ritual improprieties of the Three Families that also tell us much about ritual in general. A related theme is the need for cultural refinement (wen 文) to be accompanied by native substance (zhi 質)—that is, traditional practices must be informed by genuine feeling if they are to be more than mere empty gestures. The problem with Confucius' contemporaries is not only that they flouted proper ritual forms (cf. 3.1, 3.2, 3.6, 3.10, 3.11, 3.15, 3.17, 3.18), but also that even when they observed them they did so insincerely (cf. 3.3, 3.4, 3.12, 3.26). They are thus lacking when it comes both to cultural refinement and native substance.

3.1 Confucius said of the Ji Family, "They have eight rows of dancers performing in their courtyard. If they can condone this, what are they *not* capable of?"

According to later ritual texts, different ranks in society were allowed different numbers of dancers to perform outside the ancestral hall during ceremonial occasions: the Son of Heaven allowed eight rows of eight dancers, feudal lords six rows, ministers four rows, and official two rows. Although he was *de facto* ruler of Lu, the head of the Ji Family officially held only the position of minister, and his use of eight dancers thus represented an outrageous usurpation of the ritual prerogatives of the Zhou king.

3.2 [When making offerings to their ancestors], the Three Families had the *yong* ode performed during the clearing away of the sacrificial vessels. The Master quoted a line from the ode,

> "Assisting were the Feudal Lords,
> The Son of Heaven, solemn and stately,".

adding, "What relevance could this possibly have to the ancestral hall of the Three Families?"

The *yong* ode is number 282, and—as Confucius points out by quoting one of its couplets—describes the court of the Son of Heaven. As Brooks and Brooks note, "The two preceding lines in the stanza are 'Slow and solemn they draw nigh/till all are ranged in panoply.' As a recessional hymn, it was probably sung by a chorus, who narrated, as though it were happening, the sacrifice that had just concluded" (1998: 79). Here again we have an instance of the Three Families usurping the ritual prerogatives of the Zhou king.

3.3 The Master said, "A man who is not Good—what has he to do with ritual? A man who is not Good—what has he to do with music?"

Although it serves as a general statement concerning the relationship of internal disposition to Confucian practice (cf. 3.12 and 17.11), this comment is probably more
specifically directed at the head of the Ji Family and the other leading families of Lu
criticized in 3.1 and 3.2. A passage in the *History of the Han*, after quoting this line,
explains,

> The point is that a person who is not Good does not have the means to apply himself . . . not
> having the means to apply himself, he is unable to practice ritual and music. Even if he has
> many other talents, they will only be used to do no good. During the Master's age, ritual and
> music were under attack by the ministers [of Lu], who greedily usurped the prerogatives of
> the king and mutually followed the established habits of corruption, and practiced wrong-
> ness so that it triumphed over what was right.

3.4 Lin Fang asked about the roots of ritual.

The Master exclaimed, "What a noble question! When it comes to ritual, it
is better to be spare than extravagant. When it comes to mourning, it is better
to be excessively sorrowful than fastidious."

Lin Fang is usually identified as a man of Lu, and presumably shared Confucius'
concern that his fellow citizens were neglecting the "roots" and attending to the superficial "branches" of ritual practice, which is why he is commended by Confucius for his
question. When it comes to ritual is it harmony that is valued (1.12), but if one is to err,
it should be on the side of the "roots"—that is, the emotions that ideally inform and moti-
vate the ritual forms. Sparse ritual paraphernalia backed by genuine respect is better
than empty ritual excess, and grief-induced lapses in ritual forms of mourning (e.g.,
Confucius' own excesses upon the death of Yan Hui; see 11.10) are more easily countenanced than cool, emotionless perfection. Zhu Xi is probably correct in linking this
theme to the relationship of emotional substance over cultural form described in 6.18.
Although here in Book Three the importance of substance over cultural form is emphasized by Confucius (cf. 3.3, 3.4, 3.8, 3.12, 3.26), in other passages we see form being
stressed over substance. Probably the desirability of both being balanced that is
expressed in 6.18 is Confucius' ultimate position, and his favoring of one over another
is merely a response to the pedagogical needs of the moment (11.22).

3.5 The Master said, "The Yi and Di barbarians, even with their rulers, are still
inferior to the Chinese states without their rulers."

The Yi and Di were tribes living to the east and north, respectively, of China proper
in Confucius' time. They had some sort of political organization but did not follow
the rituals of the Zhou. Huang Kan and others are probably correct in seeing this as
another jibe at the Three Families of Lu. They wield political power as do the barbarian rulers, but their breaches of ritual propriety make them no better than the Yi
or Di, and it would be preferable for Lu to remain ritually correct (and thus "Chinese"
in the proper sense), even if this meant going without any ruler at all.

3.6 The head of the Ji Family made a sacrificial pilgrimage to Mt. Tai. The
Master said to Ran Qiu, "Were you not able to prevent this?"

Ran Qiu replied, "I was not."

The Master exclaimed, "Oh! That one would ever have to say that Mt. Tai
was not the equal of Lin Fang!"

Mt. Tai is one of the sacred mountains of China, located in present day Shandong Province. The offering of sacrifices to sacred mountains in the form of food and jade items (which were ritually arranged and then buried) was the prerogative of the feudal lord who ruled the region in which the mountain was located. Mt. Tai straddled the border of Lu and Qi, and received offerings from both states. The head of the Ji Family, of course, was a minister and not a feudal lord, and so his offering represented a violation of ritual norms. At the time, Ran Qiu was serving as an official under the head of the Ji Family, and thus was in a position to dissuade him from this ritual error, but he apparently lacked the courage (2.24) or influence. Bao Xian explains the Master's closing comment, "Spirits do not accept offerings that violate ritual. Even Lin Fang previously knew enough to ask about ritual, so how could anyone imagine that the spirit of Mt. Tai would somehow be less perspicacious than he? It was with a desire to slander of Mt. Tai that this sacrifice was performed."

3.7 The Master said, "Surely archery can serve as an illustration of the fact that the gentleman does not compete! Before mounting the stairs to the archery hall, gentlemen bow and defer to one another, and after descending from the hall they mutually offer up toasts. This is how a gentleman 'competes.'"

Archery was one of the classic six arts in which a gentleman was trained. It was a highly ritualized activity, with careful attention being given to age and rank, and everyone participating in a formal drinking ceremony at the conclusion of the competition. Archery also served in the Warring States as a standard metaphor for the overall task of self-cultivation (3.16 and *Mencius* 2:A:7 and 5:B:1). The word for "hitting the bulls-eye" (*zhong* 中) was most commonly understood in its metaphoric meaning of "the mean" of virtue, and—as with virtue—success in archery could only be obtained by a person focused on their his inner state rather than external success. As Luan Zhao explains,

> When it comes to archery, the gentleman focuses upon his art as a means of illuminating the lessons he has learned and scrutinizes his Virtue in order to monitor his moral worthiness. He repeatedly bows and defers to others in order to perfect ritual propriety, and venerates the five excellences [of archery][1] in order to inspire others to be morally instructed. . . . Competing does not at all help one to achieve victory. One must seek for victory within oneself. . . . This is why the etiquette of archery dictates that, "If you miss the center of the target, turn and look for the cause within yourself." One seeks the bulls-eye by means of deference and self-cultivation, not for the sake of competing for victory in order to shame others.[2] Thus, we also read, "Archery is the way of benevolence (*ren*). If one shoots but does not hit the bulls-eye, one does not begrudge one's victorious opponent, but rather simply looks within [*Mencius* 2:A:7]."

3.8 Zixia asked, "[An ode says,]

> 'Her artful smile, with its alluring dimples,
> Her beautiful eyes, so clear,
> The unadorned upon which to paint.'

---

[1] According to Han ritual texts, the "five excellences" of archery were lack of contentiousness or equanimity, general ritual deportment, skill in hitting the target, singing, and dancing. This will give the reader some sense of the scope of the archery ritual.

[2] This is all a paraphrase of the "Etiquette of Archery" chapter of the *Record of Ritual*; Legge 1967, vol. 2: 446–453.

What does this mean?"

The Master said, "The application of colors comes only after a suitable unadorned background is present."

Zixia said, "So it is the rites that come after?"

The Master said, "It is you, Zixia, who has awakened me to the meaning of these lines! It is only with someone like you that I can begin to discuss the *Odes*."

Again we have a disciple making the sort of conceptual leap that Confucius required of his students (cf. 1.15, 7.8). The point grasped by Zixia is that the adornment provided by the rites is meant to build upon appropriate native emotions or tendencies. Just as all of the cosmetics in the world are of no avail if the basic lines of the face are not pleasing, so is the refinement provided by ritual forms of no help to one lacking in native substance. Cf. 3.4, 5.10 and 6.18. An even stronger expression of the importance of substance is found in the *Record of Ritual*: "Just as that which is naturally sweet can be further harmonized through cooking, and just as colors may be applied to a white background, so a person who is dutiful and trustworthy can be allowed to learn the rites."[3] Here the virtues of dutifulness and trustworthiness are presented as native talents that are the prerequisites for moral education.

3.9 The Master said, "As for the rites of the Xia Dynasty, I can speak of them, but there is little remaining in the state of Qii to document them. As for the rites of the Shang Dynasty, I can speak of them, but there is little remaining in the state of Song to document them. This is because there is not much in the way of culture or moral worthies left in either state. If there were something there, then I would be able to document them."

Qii was a minor state in which the remnants of the Xia royal line were enfeoffed after their defeat by the Shang, and Song was the state where the remnants of the Shang were enfeoffed after their defeat by the Zhou. Neither of these states was successful in preserving their cultural traditions, unlike the state of Lu—the home of the Zhou cultural tradition—where the essence of Zhou culture could still be found. The most cogent interpretation of this passage is that of Zheng Ruxie, who explains:

Qii and Song had lost the ritual practices of the Xia and Shang, as evidenced by the fact that there was no remaining culture or moral worthies left in these states that could document these cultures. Lu, on the other hand, was not like this: with regard to culture, it still possessed the classic documents, and with regard to worthiness, it possessed the Master. How is it that none of the rulers and ministers of Lu saw fit to examine this evidence? Thus, in making this comment the Master did not really have Qii or Song in mind, but was instead using the examples of Qii and Song to express his opinion, for it is in fact particularly with regard to Lu that the subtle point of his words are directed.

Here again, we have a rebuke of the Lu leadership for its neglect or flouting of its cultural heritage. Also compare this passage with a later, slightly elaborated version in the *Record of Ritual*.[4]

---

[3] Chapter 10 ("Rites in the Formation of Character"); Legge 1967, vol. 1: 414.

[4] Chapter 9 ("Ritual Usages"); Legge 1967, vol. 1: 368.

3.10 The Master said, "As for that part of the *di* sacrifice that comes after the pouring of the ceremonial libation, I have no desire to witness it."

There is a great deal of debate over how to understand this passage. There is general consensus that the *di* 禘 sacrifice was a special type of ancestor sacrifice, directed toward the ultimate progenitor of one's ancestral line. Some commentators believe that all aristocratic lines had their own *di* sacrifice that they were authorized to perform, and that Confucius' disapproval is directed toward the *manner* in which the sacrifice was being carried out in Lu: either sloppily or with an usurpation of paraphernalia, music and dance that were properly the prerogative of the Zhou king. Others, citing a line found in two chapters of the *Record of Ritual* that says, "According to ritual, only a king can perform the *di*,"[5] argue that the *di* mentioned here is a specific ritual directed to the progenitor of the Zhou royal line[6] and properly performed only in the Great Ancestral Temple of Lu mentioned in 3.15. The performance of this ceremony, under this reading, was the sole prerogative of the Zhou royal line. As Mao Qiling puts it,

> The *di* is fundamentally a grand sacrifice limited to kings. Both the "Places in the Bright Hall" and "Summary Account of Sacrifices" [chapters of the *Record of Ritual*][7] say, "Because he viewed him as having made the most meritorious contributions in the entire world, King Cheng dedicated to the Duke of Zhou an important sacrifice." Thus, he sacrificed to the originating progenitor of his line, establishing the ancestral hall of the founding king, where from the beginning the ritual and music appropriate to the Son of Heaven could be performed. However, [in Confucius' time] the various lords began randomly employing this sacrifice. Their action thus fell under the category of ritual violation, and this is why the Master had no desire to witness it. This accords completely with the complaint attributed to the Master in the "Ritual Usages" [chapter of the *Record of Ritual*]:[8] "The border sacrifice (*jiao* 郊) and *di* as performed in Lu are in violation of ritual—oh, how the Duke of Zhou's legacy has declined!"

3.11 Someone asked for an explanation of the *di* sacrifice. The Master said, "I do not understand it. One who understood it could handle the world as if he had it right here," and he pointed to the palm of his hand.

Of course the unspoken implication is that there is *no one* in Lu who really understands the *di*, especially the Three Families, who have been shamelessly performing it in gross violation of ritual norms. The ability of a properly performed ritual—especially those having to do with filial piety, such as the *di* sacrifice to one's ancestors—to order the entire world in an wu-wei fashion is expressed particularly strongly here, but has parallels in such passages as 1.2, 2.21, and 12.11.

3.12 "Sacrifice as if [they were] present" means that, when sacrificing to the spirits, you should comport yourself as if the spirits were present.

---

[5] Found in Chapters 15 ("Record of Smaller Matters Regarding Mourning Dress") and 16 ("Great Treatise"); see Legge 1967, vol. 2: 44 and 60.

[6] Sometimes identified by commentators as the Duke of Zhou or the legendary emperor Ku 嚳, but more probably Hou Ji, "Lord Millet," the first figure in Chinese historiography to bear the name Ji 姬, which is the clan-name of the Zhou.

[7] Chapters 14 and 24, respectively; see Legge 1967, vol. 2: 31–32 and 253.

[8] Chapter 9; see Legge 1967, vol. 1: 372.

The Master said, "If I am not fully present at the sacrifice, it is as if I did not sacrifice at all."

To sacrifice "as if the spirits were present" means to do so with an attitude of reverence and awe. There is no attribution for the first line, and its form (cryptic text followed by an expanded, explanatory version) suggests that it might be a fragment from a lost ritual text interpolated by a later editor. Whether the Master's words or not, it nonetheless clearly harmonizes with the comment from Confucius that follows. Although some commentators take "being present" in the second line in its literal sense (i.e., being physically present at the sacrifice, not sending a proxy in one's stead), the sense of the first line suggests that what is at issue is psychological or inner presence.

3.13 Wang-sun Jia asked, "What do you think about the saying,

'It is better to pay homage to the kitchen stove
Than to the corner shrine.'

The Master replied, "This is not so. Once you have incurred the wrath of Heaven, there is no one to whom you can pray for help."

There are many ways to understand this passage. Taken literally, it is a "cynical piece of peasant lore" (Waley 1989: 97) meaning that it is better to be well-fed than to waste food on sacrifices to the ancestors. Despite Confucius' agnosticism concerning the existence of the spirits, such a crudely pragmatic argument against ritual traditions would clearly be anathema to him (cf. 3.17). There are also a host of metaphorical interpretations of the passage that take the folk saying as a coded reference to the current state of affairs in Wei, where the questioner, Wangsun Jia, was a minister. The corner shrine was traditionally located in the southwest corner of one's house, and was a specially venerated location where sacrifices to one's ancestors were carried out. The kitchen stove, on the other hand, was of no particular ritual significance, but was the focus of the family's everyday attention, and was therefore of much more practical importance. Some interpretations argue that the "corner shrine" refers metaphorically to the respected inner circle of ministers around the lord of Wei (Kong Anguo's view) or to the Lord of Wei himself (Zhu Xi's view), who had in fact only nominal power, and that the "kitchen stove" refers to the real wielder of power in Wei, Wangsun Jia. Under this reading, Wangsun is advising Confucius, who had just arrived in Wei (possibly seeking an official position after losing his position in Lu (1.10 and 3.24), to pay homage to him rather than to his nominal superiors. This, however, would be a violation of ritual (and thus a crime against Heaven), and Confucius therefore rebukes him. Other interpretations see this saying as Wangsun's attempt to justify his abandoning service under the remnants of the Zhou royal line to take up a position with the much more powerful feudal lord of Wei. As Luan Zhao explains,

[The saying means that, in theory,] the corner shrine is honored, but is not actually served in practice, whereas the kitchen stove—nominally not worthy of respect—is where one focuses one's attention. At the time the house of Zhou was weak and in decline, and real power was in the hands of the feudal lords. Wangsun gave up service under the Zhou to take up a position under the Wei, and therefore uses this saying as a way to justify his actions to Confucius. Confucius' answer . . . is intended to make it clear that, just as there is nothing greater than Heaven and the spirits, no one should be honored more than one's king—that is, that one should in fact serve that which one honors in theory and not pay homage to that which is not worthy of respect.

3.14 The Master said, "The Zhou gazes down upon the two dynasties that preceded it. How brilliant in culture it is! I follow the Zhou."

The metaphoric image of the Zhou gazing down upon the Xia and Shang Dynasties, as if from a summit, is meant to express the fact that its culture incorporated elements of the cultures that preceded it—presumably the best elements. Lu represented the depository of Zhou culture during Confucius' age, and a related passage in the *Record of Ritual* ("Confucius said, 'I look toward the Way of Zhou . . . Were I to abandon Lu, where would I go?'")[9] suggests that part of the purpose of this passage is to emphasize the moral and cultural preeminence of Lu among the feudal states of the time, even though Lu was in fact relatively small and comparatively weak politically, economically, and militarily.

3.15 When the Master went into the Great Ancestral Temple, he asked questions about everything that took place.

Someone said, "Who said that this son of a man from Zou understands ritual? When he went into the Great Ancestral Temple, he had to ask questions about everything."

The Great Ancestral Temple was located in the state of Lu, was dedicated to the Duke of Zhou, and was the site of the traditional *di* sacrifice mentioned in 3.10 and 3.11. Confucius' father was supposedly from Zou.

When this comment was reported to the Master, his reply was, "This asking is, in fact, part of ritual."

The simplest way to understand this passage is that ritual demands that one ask polite questions upon entering someone else's ancestral temple, or that one not display one's superior knowledge of ritual. As Kong Anguo puts it, "Although Confucius knew the ritual, it was appropriate for him to ask questions about it nonetheless—this is the height of carefulness." Others read it together with 3.10 and 3.11 as a subtle condemnation of the manner in which the *di* sacrifice was being performed in Lu. As Liu Fenglu explains,

> From the time of Duke Xi the rulers of Lu began usurping the [Zhou king prerogative] of practicing the *di* sacrifice in the Great Ancestral Temple. They employed ritual vestments, vessels, and officers of the Four Dynasties [appropriate only to the Son of Heaven], and were subsequently emulated by their ministers, who also usurped the great rituals. By asking about everything when he entered the Great Ancestral Temple, Confucius avoided directly criticizing this usurpation: he pretended to ask innocently, out of ignorance, such things as, "When was the precedent for this practice established?" or "What is the justification for this practice?" in order to indicate obliquely that Lu had no right to usurp the practices of the Son of Heaven.

3.16 The Master said, "It is said, 'In archery, one does not emphasize piercing the hide of the target,' because people's strengths differ. Such is the ancient Way."

The quoted phrase is probably a proverbial saying. Confucius' reference to strength indicates a slightly different take on the saying: crude physical strength (i.e., the ability

---

[9]Chapter 9 ("Ritual Usages"); Legge 1967, vol. 1: 372.

to pierce the hide of the target) is not relevant, although aim might still be a consideration. This may indicate a desire to divorce the gentlemanly practice of archery from its practical military application, where shooting with sufficient strength to pierce the opponent's leather armor was a crucial consideration. This is how the passage is understood by Zhu Xi, who makes reference to the ideal that, after King Wu's defeat of the Shang, the Zhou gave up the practice of military force and relied solely upon the power of their Virtue to maintain order:

> The ancients engaged in archery in order to observe a person's virtue, and therefore were concerned with hitting the center of the target rather than piercing its hide. . . . The saying in the *Record of Ritual*, "After King Wu defeated the Shang, he demobilized his troops and hosted an archery contest outside of the city walls, and the practice of shooting to pierce the target came to an end,"[10] refers precisely to this. Once the Zhou declined and ritual fell into disuse, however, the various states turned again to military strife, and the practice of shooting to pierce the target was revived. Hence Confucius' lament.

3.17 Zigong wanted to do away with the practice of sacrificing a lamb to announce the beginning of the month.

The Master said, "Zigong! You regret the loss of the lamb, whereas I regret the loss of the rite."

According to commentators, this lamb sacrifice had originally been part of a larger ritual in the state of Lu to mark the official beginning of the new month, and which—according to the *Annals* (Legge 1994d: 243)—was discontinued during the reign of Duke Wen. According to Huang Kan, although the larger ritual itself was no longer being practiced by the rulers of Lu, the practice of sacrificing the lamb was being kept alive by traditionally-minded government functionaries. Zigong does not see the point of continuing this vestigial, materially wasteful practice in the absence of its original ritual context. Insisting upon the continuance of this practice, however, is Confucius' way of mourning the loss of the original rite and keeping its memory alive, which in his view is worth the cost of an occasional lamb. The valuing of ritual propriety over pragmatic or financial considerations links this passage to 3.13, and the fact that Lu—as the inheritor of Zhou culture—still preserved at least the forms of the ancient rites links it to 3.9 and 3.14.

3.18 The Master said, "If in serving your lord you are careful to observe every detail of ritual propriety, people will [wrongly] think you obsequious."

Ritual practice had so degenerated by Confucius' age that a proper ritual practitioner was viewed with suspicion or disdain. As many commentators note, an example of observing every detail of ritual propriety is found in 9.3, where Confucius stubbornly insists upon bowing before ascending the stairs to have an audience with a ruler, as ritual demands, rather than following the more casual contemporary practice of bowing after ascending the stairs. Such archaic manners were no doubt received by his contemporaries with precisely the sort of amusement or cynicism mentioned here.

---

[10] This is a paraphrase from the "Record of Music" chapter, which describes King Wu's conversion from a military to civil culture: "war chariots and armor were smeared with blood and put away in the arsenal, never to be used again," shields and spears were symbolically inverted, military commanders were appointed as civil feudal lords, and King Wu announced that he would never resort to war again. He then demobilized his troops and held an archery contest where his officers cast off their swords, donned civilian clothes, shot to the sound of ritual music, and no longer had as their aim penetrating the hide of the target. See Legge 1967, vol. 2: 123–124.

3.19 Duke Ding asked, "How should a lord employ his ministers? How should a minister serve his lord?"

Confucius replied, "A lord should employ his ministers with ritual, and ministers should serve their lord with dutifulness."

Again we have a general observation about ritual and virtue that probably has a more specific target as well. As Jiao Hong explains, "In the *Annals of Master Yan* we read, 'Only by means of ritual can one govern a state.' Ritual is the tool employed by the Former Kings when they considered titles and social distinctions and thereby eliminated the seeds of disorder. Duke Ding was the kind of ruler who 'held the blade of the sword and offered the handle to his enemies,'[11] and therefore Confucius wants him to protect himself by means of ritual. The Three Families were the type of ministers of whom one might say, 'the tail is too big to wag,'[12] and therefore Confucius wishes to instruct them in the ways of dutifulness."

3.20 That Master said, "The 'Cry of the Osprey' expresses joy without becoming licentious, and expresses sorrow without falling into excessive pathos."

The "Cry of the Osprey" is the first of the *Odes*, and sometimes stands in metonymically for the *Odes* as a whole. There are two equally plausible interpretations of this passage, depending upon whether one thinks that it is the text of Ode 1 in particular or the music of the ode (and possibly the *Odes* in general) that is being praised. The text describes a young gentleman longing for and passionately seeking out a beautiful, virtuous young woman. Although originally the young woman in question was probably the anonymous subject of a peasant folk song, in the commentarial tradition that grew up around the *Odes* she became associated with the royal consort of King Wen, and the poem thus came to be seen as a model of restrained, honorable relations between the sexes. Huang Kan, for one, relies upon the text of Ode 1 to gloss this passage: "The mere prospect of joy in meeting this 'chaste woman' is why 'the gentleman loves to pursue her'—it is not because he lusts after her beauty. 'Tossing and turning at night he thinks of her'—he experiences sorrow at the fact that nowhere in this world can he find the person of his dreams, but does not allow this sorrow to diminish his affection for her." Kong Anguo, on the other hand, understands this passage as referring to the music of the ode: "'Expressing joy without becoming licentious, expressing sorrow without falling into excessive pathos' refers to the perfect harmony [of the music]." In either case, we see in the *Odes* the perfect balance of emotion and restraint that characterizes the gentleman.

3.21 Duke Ai asked Zai Wo about the altar to the soil.

Zai Wo replied, "The clans of the Xia sovereigns used the pine tree,[13] the Shang people used the cypress tree, and the Zhou people used the chestnut tree (*li* 栗). It is said that they wanted to instill fear (*li* 栗) in the people."

---

[11] A colloquial saying (literally 'to hold *tai-a* 太阿 [a famously sharp sword] backward') meaning essentially "to give someone the stick with which to beat you." The phrase first appeared in the *History of the Han*.

[12] That is, those in a normally inferior position have grown more powerful than those in a normally superior position—not too far in general meaning from the English saying, "The tail wagging the dog." The original reference is to the *Zuo Commentary* (Legge 1994d: 635).

[13] The altar of the soil, one of the most important religious sites in a state, was marked with a sacred tree.

Having been informed of this, the Master remarked, "One does not try to explain what is over and done with, one does not try to criticize what is already gone, and one does not try to censure that which is already past."

The *Annals* tells us that the altar to the soil in the state of Lu was destroyed by fire during the fourth year of the reign of Duke Ai (Legge 1994d: 804). This is probably the reason for his questioning of Zai Wo, who at the time was apparently being employed by the Duke as a ritual specialist. In his answer, Zai Wo is playing upon a graphic pun between *li* 栗 "chestnut" and *li* 栗 "fear, awe" (later distinguished with the heart radical, *li* 慄).[14] There are many ways to understand this passage. Perhaps the simplest interpretation is that of Kong Anguo and others, who see it as a rebuke of Zai Wo's reckless speculation: different states used different trees to mark their altars because of variations in local growing conditions; to derive significance from a pun as Zai Wo does is both foolish and insulting to the ancients. Alternately, Confucius saw Zai Wo's comment as being critical of the Zhou, and thus a violation of ritual propriety—especially when speaking to one of the Zhou's direct descendents, Duke Ai. Perhaps more interesting are interpretations that see this exchange as a coded reference to current affairs. In addition to their sacrificial function, altars to the soil doubled as sites of public executions. Some commentators see the Duke's question as an oblique way of suggesting that he use force against those in the state who oppose him, and Zai Wo's answer ("it is said they wanted to instill fear in the people") as an implicit approval of this strategy. There is some variation in which commentators identify as the specific players in this drama, but the explanation of Liu Baonan is representative:

It seems to me that "that which is already past" refers to the actions of Ji Pingzi.[15] Pingzi did not act as a minister should, even going so far as to force Duke Zhao from power. No doubt Duke Ai saw this "past action" of Pingzi's as the root of his current troubles, and wished to announce his crime in order to bring punishment down upon his descendents. This is an example of "trying to censure what is already past." However, the loss of favor experienced by the Ducal House and the devolvement of real power into the hands of the ministers was not brought about in a single day. Duke Ai does not yet realize that "one should employ one's ministers in accordance with ritual" (3.19), and furthermore he was not yet capable of employing Confucius. Instead, he impatiently wants to make a show of power in order to vent his anger, and thinks he can rely upon this to recapture his lost power and influence. This, of course, will not work at all, and this is why the Master tries to restrain him with his comment.

3.22 The Master said, "Guan Zhong's vessel was of small capacity."

Someone asked, "Do you mean that he was frugal?"

The Master replied, "Guan maintained three separate residences and had a separate staff member for each duty. How could he be called frugal?"

"Well, then, do you mean to say that Guan Zhong understood ritual?"

---

[14] It is possible that the other tree names had similar double meanings as the result of puns: "pine" (*song* 松) being graphically similar to *rong* 容 ("accommodating") and having the phonetic *gong* 公 ("just, public"; "lord") and "cypress" (*bo* 柏) being similar to *po* 迫 ("to press") or *pa* 怕 ("quiet, still"; "to fear").

[15] The Ji Family head who is the probable target of 3.1 and who, with the help of the other infamous Three Families, attacked his lord, Duke Zhao, and forced him from office.

The Master replied, "The lord of a state erects a wall in front of his gate, and Guan did the same. The lord of a state, when entertaining other lords, has a stand upon which to place the drinking cups after the toast, and Guan also had one of these. If Guan understood ritual, who does not understand it?"

Qi 器 refers literally to a ritual vessel, and Confucius' helpfully obtuse questioner is apparently taking his statement at face value: perhaps Confucius means that Guan Zhong was frugal and used small, unelaborated ritual implements, or perhaps that he used small ritual vessels because this is what was ritually proper to do. Both questions give Confucius an opportunity to remark upon Guan Zhong's moral failings, and to make it clear that he means *qi* in the metaphorical sense we saw in 2.12: a person who is a narrow specialist or technician. Guan Zhong was a seventh century B.C.E. statesman who encouraged Duke Huan of Qi to dispense with the traditional Zhou feudal state structure and helped him reorganize Qi along more technocratic, efficient lines. This caused Qi to become quite powerful economically and militarily, allowing Duke Huan to officially subordinate other Zhou states under his rule and thus become the first of the officially recognized hegemons (*ba* 霸). Although Confucius expresses admiration for Guan Zhong in 14.16 and 14.17 (and perhaps in 14.9), at a deeper level he disapproves of his narrowly pragmatic approach and flouting of traditional norms and institutions.

3.23 The Master was discussing music with the Grand Music Master of Lu. He said, "What can be known about music is this: when it first begins, it resounds with a confusing variety of notes, but as it unfolds, these notes are reconciled by means of harmony, brought into tension by means of counterpoint, and finally woven together into a seamless whole. It is in this way that music reaches its perfection."

Music thus serves as a model or metaphor for the process of self-cultivation: starting in confusion, passing through many phases and culminating in a state of wu-wei perfection.

3.24 A border official from the town of Yi[16] requested an audience with the Master, saying, "I have never failed to obtain an audience with the gentlemen who have passed this way." Confucius' followers thereupon presented him.

After emerging from the audience, the border official remarked, "You disciples, why should you be concerned about your Master's loss of office? The world has been without the Way for a long time now, and Heaven intends to use your Master like the wooden clapper for a bell."

Most commentators take this as a reference to Confucius' loss of the office of Criminal Judge in the state of Lu; this is presumably the reason that Confucius and his disciples are leaving the state. The ability of the border official to see Confucius' true mission is taken by many commentators as an indication that he is a sage in hiding: a virtuous man who has taken a lowly position in order to protect himself in chaotic and unvirtuous times. The bell referred to is (depending on which source

---

[16] In the state of Wei, on the border with Lu.

one consults) the kind used either by itinerant collectors and transmitters of folk songs or functionaries who circulated around the countryside promulgating official announcements. In either case, the border official's point is thus that Heaven has deliberately caused Confucius to lose his official position so that he might wander throughout the realm, spreading the teachings of the Way and waking up the fallen world.

3.25 The Master said of the Shao music, "It is perfectly beautiful, and also perfectly good (*shan* 善)."[17] He said of the Wu music, "It is perfectly beautiful, but not perfectly good."

The Shao was the court music of the sage-king Shun, and the Wu the music of King Wu, the Zhou king responsible for overthrowing the last of the Shang kings, the evil Zhow. Huang Kan plays on the standard graphic pun between "joy" (樂 AC: *lak*) and "music" (樂 AC: *ngåk*) in glossing this passage:

> All of the myriad things in the world felt joy when Shun succeeded Yao, and Shun followed the people's will in accepting the office. His orchestral music thus harmonized with the spirit of the times, and this is why the Master calls it perfectly beautiful. The succession occurred with proper bows and deference, without the slightest violation of the principles of behavior, and this is why the Master calls it perfectly good. All the world felt joy when King Wu followed the people's will in attacking Zhow. His orchestral music thus harmonized with the spirit of the times, and this is why the Master calls it perfectly beautiful. However, a minister attacking his lord represents a violation of the principles of behavior, and this is why he says that it is not perfectly good.

The idea is that one's moral character is apparent in the music one creates: King Wu found it necessary to resort to force in deposing King Zhow—rather than obtaining the world through wu-wei, as did Shun (15.5)—because of a slight flaw in his character that is revealed in his music and apparent to the subtle ears of Confucius. For the idea of music revealing one's character, see 14.29, and for additional comments on Confucius' view of the Shao music, see 7.14.

3.26 The Master said, "Someone who lacks magnanimity when occupying high office, who is not respectful when performing ritual, and who remains unmoved by sorrow when overseeing mourning rites—how could I bear to look upon such a person?"

Huang Kan observes that "this passage is meant to criticize the unvirtuous rulers of Confucius' age" (2.24). In 3.10, Confucius wished to avoid the sight of egregious violations of proper ritual form; here, he is disgusted by the prospect of form unaccompanied by emotional substance. See also 2.7, 3.4, 3.8 and 3.12.

---

[17] "Good" in the sense of "good at something" (*shan*) (elsewhere translated as "excellent," here meaning something like "good for people to listen to"—i.e., having a good effect on them), to be distinguished from "Good" (*ren* 仁) in the sense of "morally good, good as a person, highest moral virtue."

BOOK FOUR

Many of the passages in this book concern the supreme virtue of Goodness. Those who are truly Good love the Confucian Way and embody it in an wu-wei fashion—completely unselfconsciously and effortlessly—as opposed to those who pursue the Way because of ulterior motives. Such true gentlemen require nothing from the world but the genuine joy and satisfaction they derive from virtue, as opposed to "petty people" who are motivated by considerations of profit or other external goods. This Book also contains a series of statements (4.19–4.21) on filial piety that flesh out the treatment in Book One.

4.1 The Master said, "To live in the neighborhood of the Good is fine. If one does not choose to dwell among those who are Good, how will one obtain wisdom?"

There are two main interpretations of this passage—one literal, the other more metaphorical—and each is reflected in the two Warring States followers of Confucius. We see echoes of the more literal take in the *Xunzi*: "Therefore, when it comes to his residence, the gentleman is necessarily picky when choosing his village, and in his travels he seeks out the company of other scholars. He does so in order to guard against depravity and crudeness, and stay close to the right path of the mean."[1] Understood in this way, the focus of the passage is the importance of one's social environment for the development of one's character. A slightly different interpretation is found in *Mencius* 2:A:7, where a quotation of 4.1 is prefaced with the following:

> Is an arrow-maker not less benevolent (*ren*) than the armor-maker? The arrow-maker is concerned solely with harming others, while the armor-maker is concerned solely with making sure others are not harmed. With shaman-doctors and coffin-makers it is the same.[2] Therefore, one cannot but be careful in the choice of one's profession.

Although here one's "dwelling place" is understood metaphorically as one's general sphere of activity, the general idea is similar: one must be careful when choosing one's environment.

4.2 The Master said, "Without Goodness, one cannot remain constant in adversity and cannot enjoy enduring happiness.

"Those who are Good feel at home in Goodness, whereas those who are clever follow Goodness because they feel that they will profit (*li* 利) from it."

---

[1] Chapter 1 ("Encouraging Learning"); Knoblock 1988: 137.

[2] I.e., the same situation as that of the arrow-maker: they both profit off the misfortune or suffering of others.

Regarding the first half of this saying, Kong Anguo comments, "Some cannot remain constant in adversity because sustained adversity motivates them to do wrong, and cannot enjoy enduring happiness because they inevitably fall into arrogance and sloth." The second half is an explanation of the first: those who are truly Good are spontaneously and unselfconsciously Good—they "feel at home" in virtue, having internalized it to the point that externalities no longer matter. Both Confucius (7.16, 7.19) and Yan Hui (6.7, 6.11) illustrate this quality. Those who are merely clever are motivated by the external benefits of being virtuous, and therefore follow Goodness in a more self-consciously goal-oriented manner. The problem with this is that virtue does not always pay (4.5), so when the going gets rough these people lack the genuine inner commitment to remain upon the Way. Alternately, when virtue does end up paying off with social acclaim, wealth, and official position, these clever people— having attained their external end and lacking any commitment to the Way as an end in itself—fall into immoral arrogance and idleness. A more elaborate version of this passage in the *Record of Ritual* adds a third level of self-consciousness and effort: "Those who are Good are at ease in Goodness, those who are clever follow Goodness because they know that they will profit from it, and those who are afraid of punishment force themselves to follow Goodness."[3] See also 6.20, "One who knows it is not the equal of one who loves it, and one who loves it is not the equal of one who takes joy in it."

4.3 The Master said, "Only one who is Good is able to truly love others or despise others."

Jiao Xun, elaborating upon Kong Anguo's commentary, explains, "The Good person loves what is really worthy of admiration in others and despises that which is genuinely despicable in them. This is why such a person is said to 'be able to love others and despise others.'" Only the Good person is an accurate and impartial judge of character, able to love virtue in others without envy and despise vice in others without malice.

4.4 The Master said, "Merely set your heart sincerely upon Goodness and you will be free of bad intentions."

There are at least two other ways to render the second half of this line: "free of hatred (reading 惡 in falling tone, as in 4.3) or "free of wrong doing" (Zhu Xi). The first seems ruled out by the sense of 4.3: the Good person does in fact despise or hate when such an emotion is appropriate. Kong Anguo's reading ("if you are able to set your heart sincerely upon Goodness, then in other respects you will forever be free of badness") may endorse the second reading, but is somewhat ambiguous. Li Wei argues against the second reading, noting that "if the passage means that one who has set his heart sincerely upon Goodness will be 'free of wrong doing,' what would be the point of saying it? Of course a person who has set his heart sincerely upon Goodness will be free of wrong doing! It is more likely that the original meaning is that one will be free of bad intentions." This accords better with 4.2: even a clever person can act in accordance with Goodness (i.e., remain "free of wrong doing"), but only a truly Good person thoroughly and spontaneously embodies it in action, emotion, and thought (cf. 2.4, 7.4, 7.5).

---

[3] Chapter 31 ("The Record of Examples"); Legge 1967, vol. 2: 333.

4.5 The Master said, "Wealth and social eminence are things that all people desire, and yet unless they are acquired in the proper way I will not abide them. Poverty and disgrace are things that all people hate, and yet unless they are avoided in the proper way I will not despise them.

"If the gentleman abandons Goodness, how can he merit the name? The gentleman does not go against Goodness even for the amount of time required to finish a meal. Even in times of urgency or distress, he necessarily accords with it."

> The true gentleman is dedicated to the Way as an end in itself, and does not pursue it for the sake of external goods (1.14, 4.9, 7.12, 8.12). As a result, he embodies the Way unselfconsciously and effortlessly, and derives a constant joy that renders him indifferent to externalities (7.16, 7.19, 9.29). Cf. the *Xunzi*: "Where there is Goodness there is no poverty or hardship, and where Goodness is lacking there is no wealth or honor."[4]

4.6 The Master said, "I have yet to meet a person who truly loved Goodness or hated a lack of Goodness. One who truly loved Goodness could not be surpassed, while one who truly hated a lack of Goodness would at least be able to act in a Good fashion, as he would not tolerate that which is not Good being associated with his person.

"Is there a person who can, for the space of a single day, simply devote his efforts to Goodness? I have never met anyone whose strength was insufficient for this task. Perhaps such a person exists, but I have yet to meet him."

> In 7.30 we read, "Is Goodness really so far away? If I merely desire Goodness, I will find that Goodness is already here," and in 9.30, "I have yet to meet a man who loves Virtue as much as the pleasures of the flesh." A bit of frustration is apparent in all of these passages: we all have the ability to be Good if we would simply love it as we should, but how can one instill this love in someone who does not already have it (or who loves the wrong things)? This problem comes again in 6.12, when the disappointing disciple Ran Qiu claims to love the Way but complains that he lacks the strength to pursue it. Confucius sharply rebukes him in words that echo 4.6: "Those for whom it is genuinely a problem of insufficient strength end up collapsing somewhere along the Way. As for you, you deliberately draw the line." This is the heart of a paradox that Confucius faced—we might refer to it as the "paradox of wu-wei," or problem of how to consciously develop in oneself or instill in others genuine unselfconscious spontaneity—that will come up again and again in the *Analects* (cf. 5.10, 7.34, 16.5). We also see in this passage the hierarchy of moral attainment: positive, unselfconscious love of Goodness being superior to a mere aversion to immorality.

4.7 The Master said, "People are true to type with regard to what sort of mistakes they make. Observe closely the sort of mistakes a person makes—then you will know his character."

> Understood in this way, the point of this passage is that it is in unpremeditated, unconscious actions that one's true character is revealed (cf. 2.9, 2.10), and this seems to fit

---

[4]Chapter 23 ("Human Nature is Bad"); Knoblock 1994: 161.

well with the overall sense of Book Four. The pre-Tang commentators, however, take this passage as a comment on rulership and the need for understanding (*shu* 恕). Kong Anguo, for instance, remarks, "The fact that petty people are not able to act like gentlemen is not their fault, and so one should be understanding and not blame them. If you observe their mistakes, you can put both the worthies and the fools in their proper places, and this is what it means to be Good." The link between Goodness and understanding that we find elsewhere (6.30, 12.2, 15.24) makes this a plausible reading, and it is reinforced by the fact that many pre-Tang versions of the text have *min* 民 "common people" as the subject of the first clause. Understood this way, the last part of the passage should be rendered something like, "this is what it means to understand Goodness."

4.8 The Master said, "Having in the morning heard that the Way was being put into practice, I could die that evening without regret."

The pre-Tang commentators take the passage in the manner reflected by the translation. He Yan's commentary reads, "The point is that [Confucius] is approaching death and has yet to hear that the world has adopted the Way." Luan Zhao says:

> The Way is what is employed in order to save the people. The sage preserves his self in order to put the Way into practice. The point is to save the people with the Way, not to save one's self with the Way. This is why we read that if the Way were genuinely heard by the world in the morning, even if one died that evening it would be alright. [Confucius] is pained that the Way is not being put into practice, and moreover makes it clear that he is more concerned about the world than his own self.

Zhu Xi, on the other hand, understands the passage to mean: "Having in the morning learned the Way, one could die that evening without regret." He comments, "If one were able to hear the Way, one's life would flow easily and one's death would come peacefully, and there would be no more regrets." Both interpretations are plausible.

4.9 The Master said, "A scholar-official who has set his heart upon the Way, but who is still ashamed of having shabby clothing or meager rations, is not worth engaging in discussion."

Li Chong comments, "Those who value what lies within forget about what lies without. This is why in past ages those who possessed the Way were able to put it into action, caused their family members to forget about their poverty, and caused kings and dukes to forget about glory—how much less would they have worried about clothing and food?" Cf. 1.14.

4.10 The Master said, "With regard to the world, the gentleman has no predispositions for or against any person. He merely associates with those he considers right."

The verbs of this passage all have to do with social associations, but it can be (and often is) understood more metaphorically and abstractly: "the gentleman has no predispositions for or against anything, and merely seeks to be on the side of the right." In either case, we see here an indication of the situational responsiveness of the gentleman, who relies upon his internal moral sense—rather than conventional social prejudice—when judging people or affairs. Confucius' approval of his conventionally tabooed son-in-law in 5.1 and his suspicion of unexamined social judgments in 13.4 can serve as a practical illustrations of this principle.

4.11 The Master said, "The gentleman cherishes virtue, whereas the petty person cherishes physical possessions. The gentleman thinks about punishments, whereas the petty person thinks about exemptions."

Some commentators, such as Li Chong, take this passage to be referring to virtuous government and the relationship between the ruler and the people: when the ruler is virtuous, the people cherish their abodes; when the ruler pays attention to enforcing the laws, the people cherish the favors that such good government brings to them. This is possible, but the sense of the passages that surround it favor the second common reading, advocated by Zhu Xi and others, that the issue is the gentleman's public, impartial orientation versus the petty person's penchant for personal gain and favoritism. As Cheng Shude puts it,

> Everyone has a different explanation of this passage, but it seems to me appropriate to indicate my humble opinion of its general gist. The question that occupies the mind of the gentleman all day is how to improve his Virtue and perform his job, whereas the petty person pursues nothing more than his livelihood and worries about nothing other than his material needs. The gentleman is comfortable with social distinctions and holds fast to the norms, whereas the petty person has his mind focused upon nothing but profit and, if he falls afoul of the law, tries to avoid punishment without giving it a second thought.

4.12 The Master said, "If in your affairs you abandon yourself to the pursuit of profit, you will arouse much resentment."

As Master Cheng explains, "If you wish to obtain profit for yourself, you will inevitably harm others and thereby arouse much resentment." The gentleman is to be guided by considerations of what is right, not what is profitable (4.16, 14.12).

4.13 The Master said, "If a person is able to govern the state by means of ritual propriety and deference, what difficulties will he encounter? If, on the other hand, a person is not able to govern the state through ritual propriety and deference, of what use are the rites to him?"

Here we see two themes emphasized. The first concerns the efficacy of Virtue-based government, as opposed to government by force or reward and punishment, and is related to the distaste for contention and considerations of profit expressed throughout this Book. A passage from the *Zuo Commentary* describes the importance of ritual and deference for the functioning of the state:

> Deference is the mainstay of ritual propriety. In an ordered age, gentlemen honor ability and defer to those below them, while the common people attend to their agricultural labors in order to serve those above them. In this way, both above and below ritual prevail, and slanderers and evil men are dismissed and ostracized. All of this arises from a lack of contention, and is referred to as "excellent Virtue." Once an age declines into disorder, gentlemen strut about announcing their achievements in order to lord over the common people, and the common people boast of their skills in order to encroach upon the gentlemen. Both above and below there is a lack of ritual, giving birth simultaneously to disorder and cruelty. All of this arises from people contending over excellence, and is referred to as "darkened Virtue."

It is a constant principle that the collapse of the state will inevitably result from such a situation.[5]

The second theme is related to the sort of anti-Ivory-Tower attitude expressed in 13.5: traditional practices are meant to be applied to the real world, not merely studied theoretically.

4.14 The Master said, "Do not be concerned that you lack an official position, but rather concern yourself with the means by which you might become established. Do not be concerned that no one has heard of you, but rather strive to become a person worthy of being known."

Again we see a distaste for self-assertion, self-aggrandizement, and contention for external goods. The gentleman focuses solely upon achieving the internal goods of the Confucian Way. External recognition should and may follow, but is subject to the vagaries of fate and is not inevitable (especially in a disordered or corrupt age), and in any case is not a worthy object of concern. Cf. 1.16, 12.20, 14.30, 15.19.

4.15 The Master said, "Master Zeng! All that I teach can be strung together on a single thread."

Guan 貫 means "thread," and Huang Kan reads it as a metaphor: everything that the Master teaches is unified theoretically by one principle, like objects strung on a single thread. The *Analect*'s emphasis on practice over theory makes it likely, however, that the "single thread" is a kind of consistency in action rather than a unified theoretical principle, and this is supported by Master Zeng's elaboration below. See the commentary to 15.3 for more discussion of the "single thread."

"Yes, sir." Master Zeng responded.
   After the Master left, the disciples asked, "What did he mean by that?"
   Master Zeng said, "All that the Master teaches amounts to nothing more than dutifulness (*zhong* 忠) tempered by understanding (*shu* 恕)."

Although there is a general agreement upon the meaning of *shu*, commentators differ considerably regarding their understanding of *zhong*. There are quite a few passages in the *Analects* directly or indirectly concerned with *shu* (5.12, 6.30, 12.2, and 15.24), and it is clear that this virtue involves some sort of considerations of others—an ability to imaginatively project oneself into another's place. There is more debate about *zhong*. One dominant line of interpretation begins with Wang Bi, who defines *zhong* as "fully exhausting one's emotions" and *shu* as "reflecting upon one's emotions in order to have sympathy with other beings." Zhu Xi and others belong to this line of thinking in defining *zhong* as "exhausting oneself" or "doing one's utmost" (*jinji* 盡己). Relying solely upon relevant passages from within the *Analects* (3.19, 5.19), however, it would seem that *zhong* involves a kind of attention to one's ritual duties, particularly as a political subordinate. Understood this way, being "dutiful" (*zhong*) involves fulfilling the duties and obligations proper to one's ritually-defined role. This virtue is to be tempered by the virtue of "understanding" (*shu*): the ability to, by means of imag-

---

[5] Duke Xiang, Year 13 (559 B.C.E.); Legge 1994d: 438.

inatively putting oneself in the place of another, know when it is appropriate or "right" (*yi*) to bend or suspend the dictates of role-specific duty. *Zhong* is often translated as "loyalty," but "dutifulness" is preferable because the ultimate focus is upon one's ritually-prescribed duties rather than loyalty to any particular person, and indeed *zhong* would involve opposing a ruler who was acting improperly (13.15, 13.23, 14.7).

4.16 The Master said, "The gentleman understands rightness, whereas the petty person understands profit."

Again, the gentleman is motivated by the inner goods of Confucian practice rather than the promise of external goods. Cf. 4.2, 4.5, 4.9, 4.11, and 4.12. Some commentators argue that the distinction between the gentleman and the petty person (*xiaoren* 小人) should be understood in terms of social class, because *xiaoren* is often used in Han texts to indicate simply the "common people." It is clear, though, that Confucius felt anyone from any social class could potentially become a gentleman (6.6, 7.7) and that social status did not necessarily correspond to actual moral worth. It is apparent that—in the *Analects* at least—the gentleman/*xiaoren* distinction refers to moral character rather than social status.

4.17 The Master said, "When you see someone who is worthy, concentrate upon becoming their equal; when you see someone who is unworthy, use this as an opportunity to look within yourself."

That is, one is to emulate the virtues and avoid the vices observed in others; cf. 7.22. The emphasis here is upon action: not just seeing the qualities of others, but also using this insight as an opportunity for self-improvement. As Jiao Yuanxi explains, "The 'seeing' mentioned in this passage refers to that which any person can easily perceive— the difficulty lies entirely in actually beginning to do something about it. The intention of the sage [Confucius] in establishing this teaching was not merely to criticize people for not having true knowledge [of what is right], but rather to upbraid them for lacking sincerity of commitment or the courage to put their will into practice."

4.18 The Master said, "In serving your parents you may gently remonstrate with them. However, once it becomes apparent that they have not taken your criticism to heart you should be respectful and not oppose them, and follow their lead diligently without resentment."

One owes one's parents a unique level of obedience—one that transcends legal responsibilities (13.18) and that exceeds even the demands of dutifulness in the political realm. As Zheng Xuan explains,

> The "Patterns of the Family" [chapter of the *Record of Ritual*] says, "With a regard to a son serving his parents, if he remonstrates three times and is not heeded, there is nothing left to do but, with crying and tears, go along with their wishes." However, it also says, "With regard to a minister serving his lord, if he remonstrates three times and is not heeded, he should leave his lord's service and [turn to study of the classics?]"[6] ... Why is this? Father and son

---

[6] The quoted passages do not appear in the "Patterns of the Family" chapter of the extant *Record of Ritual*, although almost identical variants do appear in Chapters 1–2 ("Summary of Ritual"); Legge 1967, vol. 1: 114.

are genuinely linked to one another—with regard to our Heavenly nature, there is no relationship like it . . . Lord and minister, however, are brought together by considerations of
rightness, and it is thus natural that they should have points of divergence.

Other commentators are also fond of quoting a passage from the "Patterns of the
Family" chapter,

If a parent commits a transgression, the son should—with bated breath, a neutral expression,
and in a gentle voice—remonstrate with them. If the remonstration is not heeded, he should
summon up even more respect and filiality, and once the parent is pleased again, repeat the
remonstration. If the parent is not pleased, it is preferable that the son should strongly remonstrate with them than allow them to commit a crime against the village or county. If the
parent subsequently becomes angry and displeased, and hits the son so fiercely as to draw
blood, the son should not dare to take offense, but should summon up even more respect
and filiality.[7]

Also see *Mencius* 4:A:28, 5:A:2–4, and 7:A:35.

4.19 The Master said, "While your parents are alive, you should not travel far,
and when you do travel you must keep to a fixed itinerary."

Going on an extended journey would entail neglecting one's filial duties. As for the
issue of itinerary, Huang Kan comments:

The "Summary of Ritual Propriety" [chapter of the *Record of Ritual*] says, "The ritual propriety proper to a son dictates that when he goes out, he must inform his parents, and that
when he returns, he must report to them personally, and that in all of his travels he must
keep to a fixed itinerary"[8] . . . If one travels and does not have a fixed itinerary, this will cause
one's parents undue worry.

4.20 The Master said, "One who makes no changes to the ways of his father for
three years after his father has passed away may be called a filial son."

This is a repetition of the second half of 1.11; see Book One for commentary.

4.21 The Master said, "You must always be aware of the age of your parents. On
the one hand, it is a cause for rejoicing, on the other a source of anxiety."

There are various ways to understand this, but the most plausible is that the age of
one's parents is a cause for rejoicing that they have lived so long, while also a source
of anxiety because of their advancing years.

4.22 The Master said, "People in ancient times were not eager to speak, because
they would be ashamed if their actions did not measure up to their words."

Again we see the suspicion of glibness and an emphasis on action over speech. Huang
Zhen comments, "The distinction between the gentleman and the petty person lies

---

[7] Legge 1967, vol. 1: 456–457.

[8] Legge 1967, vol. 1: 68.

in whether or not their words and actions are consistent, and whether or not their words and actions are consistent depends upon whether or not their hearts are capable of knowing shame." Wang Yangming adds sharply, "The ancients valued action, and were therefore shy with their words and did not dare to speak lightly. People nowadays value words, and therefore loudly flap their tongues and blabber nonsense at the slightest instigation." Cf. 1.14, 2.13, 4.24, 12.3, 14.20, and 14.27.

4.23 The Master said, "Very few go astray who comport themselves with restraint."

There are two slightly different ways to take this passage. Some, such as Zhao You, take restraint (*yue* 約) to be a supreme virtue:

> With regard to the Heavenly Way and human affairs, there has never been anything that did not begin with restraint and end with restraint. Restraint that falls into extravagance cannot last, whereas extravagance tempered by restraint can endure. The "Summary of Ritual Propriety" [chapter of the *Record of Ritual*] says, "Arrogance cannot be allowed to endure, desires cannot be indulged, self-satisfaction cannot be countenanced, and joy cannot be taken to extremes."[9] All of this refers to the Way of restraint.

Another way to understand restraint is as a quality that—while falling somewhat short of constituting full virtue—will at least keep one out of serious trouble (cf. 1.13). This second reading is more plausible, and is reflected in Kong Anguo's commentary: "Neither [i.e., restraint or excess] hits upon the mean. If one is extravagant, then one's arrogance and excessiveness will call down disaster, whereas frugality and restraint allow one to at least be free of troubles or concerns."

4.24 The Master said, "The gentleman wishes to be slow to speak, but quick to act."

Here again we see a concern about one's words exceeding one's actual virtue; cf. 4.22. As Wang Fuzhi comments,

> With regard to faults that can afflict the student, none is more troubling than carelessness, and few tasks are begun or completed by those who are casual in their behavior. Carelessness reveals itself in speech—speech that flows like water, that resounds like the tongue of a reed organ, that is blabbered everywhere without one even noticing what one is saying. Proof of excessive casualness is found in one's affairs—in behavior that is overly forward or excessively withdrawn, that is erratic and disrespectful, that is timid and cowardly without one even realizing it. It is only this lack of inclination to be slow to speak and quick to act that prevents the settled ambition of the gentleman from flourishing.

4.25 The Master said, "Virtue is never solitary; it always has neighbors."

A few commentators (such as Liu Baonan) believe that what it means for Virtue not to "be alone" (literally, "orphaned") is that Virtue is never one-sided in a true gentleman: he is both internally respectful and outwardly righteous. A more likely interpretation is that the reference is to the attractive power of Virtue upon others. As the *History of the Han* explains:

---

[9] Legge 1967, vol. 1: 62.

When a minister learns of a king who has received the great commission from Heaven, he will be naturally drawn to him, in a manner beyond what human beings are capable of bringing about. This is the sort of good omen that manifests itself when one has received the Mandate. All of the people in the world will, with one heart, return to such a king, like children returning to their parents. Thus, the auspicious signs of Heaven are brought about through sincerity . . . When Confucius says, "Virtue is never alone; it always has neighbors," he is referring to the effects caused by accumulating goodness and piling up Virtue.

For this interpretation, cf. 2.1 and 15.5. Reading this passage together with 4.1, the point might also be that one requires Good neighbors and friends in order to develop Virtue; for this interpretation, cf. 1.8, 9.30, 12.24.

4.26 Ziyou said, "Being overbearing in service to a lord will lead to disgrace, while in relating to friends and companions it will lead to estrangement."

The word translated as "overbearing" here (*shu* 數) means literally "to count," and although there is a great deal of commentarial controversy about how exactly to understand it, most of the proposed readings are extensions of the sense of "to count": to enumerate (either one's own achievements or the faults of others), to be petty, to pay excessive attention to detail, etc.

BOOK FIVE

Much of the Book is dedicated to discussions of the various virtues that charac-terize the perfected Confucian gentleman, and it is therefore no surprise that most of the passages consist of descriptions of the behavior of historical or contemporary individuals, usually coupled with moral judgments delivered by Confucius. This sort of teaching by means of moral models is a crucial component of any virtue ethic: positive exemplars teach one about the virtues and provide behavioral models for the student to emulate, while negative examples teach one about vice and serve as cautionary tales.

5.1 The Master said of Gongye Chang, "He is marriageable. Although he was once imprisoned as a criminal, he was in fact innocent of any crime." The Master gave him his daughter in marriage.

The identity of Gongye Chang is not clear. Although he is identified by the *Record of the Historian* as a man from Qi, Kong Anguo and others describe him as a disciple of Confucius from Lu. It is not clear what his offense was, but his name later became associated with a variety of legends attributing to him the ability to understand the language of birds and other animals, including an amusing story that describes him being falsely accused of murder because he overheard a group of birds discussing the location of the body of a murder victim. He is freed only after having demonstrated his supernatural abilities to his jailor. Whatever the actual identity or supposed offence of Gongye Chang, the point of this passage is Confucius' independence from con-vention. The social stigma attached to former criminals in early China was enormous and inescapable, since criminals were prominently branded, tattooed, or physically mutilated. In giving his daughter in marriage to a former criminal, Confucius is flout-ing conventional mores and making a powerful statement concerning the independ-ence of true morality from conventional social judgments. As Fan Ning explains, "In giving his daughter in marriage to Gongye Chang, Confucius' intention was to make quite clear the corrupt and excessive manner in which punishments were adminis-tered in his fallen age, and to provide future encouragement to those who truly held fast to rectitude." Fu Guang adds:

> If I have within me the Way of innocence, and yet unfortunately have guilt imposed upon me from the outside, what do I have to be ashamed of? If I have within me the Way of guilt, how can I consider myself worthy of honor, even if by dint of good luck I somehow manage to avoid being externally punished? Therefore, when the gentleman commits even a minor offense behind closed doors, in complete privacy, in his heart he is as mortified as if he had been publicly flogged in the market square. If, on the other hand, he is unfortunate enough to meet with disaster through no fault of his own, and to be pun-ished in the market square or exiled to the barbarian lands, he will accept it all without the slightest bit of shame.

5.2 The Master said of Nan Rong, "When the state possesses the Way he will not be dismissed from office, and when the state is without the Way he will manage to avoid punishment or execution." He gave the daughter of his elder brother to him in marriage.

Nan Rong is usually identified as the style-name of the disciple Nangong Tao of Lu, and later traditions explain that Confucius' older brother was a cripple, which is why the responsibility for marrying off his daughter devolved to Confucius. Zhu Xi comments of Nan Rong that "because he was cautious when it came to both his words and actions, he would be able to find employment in a well-ordered court and would avoid misfortune during a disordered age." Cf. 11.6 shows further evidence of Nan Rong's cautiousness and an alternate explanation for the Master's decision is given.

5.3 The Master said of Zijian, "What a gentleman he is! If Lu were really without gentlemen, where did he learn how to be like that?"

Zijian is the style-name of the disciple Fu Buqi of Lu, who became governor of Shanfu. Most commentators see this passage as praise of the generally high moral character of the state of Lu, no doubt because of its preservation of Zhou culture. Incidentally, it may also be intended as a criticism of the ruler of Lu: having inherited the culture of the Zhou and enjoying the presence of moral worthies, there is no excuse for him not becoming a true king. Cf. 3.9, 3.14.

5.4 Zigong asked, "What do you think of me?"
    The Master replied, "You are a vessel."
    "What sort of vessel?"
    "A *hu* 瑚 or *lian* 璉 vessel."

Of course, "the gentleman is not a vessel" (2.12)—i.e., the true gentleman is more than a mere specialist. According to commentators, the *hu* and *lian* were precious jade food-offering vessels that were the most important ritual vessels in the ancestral temples of the Xia and Shang dynasties, respectively. Commentators point out that Confucius' elaboration is double-edged: comforting, in that Zigong is no ordinary vessel, but perhaps even more critical because the *hu* and *lian* vessels were both archaic curiosities (no longer used in the Zhou rites) and extremely specialized (thus seldom used even during Xia and Shang times). Zigong was a highly accomplished statesman, skillful speaker (11.3), and successful businessman (11.18), but Confucius seems to have felt that he lacked the flexibility and sympathy toward others characteristic of Goodness. This is perhaps why Confucius uses Zigong as his audience for his teaching about understanding in 6.30 and singles out Zigong for his message that "be understanding" is the one teaching that can serve as a life-long guide in 15.24. Zigong seems to be the disciple designated throughout the *Analects* to illustrate the shortcomings of dutifulness uninformed by understanding. Here, his fastidious adherence to the rites leads Confucius to dub him a "sacrificial vessel" of limited capacity; in 5.11, his claim to be understanding is sharply dismissed by the Master; in 5.18, a person he presumably admires is dismissed as being dutiful but not Good; and in 14.29, he is criticized by Confucius for being too strict with others (i.e., for not moderating his duty-based demands on others with understanding). See also 9.6, 9.13, 11.13, 13.20, 14.17, 17.19.

5.5 Someone said, "Zhonggong is Good but not eloquent (*ning* 佞)."

The Master said, "Of what use is 'eloquence'? If you go about responding to everyone with a clever tongue you will often incur resentment. I do not know whether or not Zhonggong is Good, but of what use is eloquence?"

As mentioned in the commentary to 1.3, *ning* ("beautiful of speech") was in early Zhou times the verbal counterpart to *ren* (physically beautiful or impressive), both being desirable qualities of the gentleman. For Confucius, however, *ren* referred to moral excellence in general ("Goodness"), and we have seen how he attempts to drive a wedge between the two qualities: *ren* now stands for true inner virtue and *ning* for its superficial counterfeit—rendered "glibness" elsewhere in this translation. Here we have a speaker confronting Confucius who is still using *ning* in its older, positive sense (hence "eloquence"), and who must therefore be corrected. Even though Confucius is apparently not ready to pronounce Zhonggong Good (his "I do not know" is usually taken as a polite negative), he is to be praised rather than criticized for not being *ning*.

5.6 The Master gave Qidiao Kai permission to take office.

Qidiao Kai replied, "I cannot yet be trusted with such a responsibility."

The Master was pleased.

Qidiao's reply could also be rendered, "I am not confident about it [i.e., that I am ready for the responsibility]." The sense is similar in either case; as Huang Kan puts it, the point is "that Qidiao Kai means that his studies are not yet far enough along, that he is not yet adequately well-versed in the Way. Therefore he would not enjoy the trust of the common people and cannot bear to take office." Confucius is pleased with his humility and realistic assessment of himself. Or, as Fan Ning suggests, "Confucius is pleased with the depth of his commitment to the Way, displayed by the fact that he is not eager to obtain glory or official salary." Other commentators understand the "cannot be trusted" as referring to the rulers of the time; Huang Kan reports such an alternate interpretation: "What Qidaio Kai means is that the ruler of the time were not trustworthy, and he therefore could not take office under them." In this case, Confucius is presumably pleased at Qidiao's accurate assessment of the moral qualities of the Lu rulers and/or his refusal to become associated with unvirtuous behavior.

5.7 The Master said, "If the Way is not put into practice, I will set off upon the sea in a small raft. And the one who would follow me—would it not be Zilu?"

Upon hearing this, Zilu was happy.

The Master commented, "Zilu's fondness for courage exceeds mine. But where can I find some really suitable material (*cai* 材)?"

Most commentators see Confucius' initial remark as related to the sentiment expressed in 9.14. Since his contemporaries are not implementing the Way, he wishes to wash his hands of them and withdraw from public life. There is more disagreement about the second comment. The translation above follows Luan Zhao and others who take *cai* metaphorically as referring to "moral stuff," and understand Confucius to be complaining about Zilu's character. A former warrior, Zilu was admired by Confucius for his courage, but seems to lack other virtues (such as good judgment) that would balance out his courage. Understood this way, the point of this passage is that a virtue such as courage that is entirely uninformed by other virtues becomes a vice (cf. 8.2, 17.8, and 17.23). A similar interpretation is advanced by Zhu Xi, who reads *cai* 材 as *cai* 裁 ("judgment"); in this case, the line might be rendered, "Zilu loves courage more than I do, but has no basis for making good judgments." Finally, some early commentators take *cai* quite literally as material for making a raft. Understood this way, Confucius' second comment is a gentle joke ("but where would I get the lumber?") at the expense of Zilu, who is not bright enough to realize that the Master is not really serious about floating off to sea.

5.8 Meng Wubo asked, "Is Zilu Good?"

Meng Wubo was the son of a minister of Lu, and also appears in 2.6.

The Master replied, "I do not know."
Meng Wubo repeated his question.
The Master said, "In a state of one thousand chariots, Zilu could be employed to organize the collection of military taxes, but I do not know whether or not he is Good."
"What about Ran Qiu?"
"In a town of one thousand households, or an aristocratic family of one hundred chariots, Ran Qiu could be employed as a steward, but I do not know whether or not he is Good."
"What about Zihua?"
"Standing in his proper place at court with his sash tied, Zihua could be employed to converse with guests and visitors, but I do not know whether or not he is Good."

The fact that Goodness functions as the ultimate *telos* defining the narrative arc of one's life means that no final judgment concerning whether or not a given person possesses Goodness can be delivered until that life has been completed. This is why Goodness is portrayed as a dimly perceived and ever-receding goal to a work eternally in progress in 9.11, and why Confucius is reluctant here and elsewhere (5.19, 7.26, 7.33, 14.1) to pronounce anyone truly Good, including himself (7.34). There is probably also a secondary concern that seeing oneself as having already achieved Goodness would make one complacent and lazy. As Cheng Yaotian observes, "Goodness is both the most important thing in the world and the most difficult to achieve. This is why it is said that Goodness must be carried by oneself, that it is a heavy burden, that only after death will one find rest, and that the Way is long.[1] If a person thought that he himself had already achieved this goal, and could therefore rest before having reached the end of his life, this is certainly a sentiment of which the sage would not approve."

5.9 The Master said to Zigong, "Who is better, you or Yan Hui?"
Zigong answered, "How dare I even think of comparing myself to Hui? Hui learns one thing and thereby understands ten. I learn one thing and thereby understand two."
The Master said, "No, you are not as good as Hui. Neither of us is as good as Hui."

---

[1] All references to *Analects* 8.7.

Zigong's hearing one thing and being able to grasp two is possibly a reference to 1.15 (when discussing the *Odes* and "informed as to what has gone before," Zigong is able to "know what is to come"). Zigong is realistic enough to know that even this admirable ability pales in comparison to the almost preternatural talent of Yan Hui, who apparently knows what is being taught even before he is taught it (2.9, 11.4). Some commentators believe that Confucius' last comment is intended merely to comfort Zigong, but it is possible that it is meant sincerely: Confucius was not "born knowing it" (7.20), and passages such as 2.9, 6.7, and 11.4 suggest that Yan Hui was one of those rare and superior people who are born already good (16.19).

5.10 Zai Wo was sleeping during the daytime. The Master said, "Rotten wood cannot be carved, and a wall of dung cannot be plastered. As for Zai Wo, what would be the use of reprimanding him?"

The Master added, "At first, when evaluating people, I would listen to their words and then simply trust that the corresponding conduct would follow. Now when I evaluate people I listen to their words but then closely observe their conduct. It is my experience with Zai Wo that has brought about this change."

Zai Wo obviously lacks the "native substance" (*zhi*) that serves as the background on which the "color" of Confucian self-cultivation is to be applied (3.8). As Huang Kan comments,

> Even when it comes to a famous craftsman or skilled carpenter, his carving is totally dependent upon having good wood to work with if he is to produce a perfect product. If he tries to apply his efforts to a piece of rotten wood, the result will be imperfect. Similarly, when trowelling a wall, if the earth that the wall is made out of is hard and solid, then it is easy to apply an even layer of plaster to create a smooth, clean veneer. If you try applying your trowel to a wall made out of dung, on the other hand, the plaster will crumble and fall off, resulting in an irregular surface. Confucius' purpose in invoking these two metaphors is to tell Zai Wo that if he is the kind of person who sleeps during the daytime then it is impossible to teach him anything.

The first half of the passage emphasizes the importance of native substance. The second has to do with the suspicion of language we have seen several times already: many people talk about virtue, but few actually strive to attain it in practice. As Wang Fuzhi remarks, "When it comes to learning, nothing is more crucial than actual exertion and practice. What one says is not worth paying attention to. Whether or not one gets it through exertion and practice, in turn, depends solely on whether one is diligent or lazy. A person who is able to talk well and is subsequently said to be able to understand, and who then considers himself to have already understood and thus is no longer diligent when it comes to exertion and practice—such a person is profoundly despised by the gentleman." Here, again, we see hints of the "paradox of wuwei" mentioned in the commentary to 4.6: one can only attain virtue if one genuinely desires to attain it, but how does one inspire such a genuine desire in someone who does not already have it? Cf. 6.12.

5.11 The Master said, "I have yet to meet someone who is genuinely resolute."
Someone responded, "What about Shen Cheng?"
The Master said, "Cheng is full of desires, how could he be resolute?"

We know little about Shen Cheng; early commentators report that he was a man from Lu, and many identify him as a disciple of Confucius. Huang Kan sheds some light on the relationship between resoluteness (*gang* 剛) and desires: "A person who is iron-willed is by nature not greedy, whereas Shen Cheng by nature was full of emotions and desires. When you are full of emotions and desires, you demand or seek things from other people, and when you are driven to demand or seek things from others you cannot be resolute." Shen Cheng's fault, then, is that he desires external goods (salary, physical comfort, sex, fame), which serves to undermine his commitment to the Confucian Way. Sun Qifeng relates this passage to 5.7, characterizing the sort of unreflective courage displayed by Zilu as a semblance of the true virtue of being res-olute: "The manly virtue of resoluteness consists entirely in overcoming selfishness and elevating one's heart above material things . . . The sort of rigid strength displayed by Zilu resembles resoluteness, but is not the same. Only when one can stand firmly in the mean—without wavering, no matter what, and feel harmonious without getting carried away—do we see the true virtue manifest itself." We might also see this passage in the context of 5.4 and 5.12, contrasting strength of will with the sort of inflexibil-ity displayed by Zigong.

5.12 Zigong said, "What I do not wish others to do unto me, I also wish not to do unto others."

The Master said, "Ah, Zigong! That is something quite beyond you."

Zigong's aspiration—what has been referred to as the "negative Golden Rule"—is a formulation of the virtue of understanding: the ability to temper the strict dictates of dutifulness by imaginatively placing oneself in another's place (cf. 15.24). Zigong's aspiration to the virtue of understanding is particularly amusing to Confucius because Zigong is the most unimaginative and rigid of all the disciples (cf. 5.4, 14.29). Zhu Xi says of Zigong's aspiration, "This is the sort of thing that a genuinely Good person concerns himself with, and that he does not have to be urged or forced to do. This is why the Master considers it to be something beyond the reach of Zigong" (317).

5.13 Zigong said, "The Master's cultural brilliance is something that is readily heard about, whereas one does not get to hear the Master expounding upon the subjects of human nature or the Way of Heaven."

This passage has presented something of a puzzle to some interpreters, seeing that we can find one mention of human nature (*xing* 性) (17.2) in the *Analects*, and that—although the term "Way of Heaven" (*tiandao* 天道) appears nowhere else in the text—we do find quite a few mentions of the Mandate of Heaven or other topics having to do with Heaven's will. 17.2 might be dismissed as a late addition, and even if we include it with all the various mentions of Heaven, it remains true that Confucius focuses primarily on "this world"—that is, the human world of learning and self-cul-tivation. Thus, one way to understand this passage is that Confucius did not concern himself much with such theoretical, esoteric subjects as human nature or the Way of Heaven, but rather tried to focus his disciples' attention on the task at hand: acquir-ing the cultural refinement necessary to become gentlemen (cf. 6.22, 7.20, 11.12). A related interpretation is suggested by commentators who argue that "human nature" refers to the variable endowment one receives at birth (rather than to some theoreti-cal stance about human nature as we see in the *Mencius* and *Xunzi*), and that, in classical texts, the "Way of Heaven" often refers simply to what we might call "luck" or "fate." Understood this way, "human nature" and the "Way of Heaven" collectively refer to the range of things that are beyond human control, and the point is that the Master focused on what was within human control: commitment to learning and the Confucian Way. This harmonizes well with Confucius' comment in 7.20 that he was not born knowing it, but simply loves learning—you cannot control your inborn qualities or your external luck, but you can decide whether or not to set your mind on learning and take your stand with ritual. It also harmonizes well with other statements concerning fate (*ming* 命) in the text (4.14, 6.10, 7.3, 7.19, 11.18, 14.36,, 12.4–5, 20.3).[2]

5.14 When Zilu learned something, but had not yet been able to put it into practice, his only fear was that he would learn something new.

Most commentators understand the point of this passage to be Zilu's conscientiousness: he would not move on to a new lesson until he had successfully put into practice what he had already learned. We see here again the focus on actual practice as opposed to theoretical knowledge. Wang Yangming cites 5.14 in support of one of his standard complaints about his contemporaries: their tendency to pursue theoretical knowledge about the good to the detriment of actually putting the good into practice. "Our contemporaries are never without knowledge," he remarks. "They run about everywhere accumulated useless knowledge without ever manifesting this knowledge in action. Even if they do manage to put something into practice, they display none of the urgency shown by Zilu. They fritter away their time and carry out their duties in a perfunctory fashion, ungratefully wasting their time, and even when they come across this passage in their reading they remain unconscious of shame." An alternate reading originally proposed by Han Yu reads *wen* 聞 as "fame" rather than "learning": when Zilu gained some renown, but was not yet able to live up to this reputation in practice, his only fear was that his fame should increase.

5.15 Zigong asked, "Why was Kong Wenzi 孔文子 accorded the title 'Cultured' (*wen* 文)?"

The Master replied, "He was diligent and loved learning, and was not ashamed to ask advice from his inferiors. This is why he was accorded the title, 'Cultured.'"

Kong Wenzi ("Cultured Master Kong") is the posthumous title of Kong Yu, minister in the state of Wei (d. ca. 480 B.C.E.). Zigong is puzzled by Kong Yu's flattering posthumous title because Kong was a rather unvirtuous person, known for disloyalty and dissoluteness. Confucius' response probably serves a dual purpose. On the one hand, it serves as a statement about what constitutes the virtue of being cultured; on the other, it tells us that the sage focuses on a person's positive rather than negative qualities. As Xue Xuan observes, "The fact that the Master seizes on his inconspicuous goodness, rather than his obvious badness, illustrates the greatness of the sage's Way and the majesty of the sage's Virtue. Relying solely on the accounts of later people, one would be led to think that Kong Yu was a man unworthy of being discussed, and would thereby miss out on this chance to learn about this inconspicuous goodness."

---

[2] As Cheng Shude points out, further evidence for this interpretation can be found in an alternate version of 5.13 that appears in the *Record of the Historian*: "The Master's teachings on the Heavenly Way and inborn destiny (*xingming* 性命) cannot be heard about" (320).

5.16 The Master said of Zichan, "Of the virtues that constitute the Way of the gentleman, he possessed four: in the way he conducted himself, he displayed reverence; in the way he served his superiors, he displayed respect; in the way he cared for the common people, he displayed benevolence; and in the way he employed the people, he displayed rightness."

> Zichan is the style-name of Gongsun Qiao (d. 521 B.C.E.), a minister in the state of Zheng. Even as a young man he stood out for his virtue; *Zuo's Commentary* reports that after Zheng carried out a successful military action against another state, everyone in the state rejoiced with the sole exception of the still officeless Zichan, who declared, "for a small state [like Zheng], there is no greater misfortune than to lack civil/cultural Virtue (*wende* 文德) but to have military success." He went on to predict dire consequences for Zheng's unvirtuous behavior.[3] On his deathbed, after thirty years of virtuous rule, he gave his son and successor sagely advise about ruling the people with the proper balance of mildness and severity, and when he died, Confucius wept and declared, "In him, we could see the love passed down from the ancients."[4] Although Confucius stops short of declaring Zichan to have been a full gentleman or to have possessed the supreme virtue of Goodness, from his example we learn about important qualities that the gentleman must possess.

5.17 The Master said, "Yan Pingzhong is good at interacting with other people—even after long acquaintance he continues to treat them with respect."

> Yan Pinzhong (6th c. B.C.E.) was a virtuous minister in the state of Qi and a contemporary of Confucius, in whose name the *Annals of Master Yan* was compiled. Some versions of the final half of this passage read "even after long acquaintance others continue to treat him with respect." Huang Kan's commentary is based on this reading: "Generally speaking, human relationships are easily broken, and yet Pingzhong could associate with others for a long time and their respect for him would only become greater." Sun Chuo adds, "When it comes to relationships . . . it is easy to have an auspicious beginning, but hard to have a successful ending. The way to make a relationship endure is by means of frankness, honesty, and consistency, which are difficult to achieve. This is why Confucius holds up Pingzhong as an exemplar."

5.18 The Master said, "Zang Wenzhong housed his sacred tortoises in a hall where the column capitals were carved in the shape of mountains and the roof beams were decorated with images of water plants. How could he be considered wise?"

> Zang Wenzhong is the posthumous title of the Lu minister Zang Sunchen (fl. 7th c. B.C.E.), who apparently was known by his contemporaries as a man of wisdom. Han Dynasty commentators claim that Zang's possession of the sacred tortoises was a usurpation of the prerogatives of a feudal lord. However, Zhu Xi and others argue—based on evidence from the *Family Sayings of Confucius* (hereafter *Family Sayings*) and the *Zuo Commentary*—that housing the sacred tortoises constituted part of Zang's

---

[3] Duke Xiang, Year 8 (564 B.C.E.); Legge 1994d: 435
[4] Duke Zhao, Year 20 (521 B.C.E.); Legge 1994d: 684–685

official ministerial duties, and that his sole mistake was decorating the hall with motifs that were the ritual prerogative of the Son of Heaven. Confucius' criticism seems to have less to do with Zang's ritual violations than his lack of judgment. The giant tortoises were used in divination: the tortoise was sacrificed, questions were posed to the spirits by carving them into the tortoise shell, and a hot poker was applied to the shell. The resulting pattern of cracks revealing the spirits' answers. Zang apparently felt that lavish decorations in the divination hall would impress the spirits—an attempt at flattery that Confucius dismisses as both foolish and inappropriate. Zang Wenzhong comes in for criticism again in 15.14 below.

5.19 Zizhang said, "Prime Minister Ziwen was given three times the post of prime minister, and yet he never showed a sign of pleasure; he was removed from this office three times, and yet never showed a sign of resentment. When the incoming prime minister took over, he invariably provided him with a complete account of the official state of affairs. What do you make of Prime Minister Ziwen?"

Ziwen was Prime Minister in the state of Chu who was renown for his integrity and devotion to the state, and first took the highest office in 663 B.C.E.

The Master said, "He certainly was dutiful."
"Was he not Good?"
"I do not know about that—what makes you think he deserves to be called Good?"

"When Cuizi assassinated the Lord of Qi, Chen Wenzi—whose estate amounted to ten teams of horses—abandoned all that he possessed and left the state. Upon reaching another state, he said, 'The officials here are as bad as our Great Officer Cuizi,' and thereupon left that state. Again, after going to another state, he said, 'The officials here are as bad as our Great Officer Cuizi,' and thereupon left that state as well. What do you make of Chen Wenzi?"

Cuizi and Chen Wenzi were both ministers in the state of Qi. The former is said to have assassinated Lord Zhuang of Qi in 548 B.C.E.

The Master said, "He certainly was pure."
"Was he not Good?"
"I do not know about that—what makes you think he deserves to be called Good?"

We have here both substantive, edifying descriptions of two Confucian virtues and an indirect statement concerning the difficulty of attaining Goodness: even these ancient worthies, renowned for their particular virtues, had not necessarily attained complete moral perfection. Zhu Xi's comment on this passage is helpful:

People these days become instantly hot-headed, red in the face, at the slightest loss or gain. Ziwen was given official position and had this position taken away three times, and yet showed not the slightest sign of pleasure or resentment. These days people holding even minor posts are not willing to take the time to give a quick summary of their official actions to their successors, whereas Ziwen—holding such an exalted position— nonetheless gave an exhaustive and detailed account of the official state of affairs to the incoming prime minister. These days if people develop even the slightest ties to material things they can never manage to get free of them. Wenzi, on the other hand, possessed an immense estate of ten teams of horses and yet abandoned it without a second thought, as if it were an old pair of shoes . . . We must think about why the sage did not endorse as Goodness even the behavior of these two Masters—as elevated and exceptional as it was—and why their behavior was not seen as fully exhausting the virtue of Goodness. If we consider this carefully, and think as well upon how seldom one encounters the equals of these two Masters, it will impress upon us how rare it is to see the principle of Goodness actually realized.

5.20 Ji Wenzi always reflected three times before acting. The Master, hearing of this, remarked, "Twice would have been enough."

Wenzi is the posthumous title of Jisun Xingfu, minister in the state of Lu (d. 568 B.C.E.), who was known for his extreme caution and attention to detail. Confucius' comment is apparently sarcastic, a criticism of Ji Wenzi taking caution to such an excess that it becomes a vice. Zheng Xuan sees this passage as a comment on the problem of dutifulness being taken to an extreme: "Wenzi was dutiful and worthy in his conduct, and rarely committed transgressions in his handling of affairs, but there is no need to reflect three times before acting." Excessive reflection can lead to vacillation or hesitancy to act when the situation demands.

5.21 The Master said, "When the Way was being practiced in his state, Ning Wuzi was wise, but when the Way was not being practiced, he was stupid. His wisdom can be equaled, but no one can equal his stupidity."

The reference is to Ning Wuzi's feigned "stupidity," of course. Ning Wuzi was a minister in the state of Wei, who served during the reign of Duke Cheng of Wei (who ascended the throne in 633 B.C.E.). Although he enjoyed prominence and good repute when the age was ordered, he was wise enough to allow himself to be ignored or considered incompetent when chaos overtook his state—a sign of true wisdom, since being prominent in chaotic times was a sure route to trouble. As Sun Chuo explains,

> Human nature is such that all people are fond of fame. Everyone values wisdom and disdains stupidity, and are unable to change their habit of crudely blowing their own horns, even when an ordered age descends into chaos. Only a profoundly accomplished scholar is able to conceal his wisdom and hide his reputation in order to keep himself whole and to avert harm. It is easy to embellish one's wisdom in order to gain a reputation, but it is difficult to dispense with embellishments in order to protect one's nature.

5.22 When the Master was in the state of Chen, he sighed, "Oh, let us go home! Let us go home! Our young followers back in Lu are wild and ambitious—they put on a great show of brilliant culture, but they lack the means to prune and shape it."

Some commentators believe that this call to return home was occasioned by Lu's offer of employment for the disciple Ran Qiu (11.17, 16.1). Probably the best comment on this passage is found in *Mencius* 7:B:37, which ties it together with 13.21:

> Wan Zhang asked, "When Confucius was in Chen he said, 'Oh, let us go home! Our young scholars back in Lu are wild and ambitious. They advance and seize their objectives, but cannot forget their former ways. When Confucius was in Chen, why did he think upon the wild scholars of Lu?"

Mencius replied, "Confucius said, 'If you cannot get people who have achieved the Middle Way as your associates, you must turn to the wild or the fastidious. The wild plunge right in, while the fastidious are always careful not to get their hands dirty.'[5] Of course Confucius preferred those who had attained the Middle Way, but since he could not be assured of finding them, he thought about the second-best."

"For what reason are some people referred to as 'wild'?"

"Their ambitions are grand and their language extravagant. They are constantly saying, 'The ancients! The ancients!,' and yet if you examine their daily behavior it does not live up to their words."

Here again we have a craft metaphor for self-cultivation. Although the young followers in Lu are a bit rough around the edges, they at least have the proper "native stuff" (unlike, for instance, Zai Wo in 5.10), and merely need to have this coarse stuff shaped and properly trimmed. Their hearts are in the right place, but they need to learn discipline and restraint. In 13.21, both wildness (a preponderance of native stuff) and fastidiousness (a preponderance of cultural refinement) are presented as equally serious deviations from the Way (cf. 6.18), but *Mencius* 7:B:37 ranks the wild ones above the fastidious, and we see other passages in the *Analects* where erring on the side of native substance is preferred (3.4, 3.8, 7.33).

5.23 The Master said, "Bo Yi and Shu Qi did not harbor grudges. For this reason, they aroused little resentment."

Bo Yi and Shu Qi are semi-legendary figures (often mentioned as a pair) said to have lived at the end of the Shang Dynasty. They were both princes in the Shang state of Guzhu, sons of the ruler Mo Yi. When their father died neither wished to take the throne over his brother, with the result that the throne remained vacant. When the Shang fell to the Zhou, they went into voluntary exile and reportedly starved themselves to death, refusing out of loyalty to their former king to eat the grain of the Zhou (16.12). Their names are thus bywords for rectitude, dutifulness, and especially purity (7.14). In *Mencius* 2:A:2, 2:A:9, and 5:B:1 Bo Yi is portrayed as being perhaps excessively fastidious, whereas here the point seems to be that both he and his younger brother—unlike Confucius' own contemporaries, we are probably to understand—managed to be pure without falling into intolerance. Commenting on this passage, Zhu Xi paraphrases the stories from the *Mencius* about Bo Yi's purity and concludes, "Having been introduced to him in this fashion, we might well suppose that he was intolerant. However, his dislike of a person ceased immediately once that person was able to change his fault, and therefore others did not resent his purity." Master Cheng adds, "Not harboring grudges is the true measure of purity."

5.24 The Master said, "Who says that Weisheng Gao was upright? If someone asked him for vinegar, he would beg some from his neighbors and present it as his own."

Many commentators believe that this Weisheng Gao, identified as a man from Lu, is the same person as the Wei Sheng mentioned in many Warring States and early Han texts as a paragon of trustworthiness. As we read in the commentary for 1.13, Wei Sheng took trustworthiness to an excessive extreme, which suggests that he was not truly virtuous after all. He also had a reputation for uprightness (*zhi* 直), and no doubt

---

[5] This saying constitutes *Analects* 13.21.

performed impressive, public acts of uprightness, but it is in the small matters of every-day life where true virtue reveals itself (2.9–2.10), and here Weisheng Gao falls short. As Fan Ziyu notes,

> Saying something is right if it is right; saying something is wrong if it is wrong, saying you have something if you have it and saying you do not have it if you do not have it—this is uprightness. When the sage observes a person, he focuses on how he behaves when it comes to a trifle in order to predict how he will deal with thousand teams of horses.[6] Thus, this message that one must base one's judgments on subtle things is intended to teach people that they cannot but be careful.

We might also refer to *Mencius* 7:B:11: "A man who is after fame might be able to give away a state of a thousand chariots, but if this is not really his true character, in giving away a basket of food or a bowl of soup [his reluctance] will be visible in his face." Therefore, someone eager to acquire a reputation for a particular virtue might be capable on occasion of making grand public gestures, but the emptiness of such gestures will be revealed in the details of his everyday life.

5.25 The Master said, "Clever words, an ingratiating countenance, and per-functory gestures of respect are all things that Zuoqiu Ming considered shame-ful, and I, too, consider them shameful. Concealing one's resentment and feigning friendship toward another is something Zuoqiu considered shameful, and I, too, consider it shameful."

There is some commentarial controversy over the identity of Zuoqiu Ming, but the *Record of the Historian* and other Han texts describe him as the Grand Historian of Lu who later authored *Zuo Commentary* in order to make Confucius' intention in writing the *Annals* clear. Zhu Xi and other later scholars came to doubt this whole tradition, believing that Zuoqiu Ming was simply a famous worthy who lived before Confucius' lifetime. In any case, the point is clear: the aspiring gentleman must be constantly on guard against hypocrisy and other forms of insincerity. "Perfunctory gestures of respect" is a translation of *zugong* 足恭—literally "foot respect." The reference is to mere physi-cal gestures of respect (bowing, giving precedence) unaccompanied by genuine feeling. The phrase also appears in a chapter of *Dai's Great Record of Ritual* (hereafter *Dai's Record*): "The gentleman must have nothing to do with perfunctory gestures of respect or sagely-seeming words (lit. "foot-respect and mouth-sageliness")."

5.26 Yan Hui and Zilu were in attendance. The Master said to them, "Why do you not each speak to me of your aspirations?"

Zilu answered, "I would like to be able to share my carts and horses, clothing and fur with my fellow students and friends, without feeling regret."

Yan Hui answered, "I would like to avoid being boastful about my own abili-ties or exaggerating my accomplishments."

Zilu then said, "I would like to hear of the Master's aspirations."

---

[6] A reference to *Mencius* 5:A:7: "If it were contrary to rightness and against the Way, you could offer Yi Yin rulership of the entire world and he would ignore it, you could offer him a thousand teams of horses and he would not look at them. Similarly, if it were contrary to rightness and against the Way, he would not give away a trifle, nor would he accept one from others."

The Master said, "To bring comfort to the aged, to inspire trust in my friends, and be cherished by the youth."[7]

Yan Hui's aspiration was apparently realized before his death (8.5). Most commentators see Confucius' aspiration as the possession of all-around virtue. Huang Kan reports a family saying concerning the passage: "If the aged are comforted by you, it is necessarily because you are filial and respectful. If your friends trust you, it is necessarily because you are free of deceit. If the youth cherish you, it is necessarily because you are compassionate and benevolent." Cf. the more elaborate version of a similar conversation in 11.26.

5.27 The Master said, "I should just give up! I have yet to meet someone who is able to perceive his own faults and then take himself to task inwardly."

Zhu Xi remarks, "Rare are those who, when they make a mistake, are able to realize it. Rarer still are those who, aware that they made a mistake, are able to take themselves to task inwardly. If one is able to take oneself to task inwardly, then one's sense of repentance will be profound and urgent—a necessity if one is to change oneself. The Master laments because he himself fears he will never get to see such a person, and this should be seen as a serious warning to his students."

5.28 The Master said, "In any village of ten households there are surely those who are as dutiful or trustworthy as I am, but there is no one who matches my love for learning."

Dutifulness and trustworthiness are relatively pedestrian virtues well within the reach of the average person, but it is the Master's love for learning that sets him apart from others (7.20) and that serves as the mark of the true gentleman. Such a love for learning—a prerequisite for attaining the supreme virtue of Goodness—was unfortunately a rare quality among his contemporaries, whose passions inclined more toward money and the pleasures of the flesh (9.18, 15.13). Even among his disciples only Yan Hui was viewed by the Master as having a true love of learning (6.3). An alternate parsing proposed by Wei Guan gives the passage a more wistful than critical tone, reading the second clause as, "How is it that they do not love learning as much as I?"

---

[7] Alternately, "To comfort the aged, trust my friends, and cherish the young."

BOOK SIX

This Book focuses on judgments of disciples, other contemporaries, and historical figures, all of whom function as case studies of either the Confucian virtues being put into practice or the vices an aspiring gentleman is to avoid. Since Confucius' pedagogical goal is to instill virtuous dispositions rather than impart abstract principles, this sort of education by example is a primary strategy.

6.1 The Master said, "Zhonggong can be given a position facing south."

There is some commentarial debate concerning how this praise of the disciple Zhonggong is to be understood. "Facing south" is the proper ritual orientation of a ruler (15.5), and Han Dynasty commentators understand the point to be that Zhonggong is worthy of becoming a feudal lord or even the Son of Heaven. Qing Dynasty scholars see this as excessive praise for a disciple who—although praised along with others in 11.3 for "Good conduct"—does not feature prominently in the text. They note that even ministers who had some responsibility over people took the south-facing position when serving in an official capacity, and therefore believe this passage to be an expression of Confucius' approval of Zhonggong taking an official position under the Ji Family (13.2).

6.2 Zhonggong asked about Zisang Bozi.
  The Master replied, "He is simple, and therefore acceptable."

Presumably the Master means that Zisang Bozi is acceptable as an official or ruler. We are to read 6.2 as Zhonggong following up on the approval he was accorded in 6.1.

Zhonggong said, "To watch over the people by occupying one's position with respect and being simple in one's conduct—this is no doubt acceptable. To occupy one's position with simplicity and also to be simple in one's conduct, however, seems to me to be taking simplicity too far."

There is some debate concerning the identity of Zisang Bozi. Some people identify him with the easy-going Daoist sage Master Sanghu mentioned several times in early texts. One of these stories involves an encounter between Confucius and a casually dressed Master Zisang Bo, where the latter is dismissed as a crude rustic lacking cultivation, who "lives like an ox or a horse" rather than a proper human being. It is highly unlikely that any of these stories have any sort of actual historical connection to the person mentioned in 6.2, but they give us some sense of the kind of "simplicity" being discussed here: rustic, unrefined directness. The point is that simplicity is a virtue when it comes to one's official actions toward the people over which one rules: one's expectations and responses should be simple and clear, so that it is easy for the common people to understand them. Zizang Bozi, however, seems to have taken simplicity and straightforwardness as his only guides in life, failing to see the importance of cultural refinement, indirection, and politeness when it comes to occupying one's position—he is one of the "crude rustics" mentioned in 6.18 who possesses native substance unimproved by cultural refinement.

6.3 Duke Ai asked, "Who among your disciples might be said to love learning?"

Confucius answered, "There was one named Yan Hui who loved learning. He never misdirected his anger and never made the same mistake twice. Unfortunately, his allotted lifespan was short, and he has passed away. Now that he is gone, there are none who really love learning—at least, I have yet to hear of one."

Duke Ai (r. 494–468 B.C.E.) was the nominal ruler of Lu, which was in fact controlled by the Three Families, led by the Ji Family. Commentators and Han sources disagree on the details of Yan Hui's death, but it is clear that Yan Hui was significantly younger than Confucius, and that his premature death was a source of great sorrow for the Master (9.21, 11.9–11.10). We should note that Yan Hui's love of learning is manifested in term of virtuous action, rather than theoretical knowledge. Zhu Xi comments,

> If Yan Hui was angry at Mr. X he would never shift this anger to Mr. Y, and if he made a mistake in the past he would never repeat it in the future. The fact that Master Yan's achievement in overcoming himself reached this height is why we can say that he genuinely loved learning . . . In saying that, "Now there are none who really love learning—at least, I have yet to hear of one," the Master is probably giving expression to his profound sorrow in losing Yan Hui, while at the same time making it clear how difficult it is to find someone who genuinely does love learning.

Beginning with Huang Kan, some commentators have also seen this passage as an indirect criticism of Duke Ai, who vented his anger randomly and constantly repeated previous mistakes. Cf. the shorter version of this passage in 11.7, with Ji Kangzi as interlocutor.

6.4 When Zihua went on an official mission to the state of Qi, Ran Qiu requested a stipend of millet for his mother.

The Master said, "Give her a *fu* 釜."[1]

Ran Qiu asked that the stipend be larger.

The Master said, "Give her an *yu* 庾,[2] then."

In the end, Ran Qiu gave her five *bing* 秉.[3]

[Upon hearing of this], the Master commented, "When Zihua left for Qi he was riding a fat horse and wearing light furs. I have heard it said that the gentleman aids the needy but does not help the rich to become richer."

The disciple Zihua has traditionally been described as going on a mission under the orders of Confucius, but this is historically unlikely; as Brooks and Brooks note, "only in myth did Confucius have his own foreign policy and granary" (2000: 32).

---

[1] A measure of grain, described by commentators as the standard monthly ration for one person.

[2] Another measure of grain, enough to sustain an entire family for a month.

[3] A very large amount of grain, enough to support dozens of families for a month.

Zihua and Ran Qiu were probably both being employed by one of the Three Families of Lu (probably the Ji Family; 13.2), and Ran Qiu—the official actually in charge of distributing stipends—is thus merely consulting Confucius on the proper course of action. There is a great deal of rather dry commentarial debate about the exact significance of the amounts of grain mentioned, but the basic point is that Confucius recommends a basic subsistence stipend for the mother of Zihua, or at most enough grain to support the entire family, whereas the amount actually given by Ran Qiu is far beyond what even the entire family could consume during Zihua's absence. In Confucius' eyes, this constitutes unrighteous profiteering, and is doubly questionable in light of Zihua's already considerable wealth.

6.5 When Yuan Si was serving as steward, he was offered a salary of nine hundred measures of millet,[4] but he declined it.

The Master said, "Do not decline it! [If you do not need it yourself], could you not use it to aid the households in your neighborhood?"

Most commentators explain that the disciple Yuan Si was appointed to be steward of Confucius' household while Confucius was serving as Minister of Justice in Lu. Again, this is probably not historically accurate, and it is more likely that Yuan Si's employer is one of the Three Families. Some commentators see the point of this passage to be simply that, once one has accepted a position, it is improper to decline the salary that goes along with it, but there is probably a bit more to it than that. Reading this passage together as a partner to 6.4, and seeing it in light of the many injunctions against seeking office for the sake of material benefit found in Confucius' teachings, the disciple Yuan Si no doubt expected to be praised by the Master for declining to be paid a salary. The point of Confucius' response is that the proper course of action cannot be determined by a simple formula, but should be the result of careful reflection and consideration of the needs of others. Based on Yuan Si's one other appearance in 14.1, as well as later legends that sprung up around him, he seems to have been one of the excessively "fastidious" (*juan* 狷) who Confucius complains about in 13.21: his obsession with remaining unsullied prevents him from effectively engaging with the world.

6.6 With regard to Zhonggong, the Master said, "If the offspring of a plow-ox has a solid red coat and nicely-formed horns, even if people may think it unsuitable for sacrifice, would the spirits of the mountains and rivers reject it?"

Oxen that were mottled in color or otherwise considered unattractive were relegated to farm use, while oxen with solid red coats and pleasantly-formed horns were specially bred for sacrifice to the spirits. Early commentators believe this passage to be concerned metaphorically with Zhonggong's family background: although Zhonggong's father was a lowly-born and apparently unsavory character, this is no reason to dismiss the son, who in fact displays many admirable qualities. Although human beings may be prejudiced against a lowly-born person or ox, heaven and the spirits are concerned only with the individual's own virtues. Qing Dynasty philologists point out that

---

[4]Or, alternately, the harvest from 900 square *li* of fields; the unit of measure is not specified in the passage.

there is no independent evidence that Zhonggong came from a lowly background, and some argue that the passage in fact constitutes advice to Zhonggong as he is about to take office: when choosing subordinates to serve you, judge them solely on the basis of their own merits, rather than their family backgrounds or social prestige. In either case, the point is very much the same: in one's judgments, one must look beyond conventional social prejudices.

6.7 The Master said, "Ah, Yan Hui! For three months at a time his heart did not stray from Goodness. The rest could only sporadically maintain such a state."

Again we have Yan Hui being praised for his effortless and consistent embodiment of true virtue; cf. 2.9, 5.9, 6.11, 9.20, 11.4. "Three months" is probably meant in the general sense of "a long time" rather than in its literal sense.

6.8 Ji Kangzi asked, "Could Zilu be employed to carry out official business?"

The Master replied, "Zilu is resolute. What difficulty would he have carrying out official business?"

"What about Zigong?"

"Zigong is perceptive. What difficulty would he have carrying out official business?"

"What about Ran Qiu?"

"Ran Qiu is a master of the arts. What difficulty would he have carrying out official business?"

Early commentators and even Zhu Xi have little to say about the meaning of this passage. Later, commentators speculate that Confucius, having returned to Lu from the state of Wei, had become resigned to the fact that he was not going to be employed to his full potential, and therefore recommended some of his more promising disciples to serve under Ji Kangzi in an attempt to at least moderate the excesses of the Ji Family.

6.9 The Ji Family offered Min Ziqian the position of steward of the Ji Family fortress at Bi.

Min Ziqian said [to the messenger bringing this news], "Please courteously decline the offer for me. If they ask for me again, you can find me beyond the banks of the Wen River."

The Wen River marked the boundary between Lu to the south and Qi to the north; the disciple Min Ziqian's point is that, if Ji Kangzi insists on summoning him again, he will flee the state. Most commentators attribute his reluctance to the fact that the previous steward of Bi, a worthy man named Gongshan Furao, had been disgusted by Ji Kangzi's despicable behavior and had rebelled against him. Furthermore, Confucius' disciples, and even Confucius himself, were not adverse to serving the Ji Family in public offices, where they would be formally serving the state of Lu as a whole and—at least in theory—serving as ministers to the legitimate lords of Lu. An additional problem here seems to be that Bi was the Family's private fortress-city, and that serving as its steward would contribute nothing to the public good.

6.10 Boniu fell ill, and the Master went to ask after his health. Grasping his hand through the window, the Master sighed, "That we are going to lose him must be due to fate! How else could such a man be afflicted with such an illness, [and we left with nothing we can do?][5] How else could such a man be afflicted with such an illness?"

Early commentators explain that the disciple Boniu was suffering from a disfiguring illness and did not want anyone to see him, which is why Confucius must comfort him through the "window" (possibly referring simply to an opening in a screen set up around Boniu's bed). The main point of the passage seems to be human helplessness in the face of fate. As Huan Maoyong explains,

Whether we are successful or unsuccessful in life, and whether we live to a ripe old age or die prematurely, are things that we consign to the space between what we can know and what we cannot know. The gentleman simply cultivates that which lies within his control, and then goes along with everything else, viewing it as fate, and that is all. Fate is something that not even the sage can change or avoid . . . which is why the ancients' technique for protecting their lives consisted solely of being cautious when it came to their speech and showing restraint in their eating and drinking.

For the gentleman's attitude toward fate, see 4.14, 7.3, 7.19, 11.18, 12.4–12.5, 14.36, and 20.3.

6.11 The Master said, "What a worthy man was Yan Hui! Living in a narrow alley, subsisting on a basket of grain and gourd full of water—other people could not have borne such hardship, yet it never spoiled Hui's joy. What a worthy man was Hui!"

Here again we see the idea that the true gentleman, sustained by the internal goods of the Confucian Way, is indifferent to externalities (cf. 1.14, 4.2, 4.5, 4.9, 7.12, 7.16, 15.32). Zhou Dunyi comments, "Master Yan simply focused upon what was important and forgot what was trivial. When you focus upon what is important, your heart is at peace; when your heart is at peace, you will find satisfaction in all things." This idea of focusing on the important rather than the trivial links 6.11 with its partner passage 6.12.

6.12 Ran Qiu said, "It is not that I do not delight in your Way, Master, it is simply that my strength is insufficient."

The Master said, "Someone whose strength is genuinely insufficient collapses somewhere along the Way. As for you, you deliberately draw the line."

Ran Qiu has already decided he cannot proceed further along the Master's Way, and so does not even really try. As we read in 4.6, there is no one who really lacks the strength to pursue the Way—what is lacking among most of Confucius' contemporaries is the kind of genuine love for the Way that sustains Yan Hui and Confucius during the long and arduous journey of self-cultivation. As Hu Anguo observes

The Master praised Yan Hui for his imperturbable joy [in 6.11]. Ran Qiu heard this, and this is why he says what he says here [in 6.12]. However, if Ran Qiu really did delight in the

---

[5]The latter half of the sentence is present in the Dingzhou version, and is also part of the *Record of the Historian* version of this story.

Master's Way, it would be like the palate's taking delight in the meat of grain-fed animals:[6] he would surely exhaust his strength in pursuing it, and how could he possibly worry about his strength being insufficient?

Despite his protests to the contrary, Ran Qiu actually lacks a true passion for the Way. The problem, as we have seen, is how to instill this love in someone who does not already possess it.

6.13 The Master said to Zixia, "Be a gentlemanly *ru*. Do not be a petty *ru*."

As discussed in the Introduction, in this context *ru* is a term that refers to a class of specialists concerned with transmitting and teaching the traditional rituals and texts of the Zhou. Most commentators see this passage as advice to Zixia before he begins to accept his own disciples. There are two general lines of interpretation of this passage. Kong Anguo (followed by the Cheng brothers and Zhu Xi) takes the "petty" *ru* to be someone like the "village worthy" of 17.13: "When a gentleman serves as a *ru*, it is in order to clarify the Way; when a petty person serves as a *ru*, it is because he is greedy for fame." In other words, the petty *ru*, according to this interpretation, is someone who is after external goods and does not really love the Way for its own sake. Another line of interpretation links this passage to 13.4 and 13.20, and sees the petty *ru* as something more akin to the narrow technician or "vessel" mentioned in 2.12. As Cheng Shude explains,

> At this time Zixia was establishing a school in Xihe to transmit the *Odes* and the *Rites*, and stood out among the Master's disciples for his cultural refinement and learning. We can sincerely describe him as a *ru*. However, if one focuses one's energies exclusively on philological studies and the explication of isolated passages one will become narrow-minded, vulgar, and shallow, and one's achievements will be trivial. In advising Zixia to be a "gentlemanly *ru*," the Master is probably encouraging him to enter the realm of broad-ranging concerns and lofty understanding.

Both interpretations are plausible.

6.14 Ziyou was serving as steward of Wucheng.

The Master asked him, "Have you managed to find any worthy people there?"

Ziyou answered, "There is one named Tantai Mieming. He does not take shortcuts when conducting business, and I have never seen him in my chamber except upon official business."

Wucheng was a city located in the south of the state of Lu. The point seems to be that Tantai Mieming is entirely scrupulous in his behavior, according in every detail with his official duties and not attempting to gain personal favor with his superior. He is an exemplar of the virtue of dutifulness in action. Most likely Confucius makes this inquiry as a way of checking up on how well Ziyou has been performing in his new capacity. As Huan Maoyong remarks,

> Ziyou was renowned for his cultural refinement and learnedness, and generally among cultivated people who have accumulated some experience there are none who do not appreciate talent. However, a scholar-official who has cultivation but no practical experience

---

[6] A reference to *Mencius* 6:A:7: "Order and rightness please my heart in the same way that the meat of grain-fed animals pleases my palate."

occasionally relies upon cliques of senior officials who oppress the people. In asking whether or not he had managed to find a worthy person, the Master was really trying to gauge Ziyou's degree of common sense and practical insight. In replying with the example of Mieming, Ziyou was demonstrating that his city had at least one gentlemanly senior official worthy of serving as an example to others and capable of appearing before his superiors with an appropriate level of respect.

6.15 The Master said, "Meng Zhifan is not given to boasting. When his forces were retreating he stayed behind to defend the rear, but as they were about to enter the city gates he spurred his horses ahead, saying, 'It was not my courage that kept me back, but merely that my horses would not advance.'"

Meng Zhifan was a minister of Lu whose forces were routed by the army of Qi in a battle outside the Lu capital in 485 B.C.E. Like a true gentleman, he was virtuous in action but self-deprecating in presenting himself to others. We are to see him as a contrast to the majority of Confucius' contemporaries, who exaggerate their meager achievements and boast of qualities that they do not actually possess.

6.16 The Master said, "These days it is hard to get by without possessing either the glibness of Priest Tuo or the physical beauty of Song Chao."

Both of these figures were ministers of Wei, Priest Tuo being famous for his eloquence and Song Chao (originally an aristocrat from the state of Song) for his good looks. This utterance no doubt dates from the Master's stay in the state of Wei. Priest Tuo is accorded limited praise in 14.19, but we have already seen Confucius' suspicion of both of these qualities. Superficial appeal is rarely a sign of true virtue (1.3), and the Master's point here is to lament his contemporaries penchant for flash over substance. As Fan Ning explains,

> Priest Tuo utilized flattery in order to win the favor of Duke Ling [of Wei], and Song Chao relied upon his physical beauty in order to gain the affection of Nanzi.[7] In an age that lacks the Way, it is these two qualities than win approval. Confucius detested the corruption and confusion that characterized the people of his age, who valued nothing but glibness and beauty and would not accept or approve of genuinely dutiful and correct men.

6.17 The Master said, "Who is able to leave a room without going out through the door? How is it, then, that no one follows this Way?"

We have here an eloquent expression of the exasperation Confucius felt with his contemporaries' perverse refusal to follow the Way of the ancients. Fan Ning understands the passage as having to do with learning: "When walking, all people know that they have to go out by means of the door, and yet none realize that it is only by means of learning that they can be truly accomplished." The *Record of Ritual* relates it to the ritualization of everyday life: "Ritual encompasses the great and the small, the manifest and the subtle . . . Therefore the primary rites number three hundred, and the everyday rites number three thousand, but the destination to which they ultimately lead one is the same. There has never been a person who has entered a room without using the door."[8] In either case, the point is the same: the Way of the ancients is the only way to live a proper human life.

---

[7] The notoriously corrupt and decadent consort of Duke Ling; see 6.28.

[8] Chapter 10 ("Ritual Vessels"); Legge 1967, vol. 1: 404.

6.18 The Master said, "When native substance overwhelms cultural refinement, the result is a crude rustic. When cultural refinement overwhelms native substance, the result is a foppish pedant. Only when culture and native substance are perfectly mixed and balanced do you have a gentleman."

This passage is perhaps the earliest expression of an ideal that later became very important in Confucian writings: the doctrine of holding fast to the "mean" (*zhong* 中), introduced explicitly in 6.29. A perfect balance between native substance and cultural refinement is the ideal state, although if one is to err it should be on the side of substance (3.4, 3.8, 5.10, 5.22, 7.33, 13.27). For the ideal of the "mean," see also 1.12, 13.21, 17.8, and 20.1.

6.19 The Master said, "A person survives by being upright. If you try leading a crooked life, only blind luck will allow you to get by."

This seems to be a partner passage to the exasperated 6.16: despite the depravity of the current age, moral rectitude will see one through. As Ma Rong comments, "The point is that rectitude and uprightness are what allow one to live in the world and come to a natural end." Liu Baonan elaborates, "A crooked person expends all of his energy deceiving himself in order to deceive other people. This is what it means to turn yourself into a monster, to make your life unlivable. If you are not punished by your superiors, you will surely suffer some natural misfortune—only sheer luck would allow you to escape this fate."

6.20 The Master said, "One who knows it is not the equal of one who loves it, and one who loves it is not the equal of one who takes joy in it."

The "it" referred to is most likely the Confucian Way. There are several slightly different ways to take this passage, but what is being referred to is the increasing level of unselfconsciousness and ease that characterizes the true Confucian gentleman. Bao Xian takes the "it" in the more narrow sense of learning: "One who knows about learning lacks the sincerity of one who loves learning, and one who loves learning lacks the depth of one who takes joy in it." Zhang Shi invokes an analogy to food:

It is like the five cultivated grains. "One who knows it" knows that they are edible. "One who loves it" has eaten them and found them delicious. "One who takes joy in it" has found them delicious and has moreover eaten his fill. If you know it but are not able to love it, this means that your knowledge is not yet complete, and if you love it but are not able to take joy in it, this means that your love has not yet been consummated. Is not [joy in the Way] what strengthened the resolve of the ancients and allowed them to go forward without rest?

6.21 The Master said, "You can discuss the loftiest matters with those who are above average, but not with those who are below average."

Although some commentators understand "average" to refer to overall moral character, in an alternate version of this passage in the *Guliang Commentary* it explicitly refers to level of understanding, and this is the most likely meaning here. Most commentators see this as a rationale for Confucius' practice of "skillful means": altering his teachings to accord with the level of understanding of his listeners (11.22). As Zhang Shi says, "Altering one's teachings to fit the level of understanding of one's audience is to means by which one allows them to ask and think about issues that are relevant to them, and is also the way one leads them gradually into higher levels of understanding."

6.22 Fan Chi asked about wisdom.

The Master said, "Working to ensure social harmony among the common people, respecting the ghosts and spirits while keeping them at a distance—this might be called wisdom."

He then asked about Goodness.

The Master said, "One who is Good sees as his first priority the hardship of self-cultivation, and only after thinks about results or rewards. Yes, this is what we might call Goodness."

Many commentators believe that Fan Chi is asking for advice in preparation for taking office, and therefore understand Confucius' answers as tailored to the duties of an official. "Social harmony among the common people" is the translation of *minzhiyi* 民之義 —literally, "rightness [among] the common people." "Rightness" in this sense usually refers to observing proper social distinctions and role-specific duties, and this is the sense in which this phrase is understood in later Han texts. The *Record of Ritual*, for instance, asks rhetorically,

> What is meant by "rightness among the people" (*renyi* 人義)? Kindness on the part of fathers, filialness on the part of sons, goodness on the part of elder brothers, obedience on the part of younger brothers, rightness on the part of husbands, obedience on the part of wives, benevolence on the part of elders, compliance on the part of juniors, Goodness on the part of the ruler, dutifulness on the part of the minister—these ten things are what is meant by "rightness among the people."[9]

By himself providing an example to the common people, an official or ruler ensures that they will accord with rightness (1.2, 2.21). "Respecting the ghosts and spirits while keeping them at a distance" is understood by most as fulfilling one's sacrificial duties sincerely and in accordance with ritual (3.12), without trying to flatter the spirits or curry favor with them (2.24), and thereby also reinforcing moral behavior among the common people (1.9, 2.5). In this respect, 5.18 seems particularly relevant: Zang Wenzhong's attempt to impress the spirits with ritually inappropriate decorations is declared by Confucius to be a sign of his lack of wisdom. Confucius' comments on Goodness accord with the themes we have seen so far: the Good person focuses on self-cultivation and the inner goods of the Confucian practice rather than any potential external rewards. Also cf. 12.21 and 15.38.

6.23 The Master said, "The wise take joy in rivers, while the Good take joy in mountains. The wise are active, while the Good are still. The wise are joyful, while the Good are long-lived."

This is a famously cryptic passage. A somewhat neo-Daoist-flavored interpretation of the first two lines is provided by Bao Xian: "The wise take joy in actively exercising their talent and wisdom in governing the world, just as water flows on and on and knows no cease. The Good take joy in the sort of peace and stability displayed by mountains, which are naturally nonactive and yet give birth to all of the myriad things." The precise meaning of the last line is particularly problematic. It is unclear why only the wise (and not the Good) should be joyful, for instance. As for "the Good are long-lived" statement, some commentators attempt to reconcile it with the premature death of Yan Hui by understanding it metaphorically: it is the reputation or

---

[9]Chapter 9 ("Ritual Usages"); Legge 1967, vol. 1: 379–380.

beneficial influence of the Good person is long-lived. Others reject this strategy, arguing that—the isolated counter-example of Yan Hui aside—the Good are long-lived because they are calm and free of desire for external things. All of these interpretations are quite speculative.

6.24 The Master said, "With a single change, Qi could measure up to Lu. With a single change, Lu could attain the Way."

The state of Qi was originally founded as a fief for the Grand Duke, the head of the Jiang clan that were the Zhou's primary ally in the conquest of the Shang. It was held by rulers not directly descended from the royal Jii clan. Lu, on the other hand, was established under the rule of the Duke of Zhou's son, Count Qin. Bao Xian comments, "The point is that both Qi and Lu benefit from the residual influence of the Duke of Zhou and the Grand Duke. The Grand Duke was a great worthy, while the Duke of Zhou was a sage. Despite the fact that the government and moral teachings in each state had declined by Confucius' age, if an enlightened ruler arose Qi could be made to be the equal of Lu, and Lu could once again be as it was when the Way was being put into practice." This idea of relating the relative rankings of Qi and Lu to the relative virtue of their founders can be found in other early texts; in any case, it is clear that Lu held a special place in Confucius' mind because of its direct connection to the Duke of Zhou and, consequently, its relatively complete preservation of Zhou traditions (cf. 3.9, 3.14).

6.25 The Master said, "A *gu* 觚 that is not a proper *gu*—is it really a *gu*? Is it really a *gu*?"

A *gu* was a ritual drinking vessel. Many commentators believe that Confucius' sigh of displeasure was provoked by the fact that the sort of *gu* being made by his contemporaries was not a proper *gu* (i.e., not in accordance with ancient standards), although there is disagreement over the question of what precisely was wrong. Some claim that the offending *gu* was not of the proper size. Mao Qiling, for example, claims that the *gu* being made by Confucius' contemporaries was larger than the traditional *gu*, and sees this passage as a complaint against the excesses of Confucius' age—in this case, excessive drinking. His interpretation is supported by many of the early commentaries. Wang Su, for instance, remarks that "People of that age were besotted with wine, and thus 'a *gu* not being made like a *gu*' refers to this ignorance of ritual propriety"; Cai Mo adds, "The power of wine to disturb one's Virtue has been a concern since ancient times, which is why [ancient regulations for drinking vessel size were established], to guard against drunkenness." Many of these commentators see the loss of ritual propriety regarding drink as symbolic of more general ritual excesses. Other commentators—such as He Yan or Zhu Zhongdu—see the problem as related to the shape of the *gu* or the manner in which it was manufactured, in which case the passage is similarly understood as an illustration of Confucius' strict adherence to ancient practices, his dissatisfaction with the practices of his contemporaries, and his concern for the proper use of names (cf. 13.3). Finally, Brooks and Brooks present a compelling alternate interpretation, based on the claim of William Willets that the *gu* was an exclusively Shang vessel that was no longer being manufactured or used during Confucius' lifetime, and that had been reduced to a valued, but unused, museum-piece (1998: 36). This would somewhat change the meaning of the passage ("A *gu* that is not being used as a *gu*"), turning it into a lament on the part of Confucius that he—like the *gu*—was not being put to proper use.

6.26 Zai Wo asked, "If someone lied to a Good person, saying 'a man has just fallen into the well!', would he go ahead and jump in after him [to save the supposed man]?"

The Master replied, "Why would he do that? The gentleman can be enticed, but not trapped; he can be tricked, but not duped."

> The point seems to be that the gentleman expects the best of people and always takes them at their word, which unfortunately means that he can be taken advantage of or tricked in petty ways. Since he always follows the Way, however, he cannot be duped (*wang* 罔; literally "trapped in a net") when it comes to important matters, because such serious forms of deception require active foolishness or greed on the part of deceived (consider, for example, the phenomenon of pyramid schemes). Perhaps the best commentary on this passage is *Mencius* 5:A:2, where we read how the sage-king Shun was deceived and tricked by his evil relatives, but ultimately escaped harm and continued to expect the best of them. Such enduring good faith and optimism in others may seem like naiveté to the cynical, but it is the Way of the gentleman.

6.27 The Master said, "Someone who is broadly learned with regard to culture, and whose conduct is restrained by the rites, can be counted upon to not go astray."

> A person who has been molded by the two main Confucian traditional forms—learning and ritual training—can be relied on to act appropriately. As Zhu Xi comments, "When it comes to learning, a gentleman desires broadness, and there is therefore no element of culture that he does not examine. When it comes to self-control, he desires restraint, and his every motion must therefore be in accordance with ritual. Having been disciplined in this way, he will not go against the Way." Some commentators believe that it is the learning or culture of the gentleman that must be restrained by the rites (rather than the gentleman himself), but 9.11 supports the first reading. This passage is repeated in 12.15.

6.28 The Master had an audience with Nanzi, and Zilu was not pleased. The Master swore an oath, saying, "If I have done anything wrong, may Heaven punish me! May Heaven punish me!"

> Nanzi was the consort of Lord Ling of Wei, and a woman of bad repute. Zilu is not pleased that Confucius would seek an audience with such a person. As many commentators point out, however, it is likely that ritual dictated that when arriving in a state one request an audience with the "orphaned little lord"—i.e., the wife or consort of the local ruler. In having an audience with Nanzi on arriving in Wei, Confucius was suppressing his personal distaste for Nanzi, overcoming the disapproval of his disciples, and risking more general opprobrium in order to observe an important dictate of ritual propriety. Zilu is being presented here as similar to Chen Wenzi in 5.19: as "pure," but with a rigid fastidiousness that falls short of Goodness. Alternate interpretations of the passage see Zilu's displeasure as resulting from suspicion—either that illicit activity may have occurred during Confucius' audience with the notoriously lascivious Nanzi, or that the Master was seeking some sort of questionable political advantage in seeing her—and have Confucius defending his innocence.

6.29 The Master said, "Acquiring Virtue by applying the mean—is this not best? And yet among the common people few are able to practice this virtue for long."

An alternate reading of the final line is, "for some time now such virtue has been quite hard to find among the people." This is how He Yan and Zhu Xi take it, but alternate versions of this passage in other early texts support the reading adopted in the translation. *Yong* 庸 might also be read as "constant" rather than "application," in which case the first line would read, "acquiring Virtue through constantly holding to the mean," although the *Record of Ritual* supports the first reading when it praises the sage-king Shun: "He grasped both extremes, and applied the mean between them (*yongqizhong* 用其中) when dealing with the common people."[10] This ideal of keeping to the mean is also seen in 1.12, 6.18, 13.21, 17.8, and 20.1.

6.30 Zigong said, "If there were one able to broadly extend his benevolence to the common people and bring succor to the multitudes, what would you make of him? Could such a person be called Good?"

The Master said, "Why stop at Good? Such a person should surely be called a sage! Even someone like Yao or Shun would find such a task daunting. Desiring to take his stand, one who is Good helps others to take their stand; wanting to realize himself, he helps others to realize themselves. Being able to take what is near at hand as an analogy could perhaps be called the method of Goodness."

We see here (as in 12.2, 17.20, and especially 12.22) hints of the shift toward *ren* as the more specific and limited virtue of "benevolence" that is complete by the time of Mencius.[11] Many commentators see this exchange as an attempt to rein in excessive speculation on the part of Zigong and bring him back to the fundamentals of self-cultivation. As Huan Maoyong explains,

> Zigong discusses Goodness from some distant, esoteric perspective, while the Master discusses it as something intimate and close to home. Zigong talks about great and difficult to attain rewards—something on an order of magnitude that even Yao or Shun would find difficult. The Master talks about extending the self to reach other people—something that simply requires us to plumb our own minds and hearts, to start with what is near at hand in order to reach what is far away.

The final line of Confucius' advice sounds like a formulation of the virtue of understanding (*shu*)—something that we have already seen is apparently beyond Zigong's grasp (5.12). This sort of ability to feel compassion for others and respond to the world flexibly is a crucial element of the more general virtue of Goodness that Zigong lacks, and this description of understanding as the "method of Goodness" is probably formulated for his benefit. In 7.34, the Master describes sageliness and Goodness as things beyond even his grasp, but makes it clear that he is at least practicing the "method of Goodness": "working at it without growing tired" (taking his stand, realizing himself) and "encouraging others without growing weary" (helping others to take their stand and realize themselves). Cf. 17.5.

---

[10] Chapter 32 ("Doctrine of the Mean"); Legge 1967, vol. 2: 302.

[11] Refer to Appendix 1 for more on the development of the term *ren*.

BOOK SEVEN

A discernable common theme in this Book is the importance of a properly directed and sufficiently intense will or intention, which requires a focus upon the goods internal to Confucian practice. Such a focus leads to a sense of joy that renders one immune to the allure of externalities.

7.1 The Master said, "I transmit rather than innovate. I trust in and love the ancient ways. I might thus humbly compare myself to Old Peng."

There is a great deal of commentarial controversy concerning the meaning of the reference to "Old Peng"—even if one or two people are being referred to—but the least fantastic explanation is that of Bao Xian, who takes the reference to be to one person: "Old Peng was a great worthy of the Yin Dynasty who was fond of transmitting ancient tales. In comparing himself to Old Peng, Confucius indicates his reverence for those who merely transmit [and do not innovate]." Some commentators, such as Huang Kan, believe that Confucius refrained from innovating because he was not a ruler and did not have the authority to create new social institutions. It is more likely that transmission is all that Confucius countenanced for people in his age, since the sagely Zhou kings established the ideal set of institutions that perfectly accord with human needs—the "door" through which anyone wishing to become a gentleman must pass (6.17).

7.2 The Master said, "Remaining silent and yet comprehending, learning and yet never becoming tired, encouraging others and never growing weary—these are tasks that present me with no difficulty."

Repeated in a slightly different form in 7.34, these seemingly modest qualities represent the "method of Goodness" mentioned in 6.30, something far beyond the grasp of most people.

7.3 The Master said, "That I fail to cultivate Virtue, that I fail to inquire more deeply into that which I have learned, that upon hearing what is right I remain unable to move myself to do it, and that I prove unable to reform when I have done something wrong—such potential failings are a source of constant worry to me."

tors point out that the sort of "worry" (*you* 憂) mentioned here must be distinguished from the ordinary sorts of worries that other people have. As Jiao Yuanxi

laster speaks of being "joyful and forgetting worry" (7.18), this "worry" is the sort of ry that troubles the human mind—the same worry that is spoken of in the lines, could not have born such worry/hardship (*you*)" (6.11), "the Good person does 29), and "the gentleman does not worry and feels no fear" (12.4). The "worry" spoken of here [7.3], however, is the sort of worry mentioned in the line, "the gentleman has worries his entire life" (*Mencius* 4:B:28)—that is, the "trembling fear, cautiousness and discipline" spoken of in Zhu Xi's commentary to [*Mencius* 4:B:19]. It is this sort of "worry," and this alone, that allows a worthy or a sage to become what they are.

In *Mencius* 4:B:28, the difference between these two types of worries is formulated in terms of a distinction between being "worried" (*you*) and "concerned" (*huan* 患):

> The gentleman has worries his entire life, but is never concerned for even a single moment. Now, the sort of worries he has are of this sort: [the sage-king] Shun was a person. I am also a person. Shun served as a model for the world worth passing down to later generations, while I still cannot manage to be more than a common villager. This is indeed something worth worrying about. What is to be done about this worry? One should merely try to become like Shun, that is all. In this way, the gentleman is never concerned. If something is not Good, he does not do it; if something is not ritually correct, he does not put it into practice. Thus, even if some sort of external problem (*huan*) arises, the gentleman is not made concerned by it.

The aspiring gentleman focuses upon what is under his control (self-cultivation), and consigns the rest to fate. Cf. 4.14, 11.18, 14.36, 15.32.

7.4 In his leisure moments, the Master was composed and yet fully at ease.

Huang Shisan comments, "This passage records the manner in which the sage's bearing, even when he was merely sitting at his leisure, was harmoniously adapted to the circumstances and always appeared to be in accordance with the mean." Like the accounts of Confucius' ritual behavior that constitute Book Ten, this passage describes the effortless, unselfconscious manner in which the Master embodied the Confucian Way.

7.5 The Master said, "How seriously I have declined! It has been so long since I last dreamt of meeting the Duke of Zhou."

The point seems to be that one's immersion in the culture of the Zhou should be so complete that it penetrates even into one's dream-life. Some commentators also understand the ability to see the Duke of Zhou while dreaming as a testament to Confucius' power of concentration and his power of will (*zhi* 志). The "Vast Will" chapter of *The Annals of Lü Buwei* refers obliquely to 7.5:

> It is said that Confucius and Mo Di [Mozi] spent their entire days reciting, memorizing and practicing their lessons, to the point that, at night, they could personally see King Wen and Duke Dan of Zhou [in their dreams] and ask questions of them. With this sort of intensely focused will, what task could they not master? What action could they not bring to completion? Thus, it is said, "When you focus and immerse yourself in your studies, the spirits will come and report to you." Of course, [such achievement] is not a result of the spirits actually reporting to you, but of your focus and total immersion.[1]

7.6 The Master said, "Set your heart upon the Way, rely upon Virtue, lean upon Goodness, and explore widely in your cultivation of the arts."

We seem to have here, as in 2.4, an account of the stages of self-cultivation, although the various achievements mentioned are not necessarily in chronological order. The first line might also be rendered, "Set your will/intention (*zhi* 志) upon the Way," and (2.4) it seems to be the crucial first step in Confucian self-cultivation: a conscious and

---

[1] Knoblock and Riegel 2000: 618.

sincere commitment to the Way of the Zhou kings. Wang Yangming emphasizes the importance of this first step in his comment on this passage:

> If you set your will upon the Way then you will become a scholar of the Way and Virtue, whereas if you set your will upon the cultural arts, you will become merely a technically-skilled aesthete. Therefore, you cannot but be careful about the direction of your will. This is why, when it comes to learning, nothing is as important as focusing upon the correct goal. What the ancients referred to as the "cultural arts" were ritual, music, archery, charioteering, calligraphy, and arithmetic. These were all integral parts of their daily lives, but the ancients did not focus their will upon them—they felt that they must first establish the basics and then the rest could follow. What people nowadays refer to as the "cultural arts" are merely literature, calligraphy, and painting. What could these things possibly have to do with the needs of daily life?

The idea that the cultural arts represent the final finishing touch applied to an already substantial moral foundation is also found in 1.6 and 3.8.

7.7 The Master said, "I have never denied instruction to anyone who, of their own accord, offered up as little as a bundle of silk or bit of cured meat."

There is some debate over the exact meaning of the terms *shu* 束 and *xiu* 脩, literally "restraint/bundle" and "strip," here taken separately to mean "bundle of silk and strips [of cured meat]." The terms could also be taken as a compound, either as "bundle of cured meat" or (as in some early texts) the strip with which a man can bind his hair. Zheng Xuan explains that *shuxiu* means "over fifteen years of age," presumably because this is the age when men in ancient times began binding their hair when going out in public. In this case, the point would be that Confucius would accept anyone over age fifteen as a student. Others take the term as a metaphoric extension of the "hair tie" sense (again, relying upon precedents in early texts), understanding it as a reference to the bearing of the person seeking instruction—that is, an attitude of self-restraint and self-discipline. As Mao Qiling observes, however, the verb "offering up" in the text strongly suggests that *shuxiu* refers to a literal object, and many early texts mention *shuxiu* in a context where it is clear that the term refers to small, symbolic, ritually-dictated offerings made by a student seeking instruction. Most likely, then, we should follow Kong Anguo in seeing the point as being that Confucius' door was open to anyone who came willingly and in a ritually correct manner—that is, he did not discriminate on the basis of social status or wealth.

7.8 The Master said, "I will not open the door for a mind that is not already striving to understand, nor will I provide words to a tongue that is not already struggling to speak. If I hold up one corner of a problem, and the student cannot come back to me with the other three, I will not attempt to instruct him again."

As Zhu Xi notes, this represents the flip side of Confucius' contribution as a teacher mentioned in 7.2 ("encouraging others and never growing weary"): for education to work, the student must also contribute to the process. The ideal student should come to the project possessed by an inchoate need for what study is able to provide—something like the passion for learning that causes Confucius himself to forget to eat (7.19). While Confucius certainly saw the role of traditional knowledge as being much more essential than Socrates did, there is nonetheless a similar maieutic quality to his method. Cf. 15.16.

7.9 When the Master dined in the company of one who was in mourning, he never ate his fill.

7.10 The Master would never sing on a day when he had wept.

These two passages fit together so neatly that some commentators argue that they should be read as one passage. One way to understand them is as examples of ritually proper behavior, and the *Record of Ritual* actually quotes both lines as models for proper mourning practice.[2] It is unlikely, however, that either of the behaviors described were explicitly dictated by the ritual standards of the time, and most commentators (from He Yan down to Zhu Xi) understand the point to be about sincerity and depth of feeling. That is, while others might observe the superficial niceties of the mourning rituals and then get on with their day, Confucius *felt* the rituals (even if they were being enacted by someone else), and remained profoundly affected by the emotions they evoked. Understood this way, the point is not that Confucius consciously refrained from eating his fill or singing, but that he was actually rendered unable to eat a full meal or engage in light-hearted activities.

7.11 The Master remarked to Yan Hui, "It is said, 'When he is employed, he moves forward; when he is removed from office, he holds himself in reserve.' Surely this applies only to you and me?"

Zilu interposed, "If you, Master, were to lead the three armies[3] into battle, who would you want by your side?"

The Master replied, "I would not want by my side the kind of person who would attack a tiger barehanded or attempt to swim the Yellow River,[4] because he was willing to 'die without regret.' Surely I would want someone who approached such undertakings with a proper sense of trepidation, and who came to a decision only after having thoroughly considered the matter."

The first remark refers to the virtue of timeliness (*shi* 時): responding flexibly and appropriately to the situation with which one is confronted. As Kong Anguo puts it, it is the ability to "advance when it is appropriate to advance, and remain still when it is appropriate to remain still." Such sensitivity to context and effortless grace is the hallmark of an accomplished gentleman. Most likely Confucius' comment was intended not only to praise Yan Hui, but also to indicate to Zilu the areas in which he might best develop himself morally. Zilu misses the point, though; presumably jealous of this praise for Yan Hui, he tries to win approval from the Master for his own characteristic reckless courage (cf. 5.7). Of course, it is precisely Zilu's recklessness that the Master was trying to rein in with his initial statement, and so the Master is forced to explicitly reprimand him.

---

[2] 7.9 is repeated in Chapter 3 ("Tan Gong") of the *Record of Ritual* (Legge 1967, vol. 1: 147), and 7.10 is paraphrased ("on a day when one has wept [in mourning], one should not sing"), without reference to Confucius himself, in Chapter 1 ("Summary of Ritual") (Legge 1967, vol. 1: 89).

[3] I.e., the combined military force of a large state.

[4] A reference to Ode 195: "They do not dare to attack a tiger barehanded/Or swim the Yellow River/They know one thing/And one thing only:/To be apprehensive and careful/As if on the brink of a deep abyss/Or as if treading upon thin ice."

7.12 The Master said, "If wealth were something worth pursuing, then I would pursue it, even if that meant serving as an officer holding a whip at the entrance to the marketplace. Since it is not worth pursuing, however, I prefer to follow that which I love."

Again we have the idea that the gentleman does not pursue externalities. Some commentators see this passage as a comment on fate: wealth cannot be pursued because its acquisition is subject to fate. As in 7.16, however, there seems to be more of a normative edge here: the acquisition of wealth is indeed subject to fate, but is also in itself an unworthy object of pursuit. The point here is more about rightness than fate.

7.13 When it came to fasting, war, and illness, the Master exercised caution.

The significance of this passage is not entirely clear. Most commentators understand "fasting" to generally refer to the abstinence practiced before a sacrifice to the spirits, which included physical fasting as well as mental preparation. The mention of war is a bit odd, although some think it may be a reference to 7.11—an injunction against the sort of rashness displayed by Zilu. The best way to make sense of cautiousness regarding illness is perhaps to connect it to 10.10, where the Master refrains from tasting medicine given to him as a gift because he is ignorant of its properties.

7.14 When the Master was in the state of Qi, he heard the Shao music, and for three months after did not even notice the taste of meat. He said, "I never imagined that music could be so sublime."

The Shao is the court music of the sage king Shun; cf. 3.25. As in 6.7, we are probably to understand "three months" in the sense of "a long time" rather than literally. According to the *History of the Han*, one of the descendents of Shun, who was enfeoffed in the state of Chen, was forced to flee to Qi, bringing Shun's court music with him. We see in this passage, an association between music, joy, and forgetfulness that is also echoed by the graphic pun between the words for "joy" and "music" in ancient Chinese, which are both represented by the character 樂. The joyous rapture inspired by sublimely beautiful music is one of the internal goods of the Confucian practice that frees the gentleman from the demands of externalities. Cf. 8.15.

7.15 Ran Qiu was wondering out loud, "Does the Master support the Duke of Wei?"

The "Duke of Wei" refers to the current ruler of Wei, Duke Chu.

Zigong replied, "Well, I will go ask him."
   He went in to see the Master, and said, "What sort of people were Bo Yi and Shu Qi?"
   The Master replied, "They were ancient worthies."
   "Did they harbor any regrets?"
   "They pursued Goodness and attained Goodness, what regrets could they possible have?"

Zigong emerged and reported to the other disciples, "The Master does not support him."

In 499 B.C.E. Prince Kuai Kui, son of Duke Ling of Wei, made a failed attempt upon the life of Duke Ling's infamous consort Nanzi and was forced to flee the country, abandoning his right to succession.[5] In the summer of 493 B.C.E. Duke Ling died, and—over the protests of Nanzi—his grandson Zhe, son of Kuai Kui, was made ruler, assuming the title of Duke Chu of Wei.[6] Kuai Kui, living in exile in the state of Jin, subsequently repented his former decision and began maneuvering to have himself installed as ruler of Wei. Kuai Kui's efforts were vigorously resisted by his son, who fought to hold onto power. Confucius at this time was staying in Wei at public expense and was in no position (from either a ritual or pragmatic perspective) to directly comment upon the behavior of his host, Duke Chu, which is why Zigong frames the question to him indirectly. Bo Yi and Shu Qi, mentioned already in 5.23, were both princes in the Shang state of Guzhu. When their father died neither wished to take the throne over his brother, with the result that the throne remained vacant. Confucius' praise of these virtuous exemplars is understood by Zigong as an indirect criticism of the unseemly power struggle between father and son currently playing itself out in Wei. As Zheng Xuan explains, "This struggle between father and son for control of the state was a case of bad conduct. By praising Bo Yi and Shu Qi as being both worthy and Good, Confucius is making it clear that he had no intention of aiding the current Duke of Wei." Cf. 13.3.

7.16 The Master said, "Eating plain food and drinking water, having only your bent arm as a pillow—certainly there is joy to be found in this! Wealth and eminence attained improperly[7] concern me no more than the floating clouds."

As Huang Kan explains, the point of the last line is that "floating clouds move about on their own, up in the sky—what connection do they have with me? In the same way, what do wealth and fame improperly attained have to do with me?" We have here another expression of the gentleman's independence from externalities; cf. 1.14, 4.5, 6.11, 7.12. Some commentators also link this latter comment to 7.15: the Master does not support the Lord of Wei—even considering the prospect of a generous salary—because both the Lord and his exiled father are behaving in an improper fashion.

7.17 The Master said, "If I were granted many more years, and could devote fifty of them to learning, surely I would be able to be free of major faults."

The translation follows the Lu version of the *Analects* here in reading the intensifying particle *yi* 亦 in place of *yi* 易 ([Book of] *Changes*); the Gu version reads "If I were granted many more years, so that by the age of fifty I could complete my studies of the *Changes*, this might enable me to be free of major faults." Commentators who follow the Gu version generally see these words as spoken by Confucius in his mid-

---

[5] Duke Ding, Year 14 (496 B.C.E.); Legge 1991d: 788.
[6] Duke Ai, Year 2 (493 B.C.E.); Legge 1991d: 798.
[7] Lit., in a "not right (*yi*)" fashion.

forties—before he had reached the stage of "understanding the Mandate of Heaven" (2.4)—and explain that understanding the Mandate of Heaven is a prerequisite for delving into such an esoteric work as the *Changes*. Most later scholars, doubting that Confucius seriously studied the *Book of Changes*, prefer to follow the Lu version.

7.18 The Master used the classical pronunciation when reciting the *Odes* and the *History*, and when conducting ritual. In all of these cases, he used the classical pronunciation.

Written Chinese characters are not directly phonetic in the manner of a Roman alphabet, and the same character can be pronounced differently by speakers with different dialects. In Confucius' age, people were apparently aware that the spoken languages of the various regions of China differed significantly from the "classical pronunciation," which Liu Baonan argues must have been the dialect spoken in the Western Zhou capital. We must assume that knowledge of these pronunciations was kept alive, at least in the state of Lu, through use in formal and ritual contexts. This passage suggests, though, that Confucius' contemporaries had begun to ignore this tradition and eschew the classical pronunciations in favor of local dialect—a Christian analogy would be the abandonment of Latin in favor of services in the vernacular. This represents a departure from the Way of the Zhou that Confucius characteristically resists. No doubt part of the motivation for abandoning the classical pronunciations was that they were no longer comprehensible, and Zheng Xuan suggests that Confucius would follow his formal recitations with explanations in local dialect. Mao Qiling argues that the "classical pronunciation" (lit. "elegant speech") also involved details of cadence, demeanor, and tone of voice.

7.19 The Duke of She asked Zilu about Confucius. Zilu had no reply.

[Upon Zilu's return], the Master said, "Why did you not just say: 'He is the type of person who is so passionate that he forgets to eat, whose joy renders him free of worries, and who grows old without noticing the passage of the years.'"

The Duke of She was a high minister in the state of Chu; commentators explain that, since the Chu rulers had already usurped the title of "king," Chu ministers had begun calling themselves "dukes." There are two main explanations for why Zilu does not answer his query. Early commentators claim that Duke She was a power-hungry figure who was insistently trying to lure Confucius into his service, and that Zilu was leery of encouraging him in his efforts. Under this interpretation, one purpose of Confucius' response is to indicate that he is not interested in accepting a morally questionable position for the sake of a salary or other material rewards. Later commentators, beginning with Zhu Xi, portray the Duke as a more sympathetic figure who admires Confucius, and see Zilu's failure to respond as a result of the perceived ineffability of Confucius' lofty, mysterious virtue. In this case, Confucius' reaction is refreshingly straightforward: he is far from mysterious, being merely an ordinary man possessed by a great love for the Way of the ancients. The only thing that differentiates him from others is the object of his love; as Wang Yangming notes, "The passions of ordinary people do not extend beyond being passionate about rewards, fame, wealth, and honor . . . The nature of their passion is not different [from the Master's], it is merely the object of their passion that is different." The object, of course, makes difference. We see here again the idea that the unselfconscious joy derived from internal goods of the Confucian Way renders one indifferent to externalities.

7.20 The Master said, "I am not someone who was born with knowledge. I simply love antiquity, and diligently look there for knowledge."

This passage serves as an elaboration of 7.19: Confucius is not especially gifted by nature, he simply knows where to look for knowledge and has the passion to sustain him in this quest. As Zheng Xuan notes, another purpose of this passage "is to encourage others to pursue learning." Cf. 7.1 and 16.9.

7.21 The Master did not discuss prodigies, feats of strength, disorderly conduct, or the supernatural.

Confucius' sole object of concern was self-cultivation—he did not waste time on irrelevant frivolities. As Wang Bi explains,

> "Prodigies" refers to strange or unusual events; "feats of strength" refer to things like Ao's ability to handle warships or Wu Huo being able to lift a thousand pounds; "disorderly conduct" refers to a minister killing his lord, or a son killing his father; and "the supernatural" refers to the service of the ghosts and spirits. These things either have nothing contribute to one's moral education, or are simply things the Master found distasteful to talk about.

For another comment on Ao, see 14.5; Wu Huo was a famous strong man (cf. *Mencius* 6:B:2). For more on topics that the master did not deign to discuss, cf. 5.13.

7.22 The Master said, "When walking with two other people, I will always find a teacher among them. I focus on those who are good and seek to emulate them, and focus on those who are bad in order to be reminded of what needs to be changed in myself."

Alternately, Confucius may be referring to discrete qualities in his companions rather than their overall characters: in any person he can find both virtues to emulate and vices to avoid. Model emulation is the primary method of moral education for Confucius, and the implication here is that the process of education is never completed: even the Master always has something to learn. Cf. 4.17, 16.11.

7.23 The Master said, "It is Heaven itself that has endowed me with virtue. What have I to fear from the likes of Huan Tui?"

Huan Tui was a military minister in the state of Song who apparently wished to do Confucius harm. According to an account in the *Record of the Historian*, while in Song Confucius and his disciples were one day practicing ritual beneath a large tree when Huan Tui, in an attempt to kill Confucius, cut the tree down. The assassination attempt failed, and when the disciples urged the Master to make haste in escaping the state he delivered the remark reported here. Confucius is on a mission from Heaven (3.24), and is therefore subject only to Heaven's command (*ming*). Human beings do not have the power to alter fate, and Confucius therefore accepts whatever may befall him with equanimity, viewing it as Heaven's will. Very similar sentiments are expressed in 9.5 and 14.36.

7.24 The Master said, "Do you disciples imagine that I am being secretive? I hide nothing from you. I take no action, I make no move, without sharing it with you. This is the kind of person that I am."

We should probably relate this passage to 5.13 and 7.21: since the Master did not speak of certain topics, some of his disciples apparently felt that he was keeping some sort of esoteric knowledge from them. This is not at all the case, since all that the Master taught had to do with learning from the ancients and putting this learning into practice—a lesson that he taught every moment through his own actions and comportment. Wang Yangming's comment on this passage is quite helpful:

> When it comes to teaching disciples, there are two approaches: theoretical teaching (*yanjiao* 言教; lit. "teaching through words") and teaching by example (*shenjiao* 身教; lit. "body/personal teaching"). Theoretical teaching is certainly useful for teaching one how to act, but it cannot match the sort of profound affect that one can achieve through teaching by example . . . With his behavior, the Master provided the students with a model to emulate, but there were disciples who were only interested in theoretical teaching. This is why the Master had to make it clear that he was, in fact, not hiding anything from them. This was to serve as a warning to the disciples. The sense is quite similar to that expressed [17.19]: "I wish I did not have to speak (*yan* 言), what does Heaven ever say?"

Confucius' response thus also serves as a warning to the disciples not to fixate on theoretical problems, but rather to focus on the task of actual moral practice. Cf. 16.13, where Boyu, the son of Confucius, is suspected of having received esoteric training, but responds that all that he learned from his father was to study the *Odes* and to learn ritual.

7.25 The Master taught four things: cultural refinement, comportment, dutifulness, and trustworthiness.

This is a companion to 7.24. He Yan remarks, "All four of these things are concrete and observable, and therefore can be held up as models for teaching." There is some debate over what precisely "culture" or "cultural refinement" (*wen* 文) refers to here. Although some commentators understand it as referring to study of the classics and cultural arts. He Yan sees it as referring to the cultural refinement expressed in the Master's demeanor.

7.26 The Master said, "A sage I will never get to meet; if I manage to meet a gentleman, I suppose I would be content. An excellent person I will never get to meet; if I manage to meet someone with constancy, I suppose I would be content. [Yet all I see around me is] nothing masquerading as something, emptiness masquerading as substance, limitation masquerading as grandness. I think even constancy will be hard to find."

This is a typical complaint about the corruptness of Confucius' contemporaries. Many commentators understand the reference to be to the quality of the rulers of the time; this is plausible considering that two of the other three references in the text to the "excellent person" (*shanren* 善人) are clearly to someone serving in a ruling capacity.[8] The final comment, however, favors a broader reference: the problem is people in general. Huang Kan, taking the passage in this more general sense, remarks,

> Confucius' age was corrupt and chaotic. People were all given to boasting and exaggeration, pointing to nothing and saying it was something, taking pleasure in emptiness as if it were substance, and ostentatiously masquerading as wealthy even if their households were poor. All of this represents the opposite of constancy, which is why the Master laments that constancy will be hard to find.

7.27 The Master would fish with a hook, but not with a net.[9] He would shoot with a corded line, but would not aim at roosting birds.

> There are at least two general ways to understand this passage. The first, which accords better with the sense of 7.26, is that the Master adhered to traditional standards of sportsmanship when fishing and hunting, unlike his greedy, unprincipled contemporaries who were intent only upon gain. Some later commentators shift the focus to Confucius' treatment of animals. Hong Xingzu, for instance, remarks, "Here we can see the original mind of the good person. Since he treats animals in this way, we can imagine how he treats people; since he is like this when it comes to minor matters, we can imagine how he is when it comes to matters of importance."

7.28 The Master said, "No doubt there are those who try to innovate without acquiring knowledge, but this is a fault that I do not possess. I listen widely, and then pick out that which is excellent in order to follow it; I see many things, and then remember them. This constitutes a second-best sort of knowledge."

> The final comment is probably a reference is to 7.20 (cf. 16.9): Confucius is not like those rare gifted individuals who are born with knowledge, but must instead seek it from ancient culture (cf. 7.1). On the other hand, he is better than those who recklessly innovate without first having grounded themselves in traditional learning, for such blind innovation is inevitably fruitless (2.15, 15.31). Some commentators—influenced by the traditional picture of Confucius as the author of the *Annals*—take *zuo* 作 as "creating literary works" rather than "innovation" in a general sense, but this is historically less plausible.

7.29 The people of Hu Village were difficult to talk with [about the Way]. Therefore, when a young boy from the village presented himself for an interview, the disciples hesitated to let him in.
    The Master said, "In allowing him to enter, I am not endorsing what he does after he retires. Why are you being so extreme? If a person purifies himself to

---

[8] See 13.11 and 13.29; the other appearance of the term, in 11.19, could also have a political reference.

[9] According to come commentators, the second reference is not to a net, but rather to a fishing device that consisted of one large rope with many hooks dangling from it on individual strings, and that could be strung or dragged across a river and bring in many fish at one time. The sense is the same in either case.

enter, I accept his purification—I make no guarantees about what he will do once he leaves."

As Waley notes, "a supplicant of any kind (whether asking a Master for teaching or Heaven for good crops) purifies himself by fasting and abstinence in order to enhance the power of his prayer."[10] Most commentators take the point of this passage to be that a sincere act of good will should be honored, no matter what a person's reputation or past behavior. Some also see here an optimism in people's ability to change for the better (cf. 17.13).

7.30 The Master said, "Is Goodness really so far away? If I simply desire Goodness, I will find that it is already here."

Bao Xian elaborates, "The Way of Goodness is not far—simply walk it and you will arrive there." Jiang Xi puts a more political spin on the passage: "If you can return to ritual for only a single day, everyone in the world will return home to Goodness—this is how extremely close Goodness is to us." The purpose of this passage is to emphasize the importance of sincere commitment to the Way, but it seems to conflict with passages such as 8.7 ("the burden is heavy and the Way is long"), and is thus symptomatic of the so-called "paradox of wu-wei" mentioned in the commentary to 4.6. For Confucius, the virtue of Goodness, as well as the power of Virtue that comes with it, can only be realized by one who truly loves them for their own sake. The point here in 7.30, however, seems to be that if one truly *does* love them, then one already has them—were a person to truly love Goodness in the same way that he loves to eat and drink, then the battle would be already won. This is no doubt the source of much of Confucius' frustration with his current age (9.18, 9.24, 15.13), as well as with disciples such as Zai Wo, who presumably gives assent to the Confucian project but nonetheless lies sleeping in bed all day (5.10). The student cannot learn from the teacher unless he is passionately *committed* to learning, and this requires possessing a genuine love for the Confucian Way. The problem is that it is hard to see how the teacher can engender this sort of love in a student who lacks it. Cf. 7.34, 9.24, and 9.31.

7.31 The Minister of Crime in the state of Chen asked, "Can we say that Duke Zhao [of Lu] understood ritual?"

Confucius answered, "Yes, he understood ritual."

Confucius then retired. With a bow, the Minister invited Wuma Qi to approach and said to him, "I have heard it said that the gentleman is not partial. Is the gentleman in fact partial after all? His lordship took as his wife a woman from the state of Wu who was of the same clan, and then called her 'Elder Daughter of Wu.' If his lordship understood ritual, who does not understand it?"

The identity of Wuma Qi is not clear, but he was later identified as a disciple of Confucius. "His lordship" is a reference to Duke Zhao.

---

[10] Waley refers to an example of ritual purification before an interview with a potential teacher in the *Guanzi*, Chapter 19, that consists of washing, burnt offerings, and a period of abstinence and fasting (Waley 1989: 129).

Later, Wuma Qi reported this conversation to Confucius. Confucius said, "How fortunate I am! If I happen to make a mistake, others are sure to inform me."

> The royal lines of both Lu and Wu traced their genealogies back to the Great Uncle, eldest son of the first King of Zhou, and thus shared the clan-name Jii 姬. It was a serious violation of ritual to take as a wife or concubine someone with the same clan-name. Therefore, when Duke Zhao took an aristocrat from Wu as his wife, he had people refer to her by the vague locution, "Elder Daughter of Wu," instead of using her proper name, hoping in this way to avoid attracting attention to his incestuous transgression. In this exchange, the Minister of Chen is probably trying to embarrass Confucius by citing some Confucian wisdom to criticize Confucius' actual conduct. "The gentleman is not partial" might be a paraphrase of *Analects* 2.14 or 15.22; the Minister is implying that Confucius is choosing loyalty to the former ruler of his home state over rightness in defending the ritually improper Duke Zhao. Confucius' final response is ironic: although the Minister mocks Duke Zhao for ignoring ritual propriety, he fails to see that asking Confucius to criticize a former lord of his home state—especially in the presence an official of a rival state—is itself a grave violation of ritual, and that Confucius' praise of Duke Zhao was the only ritually proper response. Cf. 3.15, where Confucius is also criticized by a third party for his ignorance of ritual, but in the end demonstrates that it is, in fact, his critic who is ritually ignorant.

7.32 Whenever the Master was singing in a group and heard something that he liked, he inevitably asked to have it sung again, and only then would harmonize with it.

> Some commentators claim that responding to another's song was a dictate of ritual, but this is more likely simply a description of Confucius' willingness and ability to learn from others (cf. 7.22). Zhu Xi comments,

>> The Master would inevitably ask the other person to sing again because he wished to get the nuances and learn from the fine points. Afterward he would harmonize with them because he was happy at having gotten the nuances and grasped the fine points. Here we see the easygoing disposition of the sage: sincere in intention and cordial to the highest degree, while at the same time humble, discerning, and happy to celebrate the excellences of others.

7.33 The Master said, "There is no one who is my equal when it comes to cultural refinement, but as for actually becoming a gentleman in practice, this is something that I have not yet been able to achieve."

> This is perhaps merely a polite demurral (cf. 7.34), but it serves to emphasize the difficulty of obtaining in practice the proper balance between cultural refinement and native substance, and is no doubt meant as a warning against falling into "foppish pedantry"—the more insidious and common of the two failings described in 6.18.

7.34 The Master said, "How could I dare to lay claim to either sageliness or Goodness? What can be said about me is no more than this: I work at it without growing tired and encourage others without growing weary."

Gong Xihua observed, "This is precisely what we disciples are unable to learn."

companion passage to 7.33 with an illuminating coda: the humble love of the Way and striving after it that Confucius is willing to grant himself as a quality is itself something beyond the ability of most people. Gong Xihua's words are very revealing and get to the heart of the paradox of Confucian self-cultivation: in order to keep oneself moving forward along on the "long journey" of self-cultivation it is necessary that one genuinely desire to reach the destination, but how does one teach such desire to a person who does not already possess it?

7.35 The Master was seriously ill, and Zilu asked permission to offer a prayer. The Master said, "Is such a thing done?"

Zilu said, "It is. The *Eulogy* reads, 'We pray for you above and below, to the spirits of Heaven and of Earth.'"

According to commentators, the *Eulogy* is the title of a traditional prayer text.

The Master said, "In that case, I have already been offering up my prayers for some time now."

That is, Confucius' prayer has been his life's work. Any other sort of appeal to Heaven is unnecessary, and the Master is ready to accept whatever fate Heaven may have in store for him. We also see here the theme expressed in 3.12 and 6.22: the gentleman keeps the spirits at a distance and focuses instead upon the human world and the task of self-cultivation. Brooks and Brooks' comment on this passage is quite nice:

> It is very moving, is it not? The Master patiently lets Zilu instruct him in ritual propriety, notwithstanding the fact (or what the hearer of this saying may be presumed to have regarded as fact) that he knows much more about it than Zilu. He then rejects the suggested intercession with the deities. Instead, he offers his whole life as the secular equivalent of a prayer. (1998: 44)

An alternate version of this story, which appears in a lost fragment from the *Zhuangzi* that is preserved in the *Imperial Readings*, focuses specifically upon Confucius' comportment:

> Confucius fell ill, and Zigong went out to make a divination. Confucius remarked, "When I take my seat I do not dare to put myself first, I dwell as if practicing austerities, and I eat and drink [sparingly] as if preparing to perform a sacrifice. I have been performing my own divination for quite some time now."

The theme in this version is similar: one should live one's entire life in a disciplined and reverent manner, rather than adopting discipline and reverence only when one wants to curry favor with the spirits or receive special guidance from Heaven.

7.36 The Master said, "Extravagance leads to presumption, while frugality leads to shabbiness. Compared to presumption, though, shabbiness is to be preferred."

The reference is apparently to ritual behavior. As Kong Anguo notes, "Both are faults, but frugality is better than extravagance. Extravagance leads to the usurpation of privileges above one's station in life, while frugality causes one to fall short of full ritual propriety." The ritual presumptions of the Ji Family as described in 3.1–3.2 and 3.6

are often cited as an example of the dangers of extravagance, while 3.4 explains that, when it comes to ritual, frugality is the lesser of two evils. It is better to err on the side of substance than on the side of refinement (3.8, 5.22).

7.37 The Master said, "The gentleman is self-possessed and relaxed, while the petty man is perpetually full of worry."

The gentleman is relaxed because he is sustained by the internal goods of the Confucian practice, whereas the petty person's focus on externalities exposes him to the vagaries of circumstance. As Jiang Xi notes, "The gentleman is self-possessed and at ease, relaxed and unselfish. The petty person, on the other hand, is always scrambling after glory and fighting for personal gain, constantly anxious about success or failure, and therefore perpetually full of worry." Cf. 7.38 and 13.26.

7.38 The Master was affable yet firm, awe-inspiring without being severe, simultaneously respectful and relaxed.

This companion passage to 7.37 fleshes out the description of the perfected person, who effortlessly embodies the mean of virtue. Cf. 7.4.

BOOK EIGHT

This Book does not seem to have a clear thematic focus. Its most distinguishing feature is series of sayings from Master Zeng that constitute 8.3–8.7.

8.1 The Master said, "Surely we can say that the Great Uncle possessed ultimate Virtue! He declined rulership of the world three times, and yet remained unpraised because the common people never learned of his actions."

Tradition has it that the Great Uncle (*taibo* 太伯) was the older brother of Jii Li (posthumously known as *taiwang* 太王, or the "Great King"), the father of Jii Chang (posthumously King Wen), whose son Jii Fa (posthumously King Wu) defeated the Shang and become the first ruler of the Zhou dynasty. Although his seniority should rightfully have made his own son king, the Great Uncle knew that his father, the Ancient Duke Danfu, was impressed by the worthiness of Jii Chang and wanted him to eventually become king. The Great Uncle therefore secretly gave up his claims to the succession and, along with the middle brother Zhong Yong, went into voluntary exile to the "barbarian lands" of south China. There are various accounts of why he had to decline the succession three times, the least fantastic being that the Great King—also a virtuous man—was reluctant to take precedence over his older brother, and repeatedly attempted to dissuade him from his self-sacrifice. They went back and forth three times because this is the standard of politeness: one must decline a boon three times before accepting it. All of this was handled privately among the brothers, and the fact that the Great Uncle made no public show of his own virtue is what makes him so truly virtuous in Confucius' eyes. The true gentleman is spontaneously and unselfconsciously good.

8.2 The Master said, "If you are respectful but lack ritual you will become exasperating; if you are careful but lack ritual you will become timid; if you are courageous but lack ritual you will become unruly; and if you are upright but lack ritual you will become inflexible.

"If the gentleman is kind to his relatives, the common people will be inspired toward goodness; if he does not neglect his old acquaintances, the people will honor their obligations to others."

Many commentators have suggested that these two sections should be split into separate passages. The first half has to do with the ability of ritual to trim and shape native tendencies so that they fit the mean of true virtue (cf. 1.12, 11.16, 12.1, and especially 17.8, where study or learning rather than ritual training is described as the force preventing virtue from falling into vice). The second half has to do with the power of charismatic Virtue as a force for bringing about political order (cf. 1.9, 12.9). One way of making the two sections cohere is to see the first as a description of how to attain the sort of individual perfection that will then enable one to bring about the political-moral suasion described in the second section. This is how Zhang Shi understands it: "If one understands what comes first and what comes last in the Way of humans, then one can be respectful without being exasperating, careful without being timid, courageous without being unruly, and upright without being inflexible, and will thereby transform the common people and cause their virtue to return to fullness [1.9]."

8.3 Master Zeng was gravely ill and called his disciples to his bedside. "Uncover my feet! Uncover my hands!" he said to them. "The *Odes* say,

> 'Fearful and cautious
> As if looking down into a deep abyss
> As if treading upon thin ice.'[1]

Only now can I be sure of having made it through safely. Note this, my little ones!"

The purpose of uncovering the feet and hands is to see that they remain unharmed— not a given in early China, where amputation was a common punishment. Master Zeng was particularly known for his filial piety, one of the main principles of which was preserving one's body intact. As the *Classic of Filial Piety* says, "One's body, hair, and skin are a gift from one's parents—do not dare to allow them to be harmed." It is only now, on his deathbed, that Master Zeng can be sure to have made it through life without disrespecting his parents in this fashion. The quoted *Ode* is intended as an expression of the anxiety about upholding filial piety that he has felt his entire life, and also to serve as a warning to his disciples.

8.4 Master Zeng was gravely ill, and Meng Jingzi came to inquire about his health.

Master Zeng said to him, "When a bird is about to die, its call is mournful and touching. When a person is about to die, his words should be heeded. There are three things that are important for a gentleman pursuing the Way: by altering his behavioral demeanor, he avoids violence and arrogance; by rectifying his countenance, he welcomes trustworthiness; and in his choice of words and tone of voice, he avoids vulgarity and impropriety. As for the details of handling sacrificial vessels, there are minor officials to deal with that."

Meng Jingzi, son of the minister Meng Wubo who appeared in 2.6, was also a minister in the state of Lu. As Waley observes (1989: 133, n. 3), this is Master Zeng's "swan-song": his final pronouncement before going on his way, and something to be ignored only at one's own peril. According to Zheng Xuan, Meng Jingzi drew this warning from Master Zeng because of his inclination to micro-manage, focusing on minor details to the neglect of his larger duties. "The gentleman is not a vessel" (2.12)—that is, his focus should be general moral perfection and not the technical details involved in running a state, for which he has underlings. Meng Jingzi can best rule his state by ruling himself. If he can regulate his demeanor and countenance as a means of both cultivating and expressing inner moral worth, he can set the tone for the entire state of Lu. As Zhu Xi explains, "The point is that, although there is nowhere the Way is not present, the gentleman should focus his attention solely upon these three tasks. They represent the essentials of self-cultivation and constitute the root of good government."

---

[1] Ode 195; cf. Ode 196.

8.5 Master Zeng said, "Able, and yet asking questions about abilities that one does not possess; using what one has much of in order to ask about what one lacks; having, yet seeming to lack; full, yet seeming empty; offended against, and yet feeling no need to retaliate. I once had a friend who was like this."

The friend Master Zeng is referring to is understood to be Yan Hui. The sort of humility, grace, and lack of resentment described in this passage contrasts markedly with the sort of pretension and overbearingness attributed by Confucius to his contemporaries in 7.26. Jiang Xi notes that "in praising his friend this way, Master Zeng's point is that he himself is not yet able to act in such a fashion."

8.6 Master Zeng said, "Consider someone who can both be entrusted with the care of a young orphan and charged with the command a hundred-square-*li* state, and who can be confronted with great challenges without being shaken. Is this not the gentleman? Yes, this is the gentleman."

The gentleman is able to respond appropriately to the demands of any task, no matter how large or small, with both sensitivity and courage.

8.7 Master Zeng said, "A scholar-official must be strong and resolute, for his burden is heavy and his way (*dao* 道) is long. He takes up Goodness as his own personal burden—is it not heavy? His way ends only with death—is it not long?"

This passage plays on the literal and metaphoric meanings of *dao*, which means physical path or road and the abstract moral "Way." The metaphor of self-cultivation as a life-long journey vividly illustrates the difficulty of the Confucian Way (cf. 8.3, 9.11). As Kong Anguo remarks, "Taking up Goodness as one's own personal task is a heavy burden—there is nothing heavier. Stopping only once death has overtaken you is a long journey—there is nothing longer." An alternate version of this passage found in the *Record of Ritual* is even more extreme: "The Master said, 'As a vessel, Goodness is heavy; as a way, it is long. No one is up to the task of picking it up, nor is anyone able to walk it to its end.'"[2]

8.8 The Master said, "Find inspiration in the *Odes*, take your place through ritual, and achieve perfection with music."

Here we have a more succinct version of the course of Confucian self-cultivation described in 2.4. The translation of the first phrase follows Jiang Xi's interpretation of *xing* 興 as "to inspire, stimulate": "Gazing upon the intentions of the ancients can give inspiration to one's own intention." Bao Xian takes *xing* to mean, more prosaically, "to begin": "The point is that the cultivation of the self should start with study of the *Odes*." "Taking one's place" through ritual involves, as discussed in 2.4, taking up one's role as an adult among other adults in society, something that requires a mastery of the rituals governing social interactions. Steps one and two thus represent, respectively, cognitive shaping through learning and behavioral shaping through ritual training. Finally, the joy inspired by the powerfully moving music of the ancients brings the cognitive and behavioral together into the unselfconscious, effortless perfection that is wu-wei. *Mencius* 4:A:27, which invokes the metaphor of dance, represents perhaps the best commentary on this passage:

---

[2] Chapter 32 ("Record of Examples"); Legge 1967, vol. 2: 334.

The substance of benevolence (*ren*) is the serving of one's parents; the substance of r̶
is obeying one's elders; the substance of wisdom is to understand benevolence and ri̶
and to not let them go; the substance of ritual propriety is the regulation and adorn̶
benevolence and rightness; and the substance of music is the joy one takes in bene̶v̶o̶l̶e̶n̶c̶e̶
and rightness. Once such joy is born, it cannot be stopped. Once it cannot be stopped, then
one begins unconsciously to dance it with one's feet and wave one's arms in time with it.

Some commentators take all three nouns in the passage as titles of classical texts—
"Take inspiration from the *Book of Odes*, take your place with the *Book of Ritual*, and
perfect yourself with the *Book of Music*"—but it is unlikely that such books existed in
Confucius' time.

8.9 The Master said, "The common people can be made to follow it, but they
cannot be made to understand it."

"It," of course, refers to the Way. There are several ways to understand this passage. The
most simple interpretation is that the common people can be guided along the Confucian Way—most efficaciously through the influence of the gentleman's Virtue—but
lack the cognitive ability to grasp the principles of the Way (cf. 16.9 and *Mencius* 7:A:5).
Some early commentators alternately see it as a comment on rule by Virtue as opposed
to rule by force, in which case the second clause is read more along the lines of "the
common people cannot be allowed to understand it." As Zhang Ping puts it:

> When one rules by means of Virtue, then everyone gets to fulfill their own nature, and every-
> thing in the world is put to use without being aware of it. This is why the Master says, "The
> common people can be made to follow it." If, however, one tries to rule by means of pun-
> ishments, one has to set up sanctions to prevent the common people from being bad. Once
> the common people become aware of these preventative sanctions, they will simply devise
> more clever ways of being bad [to evade the sanctions]. This is why the Master says, "They
> cannot be allowed to understand it." The point is that one should govern by means of Virtue,
> which causes the people to follow and nothing more, rather than by means of punishments,
> in which case the people become aware of one's technique.

This interpretation accords well with the sentiment of 2.3, where Confucius declares
that ruling by a publicized legal code merely inspires the common people to devise
devious ways to get around the law.

8.10 The Master said, "A person who is fond of courage but who despises poverty
will become rebellious. A person who is not Good, and who is excessively criticized for it, will also become rebellious."

The first phrase is similar in sentiment to 17.23: a person with a sense of rightness
knows better than to despise virtuous poverty, and will be content with his material
lot, whereas someone possessing physical courage but lacking the restraints of rightness will become a danger to others (cf. 14.4). The second phrase, as generally understood by commentators, has to do with the need for reforming people through gentle
virtuous example rather than force or harsh condemnation. As Zheng Xuan explains,
"Someone who is not Good should be reformed though environmental influence; if
you excessively criticize them, this will make them rebellious."

8.11 The Master said, "If a person has talents as fine as the Duke of Zhou, but
is arrogant and mean-spirited, the rest of his qualities are not worth notice."

Ability uninformed by virtue is useless. As Wang Bi notes, "The point is that even fine talent is wasted if one is arrogant and mean-spirited—how much more so considering that someone who is arrogant and mean-spirited necessarily lacks the fine talent of the Duke of Zhou?"

8.12 The Master said, "It is not easy to find someone who is able to learn for even the space of three years without a thought given to official salary."

Confucius is again lamenting the fact that the majority of his contemporaries were focused upon external goods, and saw learning as merely a means to an end: that is, an official position, and the prestige and salary that went with it. A great deal of commentarial ink has been spilled over the significance of the three-year period, but—as Huan Maoyong notes—"the sense is not three temporal periods; 'three years' simply means a long time."

8.13 The Master said, "Be sincerely trustworthy and love learning, and hold fast to the good Way until death. Do not enter a state that is endangered, and do not reside in a state that is disordered. If the Way is being realized in the world then show yourself; if it is not, then go into reclusion. In a state that has the Way, to be poor and of low status is a cause for shame; in a state that is without the Way, to be wealthy and honored is equally a cause for shame."

According to Bao Xian, the fact that a state is endangered means that disorder is imminent, and Zhu Xi explain that, although one already serving as an official has a duty to remain and try to protect an endangered state, "it is permissible for an outsider to refrain from entering into such a state." Once a state has degenerated into immoral disorder—defined by Bao Xian as a situation where ministers are assassinating lords and sons killing fathers—a gentleman's duty is to leave the state rather than sully himself by remaining. The end of the passage reiterates this theme: when there is an opportunity for virtuous service, it would be shameful for the gentleman to remain in obscurity and poverty; when nothing but immorality and corruption prevails, however, it would be equally shameful for the gentleman not to withdraw.

8.14 The Master said, "Do not discuss matters of government policy that do not fall within the scope of your official duties."

This seems to describe negative restrictions on one's actions imposed by the dictates of dutifulness. As Nan Xuan notes, it might further be understood as either a criticism of Confucius' contemporaries for infringing on the official duties of others and acting above their stations, or as an explanation for why the unemployed Confucius was not actively participating in the formulation of government policy. It is likely that both interpretations have some validity: Confucian refrains from actively "doing government" (2.21) because his duty is to provide general moral guidance rather than specific administrative advice. As Jiao Yuanxi puts it,

Confucius told Duke Ai only to "raise up the straight and put them over the crooked" [2.18]; he did not tell him that so-and-so should be promoted and so-and-so needs to be straightened out, or that anything specific should be done about the Three Families. In his conversation with Duke Jing, Confucius said only to "let the lord be a true lord, the ministers true

ministers, the fathers true fathers, and the sons true sons" [12.11], rather than giving any specific advice about how to handle [specific individuals]. This is the sense of "not discussing
matters of government policy that do not fall within the scope of your official duties."

Huan Maoyong notes the parallels to be found in *Mencius* 5:B:5 ("It is a crime for
those in a low position to discuss matters above their station") and the *Record of Ritual*:
"The gentleman does what is appropriate to his station and does not desire to go
beyond it."[3] This whole passage is repeated in 14.26, where an addition gloss ("The
gentleman's thoughts do not go beyond his office") is provided by Master Zeng.

8.15 The Master said, "From the time Music Master Zhi begins, to the closing
strains of the 'Cry of the Osprey'[4] — how one's ears are filled with a wondrous
ocean of sound!"

According to commentators, Music Master Zhi was the conductor of the state orches-
tra in the state of Lu. He is mentioned again in 18.9 and is often identified with the
Music Master mentioned in 3.23. There is a fair amount of debate about how to understand this passage, but the most reasonable interpretation takes it as describing the
progression of a classical musical performance, which supposedly opened with a solo
sung by the Music Master, followed by instrumental music, and concluding with a
grand chorus and orchestral finale where the words of the *Odes* would be sung and
their accompanying music played (cf. 3.23). For the rapture inspired in Confucius by
classical music, see also 7.14.

8.16 The Master said, "People who are wild without at least being upright,
simple-minded without at least being honest, or ingenuous without at least being
trustworthy — I simply do not understand them."

Comparing this passage with 17.16, the point seems to be the absence of any redeem-
ing qualities in many of Confucius' contemporaries. As Waley puts it, "In old days
people at any rate had the merits of their faults" (1989: 135), and Brooks and Brooks
note that "students should have virtues proper to their shortcomings" (1998: 127).
What is apparently lacking is some worthy native substance that could serve as the
basis for self-cultivation. According to 5.22, at least some of the young people in Lu
were exceptions to this unfortunate trend.

8.17 The Master said, "Learn as if you will never catch up, and as if you feared
losing what you have already attained."

An exhortation and warning to the aspiring student. He Yan comments, "Learning
enters from the outside, and can only be retained once it has been fully assimilated.
This is why the student should apply himself to learning as if he were never going to
catch up, and as if always afraid of losing what he has already attained." Li Chong
adds, "Learning involves hard work rather than material benefit, and in itself is not
the kind of thing one naturally loves or takes joy in. This is why it is easy to become

---

[3] Chapter 32 ("Doctrine of the Mean"); Legge 1967, vol. 2: 306.

[4] As mentioned in the commentary to 3.20, the "Cry of the Osprey," the first of the *Odes*, was
often used to refer to the *Odes* in general.

negligent or indolent in one's studies. Therefore one must be apprehensive as if one will never catch up, and always afraid that one will lose what has already been attained." Cf. 8.7, 9.11.

8.18 The Master said, "How majestic! Shun and Yu possessed the entire world and yet had no need to actively manage (*yu* 與) it."

There are many ways to understand this passage, depending primarily on how one understands the word *yu*. Mao Qiling (who in turn is following Wang Chong and the compilers of the Han and Jin Histories) understands *yu* as *yu* 預 ("participate, prepare"), seeing the passage as a description of ruling by means of "institutional wu-wei": "the point is that if one employs others to take care of the government, one does not have to personally participate—this is what is referred to as 'ruling through wu-wei.'" A variant of this passage is quoted in *Mencius* 3:A:4 and understood similarly as referring to a kind of division of labor. A related interpretation that fits better with the rest of the *Analects* is to see this as praise for ruling by means of Virtue rather than force or conscious effort (cf. 2.1, 12.19, 15.5). He Yan takes this tack in understanding *yu* as *yuqiu* 與求 ("actively pursue/desire"): "Confucius praises Shun and Yu because they did not themselves actively seek [rulership of] the world and yet attained it"; Zhu Xi similarly takes *yu* to mean *xiangguan* 相關 ("concern oneself with"): "Shun and Yu possessed the entire world and yet thought nothing of it." Finally, some Jin Dynasty commentators take *yu* as "together with," understanding this passage quite differently as a lament on the part of Confucius that he was born too late to witness in person the majesty of Shun and Yu. The "ruling by means of Virtue" interpretation seems the most plausible, especially because it fits together well with the passage that follows.

8.19 The Master said, "How great was Yao as a ruler! So majestic! It is Heaven that is great, and it was Yao who modeled himself upon it. So vast! Among the common people there were none who were able to find words to describe him. How majestic in his accomplishments, and glorious in cultural splendor!"

The common people were "not able to put a name to it" because the influence of Yao's Virtue was so subtle and pervasive that the people were transformed naturally, without being aware of what was happening. Compare this to Heaven's manner of ruling "without the need for words," as described in 17.19. As Kong Anguo observes, "Yao is being praised for modeling himself on Heaven and thereby transforming the people." Cf. *Mencius* 7:A:13:

The subjects of a hegemon are happy, while the subjects of a true king are expansive and content like the heavens. The king can execute them without stirring up resentment, and can benefit them without receiving credit for it. The common people move daily toward goodness without being aware of who is bringing it about. This is because everything the gentleman passes by is transformed; everywhere he dwells is infused with spiritual power (*shen* 神), and above and below he joins together with the flow of Heaven and Earth.

8.20 Shun had five ministers and the world was well governed.
   King Wu said, "I have ten ministers in charge of establishing order."
   The Master commented, "It is said that talent is difficult to find—is it not the case? Virtue flourished as never before after the reigns of Yao and Shun, and yet [even among King Wu's ten ministers] there was a woman included, so he really only had nine good men."

There is a great deal of commentarial controversy concerning the meaning of this last phrase, as well as the identity of the ten ministers of King Wu, who were most likely his nine brothers and either his mother or wife. It is not entirely clear whether Confucius' dismissal of the woman who served King Wu is due to misogyny (as one might conclude after reading 17.24) or simply to the fact that, in his own time, a woman would not be found serving as a minister.

"Two-thirds of the world had already turned to [King Wen],[5] and yet he still continued to defer to and serve the Shang. The Virtue of the Zhou—surely it can be said to represent ultimate Virtue?"

This is a rather difficult passage, and many commentators feel that important connecting text is missing. In addition, some believe that the final paragraph should be read separately. What the meaning of the first half may be beyond the sentiment that "good men are hard to find" is difficult to say with certainty, but commentators are a bit more clear about the final paragraph. As Bao Xian explains it, "King Zhow of the Shang was dissolute and undisciplined, whereas King Wen became the Count of the West and possessed sagely Virtue. Two-thirds of the world turned to the Zhou, and yet King Wen still continued to defer to and serve the Shang. This is why we can say that the Zhou represents the ultimate in Virtue." Even though he possessed the military and political power to easily overthrow the Shang, King Wen was loyal and dutiful, and did not dare to defy even so manifestly unworthy a ruler as King Zhow. We are to understand that it was only the continuously increasing vice of Zhow and the resulting displeasure of Heaven that motivated King Wen's son, King Wu, to finally depose the last Shang king. In contrast to the interpretations of Bao Xian and (presumably) Confucius, a figure in the *Zuo Commentary* understands King Wen's continued loyalty to Zhow more cynically, observing that "King Wen led the rebelling states of the Shang to serve Zhow, because he knew how to wait for the right time."[6]

8.21 The Master said, "I can find no fault with [the legendary sage-king] Yu. He subsisted on meager rations, and yet was lavishly filial in his offerings to the ancestral spirits. His everyday clothes were shabby, but his ceremonial headdress and cap were exceedingly fine. He lived in a mean hovel, expending all of his energies on the construction of drainage ditches and canals. I can find no fault with Yu."

Yu is the legendary sage-king who, through ceaseless effort, tamed the floodwaters and made China habitable. His heroic selflessness also won him praise from the Mohists, for whom he represented the embodiment of the doctrine of "impartial caring." Confucius here describes him as denying himself everyday pleasures in order to fulfill his ritual and moral duties to others, indicative of an admirable selflessness and dedication to the Way. An alternate way to read the first and last lines is to follow Kong Anguo and understand Confucius as saying, "Yu—I am not worthy to be counted his equal."

---

[5] King Wen is not mentioned in the *Analects* version of this line, but he clearly must be meant in this context (since his son, King Wu, did overthrow the Shang), and he is named in an otherwise identical version of this line in the *Later History of the Han*.

[6] Duke Xiang, Year 4 (568 B.C.E.); Legge 1991d: 423.

BOOK NINE

Most of the passages in this Book consist of the Master's pronouncements con-
cerning the importance of focus, sincerity, and perseverance in the pursuit of learn-
ing and virtue. In contrast are other passages where Confucius expresses his
frustration with his contemporaries for failing to embrace the Way that he has been
fated by Heaven to proclaim to the world.

9.1 The Master openly expressed his views on profit, the Heavenly Mandate, and Goodness.

> The most common way to read this passage, assuming the generally accepted mean-
> ings of the words involved, is: "The Master seldom (*han* 罕) discussed profit, the
> Heavenly Mandate, and Goodness." This reading has presented notorious difficulties
> for commentators, since Confucius discusses all of these topics in multiple places
> throughout the *Analects*. The only really plausible suggestion seems to be that of
> Huang Shisan, who focuses on the term *han*. Although this word means "seldom/
> rarely" in later classical Chinese, this is its sole appearance in the *Analects*, and it is
> also rare in other Warring States texts. Huang argues that *han* is being used in this
> passage as a loan for the similar character *xuan* 軒 (one of the basic senses of which
> is "open, wide"), and provides an example of these two characters being used inter-
> changeably in the Zuo and Gongyang commentaries. Understanding *han* in this way
> allows us to read the passage straightforwardly and still have it make sense: the Master
> does make his views on all three of these topics eminently clear in the *Analects*.

9.2 A villager from Daxiang remarked sarcastically, "How great is Confucius! He is so broadly learned, and yet has failed to make a name for himself in any particular endeavor."

> Daxiang is said by commentators to be the name of a small hamlet.

When the Master was told of this, he said to his disciples, "What art, then, should I take up? Charioteering? Archery? I think I shall take up charioteering."

> According to one understanding of this passage, Confucius' response is equally sarcastic
> as the question, expressing his contempt for limited or merely technical skills. Han and
> Jin Dynasty commentators, however, generally understand the villager from Daxiang as
> being sincere in his praise ("How great is Confucius! He is broadly learned, and yet does
> not achieve fame by means of any one particular art") and Confucius' answer as genuine
> self-deprecation—something along the lines of, "oh, perhaps I should specialize in
> something and make myself useful." Charioteering was the least respectable of the gen-
> tlemanly arts, and so his choice is seen as especially humble. Under either interpretation,
> the sense of the passage accords with the 2.12, 9.6, 19.4, and 19.7, but—as Waley
> notes (1989: 244)—the first seems to make better sense of Confucius' response.

9.3 The Master said, "A ceremonial cap made of linen is prescribed by the rites, but these days people use silk. This is frugal, and I follow the majority. To bow before ascending the stairs is what is prescribed by the rites, but these days people bow after ascending. This is arrogant, and—though it goes against the majority—I continue to bow before ascending."

> According to commentators, the linen cap specified by ritual was an elaborate affair—consisting of many layers and involving intricate stitching—and Confucius' contemporaries had begun replacing it with a simpler silk version. Confucius apparently feels that this does not interfere with its basic function. When approaching a ruler or other superior sitting on a raised dais, ritual dictates bowing before ascending the stairs, but Confucius' contemporaries had taken to ascending the stairs and only bowing when directly before their ruler. This is a more substantial change—as Brooks and Brooks note, "the 'below' option implies *asking* permission to ascend; the 'above' option *presumes* it" (1998: 51)—and Confucius rejects it as not ritually proper. This passage describes the sort of judgment and flexibility that can be exercised by an accomplished ritual practitioner. It is possible to exaggerate the iconoclastic character of this passage—we should note that the one change Confucius accedes to is a rather minor one, and that he does not actually *propose* changing the rite, but simply goes along with the popular practice (with possibly a hint of reluctance). Nevertheless, we can appreciate the sense of it without ignoring Confucius' profound conservatism: rites are expressive of a certain sense or feeling, and thus an alteration in the actual rite is permissible if it will not—in the opinion of one who has fully mastered the rites—alter its essential meaning.

9.4 The Master was entirely free of four faults: arbitrariness, inflexibility, rigidity, and selfishness.

> There are several ways to understand the faults listed; the translation follows He Yan's commentary:
>
> > [Confucius] took the Way as his standard, and thus was free of arbitrariness. If he was employed, then he put himself forth; if dismissed, he went into seclusion. Thus, he was not inflexible. He had no pre-determined ideas about what was acceptable and what was not [4.10], and therefore was not rigid in his conduct. He transmitted the [teaching of the] ancients and did not introduce his own innovations [7.1]; he flocked together with others without having to stand out, and "followed nothing but the Way" [*Laozi*, Ch. 21]. Thus, he was not filled up with his own self.
>
> Compare the critiques of the "inflexible petty person" in 13.20 and of rigidity (*gu* 固) in 14.32. Some commentators argue that *yi* 意 ("arbitrariness") should be understood in the sense of *yi* 億 ("expect, anticipate"), pointing to 14.31 ("not expecting untrustworthiness in others") as evidence.

9.5 The Master was surrounded in Kuang. He said, "Now that King Wen 文 is gone, is not culture (*wen* 文) now invested here in me? If Heaven intended this culture to perish, it would not have given it to those of us who live after King Wen's death. Since Heaven did not intend that this culture should perish, what can the people of Kuang do to me?"

> As the *Record of the Historian* tells the story,

> Confucius was leaving Wei, and was passing through the town of Kuang on his way to Chen. There was a person named Yang Hu who had in the past done violence to the people of Kuang, and they therefore detained Confucius, because he physically resembled this Yang Hu. Confucius was imprisoned there for five days.

The account goes on to note that Yan Hui had fallen behind on this journey and was finally reunited with Confucius in Kuang, providing the context for 11.23. Bao Xian also claims that, to add to the confusion, one of Confucius' disciples was a known associate of Yang Hu, and happened to be driving Confucius' chariot as he passed through Kuang, further rousing the suspicions of the Kuang people. As for Confucius being the bearer of culture, the *Guliang Commentary* for Duke Ai, Year 14 (482 B.C.E) cites Confucius as saying: "The Way of Kings Wen and Wu has not fallen to the ground—it still lives on in us.[1] King Wen having passed away, is not his Way of being cultured truly to be found in me?" For this theme of Confucius being the Heaven-appointed bearer of Zhou culture—and therefore enjoying its special protection—see also 3.24, 7.23 and 14.36.

9.6 The Prime Minister asked Zigong, "Your Master is a sage, is he not? How is it, then, that he is skilled at so many menial tasks?"

Zigong replied, "Surely Heaven not only not intends him for sagehood, but also gave him many other talents."

When the Master heard of this, he remarked, "How well the Prime Minister knows me! In my youth, I was of humble status, so I became proficient in many menial tasks. Is the gentleman broadly skilled in trivial matters? No, he is not."

There is a great deal of commentarial debate over the identity of the Prime Minister mentioned here, but none of the arguments offered are entirely convincing. The Prime Minister was presumably familiar with Confucius' many technical abilities, and apparently has trouble reconciling this with Confucius' own teaching that "the gentleman is not a vessel" (2.12). Zigong attempts to finesse the issue, but Confucius has no patience for this: his technical skills are the result of his humble background rather than being desiderata for an aspiring gentleman (cf. 9.2, 19.4, 19.7). Although—as implied in the elaboration 9.7—technical skills might come in handy for one who has yet to be properly employed.

9.7 Lao said, "The Master once remarked, 'I have not been employed, and therefore have become accomplished in the arts.'"

A less elaborate pair to 9.6: here Confucius' technical achievements are presented as due to a lack of more appropriate official employment as an adult, rather than to his humble background. As James Legge notes, "It is supposed that when these conversations were being digested into their present form, someone remembered that Lao had been in the habit of mentioning the remark given, and accordingly it was appended to [9.6]" (1990a: 219). There is some debate over the identity of "Lao," but he is usually identified as a disciple of Confucius, whose style-name was Zikai.

---

[1] This line also forms part of *Analects* 19.22.

9.8 The Master said, "Do I possess wisdom? No, I do not. [For example, recently] a common fellow asked a question of me, and I came up completely empty. But I discussed the problem with him from beginning to end until we finally got to the bottom of it."

This remark is probably occasioned by someone praising Confucius as omniscient or exceptionally wise and is one of several points in the text where Confucius denies possessing extraordinary qualities (cf. 7.20, 7.33): he simply works hard and loves the Way. The point, of course, is to instill in his disciples a sincere desire to learn, since the Master's apparent wisdom is not the result of innate intelligence or sageliness, but merely of sheer persistence.

9.9 The Master said, "The phoenix has not appeared, the [Yellow] River has not produced its chart—it is all over for me, is it not?"

Both the phoenix and chart were auspicious omens sent by Heaven in the past to indicate that a sagely ruler was arising to bring peace to the world. Phoenixes supposedly appeared during the reign of Shun, and traditional stories tell of a strange creature with a horse's body and dragon's head that emerged from the Yellow River in the time of the legendary Fu Xi. On this creature's back were markings that supposedly inspired Fu Xi to create both the Chinese writing system and the hexagrams that constitute the core of the *Book of Changes*. Confucius is here lamenting the fact that no sagely king was going to arise to employ him and order the world by putting the Confucian Way into practice. As the *History of the Han* tells it,

The Way of the Zhou declined, having been ruined by Kings You and Li,[2] and ritual, music and punitive expeditions became the prerogatives of the feudal lords. This deterioration progressed for over two hundred years before Confucius arose. Bringing sagely Virtue but born into the wrong age, he knew that his teachings would not be accepted and the Way would not be put into practice, and therefore he voiced the lament [recorded in 9.9].

9.10 Whenever the Master saw someone who was wearing mourning clothes, was garbed in full official dress, or was blind, he would always rise to his feet, even if the person was his junior. When passing such a person, he would always hasten his step.

Hastening one's step, like rising to one's feet, is a sign of respect. What is being emphasized here is probably, as Fan Ziyu says, not merely Confucius' respectfulness, but also the sincere, wu-wei fashion in which it manifested itself: "The mind of the sage is such that he grieves along with those who are in mourning, feels respect for those who hold official rank, and feels pity for those who are disabled. It is likely that the Master rose to his feet and hastened his step spontaneously, without having consciously intended it." Like 7.9–7.10, this passage resembles the descriptions of ritual behavior found in Book Ten.

---

[2] The twelfth and tenth Zhou kings, respectively, both notorious for bad conduct.

9.11 With a great sigh Yan Hui lamented, "The more I look up at it the higher it seems; the more I delve into it, the harder it becomes. Catching a glimpse of it before me, I then find it suddenly at my back.

"The Master is skilled at gradually leading me on, step by step. He broadens me with culture and restrains me with the rites, so that even if I wanted to give up I could not. Having exhausted all of my strength, it seems as if there is still something left, looming up ahead of me. Though I desire to follow it, there seems to be no way through."

The "it" referred to by Yan Hui is most likely the Confucian Way. This passage represents the most dramatic expression in the text of the difficulty of self-cultivation and the incredible strength of will needed to remain on the path—especially because it comes from the mouth of Yan Hui, the most naturally gifted of Confucius' disciples. Many esoteric and mystical interpretations of Yan Hui's words have been offered by traditional commentators, but Huang Gan is correct in rejecting them:

The Way of the sage is certainly high and brilliant, expansive and great, so that it is indeed difficult to reach, but it still does not transcend our basic human nature. The details of one's movements and expressions; the tasks of eating and drinking, rising and resting, interacting with others and meeting one's social responsibilities; the standards that govern relations between ruler and minister, father and son, elder and junior, and husband and wife; going out in public or remaining at home, resigning or accepting office, declining or accepting reward, taking this and discarding that, along with everything else up to the implementation of government regulations— none of this lies outside the scope of the Way.

The difficulty does not lie in the Way's transcendental nature, for it is right in front of us (7.30), in the details of everyday life. The true challenge is the almost superhuman stamina and determination required to walk it to its end. Cf. 8.7 and 9.19.

9.12 The Master was gravely ill, and Zilu instructed his fellow disciples to attend Confucius as if the disciples were his ministers.

That is, following the rites proper to a minister attending to a lord—which, of course, Confucius was not.

During a remission in his illness, the Master [became aware of what was happening and] rebuked Zilu, saying, "It has been quite some time now, has it not, that you have been carrying out this charade! If I have no ministers and yet you act as if I have, who do you think I am going to fool? Am I going to fool Heaven? Moreover, would I not rather die in the arms of a few of my disciples than in the arms of ministers? Even if I do not merit a grand funeral, it is not as if I would be left to die by the side of the road!"

Zilu means to honor his Master—and perhaps incidentally raise his own status—by having him attended as if he were a feudal lord, but this represents a serious abuse of ritual. As Li Ao explains, Confucius' concern over the ritual violations of the Ji Family—who, as we have seen, were usurping the ritual prerogatives of the Zhou kings in an attempt to impress their contemporaries and curry favor with Heaven (3.1 and 3.6)—no doubt accounts for some of the harshness of his rebuke, which is then softened somewhat by his final remarks. As Brooks and Brooks note, although the disciples are ashamed of their Master's lack of office and humble circumstances, Confucius himself "insists on his low rank, with devoted disciples and not sullen lackeys at his gate. Even a modern reader can hardly miss the note of intense, reproving affection" (1998: 53).

9.13 Zigong said, "If you possessed a piece of beautiful jade, would you hide it away in a locked box, or would you try to sell it at a good price?"

The Master responded, "Oh, I would sell it! I would sell it! I am just waiting for the right offer."

The gentleman should share his virtue with the world by taking public office, but only under a virtuous king and when approached in accordance with the Way. Confucius thus refuses to actively peddle his wares on the market, waiting instead for his virtue to be recognized by a ritually correct and morally cultivated ruler. As Fan Ziyu puts it, "The gentleman is never unwilling to serve in office, but also despises any offer that is not in accordance with the Way. The scholar waiting for the ritually proper approach is like a piece of jade waiting for the right price . . . he is certainly not going to compromise the Way in order to gain human rewards, or 'brag about his jade in pursuit of a sale.'" Although clearly frustrated, Confucius seems somewhat less pessimistic here than in 9.9, where he has completely given up hope of finding a proper buyer for his wares.

9.14 The Master expressed a desire to go and live among the Nine Yi Barbarian tribes. Someone asked him, "How could you bear their uncouthness?"

The Master replied, "If a gentleman were to dwell among them, what uncouthness would there be?"

The Nine Yi tribes were a group of "barbarians" who lived along the Eastern coast of present day China, possibly including the Korean peninsula. Many commentators link this passage to 5.7, where Confucius expresses a wish (facetious or not) to float away from China on a raft, and both passages are related to 9.9 and 9.13 in being expressions of frustration at having failed to find employment under a virtuous ruler in China proper. This passage is also a testament to the transformative power of the gentleman's Virtue (cf. 12.19; as Ma Rong puts it, "Everywhere the gentleman dwells is transformed"), as well as the universality of the Way's power: even non-Chinese barbarians are subject to its influence (cf. 13.19).

9.15 The Master said, "Only after I returned to Lu from Wei was music rectified, with both the Ya and Song put into proper order."

The Ya and Song refer to sections of the *Book of Odes*. Some commentators believe that this passage is about Confucius editing the text of the *Odes*, while others think the reference is to the music to which the *Odes* were sung. The latter interpretation seems more likely: "music" rather than a classical text is what is being rectified, and it is when Confucius was abroad (in the state of Qi) that he heard the great court music of the sage-king Shun (7.14), where it had been preserved and passed down from antiquity. It is possible that, although the text of the *Odes* was extant in Lu, the accompanying music had been lost or corrupted, and it is only after he returned from his trips abroad and finally settled again in Lu that he was able to restore it. In 8.15, we have already seen Confucius enjoying the fruits of his labor, taking joy in the perfect execution of Lu's Music Master Zhi. The correction of music was an important moral task; in the *Huainanzi*, we read, "The regulating models of the Former Kings were instituted in response to the desires of the common people, as a means of restraining and cultivating them. In response to people's love of female beauty the ritual of marriage was instituted, so that there might be proper distinction between man and woman. In response to people's love of musical sounds, the airs of the Ya and Song were rectified so that their style would not be dissolute."

9.16 The Master said, "When in public, serving the Duke and his ministers; when at home, serving my father and elders; not daring to not exert myself to the utmost in performing funerary tasks; and not allowing myself to be befuddled by wine—these sorts of things present me with no trouble."

> This is a somewhat opaque passage. Perhaps the most sensible interpretation of it is that of Zhang Zhentao, who see it as a rebuke of those among Confucius' contemporaries who "though humble, were not willing to serve those who were noble; though young, were not willing to serve those who were elder; and who moreover were perfunctory and sloppy in their funeral arrangements and often besotted with wine."

9.17 Standing on the bank of a river, the Master said, "Look at how it flows on like this, never stopping day or night!"

> Another rather opaque passage, with at least two plausible interpretations. Jin Dynasty commentators generally take it as a lament on the passage of time and Confucius' sense of personal failure. Sun Chuo, for instance, comments: "The river flows on without stopping like the years ceaselessly passing away; the time is already late, and yet the Way has still not been put into practice. This is the cause of Confucius' lament." This sense ties 9.17 together with 5.7, 9.9, and 9.14. Perhaps more compelling is the interpretation of the *Luxuriant Dew of the Annals*, which claims that the river's unremitting and thorough progress toward the sea is a metaphor for the ideal student's progress along the Way toward the goal of Goodness, with all of the river's qualities mapping onto human virtues: "in never ceasing day or night, it is like one who is strong; in filling up every hollow before it proceeds, it is like one who is well-balanced; . . . in following the gorges and valleys without getting lost, and traversing ten thousand miles while inevitably arriving at its goal, it is like one who is wise; . . . plunging over a towering cliff without the slightest hesitation, it is like one who is courageous," etc. This is how Zhu Xi takes the passage, "the Master made this pronouncement and pointed this out to people because he wanted the student to engage in constant reflection and examination without letting up for even a moment," and fits it together with the many other passages in the text that emphasize the importance of perseverance and hard work, such as 9.11.

9.18 The Master said, "I have yet to meet a man who loves Virtue as much as he loves female beauty."

> There are two slightly different ways to take this passage. He Yan sees it as a criticism of Confucius' contemporaries: "The Master is complaining that his contemporaries

viewed Virtue lightly and instead focused upon the pursuit of female beauty." This is how Sima Qian understands it as well, claiming in the *Record of the Historian* that 9.18 was inspired by an event in Confucius' life when he was publicly humiliated by Duke Ling of Wei, who honored his consort—the infamous Nanzi—over Confucius himself. Li Chong, on the other hand, sees the passage as more of a general statement about self cultivation, a claim that "if people simply loved Virtue as much as they love female beauty, then they would discard immorality and return to rectitude." Most likely both points are intended: if only people could love the Way in the same spontaneous, wu-wei fashion that they love the pleasures of the flesh, Confucius' job would be done, but he was not optimistic about this happening anytime soon with his contemporaries. As Xie Liangzuo explains: "Loving a beautiful woman or hating a foul smell—these are examples of sincerity. If one could only love Virtue the way one loves female beauty, this would mean sincerely loving Virtue. Unfortunately, few among the people are able to do this." Both points are also clearly intended in the very similar, but slightly more explicit, 15.13; cf. 9.24, 15.16.

9.19 The Master said, "[The task of self-cultivation] might be compared to the task of building up a mountain: if I stop even one basketful of earth short of completion, then I have stopped completely. It might also be compared to the task of leveling ground: even if I have only dumped a single basketful of earth, at least I am moving forward."

The first half of this passage echoes 1.15, 8.7, and 9.17 in emphasizing the need for constant effort and indefatigable determination if one is to completely walk the long and arduous Confucian Way. As Zhu Xi puts it, "If the student is able to steel himself and not desist, then his accumulated small efforts will result in great success. If, on the other hand, he stops halfway down the road, then he has thrown away everything he has already achieved." The second half provides some encouragement, somewhat balancing out Yan Hui's lament in 9.11: the Way is long, but with every step one is making progress. An ancillary point is that, when it comes to self-cultivation, it is the internal decisions of the individual that determine success or failure; as Zhu Xi explains, "The decision to stop or move forward lies entirely within me, and is not determined by others" (cf. 12.1). 9.20 and 9.21 seem to flesh this passage out by providing a model of one who never grew tired or stopped in his forward progress: the perfect disciple Yan Hui.

9.20 The Master said, "One with whom I could discourse without his growing weary—was this not Yan Hui?"

The language is ambiguous; a possible alternate rendering is: "One with whom I could discourse without my growing weary." The first rendering is more likely, though: the point is that Yan Hui immediately comprehended what he was taught (2.9) and therefore never grew weary of hearing new things. As Liu Kai explains,

"Discoursing" involves instructing people in what they have not yet understood. Because the principles involved are sometimes conceptually difficult, one does not always grasp them in one's mind, and so it is easy to become weary. Only Yan Hui could hear the Master's teachings and immediately comprehend every point, never going against them and yet never having to ask any questions [2.9].

Cf. 5.9, 11.4.

9.21 The Master said of Yan Hui, "Alas! I watched his advance, and never once saw him stop."

The Master expresses regret, of course, because Yan Hui passed away before being able to realize his full, exceptional potential. This is possibly also the subject of 9.22; cf. 6.3, 6.7, 6.11, 11.9.

9.22 The Master said, "Surely there are some sprouts that fail to flower, just as surely as there are some flowers that fail to bear fruit!"

Commentators from the Han to the Tang take this passage together with 9.20 and 9.21 as specifically referring to Yan Hui's untimely death. Zhu Xi, on the other hand, takes it together with 9.17 and 9.19 as a general comment on self-cultivation: "Learning that is not completed is like this, which is why the gentleman values self-motivation." As Huan Maoyong notes, an argument in favor of this latter interpretation is that it also makes 9.22 fit well with 9.23. Both interpretations are plausible.

9.23 The Master said, "We should look upon the younger generation with awe because how are we to know that those who come after us will not prove our equals? Once, however, a man reaches the age of forty or fifty without having learned anything, we can conclude from this fact alone that he is not worthy of being held in awe."

This forty or fifty year-old never-do-well is perhaps an example of the "sprout that fails to flower" or "flower that fails to fruit" mentioned in 9.22. Most early commentators take *wen* 聞 ("learning") as "reputation," but, as Wang Yangming observes, "Confucius himself said, 'This is reputation, not achievement,' so why would he consent to using reputation as a standard for evaluating a person?" Wang is referring to 12.20, where Confucius rejects public reputation as an indication of a scholar's level of achievement, and instead directs his questioner to look to a person's actual comportment and level of personal virtue. We see other passages where Confucius is suspicious of public opinion as a measure of true attainment (13.24), and that fact combined with the common theme of learning in the surrounding passages argue for *wen* as "learning."

9.24 The Master said, "When a man is rebuked with exemplary words after having made a mistake, he cannot help but agree with them. However, what is important is that he change himself in order to *accord* with them. When a man is praised with words of respect, he cannot help but be pleased with them. However, what is important is that he actually *live up* to them. A person who finds respectful words pleasing but does not live up to them, or agrees with others' reproaches and yet does not change—there is nothing I can do with one such as this."

As Sun Chuo comments, "The Master is criticizing those who consent superficially but do not transform their hearts." Nominal assent to the Confucian Way is insufficient—one must love the Way and strive to embody it in one's person. The problem is what the teacher is to do with a student who intellectually understands or superficially agrees with the Way but cannot summon up the genuine commitment required of the gentleman. Confucius' lament here is clearly related to the sarcastic 9.18: none of his contemporaries seems to have a problem finding the motivational energy required for the pursuit of sex, but their enthusiasm seems to flag when the object of pursuit is the Way. Cf. the Master's difficulties with unmotivated disciples in 5.10 and 6.12, and his comment in 15.16.

9.25 The Master said, "Let your actions be governed by dutifulness and trustworthiness, and do not accept as a friend one who is not your equal. If you have committed a transgression, do not be afraid to change your ways."

This is a repeat of the second half of 1.8; see 1.8 for commentary.

9.26 The Master said, "The three armies[3] can have their general taken from them by force, but even a commoner cannot be deprived of his will in this fashion."

As Kong Anguo comments, "Although the three armies are numerous, people's hearts are not unified, and therefore you can forcibly deprive such a group of their general and thereby take them. Although a common person is negligible, if he manages to hold firmly to his will, one will not be able to take it from him." For a similar metaphor of the will as military "general" in charge of guiding the rest of the self, see *Mencius* 2:A:2. Hu Bingwen relates 9.26 to the passages that precede it by arguing that it has to do with dedication to learning:

> The ten passages from 9.17 to 9.26 all have to do with encouraging people and urging them on in the task of learning. When it comes to learning, there is nothing more crucial than "setting your heart [will] upon it."[4] If you have set your heart upon learning you can move forward [9.19], which must necessarily be unremitting like the flow of the river toward the sea [9.17]. Without such a will you will stop short, which will necessarily leave the mountain uncompleted [9.19]. Thus, those who engage in learning but who are in the end taken by some external object are simply lacking in willpower .

Part of the point of this passage is thus that all people possess their own, self-determined will, which means that there is simply no excuse for not directing it toward self-cultivation. Cf. 6.12, 9.31.

9.27 The Master said, "Clad only in a shabby quilted gown, and yet unashamed to stand side-by-side with someone dressed in expensive furs—does this not describe Zilu?

'Not envious, not covetous,
How could he not be good (*zang* 臧)?'"[5]

Zilu took to reciting this stanza constantly. The Master thereupon remarked, "The Way summed up in these lines is hardly worth treasuring (*zang* 臧) so."

---

[3]I.e., the combined forces of an entire state; cf. 7.11.

[4]A reference to 2.4, where *lizhi* 立志 (more literally "establishing one's will [with regard to]") was translated as "setting one's heart [upon]."

[5]The Master is quoting Ode 33 in praise of Zilu.

Confucius is probably playing on the dual meaning of *zang*: both "good" and "to store up, treasure" (the second meaning is distinguished as a separate character, *cang* 藏, in modern Chinese). The rebuke is possibly in response to Zilu's unseemly dwelling upon the Master's praise; as Zhu Xi explains, "Zilu was constantly reciting the stanza [used to praise him], which indicates that he was very self-satisfied concerning his own abilities and thus might not be sufficiently pursuing further progress along the Way." Alternately, the Master may—as in 5.7, 5.8, 7.11, 11.15, 13.3—have been simply putting Zilu in his place: as Liu Fenglu interprets it, the point of the rebuke is that "being free of flattery and free of arrogance is still not as good as taking joy in the Way or loving ritual." Zilu has reached a certain level of moral attainment, but falls short of being a complete gentleman.

9.28 The Master said, "Only after Winter comes do we know that the pine and cypress are the last to fade."

This is possibly a traditional saying, the sense of which is that it is in times of adversity that the gentleman shows his true colors. As He Yan explains, "The point of the metaphor is that even ordinary people are able to be self-possessed and orderly— and thus apparently similar to the gentleman—when living in a well-governed age, but it is only in a chaotic age that we recognize the gentleman's rectitude and air of unwavering integrity."

9.29 The Master said, "The wise are not confused, the Good do not worry, and the courageous do not fear."

As Sun Chuo comments, "The wise are able to clearly distinguish between things, and therefore are not anxious. One who is at ease in Goodness is constant in his joy, and therefore is free of anxiety"; Miao Xie adds, "[The courageous person] sees what is right to do and does it, without being intimidated by physical force or threats, which is why he does not fear." Alternately, reading this passage together with 2.4, the wise are free of anxiety because they understand the Confucian Way or the Mandate of Heaven; comparing it to 12.4, the Good are free of worry because they examine themselves inwardly and find nothing to fault. A slightly different interpretation is provided by Brooks and Brooks, who read it as a pair with 9.28: "It is left to the reader to supply the qualifications: the *truly* wise, *ren*, and brave; this nuance links 9.29 with 9.28. Doubts, anxieties, and fears are vacillations that negate virtues" (1998: 56). This saying is repeated in 14.28, where these qualities are all attributed to the gentleman, and presented as something beyond the Master's capabilities.

9.30 The Master said, "Just because someone is able to learn with you does not necessarily mean that they can travel the Way in your company; just because they can travel the Way in your company does not necessarily mean that they can take their place alongside you; just because they can take their place alongside you does not necessarily mean that they can join you in employing discretion."

Using 8.8, 16.3, and 20.3 as references, taking one's place (*li* 立) probably refers to assuming one's role in society alongside others through the mastery of ritual propriety, although some commentators take it to mean having a firm cognitive grasp of right and wrong. Most commentators understand "discretion" (*quan* 權; lit. "weighing") in the sense in which it is used in *Mencius* 4:A:17, where this virtue allows one to realize that, although the rites forbid touching a woman who is not your wife, it is appropriate to ignore them in order to rescue a drowning sister-in-law. "Discretion" thus refers to a kind of cognitive flexibility that allows one to amend or bend the rules in response to changing or unique circumstances (cf. 9.3). Though 9.30 is most directly a comment about virtue and friendship (cf. 1.8, 9.25), its larger purpose is probably to emphasize that the journey of self-cultivation is long and requires many steps. As Zhang Ping comments,

> The point of this passage is to indicate the order of the gradually progressive steps involved in learning. You begin my setting your heart upon learning [2.4], seeking to enlighten yourself in areas where you are ignorant, but not yet clear about where you are going. Once you are clear about where you are going, your faith in the Way is still not yet firm, and therefore you do not have a solid foundation upon which to take your place. Once you have a solid foundation, you still have yet to attain the ability to, by means of discretion, comprehend the changing nature of things.

9.31

> "The flowery branch of the wild cherry
> How swiftly it flies back![6]
> Of course I am thinking of you,
> It is just that your house is so far away."

The Master said, "He was not really thinking of her. If he were, what difference would the distance make?"

This lost ode ostensibly describes the longing of the poet for his far-away lover, but—in keeping with the Confucian tradition—has traditionally been interpreted metaphorically by commentators, and was presumably understood this way by Confucius himself. Early commentators read this passage together with 9.30, and understood the metaphorical object of the poet's attention to be the virtue of "discretion" mentioned in the final line of that passage. Since at least the time of Su Shi, however, commentators have begun suggesting that 9.31 be read as a separate passage having to do more generally with attaining the Confucian Way or the virtue of Goodness, which makes more sense and avoids the tortuous interpretive acrobatics required to present 9.31 as a commentary on 9.30. Understood this way, the sense of this passage is very similar to 7.30: if you sincerely love virtue, virtue will be yours. Like the insincere author of the poem, people who complain about the difficulty of self-cultivation or claim to be incapable of it simply lack genuine commitment (cf. 6.12, 9.24).

---

[6] I.e., when one pulls on it to pluck a blossom and then releases it. The translation here follows Waley 1989: 145, who refers the reader to Ode 268 for this "image of things that are torn apart after a momentary union." This rendering makes best sense of the poem, which is not found in the extant *Book of Odes*.

BOOK TEN

Based on their style, lack of explicit subject, and parallels to be found in other early ritual texts such as the Record of Ritual *or* Book of Etiquette and Ritual, *scholars have concluded that most of the passages in this Book were probably culled from a lost ritual text that provided anonymous guidelines and injunctions for the aspiring gentleman. From earliest times, however, this Book has been viewed by commentators as an extended description of the ritual behavior of Confucius in particular, and it was probably intended by the editors of the earliest stratum of the Analects (Books 1–10) to be understood that way. The translation and commentary will reflect this understanding of the text, rendering it as descriptive rather than injunctive, and understanding Confucius as the implicit subject, although he is only explicitly mentioned in a few passages. Seen as an actual description of the Master's behavior rather than a set of impersonal ritual guidelines, Book Ten serves as a sort of capstone for the first stratum, providing a series of descriptions of the Master effortlessly embodying in his words, behavior, and countenance the lessons imparted throughout the rest of the text. What is being emphasized in this Book is the ease and grace with which the Master embodies the spirit of the rites in every aspect of his life—no matter how trivial—and accords with this spirit in adapting to new and necessarily unforeseeable circumstances. The final passage, 10.27, identifies this ability as the virtue of "timeliness" (shi 時)—that is, always according perfectly with the demands of the situation at hand. This is Confucius' forte, and he is in fact known to posterity (through the efforts of Mencius) as the "timely sage": the one whose ritual responses were always effortlessly and unselfconsciously appropriate (Mencius 5:B:1).*

10.1 In his village community, Confucius was respectful and circumspect, seeming to be at a loss for words. When in the ancestral temples or at court, however, he spoke eloquently, though always with caution and restraint.

As Zhu Xi understands it, this passage describes how Confucius' manner of speaking changed to accord with the social context:

> Seeming to be at a loss for words is a way to express humility and acquiescence, to avoid putting oneself above others by displaying one's sagely knowledge. In Confucius' home village, his elders and ancestors were present, and therefore when he was dwelling there his countenance was deferential. On the other hand, the ancestral temples are where ritual standards are preserved, and the court is where governmental affairs are decided, and therefore Confucius could not but be clear and particular in his speech: in such situations, it is necessary to inquire in detail and discuss at length, while at the same time always remaining cautious and not speaking carelessly.

Confucius' lack of eloquence at home, then, is an expression of reverence for his elders: even if he knew better than they did, he would acquiesce out of respect. In public life, however, a greater degree of forthrightness is called for. Cf. 3.15, 10.21.

10.2 At court, when speaking with officers of lower rank, he was pleasant and affable; when speaking with officers of upper rank, he was formal and proper. When his lord was present, he combined an attitude of cautious respect with graceful ease.

Confucius is traditionally said to have held the office of Minister of Justice in Lu, a relatively minor post, which means that the "officers of lower rank" were most likely his colleagues, although they may have included even more minor officials under his authority. Confucius effortlessly adapted his countenance and behavior to the demands of the social situation; he was neither overly familiar with his colleagues nor obsequious to his superiors.

10.3 When called on by his lord to receive a guest, his countenance would become alert and serious, and he would hasten his steps. When he saluted those in attendance beside him—extending his clasped hands to the left or right, as their position required—his robes remained perfectly arrayed, both front and back. Hastening forward, he moved smoothly, as though gliding upon wings. Once the guest had left, he would always return to report, "The guest is no longer looking back."

Some commentators believe that receiving guests was not part of Confucius' officials duties, but that he was specially summoned by the head of the Ji Family for this purpose because of his knowledge of ritual. As for his final report, it was the custom in ancient China for the guest to turn around and bow repeatedly as he left; the host (or the host's proxy, in this case Confucius) could return to his place only after this process was over. Here we see Confucius fulfilling his ritual duties with both precision and grace.

10.4 When entering the gate of his Duke, he would draw himself in, as if the gate were not large enough to admit him.

This is a sign of respect.

He would not come to a halt at the center of the doorway and when walking would not tread upon the threshold.

There are more and less elaborate explanations proposed by commentators for each of these behaviors. Most prosaically, one does not stand in the middle of the doorway as a courtesy to others, to avoid impeding their movement, and one does not tread upon thresholds to avoid dirtying them, which would in turn dirty the flowing robes of others. More elaborate explanations hold that ministers must enter only on the right side of a doorway (which were typically divided in two by a wooden post), and that only the ruler could stand at its center. Similarly, some commentators argue that only the ruler was permitted to tread upon thresholds, and therefore a minister doing so would represent an act of insubordination.

When passing by his appointed place, his countenance would become alert and serious, he would hasten his steps, his words falling to a whisper as if he could barely get them out.

Before Confucius can take his appointed place in the courtyard, he must pay his respects to the Duke, who is above on his dais.

When he ascended to the Duke's dais with the hem of his gown gathered in his hands, he would draw himself in, slowing his breath to the point that it seemed as if he were not breathing at all. Upon leaving the Duke's dais, his expression would relax as he descended the top stair, and he would seem at ease. On reaching the bottom of the stairs, he would hasten forward smoothly, as though gliding upon wings. When returning to his own place, he would resume his attitude of cautious respect.

Most early commentators believe this passage to be a record of Confucius' behavior when arriving at court for an audience with the Duke of Lu, who would be awaiting him on a raised dais above the courtyard.

10.5 When grasping the official jade tablet, he would draw himself in, as if he could not bear its weight. Sometimes he held it high against his forehead as if saluting, while at other times he held it low at his waist as if offering a gift. Alert and serious, his expression would be like someone about to go into battle, and he would walk with shortened steps as though each movement were carefully scripted. During the ceremonial exchange of gifts, his countenance was accommodating; when having his private audience, he seemed at ease.

The passage describes the proper behavior for a gentleman when serving as an envoy to a foreign state. The jade tablet (*gui* 圭) was a symbol of authority given to a minister by his ruler. When sent as an envoy to a foreign state, the minister would first formally announce his presence and mission to the ruler he was sent to meet by presenting this tablet. A ceremonial exchange of gifts would follow, in which the minister would present the gifts his ruler had sent with him and receive the gifts the foreign ruler wished him to take back. The mission would conclude on the next day with a private audience in which, presumably, the details of the matter at hand would be discussed, and where additional gifts would be exchanged between the minister and foreign ruler.[1] Confucius is described here as perfectly adapting his behavior and facial expressions to each phase of the visit. Regarding the private audience, for instance, Huang Kan notes, "Since this private visit did not constitute official public business, his expression and personal bearing accordingly changed to that of a person acting naturally . . . and he did not revert to the alert, serious, 'going into battle' expression." This passage is perhaps the most challenging in Book Ten to traditional commentators who want to read it as an account of Confucius' ritual behavior, since it is not likely that Confucius ever served as an official envoy to a foreign state. Chao Yuezhi notes this fact and finesses it by suggesting that this represents *advice* that Confucius once gave on serving as an envoy.

10.6 The gentleman did not use reddish-black or maroon for the trim of his garment, nor did he use red or purple for his informal dress.

"The gentleman" is understood by traditional commentators as a reference to Confucius, although this impersonal term is more likely evidence that we are reading

---

[1] Cf. the *Book of Etiquette and Ritual*, Chapter 15 ("Ritual Concerning Official Missions"); Steele 1917, vol. 1: 218–219.

fragments of a generic ritual text. According to Kong Anguo, reddish-black was used for fasting garments, while maroon was used in mourning garments; both, therefore, were inappropriate for use in everyday dress. The translation of both color terms, it should be noted, is extremely speculative. As for the second phrase, Wang Bi argues that Confucius viewed red and purple as impure, counterfeit colors, and this claim is supported by 17.16, where Confucius declares that he "hates purple for usurping the place of vermilion." Huang Kan believes that red and purple were viewed as intermediate colors between the five primary colors of green, vermilion, white, black and yellow, and that Confucius made a point of not wearing them because "in his age, many people were beginning to value red and purple and abandon the proper colors."

In the summer, he wore a single layer of linen or hemp but always put on an outer garment before going out.

As Waley notes, failing to don an outer garment would amount to "going out into the town in one's shirt-sleeves" (1989: 147, n. 5)—perhaps a less shocking concept to a modern American than to an early 20th-century British scholar such as Arthur Waley, but clearly an expression in Confucius' age of sloppiness, laziness, and/or a lack of respect for others.

With a black upper garment he would wear a lambskin robe; with a white upper garment he would wear a fawn-skin robe; and with a yellow upper garment he would wear a fox-fur robe.

Black garments were standard court attire, white garments were worn during certain ceremonies and for certain official receptions, and yellow garments were apparently worn for the special year-end *zha* 蜡 sacrifice. Each of the robes mentioned were of a color that would perfectly harmonize with the garment with which they were worn; as Kong Anguo explains, "The middle and outer layers of his dress were color coordinated."

His informal fur robe was long, but the right sleeve was short. He required that his nightgown be knee-length.

According to Kong Anguo, Confucius' robe was long for the sake of warmth, but with a short right sleeve to make performing tasks more convenient. As Legge comments, "Confucius knew how to combine comfort and convenience" (1991a: 231). As for why his nightgown was required to be knee-length—as opposed to a normal upper garment, which would come to the waist—the only remotely reasonable philosophical explanation is offered by Liu Baonan, who suggests that the added length was meant to distinguish the nightgown from garb worn during the daytime, and therefore to clearly demarcate sleeping from other activities. This accords well with the sense of 10.10 below. An alternate, more pragmatic, explanation is offered by Brooks and Brooks: "Too short nightclothes ride up during sleep" (1998: 61).

He wore thick fox and badger furs when at home. Except when he was in mourning, he never went anywhere without having all of his sash ornaments properly displayed.

Some commentators read *ju* 居 as "to sit" rather than "to be at home," and understand the thick furs to have served as a seating cushion. Sash ornaments were symbols of rank, made of jade for ordinary officers of the court. Confucius always had them properly displayed in accordance with ritual, but would remove them when in mourning. Jewelry and other ornamentation were generally forbidden during mourning, but it is not clear whether the decision to forgo the normally mandatory sash pendants was a cultivated intuition of the Master's or a formal ritual regulation. In either case, by the time of the *Record of Ritual* this principle was formalized: "Whenever one dons a sash one must also attach one's jade sash ornaments. Only during mourning should one not do so."[2]

With the exception of his one-piece ceremonial skirts, his lower garments were always cut and hemmed. He did not wear [black] lambskin robes or dark caps on condolence visits. On the day of the "Auspicious Moon," he would always put on his [black] court attire and present himself at court.

White (rather than black) was the color of mourning in ancient China, and Confucius was always careful to change out of his more formal and festive, but chromatically inappropriate, court attire when visiting someone in mourning. As Kong Anguo comments, "White is the color of mourning, and black is the color for auspicious occasions. Mourning and auspicious occasions demand distinctive clothing." Most commentators believe the occasion of the "Auspicious Moon" to be the same as the "Announcement of the New Month" mentioned in 3.17—i.e., the day of the new moon, or the first of the lunar month. As mentioned in 3.17, Duke Wen of Lu had apparently abandoned the ritual normally performed on this day, but Confucius wished to keep the observance alive. He therefore not only insisted that Zigong (who had a position as ritual functionary in Lu) continue the sacrifice of the sheep that originally went along with the ritual, but would show up at court, dressed in his best formal attire, although we are to presume that no one was actually there to meet him. This image of a formally-clad Confucius appearing punctually at court for a ceremony that would never occur powerfully exemplifies the sort of dogged adherence to traditional ritual practices in the face of public indifference that we have also heard described in the second half of 9.3. The point of the passage as a whole, of course, is not merely that Confucius was fashionable (though he certainly was), but that his perfectly refined aesthetic sense served as an expression of his inner virtue.

10.7 When fasting, he would always don a clean linen robe [after his ritual bath]. When fasting, he would always alter his diet, as well as the place where he would sit when at leisure.

Fasting involved physical purification through bathing and eliminating meat, wine, and pungent items (garlic, ginger, etc.) from one's diet. Most commentators understand "altering the place where he would sit when at leisure" to mean that Confucius would, even when at leisure, sit only in more formal postures and locations, refraining from fully relaxing in his more comfortable, customary seating places. Some take it to mean that he would refrain from sleeping in his usual, inner quarters—i.e., he would refrain from sleeping with his wife and/or concubines during the fasting period—but the text specifically refers to "sitting" rather than "sleeping."

---

[2] Chapter 13 ("Jade-Bead Pendants of the Royal Cap"); Legge 1967, vol. 2: 19.

10.8 He would not eat in excess, even when presented with refined grain or finely minced meat.

In this, Confucius showed unusual moderation and discretion; as Zheng Ruxie notes, "It is the general nature of people to eat sparingly when presented with tough meat or coarse grain, but to eat to excess when presented with refined grain or finely minced meat."

He would not eat grain that was damp or musty, fish that had gone bad, or meat that had spoiled. He would eat nothing that was discolored or foul smelling, nor anything that was improperly cooked or gathered out of season. He would not eat any meat that had been improperly butchered or anything that had not been properly seasoned.

As Brooks and Brooks notes, "Grain keeps only if stored dry. These rules, including seasonability, seem meant to avoid illness or discomfort from eating" (1998: 62). Presumably proper butchering refers to something like kosher regulations: ritual guidelines for the preparation of animal products, possibly including (at least according to Jiang Xi) the manner in which the animals were slaughtered. For example, the *Book of Etiquette and Ritual* provides detailed instructions for the proper slaughtering of animals to be used in sacrifice, including the cardinal direction in which the animals are to be positioned, the precise manner in which they are to be killed, and which specific parts of the animals are to be used.[3]

Even when meat was plentiful, he would not eat so much that it would overpower the grain. He would only enjoy wine without limit, though never to the point of disorderliness.

"Wine" has become the standard translation for *jiu* 酒, although the term refers to spirits fermented from grains (usually millet), rather than to our fruit-based wine. According to Huang Kan, Confucius did not set strict limits on his wine consumption because people vary from one another, and from time to time, in their capacity for alcohol: the point is simply not to drink to excess. Hu Anguo comments that "probably the sage was able to drink without strictly limiting his intake, while at the same time never becoming disorderly in his behavior, because of his ability to 'follow his heart's desire without overstepping the bounds' [2.4]." Excessive drinking was apparently quite a problem among the Zhou aristocracy—the *Book of Odes* and *Book of History* are full of injunctions against drunkenness, seen as one of the primary sources of personal and social disorder (also cf. 6.25 and 9.6, as well as the commentary to 10.13). Part of Confucius' sageliness lies in his ability to drink to his heart's content without crossing the line into excess.

He would not drink wine bought from a shop or dried meat purchased from the market.

There is some debate over how to understand this line, but Huang Kan offers the most straightforward interpretation: "If you have not made the wine yourself, you cannot be sure that it is pure and clean. If you have not cured the dried meat yourself, you

---

[3] Chapter 37 ("Rituals Concerning the Offering of the Smaller Set of Beasts as Food"); Steele 1917, vol. 2: 161–162.

cannot be sure what type of animal it has been made from." A gentleman was no doubt expected to have a household large enough to produce its own wine and dried meat.

Although he would not remove the ginger dish from the table, he would not consume it in excess.

Ginger was kept in a dish as a side condiment, much like the practice in modern-day sushi restaurants. Brooks and Brooks suggest that ginger as a spice for meat was still a novelty at this point (1998: 62), and may have been viewed with suspicion by a traditionally minded gentleman. Zhu Xi believes the point to be that although ginger is a salutary substance, Confucius was not greedy in his consumption of it. Alternately, some commentators suggest that this line (and perhaps the passage as a whole) refers to a fasting period, where pungent substances were forbidden, but ginger allowed because it did not have an overly strong smell.

10.9 After assisting his Duke at a sacrifice, he would not keep the portion of the sacrificial meat bestowed upon him overnight. When sacrificing at home, he would not let the meat sit for more than three days. If it had sat for more than three days, he would not eat it.

Officials who assisted at the sacrifice of their Duke were given a portion of the sacrificial meat to take home with them—in ancient times, as today, the spirits took only the "spiritual essence" of the food, leaving the material remainders for humans to enjoy. According to Zhousheng Lie, the especially sacred quality of the lordly sacrifice dictated that it be consumed immediately, so that its "spiritual benefit" was not dissipated. The meat used in domestic sacrifices was less sacred and subject only to the normal demands of hygiene.

10.10 He would not instruct while eating, nor continue to converse once he had retired to bed.

That is, he remained thoroughly focused in all of his activities. As Fan Ziyu explains, "The sage preserves his mind and is not distracted: when it is time to eat, he eats; when it is time to sleep, he sleeps. Neither of these times are appropriate for instruction or conversation."

10.11 Even though a meal was only of coarse grain or vegetable broth, he invariably gave some as a sacrificial offering, and would do so in a grave and respectful manner.

As Zhu Xi explains,

When the ancients took their meals, they would take a small portion of each type of food and place it on the ground, among the sacrificial vessels, as an offering to their ancestors. In thus sacrificing to those of previous generations—who were also once people, and thus ate and drank like them—they demonstrated that they did not forget their roots. Even when it came to relatively worthless things, Confucius would always make an offering, and would do so in a respectful manner. Such is the sincerity of the sage.

10.12 He would not sit unless his mat was straight (*zheng* 正).

Zheng means literally "straight" as well as more abstractly "correct," and possibly both meanings are intended. Fan Ning takes *zheng* in the literal sense, observing that "a straight mat is a means of expressing reverence and respect." However, he also notes that, according to some commentators, different ranks of society had different types of seating mats they were ritually sanctioned to use, each being employed in its own proper context. Therefore, we might alternately render the passage, "He would not sit unless his mat were of the correct type."

10.13 When attending village drinking ceremonies, he would leave only after the elderly people had left.

Waiting to leave until one's elders have left is a basic dictate of ritual propriety. There is some commentarial debate over what specific ceremony is referred to here, but Cheng Shude is probably right in thinking that the passage refers to a whole class of ceremonies performed at the village level. Though formal occasions, village drinking ceremonies could apparently get out of hand; in the *Record of Ritual*, Zigong returns from observing the *zha* 蜡 end of the year ceremony and complains to Confucius, "The people of the entire state behaved as if they were mad."[4] As we learned in 10.8, Confucius never drank excessively, and we presume that his observation of ritual precedence even at the end of a long drinking ceremony was intended to set an example of moderation and discipline to others.

10.14 When the villagers were performing the end of the year exorcism (*nuo* 儺), he would stand on the Eastern steps of his house dressed in full court regalia.

The Eastern steps are the proper ritual position for a host. This passage is probably to be read together with 10.13, and has a similar theme. There were three *nuo* ceremonies each year, but the one referred to here is probably the New Year's exorcism where the entire populace—rather than just the court elite—participated.[5] Held at the height of winter and meant to drive away evil spirits and noxious influences remaining from the pervious year, this *nuo* involved exorcists leading the common people around from house to house to perform purifying ceremonies. It was a loud, festive occasion, and undoubtedly involved a fair amount of alcohol consumption. As in 10.13, Confucius attempts to gently guard against excess on the part of his fellow villager by striking a formal note and injecting a note of solemnity into the proceedings. As Wang Fuzhi notes, socializing with the common people is no simple task for the gentleman, who has to serve as moral exemplar without being too overbearing, pedantic, or heavy-handed. In 10.13 and 10.14, "we observe the sage in action and see it done to perfection." An alternative interpretation is offered by Kong Anguo, who believes that Confucius is standing on the steps of his ancestral temple, rather than his home, in order to comfort his ancestral spirits during the exorcism and keep them from fleeing along with the evil spirits.

---

[4] Chapter 22 ("Miscellaneous Records"); Legge 1967, vol. 2: 167. Interestingly, in this passage Confucius excuses the drunken behavior of the common people as an understandable opportunity to "blow off steam" after a hard year of labor.

[5] See the *Zhou Ritual*, chs. 48 and 54, for an account of this ritual.

10.15 When sending his regards to someone in another state, he would bow twice to the messenger and then see him off.

The double-bow was to express respect to the acquaintance to whom he was sending the complimentary regards, which usually included some sort of gift.

10.16 When Ji Kangzi sent him a gift of medicinal herbs, he bowed [to the messenger] and accepted it, but said, "I do not know what sort of medicine this is, so I dare not taste it."

Tasting an unknown medicine could be quite dangerous, as many of them were mild poisons or dangerous if taken at an improper dosage. This gift thus put Confucius in a bind because one was usually expected to sample a gift when receiving it. As Fan Ziyu explains, "When given a gift of food one must first taste it and then bow,[6] but in the case of this medicine, Confucius did not understand [what sort of medicine it was], and so he did not dare to taste it. To accept a gift without tasting it, though, would normally express contempt for the gift, so Confucius explained himself to the messenger in this way." Here we see Confucius skillfully balancing the demands of ritual etiquette and those of common sense. Kong Anguo understands the passage somewhat differently: what Confucius does not understand is Ji Kangzi's motivation in sending the gift, and therefore he physically accepts it in order to be polite, but does not taste it in order to send a message to the illegitimate ruler of Lu that he is not to be bought. Legge apparently follows this interpretation in his comment: "Confucius accepted the gift, but thought it necessary to let the donor know that he could not, for the present at least, avail himself of it" (1991a: 234).

10.17 One day the stables burned. When the Master returned from court, he asked, "Was anyone hurt?" He did not ask about the horses.

Considering that horses were quite valuable commodities and stable hands easily replaceable, Confucius' response is both unexpected and moving—an expression, as many later commentators have put it, of Confucius' "humanism." According to the version of this passage in the *Family Sayings of Confucius*, the stables mentioned were the state stables of Lu. Most commentators, though, assume that the stables in question were those of Confucius himself, and argue that part of the point of this passage is the Master's lack of concern for his own material possessions.

10.18 When presented with a gift of food from his lord, he would taste it before even straightening his mat. When presented with raw meat, he would always have it cooked and then present it as an offering [to his ancestors]. When presented with livestock, he would always have it reared.

When attending his lord at a meal, he would taste the food his lord had sacrificed before giving it to him to eat.

---

[6] See 10.18.

According to the *Record of Ritual*, it is the ritual duty of a minister to taste a bit of all of the foods present before allowing his lord to eat them, in order to assure that they are palatable and safe.[7]

10.19 When he was sick, and his lord came to visit him, he would lay with his head to the east, draped in his court robes, with his ceremonial sash fastened about him.

Being sick, he could not rise to greet his lord or properly dress himself in court attire, but it would also be unseemly for him to receive his guest in civilian garb. He thus had himself arranged in bed so that he would be both ritually presentable and facing the door when the lord entered. Some commentators believe that the eastern orientation of the Master's head was for medical reasons—Huang Kan, for one, explains that east is the direction of *yangqi* 陽氣 ("virile/healthy-vital essence"), and thus laying in this direction when sick is advantageous for one's health. It is more likely, however, a bit of ritual decorum. The *Record of Ritual*, for instance, contains the injunction, "When sitting, the gentleman always takes a place directly facing the window, and when sleeping, his head is always towards the east."[8] Of course, this ritual injunction possibly has as its origin certain *fengshui* 風水 (Chinese geomancy; lit. "wind and water") considerations.

10.20 When summoned by his lord, he would set off on foot, without waiting for his horses to be hitched to the carriage.

Setting off immediately is a sign of respect and humbleness, and we see references to the immediate response of a vassal to the summons of his lord as early as Ode 100: "He hustles, throws on his clothes upside down/By his lord he has been summoned." This ode is quoted in Chapter 27 of the *Xunzi* ("Great Compendium") after it is explained that "when a feudal lord summons a minister, the minister does not wait for the horses to be hitched to the carriage, but throws his clothes on upside down in his haste and sets out on foot. This is ritual."[9] Some commentators explain that, since it would be unseemly for an official to travel by foot, after Confucius set out someone would hitch up the carriage and pick him up along the way. The appropriateness of Confucius' behavior as described here is discussed in *Mencius* 5:B:7.

10.21 Upon entering the Grand Ancestral Temple, he asked questions about everything.

This is a repetition of a portion of 3.15; see that passage for commentary.

---

[7] Chapter 13 ("Jade-Bead Pendants of the Royal Cap"); Legge 1967, vol. 2: 7.

[8] Chapter 13 ("Jade-Bead Pendants of the Royal Cap"); Legge 1967, vol. 2: 5.

[9] Knoblock 1994: 208. See also the *Record of Ritual*, Chapter 13 ("Jade-Bead Pendants of the Royal Cap"); Legge 1967, vol. 2: 17.

10.22 When a friend died without relatives able to take care of the funeral arrangements, he would say, "I will see to burying him properly."

Kong Anguo comments, "He valued the kindness shown to him by his friend," but probably this is simply what should be expected of a friend. A related and slightly more elaborate passage in the *Record of Ritual* expands the sphere of concern further: "When a strange guest arrived and had nowhere to lodge, the Master said, 'While he is alive in my care, I will take care of lodging him, and should he pass away in my care, I will take responsibility for burying him properly.'"[10]

10.23 When receiving a gift from a friend—even something as valuable as a cart or a horse—he did not bow unless it was a gift of sacrificial meat.

A gift of sacrificial meat carries with it a sort of ritual solemnity not possessed by a non-religious gift, no matter how sumptuous it might be. As Kong Anguo comments, "Not bowing signifies that all that has transpired is an exchange of goods." There is probably no specific clause in the rites that dictate particular response; rather, Confucius, by virtue of his sensitivity to the ritual value of sacrificial meat relative to a sumptuous—but nonsacred—gift, simply *knows* how to respond properly.

10.24 He would not sleep rigidly like a corpse, nor would he assume a formal posture when sitting at leisure.

There is some debate over the sense of the first phrase. Some, such as Bao Xian and Zhu Xi, see it as a form of superstitious avoidance of invoking the appearance of a dead person. Something like Fan Ziyu's explanation is more likely: "'Not sleeping rigidly like a corpse' has nothing to do with hating the appearance of death. The point is that if you do not allow relaxed, restful vital essence to establish itself in your body, you will never be refreshed, even if you do manage to stretch out your limbs." As for the second phrase, commentators explain that there were different traditional seating postures that corresponded to different levels of formality; what we have translated as "formal posture"—literally "sitting as if a guest" (*kezuo* 客坐)—probably refers to kneeling against a mat and then sitting with one's legs folded beneath the buttocks, still a formal seating posture in modern Japan. The point, as in the first phrase, seems to be that Confucius did not maintain rigid, formal postures at all times, but knew when and how to relax. Again, Fan Ziyu: "It is not that he sat in an indolent fashion, just that he did not sit the way he would if he were offering a sacrifice or receiving a guest—he was 'composed and yet fully at ease.'" "Composed and yet fully at ease" is a reference to 7.4, where we find a very similar theme.

10.25 When he saw someone fasting or mourning, he invariably assumed a changed expression, even if they were an intimate acquaintance. When he saw someone wearing a ritual cap or a blind person, he would invariably display a respectful countenance, even if they were of low birth (*xie* 褻).

---

[10] Chapter 3 ("Tan Gong"); Legge 1967, vol. 1: 155.

The translation follows Huang Kan, who takes *xie* as referring to someone of low birth. "Respect has to do with one's position, and ancestry does not make the man" he remarks. "Therefore one must always show a respectful countenance." This accords with the passage below where Confucius shows respect to a commoner, but an alternate reading that accords better with the phrase immediately preceding is that of Mr. Zhou, who takes *xie* as "intimate, acquainted," giving us the reading: "even if they were well-known to him" (cf. 9.10).

When riding past someone dressed in funeral garb, he would bow down and grasp the crossbar of his carriage. He would do so even if the mourner was a lowly peddler.

Facing downward and grasping the crossbar of the chariot is a sign of respect. The translation follows Yu Yue's suggestion that the obscure *fuban* 負版 ("carrying tablets") should be read as *fufan* 負販 ("porter" or "peddler"), which makes this passage accord with a related comment in the *Record of Ritual*: "Ritual has to do with humbling oneself and showing respect to others—even porters and peddlers must be shown respect, how much more so the wealthy and noble!"[11] Kong Anguo, however, understands the term *fuban* to refer to someone carrying official state documents; on this reading, the second phrase would be translated: "He would do the same when passing a messenger carrying official documents."

When presented food with full ritual propriety, he would invariably assume a solemn expression and rise from his seat.

A related passage in the *Record of Ritual* says, "When attending an elder at a meal, if the host offers one food with his own hands, one then bows and eats it. If the host does not offer the food with his own hand, then one eats it without bowing."[12] When presented with food by the host himself, then, Confucius would invariably respond with a gesture of respect.

He would also assume a solemn expression upon hearing a sudden clap of thunder or observing a fierce wind.

This is understood as a sign of respect for Heaven's power.

10.26 When mounting his carriage, he would always stand facing it directly while grasping the mounting strap. Once in his carriage, he would not let his gaze wander past the crossbar in front of him or to either side, he would not speak rapidly, nor would he point with his hand.

Many of these items of ritual etiquette are to be found in the *Record of Ritual*.[13] As in many cultures, pointing was considered rude.

10.27 Startled by their arrival, a bird arose and circled several times before alighting upon a branch. [The Master] said, "This pheasant upon the mountain

---

[11] Chapter 1 ("Summary of Ritual"); Legge 1967, vol. 1: 65.

[12] Chapter 1 ("Summary of Ritual"); Legge 1967, vol. 1: 80.

[13] Chapter 1 ("Summary of Ritual"); Legge 1967, vol. 1: 94–97.

bridge—how timely it is! How timely it is!" Zilu saluted the bird, and it cried out three times before flying away.

This poetic, somewhat cryptic passage has always been very problematic for interpreters and translators, and seems like a nonsequitur at the end of a chapter devoted to short, prosaic descriptions of ritual behavior. Legge refers to it as "a fragment, which seemingly has no connection with the rest of the Book" (1991a: 236), and Leys has even stronger words: "the obscurity of this entire passage has acted as a dangerous stimulant upon the imaginations of many commentators. It seems in fact that the original text has become hopelessly garbled and corrupt; there would be little point in insisting on making sense out of it" (1997: 168). Even the infinitely resourceful Zhu Xi admits to being stumped, and suggests that some explanatory text has been lost. A quite plausible way to understand it, however, is as a summary of the chapter as a whole: different in style from other passages in this Book, it was probably added by the editors as a thematic capstone. While it is not entirely clear *why* the pheasant is being praised for timeliness (perhaps because it knows when to arise, when to alight, and when to fly off), the ideal of "timeliness" (*shi* 時)—according perfectly with the demands of the situation at hand—sums up fairly well the general theme of Book Ten:[14] that the Master's actions accorded perfectly with the demands of ritual propriety, no matter what the circumstances. Timeliness is Confucius' particular forte, and indeed he is known to posterity (through the efforts of Mencius) as the "timely sage"—the one whose ritual responses were always appropriate to circumstances. As Mencius explains in 5:B:1:

> When Confucius decided to leave Qi, he emptied the rice from the pot before it was even done and set out immediately. When he decided to leave Lu he said, "I will take my time, for this is the way to leave the state of one's parents." Moving quickly when it was appropriate to hurry, moving slowly when it was appropriate to linger, remaining in a state or taking office when the situation allowed—this is how Confucius was . . . Confucius was the sage whose actions were timely.

Liu Fenglu understands 10.27 in this fashion, quoting *Mencius* 5:B:1 and adding, "Book Ten records the fact that the Master's words and actions all accorded perfectly with ritual, and all came at the proper time. When it comes to according perfectly with ritual, it is timeliness that is most important."

---

[14] If, that is, we see it as a set of descriptions of Confucius' behavior rather than impersonal ritual injunctions.

BOOK ELEVEN

As Liu Baonan notes, "this entire chapter is devoted to the words and actions of the disciples." Most of the passages consist of evaluations of the characters of various disciples that serve to illustrate general points about virtue and self-cultivation.

11.1 The Master said, "Those of my disciples who were first to enter into study of ritual and music with me were simple rustics, whereas those who entered later were aristocrats (*junzi* 君子). If I had to employ them [in public office], I would prefer the first."

> There are several ways to understand this passage. Many commentators take "first" and "after" to refer to historical ages—usually the Shang and the Zhou—and understand *junzi* in its ordinary Confucian sense of cultural and moral exemplar. On this interpretation, the people of earlier ages were not as culturally refined as those later ages, but had a kind of rough, simple honesty that recommended them. Considering that 11.2 and the rest of Book Eleven mostly concerns disciples of Confucius, however, it is more plausible to follow Xing Bing (following Bao Xian) in seeing "first" and "last" as referring to generations of disciples, the former being preferable because they "possessed something of the [unaffected] style of the ancients." In this understanding, the issue is the distinction between disciples from the lower, common classes, and those from the aristocratic classes, which involves reading *junzi* in its original sense of "aristocrat," in which case the point would be that Confucius preferred those from humble and even crude beginnings who rose through their own effort and ability over those who were born into their elite status. This accords well with passages such as 6.6 and 7.7.

11.2 The Master said, "None of those who followed me in Chen and Cai managed to attain official position there."

> This is a difficult passage that has inspired much commentarial ingenuity. To "attain official position" is a loose rendering of the literal to "reach the gate," and much of the debate has centered around what is meant by "gate." Beginning with Han Yu, some have read this passage together with 11.15, taking "gate" to refer to the metaphorical entranceway into Confucius' Way. On this reading, Confucius' point is that none of the disciples who were with him in Chen and Cai (when he, along with some disciples, encountered the "difficulties" mentioned in 15.2, becoming trapped without food by troops from Chen) have made much progress in their learning. This seems strange, though, considering that—at least according to the *Record of the Historian*—Yan Hui, Zigong, and Zilu were among the disciples with him at that time. Zheng Xuan takes "gate" to refer to the metaphorical gateway to public office and influence: "The point is that none of the disciples who followed me and thus encountered difficulties in Chen and Cai had been able to attain public office." Liu Baonan, elaborating on Zheng Xuan, connects 11.2 to *Mencius* 7:B:18, which reads: "The

111

gentleman [Confucius] encountered difficulties between Chen and Cai because he had no connections with those in power." Liu comments, "'Having no connections with those in power' is precisely what is meant here [in 11.2] by 'none of them reached the gate' . . . When the Master traveled around, he relied upon connections acquired through his various disciples attaining official positions, and the point here is that he was brought to such difficulties because none of his disciples had attained a post in Chen or Cai." This seems to make the best sense of the passage.

11.3 Those known for virtuous conduct: Yan Hui, Min Ziqian, Boniu, and Zhonggong. Those known for eloquence: Zai Wo and Zigong. Those known for administrative skill: Ran Qiu and Jilu. Those known for cultural learning: Ziyou and Zixia.

The version of this passage found in the *Record of the Historian* is presented as a direct quotation from Confucius, who prefaces it by noting, "Those who personally received instruction from me numbered seventy-seven, and they were all exceptionally talented scholars." We are to assume that the ten then mentioned by name were either extraordinarily talented or representative of the various types of talents to be found among the disciples.

11.4 The Master said, "Yan Hui is of no help to me—he is pleased with everything that I say."

As Zhu Xi remarks, the comment seems to be meant ironically: the Master is in fact quite happy that Yan Hui "silently comprehends" everything that he hears (cf. 2.9). The *Discourses on the Mean* comments, "Yan Hui comprehended the essence of the sage, and therefore expressed no exhaustion or difficulties. This is why he alone achieved such an exalted reputation, and ranked at the top of the seventy disciples."

11.5 The Master said, "How filial is Min Ziqian! No one can gainsay the praise lavished upon him by both parents and brothers."

Several early texts have stories concerning the filiality of Min Ziqian. All present a filial respectful son dealing selflessly with a classically evil stepmother and two pernicious stepbrothers. Min Zijian apparently lost his mother early in life, whereupon his father remarried and had two more sons with his new wife. The new wife hated Min Zijian and treated him poorly, favoring her own two sons. One cold winter day, Zijian was out driving for his father when the reins of the carriage fell from his hands; on examination, the father discovered that Zijian's hands had frozen because he was wearing only thin, unlined gloves. Returning home and inspecting the hands of his new wife and her two sons, he discovered that they were clad in warm, padded gloves, and in his anger he wished to dismiss her and disown her children. Zijian then interceded, saying, "While she is here, one son must go cold, but were she to be dismissed, three sons would be out in the cold"—i.e., without the stepmother, both Zijian *and* his two stepbrothers would be bereft of a mother's love. The father relented, and according to some versions the stepmother, shamed by Zijian's selflessness, reformed herself and became an exemplary parent. Hu Anguo comments, "His parents and brothers all praised him for his filiality and brotherliness, and others believed this praise without a hint of doubt. Probably this is because he accumulated the substance of filiality and brotherliness on the inside until it manifested itself on the outside, and this is why the master sighs in praise of him."

11.6 Nan Rong often recited the ode that mentioned the white jade tablet. Confucius gave the daughter of his elder brother to him in marriage.

The ode referred to is number 256, which reads:

> A flaw in the white jade tablet
> Can still be polished out;
> A flaw in these words of mine,
> Can never be undone.

Confucius presumably sees Nan Rong's constant recitation of this ode as evidence of his carefulness in both speech and practice. As Fan Ziyu notes, "Speech is the outward manifestation of action, and action provides the substance for speech. There has never been one who was careless in his speech and still able to be cautious in his action. The fact that Nan Rong wished so intensely to be careful about his speech means that he would certainly be able to be careful with regard to his behavior." A slightly different interpretation is presented in *Dai's Record*: "One who thinks upon Goodness when in private will speak of rightness when in public. After hearing the ode, Nan Rong three times in one day repeated the lines about 'a flaw in the white jade tablet'—such was Nan Rong's behavior. The Master therefore believed in his Goodness and accepted him as an in-law." Cf. 5.2, where an alternate explanation for the Master's decision to accept Nan Rong is given.

11.7 Ji Kangzi asked, "Who among your disciples could be said to love learning?"
    The Master replied, "There was one named Yan Hui who loved learning, but unfortunately he was fated to live a short life, and has since passed away. Now there are none who really love learning."

This is a shorter version of 6.3, where Duke Ai is the interlocutor. Some commentators see significance in the fact that different answers are given to the two different rulers, attributing it to differences in moral or political status (Duke Ai, as a legitimate ruler, merits a fuller answer than the usurper Ji Kangzi), understanding (Ji Kangzi is not capable of understanding as much as the Duke), or pedagogical needs (the extra line concerning "misdirecting anger" in 6.3 is meant as a corrective to the Duke's particular faults). Most likely, though, the discrepancy is a result of alternate transmissions of the same story, the basic point of which is to honor Yan Hui.

11.8 When Yan Hui died, Yan Lu, his father, requested the Master's carriage, so that it could be used for Yan Hui's coffin enclosure.
    The Master replied, "Everyone recognizes his own son, whether he is talented or not. When Bo Yu, my own son, passed away, he had a coffin, but no enclosure. I did not go on foot in order to provide him with an enclosure. Having held rank below the ministers, it is not permissible for me to go on foot."

As Brooks and Brooks note, "chariots in Warring States graves . . . proclaim the power and wealth of the deceased" (1998: 71). Yan Lu is asking that Yan Hui be accorded funerary honors that were normally reserved only for high-ranking officials. Confucius' response is kind, but firm: he acknowledges Yan Lu's desire to honor his son, as well as the fact that his own son, Bo Yu, was not as talented as Yan Hui. Nonetheless, Confucius managed to refrain from according his son funerary honors to which he was not ritually entitled, and he is urging Yan Lu to do the same—although gently, and couched in terms of Confucius' own need to maintain the trappings of his rank. A long line of commentators, beginning with Kong Anguo, claim that Yan Lu, being a poor man, is asking that the Master sell his carriage in order to raise money for the purchase of a *guo* 槨, which most take in the standard, possibly later, sense of "outer coffin": a secondary coffin surrounding the inner coffin that actually holds the corpse. Alternately, Huan Maoyong cites various Han ritual texts that he sees as evidence that Yan Lu is asking that Confucius provide his carriage to serve as a specially-draped hearse for Yan Hui's coffin, a request that is denied because Yan Hui, as a mere scholar (*shi* 士), does not ritually merit the use of a hearse. The second half of the passage, however, indicates that Confucius is expecting to be deprived of the use of a carriage for longer than the duration of a funeral procession if he accedes to Yan Lu's request, which suggest that Yan Lu is asking that Confucius' chariot actually be buried with the corpse or sold.

11.9 When Yan Hui passed away, the Master lamented, "Oh! Heaven has bereft me! Heaven has bereft me!"

A touching comment on the importance of Yan Hui for the Master and the affection with which he was viewed. As He Yan notes, "[The Master laments] 'Heaven has bereft me!' because losing Yan Hui was like losing himself, and the repetition emphasizes the depth of the Master's pain and sorrow." Beginning with Han Dynasty commentators, we also find the theory that Heaven provided Yan Hui as a helper and companion to the sage Confucius, which makes his loss particularly poignant and disturbing.

11.10 When Yan Hui passed away, the Master cried for him excessively. The disciples reproved him, saying, "Master, surely you are showing excessive grief!"
    The Master replied, "Am I showing excessive grief? Well, for whom *would* I show excessive grief, if not for this man?"

This is a companion passage to 11.9. Most commentators see Confucius' final comment as a defense of his behavior as appropriate to the situation; Zhu Xi, for instance, remarks, "The point is that Yan Hui's death is tragic, and therefore in wailing for him it is fitting to lose control—no other person was his equal." The Master's lack of awareness of how far he has gone, though, suggests that we have here a rare and poignant record of the sort of "minor fault" (as opposed to "major faults"; cf. 7.17) that even a gentleman cannot avoid. This may also be meant as an illustration of the observation in 3.4 that "when it comes to mourning, it is better to be excessively sorrowful than fastidious."

11.11 When Yan Hui passed away, the disciples wished to give him a lavish funeral.

Some commentators believe that it is the disciples of Yan Hui (rather than Confucius) who are meant here, which makes their disobedience of Confucius' wishes more understandable.

The Master said, "That would not be proper."
    The disciples nonetheless went ahead and buried Yan Hui lavishly.

The Master remarked, "Hui looked upon me as a father, and yet in this case I was unable to treat him as a son. This was not my choice, but rather yours, you disciples."

It seems plausible to follow commentators such as Ma Rong and Fan Ning and read this passage together with 11.8: as in 11.8, it is Yan Hui's father, Yan Lu, who is pushing for a lavish funeral, and Confucius who opposes it as ritually inappropriate, considering Yan Hui's modest station in life, and therefore unworthy of Yan Hui. Confucius' final remark reflects the fact that, despite his role as Yan Hui's spiritual father, it is Hui's actual father that has final say in the matter. Confucius is therefore powerless to prevent this violation of ritual propriety.

11.12 Zilu asked about serving ghosts and spirits. The Master said, "You are not yet able to serve people—how could you be able to serve ghosts and spirits?"

"May I inquire about death?"

"You do not yet understand life—how could you possibly understand death?"

In this passage—often cited by Western commentators as an expression of Confucius' profound "humanism"—we clearly see Confucius' practical orientation: the aspiring gentleman is to focus his energy on virtuous conduct and concrete learning rather than empty speculation (cf. 7.21). As Huang Kan remarks, "the teachings of the Zhou Dynasty and of Confucius have to do solely with the here and now." More metaphysically oriented commentators such as Zhu Xi contend that the Master did have esoteric teachings about death and spirits, but that Zilu is simply not yet ready to hear about them, and must complete more basic levels of education before he can receive the esoteric teachings. This, however, is unlikely. As Chen Tianxiang puts it, "The Way of the two sage-lords, the three kings, Duke Zhou, and Confucius focuses solely upon the exigencies of daily human existence and does not depart from them for an instant . . . nowhere do we hear of teachings concerning various levels of esoteric comprehension that must be completed so that one might understand the mysteries of death . . . The Master correctly saw that Zilu's questions were only remotely related to practical concerns, and therefore answered him [as he did]."

11.13 Min Ziqian was attending the Master, standing at his side in a straight and correct manner; [also attending were] Zilu, looking bold and uncompromising, and Ran Qiu and Zigong, both of whom appeared happy and at ease.

The Master was pleased, but remarked, "Someone like Zilu will not get to live out his years."

Some believe the Master to be pleased at having all of his disciples around him. Others, such as Zheng Xuan, identify the source of Confucius' pleasure as the fact that "each disciple [in his attitude] was fully expressing his own nature." The added warning about Zilu is a bit jarring, but not out of keeping with the characterization of Zilu elsewhere in the text (cf. 5.7, 7.11, 11.15, 11.22, 11.26, 17.23). The Master's foreboding was validated, for Zilu ended up dying a violent death during the succession battles in the state of Wei.[1] A story in a pre-Tang text called *The Hidden Meaning*

[1] See the *Zuo Commentary*, Duke Ai, Year 15 (481 B.C.E.); Legge 1991d: 843. Confucius' remark is repeated here.

of the Analects provides a moving account of his death, where Zilu's impetuousness and impulsive courage are presented in a noble light:

> Kuai Kui of Wei was in revolt, and Zilu joined the army that went to meet him. There was an opposing soldier named Hu An who asked him [from the battlements of Kuai Kui's stronghold], "You wish to enter?" Zilu replied, "Yes." From the top of the wall Hu An tossed down a hook on the end of a hemp-rope line to Zilu, [and began pulling him up]. When Zilu was halfway up the wall, Hu An asked incredulously, "Are you a soldier or a gentleman?" Zilu replied, "When dealing with gentlemen, I am a gentleman; when dealing with soldiers, I am a soldier." Thereupon Hu An dropped the rope, and Zilu fell. He broke his left leg but was not killed. Hu An opened the gate and came out, ready to kill Zilu, but Zilu's eyes flashed fiercely like the brightness of the stars. Hui An was unable to advance, and said, "Your eyes fill me with awe and dread; I would prefer that you cover them." Zilu covered his eyes with the sleeve of his gown, and thereupon Hu An killed him.

11.14 The people of Lu were planning to remodel the Long Treasury.

Min Ziqian remarked, "Why not simply restore it? Why does it need to be completely remodeled?"

The Master said, "That man does not talk much, but when he does say something he inevitably hits the mark."

Some commentators see this passage as a simple protest against needless public expense: restoration is cheaper than complete remodeling. However, commentators such as Liu Baonan and Zhai Hao are probably correct in seeing deeper meaning. The Long Treasury was originally a storehouse for precious items and weapons, but, according to the *Zuo Commentary*, it was also used by Duke Zhao in 516 B.C.E. as a stronghold from which to attack the Ji Family as part of his ill-fated attempt to wrest back control of Lu from the usurpers.[2] Many commentators argue that the Ji Family held a particular grudge against the Long Treasury because of its use against them, and also feared that—as a well-fortified stronghold—it might be used again as a staging-point for a revolt by loyalist forces. They were therefore planning to completely remodel it, both to erase bad associations and to make it less easily defensible in the future. Understood in this light, Min Ziqian's comment is a subtle jab at the Ji Family and coded expression of support for the rightful Ducal house of Lu—a loyalist sentiment sure to please Confucius, who was living in Lu during Duke Zhao's failed attempt to regain power. As Zhai Hao explains, "Min Ziqian could not be accused of directly criticizing or disagreeing with the Ji Family, but was able to satirize them using superficially agreeable words, thereby demonstrating his deep agreement with the sage's sentiment that the public good should be strengthened and private interests weakened."

11.15 The Master was heard to remark, "What is Zilu doing in my school, playing the zither the way he does?"

After this, the disciples began treating Zilu in a disrespectful manner. The Master reproved them, saying, "Although Zilu has not yet entered the inner chamber, he has at least ascended to the reception hall."

Alternate versions of this story in the *Family Sayings* and *Garden of Persuasions* explain that Zilu, following his martial predilections, was given to playing the so-called "North-

---

[2] See Duke Zhao Year 25 (516 B.C.E.); Legge 1991d: 710.

ern style" of music, which was rather crude and aggressive, whereas Confucius taught the more gentle and refined "Southern style," exemplified by the court music of the sage-king Shun. His initial complaint was probably intended as a goad, aimed at getting Zilu to take up a more appropriate style of music. As Huang Kan explains,

> Zilu was hard and unyielding by nature, and in his zither playing also displayed a vigorous, aggressive style. Confucius, knowing that he was not destined to live out the full span of his years, repeatedly tried to restrain him. "You are playing the zither in my school, but my school is cultured and elegant, not a place for displays of martial sentiment."

The other disciples mistake this attempt to moderate Zilu's hardness as a complete dismissal, and therefore Confucius is forced to correct them. As Zhu Xi explains, "He points out that, in his learning, Zilu has already reached a correct, great, and glorious stage—it is only that he has yet to enter into the subtle and mysterious final stage. Nonetheless, it is not permissible to dismiss someone or treat them with disrespect because of a single failure."

11.16 Zigong asked, "Who is more worthy, Zizhang or Zixia?"

The Master replied, "Zizhang overshoots the mark, while Zixia falls short of it."

"Then can we say that Zizhang is better?"

The Master replied, "Overshooting the mark is just as bad as falling short of it."

An alternate version of this story in the *Record of Ritual* makes it clear that the unspecified "mark" that Zizhang and Zixia are being measured against is the mean of ritual:

> The Master said, "Zizhang, you overshoot the mark, and yet Zixia falls short." . . . Zigong left his seat and, coming to face the Master, asked, "May I ask what we might take to be the mean between these two extremes?" The Master replied, "Ritual! Ritual! It is by means of ritual that we establish the mean."[3]

Huang Kan remarks, "Zizhang overshot the mark because his nature was overfull and disorderly, and so in his actions he was prone to go too far and not restrain himself. Zixia fell short because his nature was somewhat cold and detached, and so in his actions he was prone to stop himself before he had reached the mark." Based on 3.4, 3.8, or 5.22 we might be forgiven for expecting, like Zigong, that excess (erring on the side of "native substance") would be preferred to deficiency (erring on the side of "cultural refinement") by the Master, but here the emphasis is on hitting the mean (*zhong* 中) (cf. 1.12, 6.18, 6.29, 13.21, 20.1). Perhaps this is because the importance hitting on the mean is the message Zigong needs to hear (see 11.22).

11.17 The Master said, "The head of the Ji Family is wealthier than even the Duke of Zhou ever was, and yet Ran Qiu collects taxes on his behalf to further increase his already excessive wealth. Ran Qiu is no disciple of mine. If you disciples were to sound the drums and attack him, I would not disapprove."

Ran Qiu was serving as the household steward for the Ji Family under Ji Kangzi; cf. 3.6, 6.8, 16.1. An alternate version of this story appears in the *Zuo Commentary*:

---

[3] Chapter 28 ("Confucius at Home at Ease"); Legge 1967, vol. 2: 270–271.

The head of the Ji Family wanted to institute a land tax, and dispatched Ran Qiu to ask for Confucius' counsel. Confucius replied, "I know nothing about such matters." Several attempts were made, and finally the head of the Ji Family sent Ran Qiu with a message for Confucius, "You are a respected elder in this state, and I await your help in carrying out this action. How is it that you do not answer me?" Confucius did not send an official reply, but privately he remarked to Ran Qiu, "The conduct of the gentlemanly ruler is measured by ritual. In giving he is generous, in his affairs he upholds the mean, and in levying taxes he follows moderation. For a ruler like this, taxation according to the Qiu 丘 model[4] is already sufficient. However, if a ruler does not measure himself with ritual and lets his greed grow to insatiable proportions, then in the end even a land tax will not prove to be enough for him. If the Ji-sun Family head wishes to act in accordance with proper models, he has the standards passed down by the Duke of Zhou. If, on the other hand, he wants to proceed according to his own personal whims, what good will my counsel be to him?" Confucius' words were not heeded.[5]

Drums were sounded not only when going into battle, but also to summon people to witness public executions and other punishments, and some commentators try to soften Confucius' final words by suggesting that he meant only that the disciples should publicly chastise Ran Qiu—that is, they should metaphorically rather than literally attack him. A more elaborate version of this story is also found in *Mencius* 4:A:15.

11.18 Zigao is simple-minded, Master Zeng is dull, Zizhang is prone to excess, and Zilu is wildly fierce.

Probably Ge Yinliang is correct in thinking that this passage represents "occasional criticisms uttered by the Master at odd moments, which were then recorded by the disciples." There is some uncertainty about how to render the adjectives, especially Zizhang's quality of *pi* 辟 (excess). The translation follows Ma Rong's gloss, "Zizhang's natural talents surpassed others, but his fault lay in irregular excess (*xiepi* 邪僻) and overstepping the bounds of cultural refinement," which has the virtue of according with the assessment of Zizhang in 11.16. Huang Shisan believes that the faults mentioned "refer to inborn native substance, not to training"—that is, they represent the challenges each disciple was being urged by the Master to overcome rather than final character judgments.

11.19 The Master said, "How close was Yan Hui [to being morally perfected], and yet he was perpetually impoverished. [Unlike Yan Hui,] Zigong will not accept his fate,[6] and so engages in business speculation. His conjectures, though, are always on the mark."

This is a somewhat obscure passage, with a host of plausible alternate renderings. "Perpetually impoverished" (*lükong* 屢空) might also be rendered "perpetually empty/ modest," the point in either case is that, despite his moral attainment, Hui was always unassuming and unconcerned about material externalities (cf. 6.11). We are appar-

---

[4] An ancient taxation system, the details of which are the subject of long and rather tedious commentarial debate.

[5] Duke Ai, Year 11 (485 B.C.E.); Legge 1991d: 826.

[6] Alternately, "will not accept [my] teachings."

ently to contrast this behavior with Zigong, who—unable to consign to fate the attainment of external goods as a proper gentleman should (4.5, 4.9, 7.12, 7.16, 15.32)—is driven by a desire for financial success, and so focuses his energy on business speculation (lit. "hoarding goods"). The most plausible way to understand the final comment is that Zigong is always successful in his speculations, a fact that causes Confucius some regret, since if Zigong would only apply this same talent and intelligence to self-cultivation he might become a gentleman. As He Yan observes, "Probably Hui is being praised in order to encourage Zigong [to reform himself]."

11.20 Zizhang asked about the Way of the excellent person.

The Master replied, "If he does not personally follow in the footsteps [of the ancients], he will be unable to enter the inner chamber."

The excellent person (*shanren* 善人) may be presumed to possess exceptional native talent, but this does not obviate the need for hard work or the models established by the ancients. As Chen Houfu explains, "The point is that the Way of the excellent person must involve personally following in the footsteps [of the ancients], because only then can he enter into the inner chamber of sagehood . . . the point is that fine native substance alone cannot be relied upon." For the metaphor of self-cultivation as a journey through the "gate" of learning and a "receiving hall" of intermediate achievement, and then finally into an "inner chamber" of sagehood, see 11.15.

11.21 The Master said, "If someone seems sincere and serious in their conversation, does this mean they are a gentleman? Or have they merely adopted the appearance of the gentleman?"

Han commentators read this as a continuation of 11.20, and therefore describes additional qualities of the "excellent person": he is sincere and serious in speech, gentlemanly in conduct, and severe in appearance—in order, as He Yan explains, "to keep petty people at a distance." This does not make good sense of the grammar, however, and "the Master said" at the beginning suggests that 11.21 is a new passage and should be read separately from 11.20. The translation thus follows Zhu Xi, who believes that "the point is that you cannot judge a person merely from their words or appearance." Cf. Confucius' concern about the "petty *ru*" in 6.13, the "renowned person" in 12.20, or the "village worthy" in 17.13.

11.22 Zilu asked, "Upon learning of something that needs to be done, should one immediately take care of it?"

The Master replied, "As long as one's father and elder brothers are still alive, how could one possibly take care of it immediately?"

That is, one should continue to defer to the judgment of one's elders and not take the initiative.

[On a later occasion] Ran Qiu asked, "Upon learning of something that needs to be done, should one immediately take care of it?"

The Master replied, "Upon learning of it, you should immediately take care of it."

Zihua, [having observed both exchanges], inquired, "When Zilu asked you whether or not one should immediately take care of something upon learning of it, you told him one should not, as long as one's father and elder brothers were still alive. When Ran Qiu asked the same question, however, you told him that one should immediately take care of it. I am confused, and humbly ask to have this explained to me."

The Master said, "Ran Qiu is overly cautious, and so I wished to urge him on. Zilu, on the other hand, is too impetuous, and so I sought to hold him back."

For Ran Qiu's excessive caution or timidity, see 6.12; for Zilu's recklessness, see especially 5.7. This is a paradigmatic example of how the Master's teachings were variously formulated depending on the individual needs of his students. As Zheng Xuan puts it, "Each piece of advice was aimed at correcting the fault particular to each person." Han commentators and early texts take this passage as having to do with specifically with household financial decisions. Bao Xian's commentary reads, "[This passage is about] matters having to do with saving people from penury or succoring them in need," and Huang Kan elaborates by explaining that the issue is when it is necessary to consult with one's elders before providing gifts to friends in need. In contrast, later commentators and Western translators generally take the unspecified thing that is heard of or learned (*wen* 聞) to be a bit of moral teaching or knowledge. Understood this way, the questions asked by the disciples would be rendered: "learning this teaching/moral principle, should one immediately put it into practice?" This interpretation fits better with 6.13, where Ran Qiu's timidity has to do with self-cultivation, rather than practical decision making.

11.23 The Master was surrounded in Kuang. Yan Hui had fallen behind, [and when he finally caught up], the Master said, "I thought that you were dead."

Yan Hui replied, "As long as you are still here, Master, how could I dare to allow myself to die?"

As we have already seen in 9.5, Confucius was mistaken by the people of Kuang for a certain Yang Hu, whom he physically resembled and who had caused some trouble in Kuang, and he and his entourage were therefore surrounded or imprisoned for some days. Yan Hui had apparently been separated from the main group for some reason, but eventually caught up. There is disagreement on how to understand this passage, with some commentators claiming that Yan Hui did not dare to perish while the Master was still alive because he still had much he needed to learn from him. The most plausible interpretation, though, is provided by Liu Baonan, who notes the *Record of Ritual* passage, "when one's parents are still alive, one cannot pledge one's life to a friend,"[7] and observes that Yan Hui "served the Master like a son serving a father [cf. 11.11] . . . and thus since the Master was still alive, he did not dare to get himself killed. He therefore probably hid himself to escape harm, or took another, more circuitous route [to avoid capture], and this is why he was separated from the Master and only arrived later." A telling of this story in the *Annals of Lü Buwei* supports this reading:

---

[7] Chapter 1 ("Summary of Ritual Propriety"); Legge 1967, vol. 1: 69.

Serving one's teacher is like serving one's father. Zengxi[8] sent Master Zeng on a mission. When the time for him to return had passed and he still did not appear, everyone who saw Zengxi asked him, "Do you not fear for him?" Zengxi answered, "Although he may be in danger somewhere, I am still alive, so how could he dare to perish?" [*Analects* 11.23 is then quoted.] Yan Hui's relationship to Confucius was the same as Master Zeng's relationship to his father.[9]

Yan Hui's careful preservation of his own life in order to fulfill his filial duty to the Master contrasts sharply with the impetuous behavior of Zilu during the Kuang crisis, as described in a wonderful story from the Han music text, *Zither Song*, quoted by Jiao Xun:

The people of Kuang reported to the Lord of Kuang, "That Yang Hu who troubled us before has now shown up again." Thereupon they led a force to surround Confucius, and did not let him go for several days. Seized by sorrowful emotions, Zilu suddenly went into a fury, staring about him with enraged eyes, hand on his sword, shouting in a loud voice like the sounding of bells or beating of drums. Confucius said to him, "Zilu, come here. Now you want to make a name for yourself with your display of contentiousness, but such behavior will be the death of me. If you instead give vent to your emotion by singing of your sorrow, this will bring nothing but peace to my heart." Thereupon Confucius took out his zither and began to sing, and the notes that he played and words that he sang were filled with intense sorrow. With the sound of a violent storm striking, the soldiers and knights stiffly prostrated themselves on the ground in submission, and then the people of Kuang realized that Confucius was in fact a sage. At this point, their siege was broken and they departed.

11.24 Ji Ziran asked, "Could Zilu and Ran Qiu be considered great ministers?"

The Master replied, "I thought you were going to ask about some exceptional individuals, but instead you always ask about Zilu and Ran Qiu! What we call 'great ministers' are those who seek to serve their lord by means of the Way, and who resign if unable to do so. Now, Zilu and Ran Qiu are what we might call 'useful ministers' (*juchen* 具臣)."

Juchen means literally "tool-ministers" (cf. 2.12, "the gentleman is not a vessel"). Confucius probably means to imply that Zilu and Ran Qiu are minimally competent in carrying out the official duties required of them but lack the moral vision of a great minister. As we see immediately below, Ji Ranzi apparently mistakes him to mean that Zilu and Ran Qiu are "tools" that can be easily manipulated

"Then are they the type who do what they are told?"

"If it came to murdering their father or their lord, surely even *they* would not obey."

Ji Ziran was the younger brother of Ji Kangzi; the version of this passage found in the *Record of the Historian* has Ji Kangzi himself as Confucius' interlocutor. Both Zilu and Ran Qiu were serving as ministers for the Ji Family, and were clearly not displaying the sort of scruples expected of a "great minister" (cf. 3.6, 11.17, 11.23, and 16.1). As the *Record of Ritual* explains, "The ritual for one serving as a minister is to not remon-

---

[8] The father of Master Zeng, and himself one of the senior disciples of Confucius; he appears in 11.26.

[9] Book 4.2 "Exhortation to Learning"; Knoblock and Riegel 2000: 121.

strate openly. If one is not heeded after three remonstrations, one is to resign the post."[10] Huan Maoyong's interpretation of this exchange seems correct:

> The head of the Ji Family was having the *yong* hymn sung in his ancestral temple [3.2] and had eight rows of dancers in his courtyard [3.1], thereby usurping the administration of Lu—to the point that his own family matters and administration of Lu were conflated and viewed as one thing. As a youngster, how was Ziran to know that Lu had once had a legitimate lord? In taking Zilu and Ran Qiu to be great ministers, he probably seriously viewed the Ji Family and the Lu state to be one and the same. The Master elucidated the duty of a great minister to him in order to make him see matters more clearly . . . and his putting down of Zilu and Ran Qiu as mere 'useful ministers' was specifically intended to restrain the Ji Family as well. Ziran, however, misunderstands his intention, thinking that since the two disciples eat at his family trough, they will follow his direction like trained hunting falcons or dogs . . . Therefore the Master further clarifies to him the great duties concerning lords and fathers, in order to disabuse him of this notion.

11.25 Zilu dispatched Zigao to serve as the steward of [the Ji Family stronghold of] Bi.

The Master remarked, "You are harming another man's son."

Zilu replied, "There are people there for him to govern, and altars to the soil and grain for him to maintain. Why must we think that it is only by reading books that one can be considered learned (*xue* 學)?"

The Master answered, "It is for precisely this reason that I despise those who are glib."

Bi was the stronghold of the Ji Family, and thus the base of their personal power; cf. 6.7, where the virtuous Min Ziqian declines the position of steward. Zilu's point seems to be that Zigao, although young and not particularly bright or well educated (11.18), can learn on the job through practical experience, and based on 1.7 we might expect Confucius to agree with him. Confucius' rebuke can be understood in various ways. Most commentators argue that book learning is crucial to someone aspiring to take up an important official position, a view supported by a passage from the *Exoteric Commentary*: "Duke Ai asked Zixia, 'Is is necessary to first learn before it is possible to bring peace to the state and protect the people?' Zixia replied, 'There has never been one who, without first learning, was able to bring peace to the state and protect the people.'"[11] Waley also remarks that "the pertness of Zilu's remark consists of the fact that he throws in the Master's teeth a favourite Confucian maxim" (1989: 159, n. 4). Probably the point here is that Zilu is doing something that he knows at some level is wrong—pulling an inexperienced young man away from his studies and throwing him into a situation that is over his head, which will surely harm both the young man and the people under his rule—but trying to defend his behavior by citing a Confucian maxim out of context. Though clever, such behavior is morally despicable in Confucius' eyes.

11.26 Zilu, Zengxi, Ran Qiu, and Zihua were seated in attendance. The Master said to them, "Because I am older than any of you, no one is willing to employ me. Yet you, too, often complain, 'No one appreciates me.' Well, if someone were to appreciate you, what would you do?"

Zilu spoke up immediately. "If I were given charge of a state of a thousand chariots—even one hemmed in between powerful states, suffering from armed invasions and afflicted by famine—before three years were up I could infuse its people with courage and a sense of what is right."

The Master smiled at him.

The Master's smile is one of disapproval, probably of Zilu's abrupt manner as well as the content of his answer. The disciples that follow are noticeably more cautious in their responses.

He then turned to Ran Qiu. "You, Ran Qiu!" he said, "What would you do?"

Ran Qiu answered, "If I were given charge of a state sixty or seventy—or even fifty or sixty—square *li* in area, before three years were up I could see that the people would have all that they needed. As for instructing its people in ritual practice and music, this is a task that would have to await the arrival of a gentleman."

The Master then turned to Zihua. "You, Zihua! What would you do?"

Zihua answered, "I am not saying that I would actually be able to do it, but my wish, at least, would be to learn it. I would like to serve as a minor functionary—properly clad in ceremonial cap and gown—in ceremonies at the ancestral temple, or at diplomatic gatherings."

The Master then turned to Zengxi. "You, Zengxi! What would you do?"

Zengxi stopped strumming his zither, and as the last notes faded away he set the instrument aside and rose to his feet. "I would choose to do something quite different from any of the other three."

"What harm is there in that?" the Master said. "We are all just talking about our aspirations."

Zengxi then said, "In the third month of Spring, once the Spring garments have been completed, I should like to assemble a company of five or six young men and six or seven boys to go bathe in the Yi River and enjoy the breeze upon the Rain Dance Altar, and then return singing to the Master's house."

According to commentators, the Yi River was near Confucius' home, and the Rain Altar was located just above the river. The "Rain Altar" was so named because traditionally it was a site where ceremonies were performed to pray for rain during times of summer drought, although here it seems to be featuring merely as a pleasant destination for an excursion.

The Master sighed deeply, saying, "I am with Zengxi!"

The other three disciples left, but Master Zeng stayed behind. He asked, "What did you think of what the other disciples said?"

"Each of them was simply talking about their aspirations."

"Then why, Master, did you smile at Zilu?"

"One governs a state by means of ritual. His words failed to express the proper sense of deference, and that is why I smiled at him."

"Was Ran Qiu, then, not concerned with statecraft?"

"Since when did something sixty or seventy—even fifty or sixty—square *li* in area not constitute a state?"

"Was Zihua, then, not concerned with statecraft?"

"If ancestral temples and diplomatic gatherings are not the business of the feudal lords, what then are they? If Zihua's aspiration is a minor one, then what would be considered a major one?"

The point of this final remark is that Zihua's aspiration also involves high-level diplomacy and statecraft, despite the surface humility of his response. According to one plausible interpretation of this passage, the Master is equally disapproving of Zilu, Ran Qiu, and Zihua's aspirations—all of which are overly focused on statecraft techniques—although only Zilu's response is audacious enough to provoke a smile. The point is that true government is effected through the superior virtue gained by ritual practice, and the task of the gentleman is to focus on self-cultivation and attaining a state of joyful harmony with the Way. Such wu-wei harmony with the Way is exemplified by Zengxi's musical bent, his reluctance to speak about his aspirations, and the sense of spontaneous joy in the cultivated life conveyed by his answer. As Li Chong puts it, "Only Zengxi has transcendent aspirations, only he is able to stir up the sounds of Virtue and give expression to the Master's style and sensibility. His words are pure and remote, his meaning lofty and fitting, and his diligence is certainly something with which one with sagely Virtue would feel an affinity. By comparison, the answers of the other three disciples seem vulgar." It is interesting to note that the opposition to techniques of statecraft seen here becomes an even more prominent theme in Books Twelve and Thirteen, and may reflect a growing influence of Legalist (*fajia* 法家) teachings. Another, slightly different interpretation is that the passage is about the importance of "timeliness" (*shi* 時): although the various aspects of statecraft pursued by the first three disciples are important, only Zengxi perceives that the time is wrong for their application. Mr. Zhou explains that "Zengxi wins approval because he alone understands timeliness," and Huang Kan elaborates: "At that time the Way was in decline and the world was disordered, and everywhere people were striving against one another, which is why the disciples all had their hearts set on entering official service. Only Zengxi understood the vicissitudes of the age, which is why the Master approved of him." Following this line of interpretation, some commentators connect 11.16 with 5.7 and 9.14, and see it as a similar expression of Confucius' frustration with his contemporaries and desire to withdraw from public life.

BOOK TWELVE

As Legge observes, this book conveys "lessons on perfect virtue [ren], government, and other questions of morality, addressed in conversation by Confucius chiefly to his disciples. The different answers, given about the same subject to different questioners, show well how the sage suited his instruction to the characters and capacities of the parties with whom he had to do" (1991a: 250). A prominent theme is the contrast between Confucian rule by Virtue and personal example as opposed to rule by force or coercive laws.

12.1 Yan Hui asked about Goodness.

The Master said, "Restraining yourself and returning to the rites (*keji fuli* 克己復禮) constitutes Goodness. If for one day you managed to restrain yourself and return to the rites, in this way you could lead the entire world back to Goodness. The key to achieving Goodness lies within yourself—how could it come from others?"

> There is a long-running debate in the commentarial tradition concerning how to understand the phrase *keji*. The translation follows early commentators such as Ma Rong and Huang Kan in taking *ke* 克 (often "defeat," "overcome") in the sense of "cutting" or "trimming," and thus as "imposing restraint" (*yue* 約). This accords with the common metaphor of ritual as a tool for restraining, regulating, or reshaping one's native substance (see 1.2, 5.21, 6.27, 8.2, 12.15, and especially 9.11, where Yan Hui notes that the Master "restrains me with the rites"). *Ji* 己 is taken as the simple first-person object pronoun, rather than having the sense of "selfish desires" (*siyu* 私欲), as Zhu Xi and later commentators would have it. As Huang Kan explains, "The point is that if one is able to restrain and discipline oneself in order to return to the mean of ritual, this is what it means to be Good. At the time, Confucius' contemporaries tended to be extravagant and arrogant, exceeding the limits of ritual, which is why he mentions the rites." For the contrast between looking within oneself and looking to others, cf. 4.14, 14.24, 15.21.

Yan Hui asked, "May I inquire as to the specifics?"

The Master said, "Do not look unless it is in accordance with ritual; do not listen unless it is in accordance with ritual; do not speak unless it is in accordance with ritual; do not move unless it is in accordance with ritual."

Yan Hui replied, "Although I am not quick to understand, I ask permission to devote myself to this teaching."

> Liu Baonan's commentary on the second half of 12.1 is very helpful:
>
>> Looking, listening, speaking, and moving are all things that come from oneself, not from others, which is why the key to achieving Goodness lies within oneself and does not come from others . . . If only I am able to restrain myself and return to ritual, whenever I am confronted with something that is not in accordance with ritual, I will have within myself the

means to restrain my eyes and not look at it, restrain my ears and not listen to it, restrain my
mouth and not speak of it, and restrain my heart and not put it into action. This is all that
is meant by "restraining oneself and returning to ritual."

As Brooks and Brooks observe, "the four 'details' (trivialized in the Three Monkeys of
later art) make two pairs: do not promote impropriety either passively (by seeing or
hearing it) or actively (by saying or doing it)" (1998: 89).

12.2 Zhonggong asked about Goodness.

The Master said, "'When in public, comport yourself as if you were receiving
an important guest, and in your management of the common people, behave as
if you were overseeing a great sacrifice.' Do not impose upon others what you
yourself do not desire. In this way, you will encounter no resentment in your
public or private life."

Zhonggong replied, "Although I am not quick to understand, I ask permission
to devote myself to this teaching."

The first set of advice concerns the virtue of dutifulness or respectfulness, the second
that of understanding (cf. 4.15). The phrase rendered "in your public or private life"
means literally "in the state or in the family," and this line as a whole might alternately
be rendered, "do not let resentment [effect you in your dealings] in your state or in
your family."

12.3 Sima Niu asked about Goodness.

The Master said, "The Good person is hesitant to speak (*ren* 訒)."

"'Hesitant to speak'—is that all there is to Goodness?"

"When being Good is so difficult, how can one not be hesitant to speak
about it?"

Confucius is playing with a pun between *ren* 仁 and *ren* 訒. We have seen many other
passages concerning the incompatibility of Goodness and glibness of tongue (1.3, 5.5,
5.25, 15.11, 16.4,), and the extreme caution that the gentleman takes in choosing his
words, lest they exceed his actions (2.13, 4.22, 4.24, 14.20, 14.27); in 13.27, we will
also read that "reticence (*na* 訥) is close to Goodness." As Zhu Xi suggests, though,
the fact that Sima Niu draws this answer in particular suggests that the Master thought
him guilty of excessive volubility.

12.4 Sima Niu asked about the gentleman.

The Master replied, "The gentleman is free of anxiety and fear."

"'Free of anxiety and fear'—is that all there is to being a gentleman?"

"If you can look inside yourself and find no faults, what cause is there for
anxiety or fear?"

Again, although the general import of this reply—that the gentleman is free from
anxiety because he accepts his fate, does not covet external goods, and focuses solely
on what is in his control—is something we see elsewhere in the text (4.14, 7.3, 7.37,
9.29, 12.5, 14.28, 15.32), it probably also has contextual meaning. If we accept the
identification of Sima Niu with the figure of the same name mentioned in the *Zuo*

Commentary, his older brother was Huan Tui,[1] the minister of military affairs in Song who caused Confucius so much trouble when he was sojourning there (7.23). This conversation possibly took place during Confucius' visit to Song. Kong Anguo explains that Sima Niu was experiencing anxiety because at the time, Huan Tui was planning a revolt against his sovereign, in which case Confucius' response would seem to be aimed at focusing Niu's attention on his own state of moral self-cultivation rather than the indiscretions of his brother. Alternately, it is possible that the Master's reply is actually intended for Huan Tui's ears: plotting a rebellion is surely anxiety-inspiring business, but if Huan Tui could simply rid himself of evil intent he would have no cause for anxiety. Confucius' own *sang froid* in the face of Huan Tui's attack on him is a perfect illustration of this principle.

12.5 Anxiously, Sima Niu remarked, "Everyone has brothers, I alone have none."

Sima Niu came from a prominent military family in Song, and in fact left behind several brothers when he went abroad. Huan Tui planned and carried out an unsuccessful revolt against the rightful lord of Song in 483 B.C.E., and was forced to flee the state. Another of Sima Niu's older brothers, Xiang Chao, was also a military official in Song; he was apparently a somewhat arrogant and self-aggrandizing man, and was also forced to flee the state after Huan Tui's attempted revolt, along with the remaining elder Xiang brothers. Sima Niu—apparently uninvolved in the revolt or its aftermath—resigned his official post in disgust and emigrated, ending up eventually in Lu, where he presumably had the conversation with Zixia recorded here. His comment that "he alone has no brothers" is thus not meant literally: the point is either that he has no brothers truly worthy of being considered brothers, or that all of his brothers are in exile or in constant danger of losing their lives, and therefore as good as dead. Sima Niu is bemoaning the fate that has left him effectively without family, an exile from his home state.

Zixia replied, "I have heard it said, 'Life and death are governed by fate, wealth and honor are determined by Heaven.' A gentleman is respectful and free of errors. He is reverent and ritually proper in his dealings with others. In this way, everyone within the Four Seas[2] is his brother. How could a gentleman be concerned about not having brothers?"

Presumably Zixia heard this phrase from the Master. The *Garden of Persuasions* quotes Confucius as saying, "Be diligent with regard to your conduct, cultivate your ritual propriety, and then even a thousand miles away people will treat you intimately, as if they were your brothers. If you are not diligent in your conduct, or are not in accordance with ritual, then even right outside your front door you will make no progress." We see two themes at work here. The first concerns fate: if the gentleman focuses on what is in his control (self-cultivation), he has no need to be anxious or worry about things out of his control, which will take care of themselves (cf. 4.14, 7.3, 7.37, 9.29, 12.4, 14.28, 15.32). A shift of perspective may be involved here as well. As Ames and Rosemont note, Sima Niu in his initial comments effectively disowns his flesh-and-blood brothers,

---

[1] The family's ordinary surname was Xiang 向, but as descendents of Duke Huan 桓, they were also allowed to use this surname, and the military title of *sima* 司馬 (Master of the Horse) had been in the family so long that it was also used by them at times as a surname.

[2] I.e, the entire world; China was viewed as being surrounded on all sides by oceans.

"altering the unalterable by refusing to interpret 'brotherliness' in terms of 'facticity.' Zixia trumps him by insisting that the reverse can be effected—a brotherless person can alter his 'propensity of circumstances (*ming* 命)' which has rendered him brotherless by redefining what it means to have brothers ... the criterion of brotherhood can be ethical and religious rather than biological" (1998: 250, n. 192). The second theme is the universality of ethical culture: a ritually correct person will find acceptance wherever he goes—even in foreign lands—because human beings throughout the world respond to the efficacy of the Zhou rituals (cf. 9.14). As Bao Xian remarks, "The gentleman distances himself from those who are bad and befriends those who are worthy, because every person in the entire world can be made an intimate by means of ritual."

12.6 Zizhang asked about perceptiveness.

The Master replied, "He who does not base his actions upon slanders that try to seep into one's mind, or accusations that accumulate like dirt on one's skin, may be called 'perceptive.' Indeed, such a person could even be called 'far-sighted.'"

This passage apparently has to do with desirable qualities of a ruler. As Liu Baonan points out, similar passages from the *History of the Han* and the *Xunzi* present "perceptiveness" as a quality of a ruler who clearly understands the moral quality of his ministers, and therefore is not mislead by false slander or accusations. In rendering *yuan* 遠 as "far-sighted," the translation follows Zhu Xi and the commentators cited by Huang Kan in seeing the term as an extension of "perceptiveness"; alternately, one could follow Ma Rong in seeing it as a separate quality of "aloofness"—"virtuous behavior that is lofty and aloof, beyond the reach of anyone"—that preserves the ruler from noxious influences.

12.7 Zigong asked about governing.

The Master said, "Simply make sure there is sufficient food, sufficient armaments, and that you have the confidence of the common people."

Zigong said, "If sacrificing one of these three things became unavoidable, which would you sacrifice first?"

The Master replied, "I would sacrifice the armaments."

Zigong said, "If sacrificing one of the two remaining things became unavoidable, which would you sacrifice next?"

The Master replied, "I would sacrifice the food. Death has always been with us, but a state cannot stand once it has lost the confidence of the people."

Wang Yangming's comment on this passage is helpful:

Once you have lost the hearts of the people, how can the rest be relied upon? Even if you have grain, would you even get to eat it? Even if your soldiers are numerous, this may merely set the stage for a rebellion. During the Sui Dynasty, Emperor Yang [r. 604–618] caused the fortress of Luokoucang to be built, and during the Tang Dynasty, Emperor Dezong [r. 780–805] built the Qionglin Treasury. They had an overflowing abundance of riches, and piles of grain as high as mountains; when their armies took the field, it was if a forest of trees had sprung up, and their assembled armor and horsemen covered the earth like clouds. Even then, they could not avoid losing their states and ruining their families, because they did not possess the hearts of the people. One who wishes to govern skillfully should think carefully upon this!

This passage is primarily advice to the aspiring ruler. Li Chong additionally sees it as reflecting Confucius' valuing of morality and the Way over physical life itself: "Confucius valued being able to 'hear in the morning that the Way was being put into practice, and thus dying that evening without regret' [4.8], while Mencius celebrated the ability to 'abandon life in order to hold fast to rightness' [6:A:10]. From ancient times we have had the imperishable Way, and yet there have never been imperishable people. Therefore, to allow one's body to die is not to necessarily to sacrifice the [true] self, while to keep oneself alive at any cost in fact involves losing oneself."

12.8 Ji Zicheng said, "Being a gentleman is simply a matter of having the right native substance, and nothing else. Why must one engage in cultural refinement?"

Zigong replied, "It is regrettable, Sir, that you should speak of the gentleman in this way—as they say, 'a team of horses cannot overtake your tongue.'

This is a traditional sayings, meaning that foolish words, once uttered, cannot be taken back.

"A gentleman's cultural refinement resembles his native substance, and his native substance resembles his cultural refinement. The skin of a tiger or leopard, shorn of its fur, is no different from the skin of a dog or sheep."

Ji Zicheng is described as a minister of Wei, but nothing else is known about him. Zigong served as an official in Wei for some time, and this is probably when this exchange took place. Zhu Xi believes Ji Zicheng's comment to be a criticism of his contemporaries, who have carried cultural refinement to an excessive extreme, but Chen Tianxiang is probably correct in seeing it as a jab specifically directed as Zigong, known for his sedulous—if limiting—specialization, perhaps a compensation for some lack of native talent (cf. 5.4, 5.9, 5.12, 5.18, 14.29). Zigong's response invokes an interesting metaphor for the relationship of native substance and cultural refinement: although native substance is required (as an animal requires a hide), a gentleman possessing substance but unadorned by cultural refinement would be like a tiger or leopard shaved of its beautiful pelt—indistinguishable from any ordinary creature. Cf. 6.18.

12.9 Duke Ai said to Master You, "The harvest was poor and I cannot satisfy my needs. What should I do?"

Master You said, "Why do you not try taxing the people one part in ten?"

"I am currently taxing them two parts in ten, and even so I cannot satisfy my needs. How could reducing the tax to one part in ten help?"

Master You answered, "If the common people's needs are satisfied, how could their lord be lacking? If the common people needs are not satisfied, how can their lord be content?"

According to the *Annals*, the traditional ten percent tithe on agricultural production was doubled by Duke Xuan of Lu in 593 B.C.E., and then continued as standard practice. It is possible that this exchange between Duke Ai and Master You took place during the Lu famine of 484 B.C.E. (Year 14 of Duke Ai's reign), which occurred after back-to-back plagues of locusts in 484 and 483 B.C.E. Master You is thus suggesting a return to a taxation rate over one hundred years old—quite a radical cutback. Probably the best commentary on this passage is a story from the *Garden of Persuasions*:

Duke Ai of Lu asked Confucius about governing. Confucius replied, "The purpose of the government is to make the common people rich." Duke Ai asked, "What do you mean by that?" Confucius said, "Lighten the burden of levies and taxes, and this will make the common people rich." The Duke replied, "If I did that, then I myself would become poor." Confucius responded, "An ode says, 'All happiness to our gentleman-ruler/Father and mother of his people' [Ode 251]. I have never seen a situation where the children were rich and the parents poor." (844)

The point, of course, is that if the Duke comported himself as the parent of his people, as he properly should, his sole concern would be for their welfare, not his own financial needs.

12.10 Zizhang asked about accumulating Virtue and resolving confusion.

The Master said, "Make it your guiding principle to be dutiful and trustworthy, and always move in the direction of what is right. This is what it means to accumulate Virtue. If you love someone, you desire that they live; if you hate them, you desire that they perish. Now, having already desired that someone live, and then to desire that they perish—this is confusion.

'Not for the sake of wealth,

But simply for the sake of variety.'"

The final two lines come from Ode 188, which describes the complaints of a woman who has been brought a long way to marry a man, and who is then promptly neglected in favor of someone else. Many commentators have suggested that these lines are out of place—Master Cheng, for instance, recommended moving them to the beginning of 16.12—but they actually fit the context quite well, describing someone who simply cannot make up his mind what he really wants. The target is probably the inconsistent ruler, who cannot make a clear decision concerning the moral worth of a given minister, and therefore promotes or demotes him according to the dictates of momentary whim. This is the context in which 12.10 is generally cited in Han texts, such as in an encounter recorded in the Wei history of the *Record of the Three Kingdoms*:

> Ying Zhongyuan was appointed Grand Protector of Mount Tai. He was in the habit of promoting a filial and honest man to office, and then a few months later having him demoted. Bing Yuan said to him, "These filial and honest men are the finest candidates in the state. If it was right to promote them, then it is now wrong to demote them; if it is now right to demote them, then it was wrong to promote them. The *Analects* says, 'If you love someone, you desire that they live; if you hate them, you desire that they perish. Now, having already desired that someone live, and then to desire that they perish—this is confusion.' You, Sir, are extremely confused."

Zhu Xi takes the comment on confusion rather differently: life and death are beyond our control, so to wish them on someone is confusion, and to wish them inconsistently on someone is even greater confusion. The Han interpretation seems preferable, however. For another comment on "accumulating Virtue and resolving confusion," see 12.21 below.

12.11 Duke Jing of Qi asked Confucius about governing.

Confucius responded, "Let the lord be a true lord, the ministers true ministers, the fathers true fathers, and the sons true sons."

The Duke replied, "Well put! Certainly if the lord is not a true lord, the ministers not true ministers, the fathers not true fathers, and the sons not true sons, even if there is sufficient grain, will I ever get to eat it?"

In Duke Zhao, Year 25 (516 B.C.E.), Confucius arrived in Qi to find that Duke Jing, near the end of his reign, was in dire straights. His nominal minister, Chen Qi, had usurped control of the state, and the Duke's plan to pass over his eldest son for the succession had set off contention among his sons. Confucius' advice is thus very topical. His point is that if everyone would simply concentrate on conscientiously fulfilling their role-specific duties, order would result naturally—there is no need for some special technique or theory of "governing" (cf. 2.21, 13.3). Many commentators have seen this passage as concerned with the theme of "rectifying names" (*zhengming* 正名) mentioned in 13.3, whereby the actualities of one's behavior should follow the standard set by one's social role ("name"). This is the import of similar passages in the *Annals of Lü Buwei*:

> Those who govern must make establishing clear distinctions (*dingfen* 定分) their first priority. When lords and ministers, fathers and sons, and husbands and wives all occupy their proper positions, then the lower member of each pair will refrain from overstepping their place, and the higher member will refrain from behaving arbitrarily. Juniors will not be audacious or unrestrained, and seniors will not be careless or arrogant . . . The difference between what is similar and what is dissimilar, the differentiation between noble and base, and the proper distinction between elder and junior are things about which the Ancient Kings were very careful, and constitute the guiding principle for controlling disorder.[3]

As Zhu Xi observes, Confucius' attempt to advise the Duke was ultimately for naught: "Duke Jing praised Confucius' words, but did not subsequently put them into practice. In the end, he failed to clearly establish a successor, and thereby set the stage for the disaster of the Chen clan assassinating their lord and usurping control of the state."

12.12 The Master said, "Able to decide a criminal case after only hearing one side—does this not describe Zilu?"
Zilu never put off fulfillment of a promise until the next day.

Many interpretative permutations are possible with this passage. The translation follows Kong Anguo's gloss of *pianyan* 片言 as "one side [of a criminal legal case]"—normally, both sides present their cases before a decision is made, but Zilu was unique in being able to make a decision after only hearing one side. This could have a slightly negative connotation, which would accord with Confucius' criticisms of Zilu's impetuousness elsewhere in the text (5.7, 17.7, 17.23); as Dawson puts it, "It was Zilu's headstrong nature not to put things off, even if this meant making decisions on partial evidence or fulfilling promises before nightfall" (Dawson 1993: 96). Most commentators take the Master's comment as unqualified praise, however, understanding it variously as "able to have a case decided with just half a word" (he was so trusted and known for honesty that merely half a word of testimony from him would carry a decision) or "able to cause a criminal to admit his guilt with merely half a word" (he was so straightforward and honest that he inspired honesty in others). The second half of the translation follows Zhu Xi in understanding *su* 宿 as "overnight": Zilu would not wait until the next day to fulfill a promise. He Yan, however, takes it in the sense of *yu* 預 ("beforehand"), hence: "Zilu would never make a promises he could not keep"—i.e., he would never promise to do something before he was sure he would be able to carry it out.

---

[3] Chapter 25.5 ("Keeping to One's Lot in Life"); Knoblock and Riegel 2000: 637.

12.13 The Master said, "When it comes to hearing civil litigation, I am as good as anyone else. What is necessary, though, is to bring it about that there is no civil litigation at all."

A classic expression of the Confucian suspicion of rule by law; cf. 2.3, 13.12, 13.18. A good ruler morally transforms the people and renders them obedient through the suasive power of his Virtue, and therefore litigation never arises. As Wang Su notes, "One can bring it about that there is no litigation at all by transforming the people beforehand." This is similar to the manner in which a good moral example on the part of the ruler obviates the need for punishments (12.17–12.19), and is the basis of noncoercive, wu-wei government (2.1, 15.5). Fan Ziyu invokes vegetative and river metaphors to explain the priorities of a true ruler—"hearing civil litigation is like trying to fix the branches or stop a river that is already flowing: if you had simply rectified the roots or purified the source, there would simply be no litigation at all"—while Yang Shi adds a reflection on the relationship between 12.13 and 12.12: "Zilu was able to decide a case after hearing only one side, but he did not understand how to govern a state by means of ritual obedience, and therefore was never able to bring it about that there was no litigation among the people at all." 12.13 is repeated in the "Great Learning" chapter of the *Record of Ritual*, followed by the comment: "Those with frivolous complaints do not get the chance to fully air them, because the minds of the common people have a proper sense of respectful awe."[4] *Dai's Record* contrasts the subtleties of rule by ritual with the crudeness of rule by law and punishments:

> Generally speaking, people can easily understand what is past, but have trouble seeing what is to come. Ritual guards against what is yet to come, whereas laws are created after the fact to deal with what is already past. This is why the usefulness of laws is easy to see, whereas the reason for the existence of ritual is hard to perceive . . . What is valuable about ritual is that it destroys badness before it has had a chance to sprout up, inspires respectfulness in even the most trivial and easily overlooked aspects of life, and thereby daily moves the common people toward goodness and keeps them away from transgression without them even being aware of it. This is the point of Confucius' comment [in 12.13].

This valuing of social harmony over the adversarial assertion of individual interests has become an enduring feature of societies in the Confucian cultural sphere.

12.14 Zizhang asked about governing.

The Master replied, "Occupy your position without wearying and conduct your business in a dutiful manner."

Probably the best commentary on this passage consists of advice given to Zizhang in *Dai's Record*: "If you do not personally take the lead, then although you act, your scope of your effectiveness will necessarily be limited. If you do not lead them with the Way, then although they submit, this submission will necessarily be forced. Therefore, unless you are dutiful and trustworthy, you will lack the means to win the affection of the common people."

---

[4] Legge 1967, vol. 2: 416.

12.15 The Master said, "Someone who is broadly learned with regard to culture, and whose conduct is restrained by the rites, can be counted upon to not go astray."

This is a repetition of 6.27; see that passage for commentary.

12.16 The Master said, "A gentleman helps others to realize their good qualities, rather than their bad. A petty person does the opposite."

This is probably a proverbial saying; the *Guliang Commentary* says of reading the *Annals*, "They help people to realize their good qualities, rather than their bad." As *Dai's Record* observes of the gentleman, "Since the gentleman is himself excellent, he takes joy in the excellence of others; since he himself is able, he takes joy in the ability of others. The gentleman does not discuss other people's faults, but rather helps them to realize their good qualities."

12.17 Ji Kangzi asked Confucius about governing.
   Confucius responded, "To 'govern' (*zheng* 政) means to be 'correct' (*zheng* 正). If you set an example by being correct yourself, who will dare to be incorrect?"

As Zhai Hao notes, a passage in the *Book of Documents* reads: "If you are able to make yourself correct, how can others dare not to be themselves correct?"[5] This is also probably a proverbial saying and is found is various permutations in several early texts. The theme of personal perfection on the part of the potential ruler radiating out to encompass the family, the state, and then the entire world is developed in the opening of the "Great Learning" chapter of the *Record of Ritual* (Legge 1967, vol. 2: 411–412). Passages 12.17–12.19 are similar in theme, and echo the series 2.19–2.21 in Book Two; also cf. 13.6.

12.18 Ji Kangzi was concerned about the prevalence of robbers in Lu and asked Confucius about how to deal with this problem.
   Confucius said, "If you could just get rid of your own excessive desires, the people would not steal even if you rewarded them for it."

Kong Anguo comments, "The point is that the common people are transformed from above, and they do not act in accordance with what their superiors explicitly command, but rather with what their superiors themselves personally desire." A similar and more elaborate exchange is found in the *Zuo Commentary*. There we read that Lu was plagued by robbers, and that the head of the Ji Family said to Zang Wuzhong, Minister of Crime at the time, "You are the Minister of Crime, why are you not able to deal with these robbers?" Wuzhong's reply is similar to that of Confucius:

You, Sir, invite foreign robbers to come to our state and then treat them with great ritual honor—how am I supposed to put a stop to the robbery in our state? . . . Shu Qi stole cities from Zhu and arrived here, and yet you gave him wives from the Ducal line, as well as other cities, and gave gifts to all of his followers . . . I have heard it said that those above can rule others only after they have purified their own hearts, learned to treat others consistently, and

---

[5] Chapter 25 ("Jun Ya"); Legge 1991a: 580.

regulated their trustworthiness by means of models and regulations, so that their trustworthiness is clear for all to see. For the model set by the actions of their superiors is what the common people will turn to."[6]

Again, the key to political order is personal self-cultivation on the part of the ruler.

12.19 Ji Kangzi asked Confucius about governing, saying, "If I were to execute those who lacked the Way in order to advance those who possessed the Way, how would that be?"

Confucius responded, "In your governing, Sir, what need is there for executions? If you desire goodness, then the common people will be good. The Virtue of a gentleman is like the wind, and the Virtue of a petty person is like the grass—when the wind moves over the grass, the grass is sure to bend."

An alternate version of this story is found in the *Exoteric Commentary*:

The state of Lu had a case of a father and son filing civil complaints against each other, and Ji Kangzi wanted to have them executed. Confucius said, "You cannot execute them . . . When the common people do something that is not right, it is only because their superiors have lost the Way . . . If the superiors make manifest their teachings and then take the lead in obeying these teachings, the common people will then follow as if being impelled by a wind."[7]

We also find this wind metaphor for the virtuous influence of the ruler[8] in a passage from the *Garden of Persuasions*—"Those below are transformed by those above like grass bending in the wind . . . the direction from which the wind is blowing will determine the direction in which the grass bends. This is why the ruler of men must be very careful about his behavior"—and it also appears in a warning to a ruler in a portion of the *Book of Documents*: "You are the wind, and the people below are the grass."[9] In this passage, we see again a suspicion of recourse to legal means and reliance on punishment—widespread disorder among the common people is a sign of immorality among the ruling class, and in such a situation it is actually cruel and unfair to punish the people for their transgressions. Throughout traditional Chinese texts on rulership the common people are portrayed as childlike and easily influenced by their superiors, and therefore not totally accountable for their behavior. Some modern scholars of Confucianism present passages such as *Analects* 12.17–12.19 as examples of how traditional China had something like the modern Western liberal-democratic ideal of governmental accountability, but it is important not to lose sight of how distinct from modern liberal ideals the early Confucian conception actually was.

12.20 Zizhang inquired, "What must a scholar-official be like before he can be considered accomplished (*da* 達)?"

The Master replied, "What do you mean by 'accomplished'?"

"Sure to be renowned (*wen* 聞), whether serving the state or a noble family."

---

[6] Duke Xiang, Year 21 (551 B.C.E.); Legge 1991d: 490.

[7] Chapter 3.22; Hightower 1952: 100–101; see also 3.24: 105–106.

[8] Cf. the "press-frame" metaphor in 2.19 and 12.22.

[9] Book 21 ("Jun Chen"); Legge 1991a: 539. Most scholars believe that this book is a forgery dating to the fourth century B.C.E. Also cf. the quotation of 12.19 in *Mencius* 3:A:2.

The Master said, "That is merely being 'renowned,' not being 'accomplished.' Someone who is accomplished is upright in his native substance and fond of rightness. He examines other people's words and observes their demeanor, and always takes the interests of his inferiors into account when considering something—no matter whether serving the state or a noble family. Someone who is renowned, on the other hand, adopts the appearance of Goodness but violates it in his actual conduct, all the while never doubting that he deserves to be called Good. Thus, he is sure to be renowned, whether serving the state or a noble family."

Here we see again the concern with moral hypocrisy briefly raised in 11.21, which is related as well to the suspicion of public reputation voiced in 13.24 and 15.28 and the condemnation in 17.13 of the "village worthy"—the counterfeit version of the true gentleman, who adopts the external appearance of Goodness and thereby wins the praise of others. Confucius is probably also concerned that Zizhang focus on the substance of self-cultivation rather than the appearance, and we might read this passage as an elaboration of 4.14: "Do not be concerned that no one has heard of you, but rather strive to become a person worthy of being known." The accomplished person's genuine concern for others as described here also echoes the 1.16 injunction to "not be concerned about whether or not others know you; be concerned about whether or not you know others." In *Dai's Record*, a disciple asks Zizhang's question about how to be "accomplished" of Master Zeng and receives the following answer:

When unable, then learn; when in doubt, ask; in your desires and conduct, emulate the worthies; and even though you have a dangerous way before you, simply follow it until you reach the end (*da* 達).[10] Nowadays, on the other hand, you disciples dislike humbling yourself below others, are ignorant of how to serve a worthy person, are ashamed of not knowing something and therefore refuse to ask, desire to innovate even when your knowledge is insufficient, and thereby accomplish nothing but confusing, darkening, and bringing about the demise of our age.

12.21 Fan Chi was on an excursion with the Master, wandering below the Rain Dance Altar, when he asked, "May I ask what it means to, 'Accumulate Virtue, reform vice, and resolve confusion'?"

For the Rain Dance Altar, see 11.26. The quoted phrase rhymes and may be part of a traditional catechism. Li Baonan suggests that it formed part of the invocation sung during the Rain Dance ceremony, which is why Fan Chi brings it up on this particular excursion. Fan Chi's question is similar to that of Zizhang in 12.10.

The Master replied, "A noble question indeed! Put service first and reward last— is this not the way to accumulate Virtue? Attack the bad qualities in yourself rather than the badness in others—is this not the way to remedy vice? To forget yourself in a moment of anger and thereby bring ruin upon both you and your family—is this not an example of confusion?"

---

[10] Playing on the literal and metaphorical senses of *da*, which means both to reach a physical destination and to attain a metaphorical goal.

The difference between the answers given here and to the almost identical question asked by Zizhang in 12.10 is attributed by many commentators to the differing educational needs of the disciples. The fact that Fan Chi is similarly warned against acquisitiveness in 6.22 ("One who is Good sees as his first priority the hardship of self-cultivation, and only after thinks about results or rewards") suggests that this was a particular character flaw of his. For "forgetting oneself in a moment of anger," see the *Xunzi*,[11] where fighting is presented as the effect of a moment's anger that results in the direst of consequences for both oneself and one's family—as Yang Liang notes in his commentary on the *Xunzi* passage, laws governing homicide at the time probably involved punishing both the culprit and his or her relatives. As in 12.11, the explanation of how to "resolve confusion" merely gives an example of emotional befuddlement, which may be the point: simply perceiving the situation accurately is the key to resolving it.

12.22 Fan Chi asked about Goodness.
The Master replied, "Care for others."

In this passage we have the first and only hint in the *Analects* of *ren* 仁 as specifically "benevolence"—the sense it will have in later Warring States texts—rather than general moral excellence.

He then asked about wisdom.
The Master replied, "Know others."
Fan Chi still did not understand, so the Master elaborated: "Raise up the straight and apply them to the crooked, and the crooked will be made straight."
Fan Chi retired from the Master's presence. Seeing Zixia, he said, "Just before I asked the Master about wisdom, and he replied, 'Raise up the straight and apply them to the crooked, and the crooked will be made straight.' What did he mean by that?"
Zixia answered, "What a wealth of instruction you have received! When Shun ruled the world, he selected from amongst the multitude, raising up Gao Yao, and those who were not Good then kept their distance. When Tang ruled the world, he selected from amongst the multitude, raising up Yi Yin, and those who were not Good then kept their distance."

The Master explains that wisdom—here, specifically in the context of rulership—involves being a good judge of character, a theme that will be appear several times in Book Fourteen. Tang was the legendary founder of the Shang Dynasty, and Gao Yao and Yi Yin were famously virtuous ministers. Regarding this "press-frame" metaphor for virtuous influence, cf. 2.19.

12.23 Zigong asked about friendship.
The Master replied, "Reprove your friend when dutifulness requires, but do so gently. If your words are not accepted then desist, lest you incur insult."

---

[11] Chapter 4 ("Of Honor and Disgrace"); Knoblock 1988: 187.

The virtue of role-specific dutifulness governs not only the vertical relationship between social inferiors and superiors, but also the horizontal relationship between friends. Regarding the dangers of being overbearing in one's remonstration, cf. 4.26. The gentle reproof offered by a friend in virtue is no doubt one of "supports" in becoming Good mentioned below in 12.24.

12.24 Master Zeng said, "The gentleman acquires friends by means of cultural refinement, and then relies upon his friends for support in becoming Good."

Friends in virtue are drawn to each other by their common interest in learning and culture—their common love of the Way—and then support each other in these endeavors. A related passage in the *Record of Ritual* reads:

> When it comes to instruction in the great learning, every season has its appropriate subject, and when the students withdraw to rest, they are required to continue their studies at home . . . Therefore, when it comes to learning, the gentleman holds it dear, he cultivates it, he breathes it, he rambles in it. Because of this, he is at ease while learning and feels affection for his teacher, takes joy in his friends and trusts in the Way. This is why, even when separated from the support of his teacher, he does not go against what he has been taught.[12]

A passage in the *Garden of Persuasions* puts it more succinctly: "Having worthy teachers and excellent friends at his side, and the *Book of Odes, Documents, Ritual*, and *Music* spread out in front of him—few indeed ever abandon the Way and go bad in such an environment."

---

[12] Chapter 16 ("Record of Learning"); Legge 1967, vol. 2: 85.

BOOK THIRTEEN

As in Book Twelve, many of the passages in this Book focus on the theme of governing by personal example and the gentle power of Virtue rather than by means of laws or coercion. The importance of superiors knowing others so that they can employ them fairly and effectively is emphasized, as is the importance of inferiors being forthright and courageous, unafraid to contradict their lord or incur the disfavor of their colleagues. Several passages explicitly contrast the gentleman and petty person, and many others do so implicitly: the gentleman is flexible and context-sensitive, while lesser people are rigid and prone both to flattering and being flattered. Related to this theme is a suspicion of public opinion and concern about appearance and actuality, especially the danger of petty people assuming the semblance of virtue.

13.1 Zilu asked about governing.

The Master replied, "Precede the common people in accepting the burden of labor."

When asked to elaborate, he added, "Do not slacken in your efforts."

There are several plausible ways to take Confucius' initial, cryptic advice. Taking *xian* 先 in the temporal sense of "first," Kong Anguo understands the line to mean, "First guide [the common people] by means of Virtue, cause them to have confidence in you, and then get them to work. As the *Book of Changes* says, 'Joyfully employ the common people, and they will not notice their labors.'" This accords with 19.10, where Zixia explains that "Only once the gentleman has won the common people's confidence can he put them to work." Mr. Su, on the other hand, takes *xian* to mean "to take the lead"—i.e., to set a personal example. "When it comes to the behavior of the common people, one must set a personal example, and then the people will put it into action without having to be ordered." Yu Yue proposes a similar interpretation, adopted in the translation above, although he takes *xian* temporally: "precede the people in accepting the burden of the labor." This seems to best fit the grammar of the sentence and general tenor of Books Twelve and Thirteen, where personal effort directed toward the task of moral cultivation is presented as the key to winning the hearts of the people and governing effectively.

13.2 Zhonggong, who was serving as a steward for the Ji Family, asked the Master about governing.

The Master said, "First appoint your supervising officials, then overlook their petty faults and promote those who are worthy and talented."

"How can I recognize those who are worthy and talented so that I can promote them?"

"Just promote the ones you know. As for those you do not know, will others allow them to be passed over?"

As Legge notes, "a head minister should assign [the supervisory officials] their duties, and not be interfering in them himself. His business is to examine into the manner in which they discharge them. And in doing so, he should overlook small faults" (1991c: 263). Cf. 8.4, where the gentleman is advised to focus on the large task of self-cultivation and leave smaller ritual details to his underlings. For the importance of the ruler knowing others, cf. 12.22.

13.3 Zilu asked, "If the Duke of Wei were to employ you to serve in the government of his state, what would be your first priority?"

The Master answered, "It would, of course, be the rectification of names (*zhengming* 正名)."

Zilu said, "Could you, Master, really be so far off the mark? Why worry about rectifying names?"

The Master replied, "How boorish you are, Zilu! When it comes to matters that he does not understand, the gentleman should remain silent.

Lit., the gentleman should "leave a blank space" (*que* 闕). Cf. 15.26, where *que* is used in its literal sense, with the point being much the same: the gentleman should not pretend to knowledge that he does not have; also cf. 2.17, where Zilu is also the target of the lesson.

"If names are not rectified, speech will not accord with reality; when speech does not accord with reality, things will not be successfully accomplished. When things are not successfully accomplished, ritual practice and music will fail to flourish; when ritual and music fail to flourish, punishments and penalties will miss the mark. And when punishments and penalties miss the mark, the common people will be at a loss as to what to do with themselves. This is why the gentleman only applies names that can be properly spoken and assures that what he says can be properly put into action. The gentleman simply guards against arbitrariness in his speech. That is all there is to it."

Reading this passage in light of 12.11 ("let the fathers be true fathers, the sons true sons"), it can be seen as a barb against the ruling family of Wei, whose disordered family relations (discussed in 7.15) eventually threw the state into chaos. The "Duke of Wei" referred to in Zilu's initial question is thus probably Duke Chu, grandson of Duke Ling and son of Kuai Kui. As Zhu Xi observes, "At this time, Duke Chu was not treating his father as a father, and instead was performing the paternal ancestral sacrifices to his grandfather. In this way, name and actuality were confused, and this is why Confucius saw the rectification of names as the first priority." Huang Kan quotes a passage from the *Exoteric Commentary* that shows Confucius putting the rectification of names into practice in the state of Lu:

Confucius was seated in attendance at the side of the head of the Ji-sun Family. The Ji-sun's steward, Tong, said, "If you, lord, send someone to borrow a horse [from one of your ministers], would it in fact be given to you?" [Before the head of the Ji-sun could reply,] Confucius remarked, "When a lord takes something from a minister, it is called 'taking,' not 'borrowing.'" The Ji-sun head understood Confucius' point, and reproved his steward, saying, "From now on, when speaking of your lord taking something, call it 'taking,' do not call it 'borrowing.'" In this way, Confucius rectified the names involved in the expression, "borrowing a horse," and thereby established clearly a relationship of rightness between lord and minister.[1]

The passage then quotes *Analects* 13.3, as well as Ode 339: "The lord should not lightly utter his words." For other examples of the "rectification of names," see 12.11, 12.17, and 13.14, the story in the *Zuo Commentary* about Confucius bemoaning the inappropriate use of titles and ritual insignia,[2] and the "Rectification of Names" chapter of the *Xunzi*.[3]

13.4 Fan Chi asked to learn about plowing and growing grain [from Confucius].
   The Master said, "When it comes to that, any old farmer would be a better teacher than I."
   He asked to learn about growing fruits and vegetables.
   The Master said, "When it comes to that, any old gardener would be a better teacher than I."
   Fan Chi then left. The Master remarked, "What a common fellow (*xiaoren* 小人) that Fan Chi is! When a ruler loves ritual propriety, then none among his people will dare to be disrespectful. When a ruler loves rightness, then none among his people will dare not to obey. When a ruler loves trustworthiness, then none of his people will dare to not be honest. The mere existence of such a ruler would cause the common people throughout the world to bundle their children on their backs and seek him out. Of what use, then, is the study of agriculture?"

Part of the theme here is clearly the proper distinction between the vocations of the "great person," or gentleman, and the "little person," or commoner. The *Book of Documents* says that "Knowing the painful toil of sowing and reaping . . . one knows the livelihood of the commoner";[4] similarly, we read in *Mencius* 3:A:4 that plowing the fields is the "work of the commoner." There are at least two ways to understand how this relates exactly to Confucius' response. Commentators such as Li Chong read this passage together with 15.32 ("the gentleman focuses his concern on the Way, not on obtaining food"), as well as the hints of Fan Chi's acquisitiveness in 6.22 and 12.21, understanding Confucius' point to be that the gentleman does not give up the pursuit of moral excellence in order to pursue externalities such as food or money. Others, such as Cheng Shude and Jin Lüxiang, read it together with *Mencius* 3:A:4 as an attack on the so-called "Divine Farmer" (*shennong* 神農) or "primitivist" movement. This movement—which produced a host of writings recorded in the *History of the Han*, and which was probably also the incubator of the famous Daoist text *Laozi*—advocated a kind of agricultural communism: educated people should withdraw from public life into isolated agricultural communities, where social distinctions would be abolished and the educated would plow the fields alongside the commoners, everyone sharing in the tasks required to sustain life. In 3:A:4, Mencius defends Confucian social distinctions and division of labor against this "leveling" doctrine, arguing that, just as the heart-mind is the ruler of the body, those who work with their minds should

---

[1] Chapter 5.33; Hightower 1952: 190.
[2] Duke Cheng, Year 2 (588 B.C.E.); Legge 1991d: 344.
[3] Chapter 22; Knoblock 1994: 113–138.
[4] Chapter Fifteen ("Against Luxurious Ease"); Legge 1991a: 464–465.

rule over those who work with their bodies. We can see Confucius' response here as a similar counter-argument to primitivist doctrines, by which Fan Chi has apparently been at least partially seduced. This understanding of the passage is supported by 14.39, 18.6, and 18.7, which present encounters between Confucius and his disciples with disillusioned former officials who have apparently turned to the practices of primitivism. The appeal of primitivism to educated elite troubled by the chaos of the late Spring and Autumn and Warring States periods in China should not be unfamiliar to those acquainted with the various "back to nature" movements popular in the West in the 1960s and 1970s, which arose among elite, educated people disillusioned with the ills brought about by modern industrial capitalist societies—and among whom the *Laozi* was quite popular in English translation.

13.5 The Master said, "Imagine a person who can recite the several hundred odes by heart but, when delegated a governmental task, is unable to carry it out, or when sent abroad as an envoy, is unable to engage in repartee. No matter how many odes he might have memorized, what good are they to him?"

The words of the *Odes* formed part of the repertoire of an accomplished statesman of the time, who would often quote an apt phrase to make a point or invoke a relevant historical allusion (cf. 16.13, 17.9–17.10). The point here, though, is that merely memorizing the *Odes* is not enough to make one a good messenger or envoy—one must also learn to think on one's feet. As the *Book of Etiquette and Ritual* observes of serving as an envoy, "The words one are to speak cannot be determined ahead of time; one must speak in accordance with the situation."[5] A story from the *Exoteric Commentary* refers obliquely to 13.5 in its portrait of a skillful envoy in action:

> Duke Jing of Qi dispatched an envoy to Chu. The King of Chu accompanied him in ascending his nine-level throne-dais. Fixing his gaze upon the envoy, the King of Chu asked, "Does the state of Qi have a dais the equal of this?" The envoy replied, "My lord has a place to sit when dealing with governmental affairs. It has three levels of earthen stairs, a roughly-made thatched hut at the top, and unadorned wooden rafters. Even still, my lord feels that he has overworked those who made it, and worries also that he who sits in it will be overly proud. How could my lord have a dais the equal of this one?" Thereupon the King of Chu was ill at ease. Because of his ability to engage in repartee, this envoy can be said to have not disgraced his lord's commission.[6]

Here we see again the theme that learning involves not merely the acquisition of scholastic knowledge, but also the ability to flexibly apply this knowledge in a situation-specific manner (cf. 2.11).

13.6 The Master said, "When the ruler is correct, his will is put into effect without the need for official orders. When the ruler's person is not correct, he will not be obeyed no matter how many orders he issues."

A passage in the *New Arrangement* elaborates on 13.6:

> If you sing and others do not harmonize with you, or you move and others do not follow, it is invariably because there is something lacking within yourself. Therefore, do not descend from your place in order to set the world straight; simply look within yourself. [13.6.] This is

---

[5] Chapter 15 ("Rites Concerning Official Missions"); Steele 1917, vol. 1: 233.
[6] Chapter 8.12; Hightower 1952: 266–267.

the reason the Former Kings were able to simply assume a reverent posture and beckon, and have everyone within the Four Seas respond. This is a case of the regulation of sincere Virtue manifesting itself on the outside. Thus, the ode [263] says, "Because the King's plans are sincere and reliable, the people of the Xu region come immediately [and submit to his rule]."

Again, we have the theme of wu-wei rulership through personal moral perfection and the power of Virtue; cf. especially 2.1, 2.3, 2.21, 12.17, 13.13, and 15.5.

13.7 The Master said, "In their forms of government, the states of Lu and Wei are like elder and younger brother."

One interpretation of this cryptic remark is that of Bao Xian, who notes that Lu was given as a fiefdom to the descendents of the Duke of Zhou, and Wei was given to the descendents of Kang Shu—the fourth and seventh sons, respectively, of King Wen. The two states were thus founded by brothers, and presumably had similarly virtuous governments as a result. Su Shi, on the other hand, takes it as a negative comment on current affairs:

> This comment was made in Year 7 of Duke Ai of Lu's reign (489 B.C.E.), which corresponds to Year 5 of Duke Chu of Wei's reign. In the government of Wei at this time, fathers were not behaving as true fathers and sons were not behaving as true sons,[7] and in the government of Lu, the lord was not acting like a true lord, and the ministers were not acting like true ministers.[8] In the end, Duke Ai fled to Zhu and ended up dying in Yue, and Duke Chu escaped to Song and also ended up dying in Yue. Thus, their situations were not so different.

Most likely, both senses of Lu and Wei being "like brothers" is meant, and this is how Zhu Xi takes it: "Lu was the fiefdom of the descendents of Duke Zhou, and Wei of the descendents of Kang Shu, and thus, the two state were originally founded by brothers. In Confucius' age, moreover, both had declined and become disordered to the point that their governments resembled one another, and this is why the Master voices this lament."

13.8 The Master said of Prince Jing of Wei, "He is good at running a household. When he first built his house, he said, 'Oh, it seems acceptable.' After he had worked on it for a while, he said, 'Oh, it seems finished.' When he became wealthy and had improved it, he said, 'It seems beautiful to me.'"

Prince Jing was a minister in Wei and scion of the Ducal house, and thus in a position to enrich himself more or less without limit. Confucius praises him for his lack of acquisitiveness and his financial restraint—the Prince was never particularly eager to acquire greater wealth and the trappings that go along with it, and was always satisfied with what he had. As Wang Kentang notes, this praise is probably also meant by Confucius as an oblique jab of the majority of his contemporaries for their lack of similar restraint. He quotes a passage from the *Yan Family Explications*: "The *Record of Ritual* says, 'The desires cannot be given free rein, and the will should never be fully indulged.'[9] We can plumb the farthest depths of the physical universe, but the

---

[7] Refer to the commentary to 7.15 and 12.11 above.

[8] A reference to the usurpation of the Duke's rightful power by the Three Families, and the failure of the Duke to prevent it.

[9] Chapter 1 ("Summary of Ritual"); Legge 1967, vol. 1: 62.

limits of human desires cannot be known. The only way to establish limits is to reduce the desires and know when to stop." A story in the *Garden of Persuasions* is directly relevant to 13.8:

> Master Zhi Rang established his household, and Mei Shimiao came to stay the night. Count Zhi said to him, "My household is beautiful, is it not?" Mei replied, "Sure, it is beautiful enough, it is just that I am worried." "Why are your worried?" "I serve my lord as a principled historian, and have seen recorded the saying, 'The high mountains have deep springs, but no grass or trees grow there; on land where the great pine and cypress grow, the earth is not fertile.' Now, the lavishness of your household is inappropriate to your status, and I am worried that a man cannot be at ease in such a situation." Three years after his household was complete, Mr. Zhi was ruined.

This idea of reducing desires and knowing when to stop is a common theme throughout Warring States and Han texts, including the *Laozi*. The primitivist Daoists, though, tend to see anything exceeding basic survival requirements as "excessive," while the Confucians are much more generous in deciding how much is "enough." 13.8 might thus also be an oblique response to the primitivists: a virtuous man like Prince Jing can possess a wealthy, elaborate household and still not be the slave of his desires. In other words, in order to "know how to be satisfied" (*zhizu* 知足), it is not necessary for one to radically reject social luxuries and live in a dirt-floored thatched hut.

13.9 The Master traveled to Wei, with Ran Qiu as his carriage driver. [Upon arriving,] the Master remarked, "How numerous the people of this state are!"

Ran Qiu asked, "Being already numerous, what can be done to further improve them?"

The Master replied, "Make them wealthy."

"Once they are wealthy, what else can be done to improve them?"

"Instruct them."

In light of 13.29 and 13.30 below, Brooks and Brooks take the "instruction" mentioned here to be a reference to military training (1998: 100), but it much more likely that *jiao* 教 refers to moral education, and this is how traditional commentators take it. This is supported by a more elaborate version of Confucius' final response as recorded in the *Discourses on Salt and Iron* that reads: "Instruct them by means of Virtue and order them with ritual." Having a large population was desirable at this period of Chinese history, when China was relatively under-populated and the main source of state wealth and strength were taxes on peasant agricultural production and levying of peasant armies. Peasant populations were also mobile (they were not tied to the land like serfs in medieval Europe), and thus the common people could essentially "vote with their feet"—leaving states that were poorly governed and taking up residence in well-governed states. The ability to attract a large peasant population was thus an important sign of good rulership (13.4, 13.6), and apparently the rulers of Wei were not doing too badly at this point. Confucius, however, is not satisfied with merely a large population—it must be well fed and morally educated as well. It is interesting to note the order in which these two qualities are presented here, with food first and education second (in contrast to 12.7). We see here the appearance of what might be called a "proto-Mencian" theme: the people must be materially comfortable before they can be instructed in virtue (see *Mencius* 3:A:3, "the Way of the common people is such that when they have a reliable livelihood they have constant hearts; when they do not have a reliable livelihood, they do not have constant hearts").

13.10 The Master said, "'If someone would simply employ me, within a single year I could put things into some kind of order, and within three years the transformation would be complete.'"

Kong Anguo understands this to be referring to the Master's political teachings: within a year he could have his style of government implemented, and within three years he would achieve some success in ordering the state. Presumably this would involve getting the ruling class to reform itself morally and instructing the populace as mentioned in 13.9. It is interesting to observe along with Liu Baonan, however, that the *History of the Han* takes Confucius' goal to be political order through economic development: "If the people farm for three years, they will be able to accumulate an extra year's surplus. Once clothes and food are sufficient, they will come to understand renown and disgrace, honesty and deference will appear and quarreling and lawsuits will cease . . . When Confucius said, '[quotes 13.1],' this is the sort of success he had in mind."

13.11 The Master said, "'If excellent people managed the state for a hundred years, then certainly they could overcome cruelty and do away with executions'—how true this saying is!"

13.12 The Master said, "If a true king were to arise, though, we would certainly see a return to Goodness after a single generation."

These passages are probably to be read together as a contrasting pair. Liu Baonan, elaborating on Zheng Xuan, understands the "excellent person" in terms of 11.20: someone with considerable native talent, but not yet the equal of a true King. Being excellent—and thus superior to the actual rulers of Confucius' age—such a series of people could very slowly improve the common people to the point that they could do away with the most onerous of punishments, although not punishment altogether. Commentators such as Zhao Luan emphasize that transformation through the power of Virtue takes at least a generation, because it is gentle, gradual, and lasting, unlike behavioral modification through harsh laws and punishments, which may achieve more immediate—but short-lived—results.

13.13 The Master said, "If you simply correct yourself, what difficulties could you encounter in government service? If you cannot correct yourself, how can you expect to correct others?"

Essentially identical to the statements of 12.17 and 13.6, but here applying to a minister—someone who "pursues government service" (*congzheng* 從政)—rather than to the ruler.

13.14 Ran Qiu[10] returned from court.
 The Master asked, "Why so late?"

Court audiences (*chao* 朝) took place in the morning (*zhao* 朝)—a graphic pun in both classical and modern Chinese—and Ran Qiu was apparently returning sometime in the afternoon or evening.

---

[10] This is the sole point in the text where Ran Qiu is actually referred to with an honorific, "Master Ran," possibly because this passage was recorded by his disciples.

Ran Qiu replied, "There were governmental matters (*zheng* 政) to be discussed."

The Master said, "No, what you were discussing were 'private affairs' (*shi* 事). If there were governmental matters to be discussed, how would I have not received word of them, even though I am not employed?"

As we have already seen from the *Zuo Commentary* (see the passage quoted in the commentary to 11.17), Confucius, though unemployed for most of his life, was apparently considered a "state elder" by the rulers of Lu, and presumably consulted on state matters. This is not really the point of this passage, though. Although there is some debate concerning what sort of court audience Ran Qiu had attended, the Zheng Xuan line of commentary is almost certainly correct: Ran Qiu was being employed as a family steward by the Ji Family, and he was no doubt returning from an audience with them. Since the Ji were technically ministers in Lu, the only things properly discussed at such an audience should be "private affairs" (i.e., the personal affairs of the Ji Family), because the discussion of governmental matters was the sole prerogative of the Ducal Court. Of course, since the Ji had usurped control of the state, state matters *were* in fact being discussed and decided in the Ji Family court. What seems to disturb Confucius so much here is not merely that this is the case—the *de facto* control of Lu by the Three Families was long established—but that things had degenerated to the point that the Ji were no longer even trying to hide their insubordination. As Wang Fuzhi explains,

> When the relationship between superiors and subordinates becomes disordered, at first the subordinates usurp the actuality (*shi* 實) [i.e., real power], but continue to preserve the name (*ming* 名). Once the usurpation has lasted for some time, though, the name is appropriated and usurped as well, and eventually the point is reached that the subordinate appropriates the name without feeling any sense of shame. Once things have gone this far, great disorder will follow and will be impossible to resolve. If the gentleman wishes to rectify the wrong of usurpation, his most urgent priority is contesting the theft of the name.

Confucius is thus here engaged in the "rectification of names" (*zhengming* 正名; see 13.3 above), contesting the Ji Family's usurpation of the right to discuss governmental matters in the same way that he contested their usurpation of ritual prerogatives in Book Three. The only way the gentleman can hope to restore order is by setting names and ritual aright; as Zhu Xi remarks, "the distinction that the Master makes [between public and private] in thus rectifying names is intended to serve both as a powerful reproof to the Ji Family and a profound lesson to Ran Qiu."

13.15 Duke Ding asked, "A single saying that can cause a state to flourish—is there such a thing as this?"

Confucius replied, "There is no saying that can have *that* sort of effect. There is, however, something close. People have a saying, 'Being a ruler is difficult, and being a minister is not easy.' If this saying helps you to understand that being a ruler is difficult, does it not come close to being a single saying that can cause a state to flourish?"

The proverbial saying quoted here is similar to lines from Ode 236 ("It is difficult to trust Heaven/It is not easy to be a king") and from the *Book of Documents* ("If the sovereign can realize the difficulty of being a sovereign, and the minister realize the difficulty of being a minister, then the government will be well ordered, and the common people will strive diligently after Virtue").[11] The point is that, as Zhu Xi explains, "If,

---

[11] Chapter 3 ("The Counsels of the Great Yu"); Legge 1991b: 53.

as a result of this saying, one could understand the difficulty of being a ruler, then one will necessarily be 'fearful and cautious/as if skirting the edge of a deep abyss/as if treading upon thin ice' [8.3], and as a result one would not dare to handle casually even a single affair."

Duke Ding asked, "A single saying that can cause a state to perish—is there such a thing as this?"

Confucius replied, "There is no saying that can have *that* sort of effect. There is, however, something close. People have a saying, 'I take no joy in being a ruler, except that no one dares to oppose what I say.' If what the ruler says is good, and no one opposes him, is this not good? On the other hand, if what he says is not good, and no one opposes him, does this not come close to being a single saying that can cause a state to perish?"

In a passage from the *Hanfeizi*, this saying is attributed to Duke Ping of Jin:

> Duke Ping of Jin was drinking wine with his assembled ministers. Drinking to his heart's content, the Duke loudly sighed to his ministers, "I find no joy in being a ruler, except that no one dares to oppose what I say." [The blind][12] Music Master Guang was in attendance before him. Taking hold of his zither, he threw it at the Duke. Gathering up his robe, the Duke dodged and managed to avoid it, and it instead hit the wall, creating a hole. The Duke said, "At whom did the Music Master throw his zither?" The Music Master said, "Just now, some petty person was sounding off at my side; I was aiming my zither at him." The Duke replied, "That person was I." "Alas!" the Music Master sighed, "Those are not the words of a gentleman!" The attendants asked permission to repair the wall, but the Duke said to them, "Leave it. It will serve as a constant admonition to me."[13]

One of the duties of a loyal minister is to remonstrate with his lord when he has done or said something wrong. As Fan Ziyu comments, "If what the ruler says is not good and no one opposes it, then dutiful advice will never reach his ears. When the ruler is daily growing more arrogant and the ministers are daily growing more obsequious, there has never been a case when the state was not lost." Brooks and Brooks also observe that "this is one of several *Analects* passages defining the idea of the censorate, an institutionalized internal criticism that is the most recognizably Confucian of Imperial government forms" (1998: 101).

13.16 The Duke of She asked about governing.

The Master said, "[Act so that] those near to you are pleased, and those who are far from you are drawn closer."

The Duke, personal name Zigao, was lord of the walled city of She within the powerful state of Chu. Alternate versions of this encounter appear in many Warring States texts; the only significantly different one, found in the *Mozi*, gives Confucius' answer as: "Those who are good at governing draw close to them those who are far away, and renew that which is old."[14] The point seems to concern rule by Virtue, whereby

---

[12] Blind people were generally chosen to be trained as musicians in ancient China, both in order to give them a trade in which they could excel and because their sense of hearing was considered more acute than that of the sighted.

[13] Chapter 36 ("Criticisms of the Ancients, Series One"); Liao 1959, vol. 2: 149.

[14] Chapter 46 ("Geng Zhu"); Mei 1929: 216.

common people are naturally drawn to the kind and Good ruler. The message may be especially intended for the Duke of She because of the harsh legalist practices apparently practiced in the state of Chu, as well as Chu's policy of aggressive military expansion (cf. 13.18).

13.17 Zixia, who was serving as steward of Jifu, asked about governing.

The Master said, "Do not crave speed, and do not be enticed by the prospect of minor gains. If you crave speed, then you will never arrive (*da* 達), and if you are distracted by the prospect of minor gains you will never complete major tasks."

Jifu was a walled city in the state of Lu. Most commentators believe that Zixia had overly ambitious plans for reforming it on taking over as steward, and that Confucius' words are meant to restrain him. Also see the criticism of the petty scholar-official in 13.20 below ("with regard to his actions, he insists that they bear fruit") and 12.14, where Confucius advises Zizhang to be patient as a ruler: "Occupy your position without wearying, and implement your rule by means of dutifulness."

13.18 The Duke of She said to Confucius, "Among my people there is one we call 'Upright Gong.' When his father stole a sheep, he reported him to the authorities."

Confucius replied, "Among my people, those who we consider 'upright' are different from this: fathers cover up for their sons, and sons cover up for their fathers. 'Uprightness' is to be found in this."

This represents the classic statement of the Confucian valuing of familial relations over considerations of public justice that so infuriated the Mohists and statecraft thinkers such as Hanfeizi. Some commentators see this passage as a specific response to Hanfeizi (and thus of quite late provenance), but legalist tendencies probably had their beginning in China long before they were systematized by the late Warring States statecraft theorists. In the Confucian view, proper relations between father and son are the root of Goodness (1.2), and Goodness—rather than rule of law—is the only way to properly order a state (cf. 2.3, 12.13, 12.17–12.19, 13.6). Comparing 13.18 to *Mencius* 7:A:35 is also helpful:

> Tao Ying asked, "When Shun was serving as the Son of Heaven, and Gao Yao was his minister, if the Old Blind Man [Shun's father] had committed murder, what would have been done?" Mencius replied, "The Old Blind Man would simply have been apprehended." "Would Shun not have prevented it?" "How could Shun have prevented it? Gao Yao had his rightful duty to perform." "So what would Shun have done?" "Shun would have regarded giving up his rulership of the world no differently than throwing away an old pair of sandals: he would have secretly taken his father on his back and fled into exile, taking up residence somewhere along the coast. There he would have spent the rest of his days, cheerful and happy, with no thoughts of his former kingdom."

The emphasis is slightly different here, in that the rightfulness of legal punishment is not denied, but the basic theme is the same: it is the duty of the filial son to sacrifice himself in order to prevent the law from being applied to his father. Alternate versions of the "Upright Gong" story in other Warring States texts present his fault as an overly developed sense of "trustworthiness" (*xin* 信)—trustworthiness in the sense of "fidelity to one's word" being closely allied to uprightness (5.24, 17.8). In his commentary to

Mencius 4:B:11 ("The great person is not always necessarily true to his word (*xin*), because he is concerned only with rightness"), Zhao Qi observes that "the fact that rightness sometimes involves not necessarily being true to one's word is shown by the example of son covering up for the father," and the *Zhuangzi* similarly remarks that "Upright Gong reporting his father and Wei Sheng allowing himself to drown are examples of the dangers of trustworthiness."[15] For other criticisms of the virtue of trust-worthiness becoming a vice through excess, see the commentary to 1.13, 13.20, and 17.8, where the danger of excessive trustworthiness is described as "harmful rigidity," and the danger of excessive uprightness as "intolerance."

13.19 Fan Chi asked about Goodness.

The Master replied, "When occupying your place, remain reverent; when per-forming public duties, be respectful; and when dealing with others, be dutiful. These are virtues that cannot be abandoned, even if you go to dwell among the Yi or Di barbarians."

Goodness is defined in terms of three lesser virtues; cf. 13.27, 14.4, 15.6, 17.6. For the Yi and Di barbarians, see the commentary to 3.5. In contrast to "definitionalist" pas-sages such as 12.1, where Goodness is understood in terms of ritual mastery, here it appears as a character trait independent of Chinese culture. As Bao Xian remarks, "Even if you go to regions lacking ritual, such as those of the Yi and Di, these are still qualities that you cannot abandon nor fail to put into practice."

13.20 Zigong asked, "What does a person have to be like before he could be called a true scholar-official?"

The Master said, "Conducting himself with a sense of shame, and not dis-honoring his ruler's mandate when sent abroad as a diplomat—such a person could be called a scholar-official."

"May I ask what the next best type of person is like?"

"His lineage and clan consider him filial, and his fellow villagers consider him respectful to his elders."

"And the next best?"

"In his speech, he insists on being trustworthy, and with regard to his actions, he insists that they bear fruit. What a narrow, rigid little man he is! And yet he might still be considered the next best."

"How about those who today are involved in government?"

The Master exclaimed, "Oh! Those petty functionaries are not even worth considering."

Here again the flexibility and true grace of the gentleman is contrasted with those who are simply "renown" (cf. 12.20, 17.13, 17.18), and those who are too narrowly focused on trustworthiness (cf. 1.13, 13.18) or attaining results (cf. 13.17). As *Mencius* 4:B:11 observes, "The great person is not always necessarily true to his word (*xin*), because he is concerned only with rightness." Apparently even such narrow, rigid officials are to be preferred to the "vessels" (2.12) or "petty functionaries"— *doushaozhiren* 斗筲之人, lit. "peck and basket men," which we might have rendered more colloquially as "bean counters"—who dominated public life in Confucius' age.

---

[15] Chapter 29 ("Robber Zhi"); Watson 1968: 334. For Wei Sheng, see the commentary to 1.13.

13.21 The Master said, "If you cannot manage to find a person of perfectly balanced conduct to associate with, I suppose you must settle for the wild or the fastidious. In their pursuit of the Way, the wild plunge right in, while the fastidious are always careful not to get their hands dirty."

In the commentary to 5.22 we have already cited portions of *Mencius* 7:B:37, which discusses both 5.22 and 13.21. The "wild" (*kuang* 狂) have a preponderance of native substance insufficiently shaped by refinement (5.22), while the "fastidious" (*juan* 狷) lack the passion, flexibility, and courage possessed by a true gentleman. Zilu might serve as an example of the former, while examples of the latter include the excessively "pure" Chen Wenzi in 5.19, the overly cautious Ji Wenzi in 5.20, the excessively scrupulous disciple Yuan Si in 6.5 and 14.1, or the various principled recluses presented in Books Fourteen and Eighteen. These two types represent extremes of the ethical spectrum, and each has its strengths, but it is the mean between these two extremes that is truly desirable.

13.22 The Master said, "The Southerners have a saying, 'The fate of a person who lacks constancy cannot be diagnosed by the shaman-healers (*wuyi* 巫醫).' How well put!"

[It is also said,] "One inconstant in Virtue will probably incur disgrace." The Master commented, "It simply cannot be foretold through divination."

In classical times, the South (the region of Chu) was associated with shamanism, and these shamans apparently served as combination healers and fortune-tellers. The second quotation appears in the *Book of Changes* (Hexagram 32, "Constancy"), a traditional divination text, and this is the first real hint in the *Analects* of the existence of this text. This passage is rather cryptic. It helps somewhat to read it together with a similar passage from the *Record of Ritual*, which quotes Confucius as observing: "The Southerners have a saying, 'A person who lacks constancy cannot have his fortune told with the yarrow stalks.'[16] This is no doubt a saying passed down from the ancients. If a person cannot be known even by the turtle shells and yarrow stalks, how much less so can he be known by other people!"[17] Zheng Xuan's commentary on this passage reads, "'He cannot have his fortune cast' means that the evidence of the hexagrams cannot reveal his essential nature, nor determine if he is to have good or bad fortune." In 7.26, constancy (*heng* 恆) is contrasted with the superficial appearance of virtue, so it is plausible to take the point here to be that it is difficult to distinguish between true virtue and its counterfeit (17.13, 17.18), even by supernatural means. This also harmonizes well with 13.24.

13.23 The Master said, "The gentleman harmonizes (*he* 和), and does not merely agree (*tong* 同). The petty person agrees, but he does not harmonize."

The best commentary on this passage is a story from the *Zuo Commentary*:

---

[16] Divination utilizing the hexagrams of the *Book of Changes* was (and still is) performed by means of yarrow stalks; the use of yarrow-stalk divination by shamans is revealed by the graphic relationship between the characters for yarrow stalk (*shi* 筮) and shaman (*wu* 巫).

[17] Chapter 33 ("Black Robes"); Legge 1967, vol. 2: 363.

The Marquis of Qi had returned from a hunt, and was being attended by Master Yan at the Chuan pavilion when Ran Qiu came galloping up to them at full speed. The Marquis remarked, "It is only Ran Qiu who harmonizes (*he*) with me!" Master Yan replied, "Certainly Ran Qiu agrees (*tong*) with you, but how can you say that he harmonizes with you?" The Marquis asked, "Is there a difference between agreeing and harmonizing?" Master Yan answered, "There is a difference. Harmonizing is like cooking soup. You have water, fire, vinegar, pickle, salt, and plums with which to cook fish and meat. You heat it by means of firewood, and then the cook harmonizes the ingredients, balancing the various flavors, strengthening the taste of whatever is lacking and moderating the taste of whatever is excessive. Then the gentleman eats it, and it serves to relax his heart. The relationship between lord and minister is just like this. If in what the lord declares to be acceptable there is something that is not right, the minister submits to him that it is not right, and in this way what the lord declares acceptable is made perfect. If in what the lord declares to be wrong there is something that is, in fact, acceptable, the minister submits to him that it is acceptable, and in this way the inappropriate aspects of what the lord declares wrong are discarded. In this way, government is perfected, with no infringement upon what is right, and the common people are rendered free of contentiousness . . . [An extended musical metaphor follows, where different notes are brought together and harmonized to please the heart of the gentleman.] Now, Ran Qiu is not like this. What his lord declares acceptable, he also declares acceptable; what his lord declares wrong, he also declares wrong. This is like trying to season water with more water—who would be willing to eat it? It is like playing nothing but a single note on your zither—who would want to listen to it? This is why it is not acceptable for a minister to merely agree."[18]

For the danger caused to a state by a minister who merely agrees, also see 13.15.

13.24 Zigong asked, "What would you make of a person whom everyone in the village likes?"

The Master said, "I would not know what to make of him."

"What about someone whom everyone in the village hates?"

"I would still not know. Better this way: those in the village who are good like him, and those who are not good hate him."

We see again the suspicion of public opinion voiced in 12.20, 15.28, 17.13, and 17.18. This is related to the deeper problem of separating appearance from substance that motivates both Confucius' suspicion of glibness and flattery and his tendency to favor native substance over refinement. These themes also appear in 13.25 and 13.27.

13.25 The Master said, "The gentleman is easy to serve, but hard to please. If you attempt to please him in a manner not in accordance with the Way, he will not be pleased, but when he employs others, he does so in consideration of their particular capacities. The petty person is hard to serve, but easy to please. If you attempt to please him, he will be pleased, even if it is in a manner not in accordance with the Way, but when it comes to his employment of others, he demands everything from them."

Here we have the contrast between the gentleman and petty person as managers of others. The gentleman is only pleased by rightness and proper behavior, but is fair in his use of others—as Kong Anguo explains, "He assigns people to offices only after

---

[18] Duke Zhao, Year 20 (521 B.C.E.); Legge 1991d: 684.

having gauged their abilities"—and is thus ultimately easy to work under. The petty person, on the contrary, is easily and temporarily swayed by flattery or bribes, but has as his ultimate aim squeezing his subordinates dry in order to serve his own purposes—often very much to the detriment of those he is using. As Brooks and Brooks put it, "the right kind of officer uses people appropriately, whereas the little man is indiscriminate in his use of men, and, so to speak, uses the screwdriver to open the paint can, thus spoiling it as a screwdriver" (1998: 104). The translation reads the character 説 in the sense of "pleased" or "happy" (pronounced *yue* in modern Mandarin, and sometimes distinguished graphically by the use of the heart rather than the speech radical, 悦). Some early commentators read it as "speak, persuade" (pronounced *shuo* in modern Mandarin), but the sense is more or less the same. For instance, a passage in the *Record of Ritual* reads, "Do not speak inappropriately to others,"[19] and Zheng Xuan's commentary quotes 13.25, playing upon both senses of 説: "[Speaking inappropriately] is close to glibness or flattery, and 'if the gentleman is spoken to (*shuo* 説) in a manner not in accordance with the Way, he will not be pleased (*yue* 説).'"

13.26 The Master said, "The gentleman is grand, but never arrogant; the petty person is arrogant, but never grand."

As He Yan explains, "The gentleman is uninhibited and grand, which could appear to be arrogance, but is not arrogance. The petty person is restrained and afraid to give offense, but in actuality is secretly arrogant and proud." Cf. the contrasting manners of the gentleman and petty person as presented in 7.37 ("The gentleman is self-possessed and relaxed, while the petty man is perpetually full of worry"). In this passage, we see again the problem of appearance and actuality.

13.27 The Master said, "Resolute, decisive, straightforward, and reticent—these qualities are close to Goodness."

For "resoluteness" (*gang* 剛), cf. 5.11. "Straightforward" is the translation of *mu* 木—lit. "like a tree." It is glossed by Wang Bi as "simple-unadorned native substance" (*zhipu* 質樸) (941), and the sense is something like "simple," "honest," or "unpretentious." For the relationship of reticence (*na* 訥) to Goodness, see 4.24 ("The gentleman wishes to be slow to speak (*na* 訥) but quick to act") and 12.3 ("The Good person is hesitant to speak (*ren* 認)"). Here we have Confucius again favoring the rustic virtues of native substance over the adornments of cultural refinement, presumably because the latter are easier to counterfeit. For other examples of this bias, see 3.4, 3.8, 5.10, 5.22, and 7.33.

13.28 Zilu asked, "What does a person have to be like to be considered a true scholar-official?"
  The Master replied, "He must be earnest and critical, but also affable—earnest and critical with his friends, and affable with his brothers."

Earnest criticism between friends is desirable (12.23), but this sort of taking to task has no place in the family. As we read in *Mencius* 4:A:19 "Father and son do not crit-

---

[19] Chapter 1 ("Summary of Ritual"); Legge 1967, vol. 1: 62.

icize each other's moral conduct; moral criticism is the Way of friendship. If father and son were to criticize each other's moral conduct, this would cause great harm to their mutual affection."

13.29 The Master said, "Having been instructed by an excellent person for seven years, the common people will be ready for anything, even the taking up of arms."

The intensifying *yi* 亦 suggest that taking up arms is not the specific goal of instruction, but rather a by-product—the most difficult task a ruler can expect from his people, something they will be capable of only after they have been properly instructed in moral principles. In *Mencius* 1:A:5, King Hui of Liang complains about having suffered military defeats at the hands of the two great powers of the time, Qin in the west and Chu in the south. He then asks Mencius's advice about how to improve his army, and Mencius replies as follows:

> If your majesty can apply benevolent government to the people, lessen punishments and reduce taxes, get the people to plow deeply and weed regularly, and see to it that those in their prime use their spare time to cultivate filial piety, respect for elders, dutifulness and trustworthiness—so that at home they will serve their fathers and older brothers, and abroad they serve their elders and superiors—you can bring it about that they will be able to defeat the strong armor and sharp weapons of Qin and Chu armed with nothing more than wooden staves.

This sort of combination of practical and moral instruction is probably what is intended here in 13.29.

13.30 The Master said, "Leading people who have not been instructed into battle—this is called, 'throwing them away.'"

A similar passage occurs in the *Guliang Commentary* for Duke Xi, Year 23 (636 B.C.E.):

> Duke Cifu of Song died. Why was he not mourned? Because he lost the common people. How did he lose the common people? Because, by letting uninstructed commoners be lead in to battle, he threw away his troops. If you are a ruler of men and yet throw away your troops, how can your people look up to you as a true ruler?

Some commentators take the "instruction" (*jiao* 教) to refer to military training, and a passage in the *Zhou Ritual* uses the term *jiao* in describing a military official, the "Horse Commander" (*sima* 司馬), drilling commoners in military formations. Most commentators, however, believe "instruction" to have a broader reference—perhaps including military training, but primarily focusing on moral education. Cf. *Mencius* 6:B:8.

BOOK FOURTEEN

Most of the passages in this Book concern themselves in some way with the respective duties of ruler and minister. Here the key to rulership is presented as employing people correctly, which requires that one be a good judge of character—a potentially difficult task, since often a person's outward presentation does not always match their inner character or actual behavior (14.4, 14.6, 14.13–14.14, 14.20, 14.24, 14.27). A large portion of the Book (14.8–14.19) is dedicated to case examples of how one would go about judging the character of others, with the Master evaluating the behavior of various historical figures, noting both their strengths and weaknesses, and thereby illustrating the perceptive powers of a gentleman. On the minister's side, one must be dedicated to the Way and not to the pursuit of salary, honest with oneself and others, and courageous in remonstrating with one's ruler when it comes to matters of rightness. A good minister also persists in holding to rightness even when the situation seems hopeless (14.21, 14.38–14.39), and this probably accounts for the series of passages at the end of the Book (14.32, 14.37–14.39, 14.43) where Confucius rebukes (either verbally or by example) recluses or nonconformists of various types, who have given up the Confucian Way and withdrawn into private life.

14.1 Yuan Si asked about shame.

The Master said, "When the state has the Way, accept a salary; when the state is without the Way, to accept a salary is shameful."

"To refrain from competitiveness, boastfulness, envy, and greed—can this be considered Goodness?"

The Master said, "This can be considered difficult, but as for its being Good, that I do not know."

Yuan Si is the disciple who, serving as a steward for one of the Three Families in 6.5, makes a show of declining his salary, and is then reproved for it by the Master. According to the later legends that sprang up around Yuan Si, he became a recluse and led a strict, ascetic lifestyle. An account in the *Record of the Historian* reads:

> Yuan Si lived in an obscure, humble abode, reading books and embracing the solitary enactment of gentlemanly Virtue. He was righteous and would not compromise with his contemporaries, and in return his contemporaries mocked him. Therefore, he lived out his days without complaint in an empty room with a thorn-wood gate, clad in hemp and subsisting on vegetables and millet. It has now been over four hundred years since his death, and still the memory of him has not died out among his disciples.

The Master's answer to Yuan Si's initial question (cf. 8.13) seems to be an endorsement of his reclusive tendencies, which is perhaps why he is emboldened to offer his other achievements for the Master's approval. This approval is, of course, denied (as in modern Japanese, we have the polite locution, "I do not know," to soften the impact of the real message, "No"). As mentioned in the commentary to 6.5, Yuan Si's extreme and rigid adherence to principle seems to mark him as one of the overly "fastidious" criticized by the Master in 13.21. Yuan Si's achievements, though impressive, are all purely negative—the truly Good person displays a degree of flexibility, creativity, and positive concern for others lacking in the fastidious or "pure" (*qing* 清). Jiao Xun expresses this sentiment quite well:

> Insisting on dismissing one's concubines and scrimping on clothes and food, while at the same time remaining aloof from the hunger, cold, and separation experienced by the common people, is the behavior of an inflexible prude (*jianhu* 堅瓠; lit. "rigid gourd"). This is why Confucius did not accept this sort of bitter-minded, holier-than-thou scholar-official focused solely on being free of competitiveness, boastfulness, envy, and greed. It is better to allow oneself to feel some desire, so as to, by extension, better understand the desires of others; similarly, it is better to allow oneself to feel what one does not desire, so as to, by extension, understand what other people do not desire.[1] To take as one's model the measuring line or carpenter's square is not so difficult a feat, but Goodness is much more than that. To completely cut off one's own desires to the point that one is unable to understand the aspirations of the rest of the world can certainly not be considered Goodness.

14.2 The Master said, "A scholar-official who cherishes comfort is not worthy of the name."

"Comfort" here translates *ju* 居—literally "dwelling," "leisure," "to sit"—and seems to encompass both physical and economical comfort. As He Yan remarks, "The scholar-official should set his heart upon the Way rather than pursuing comfort or ease (*an* 安); one who cherishes his dwelling is not a true scholar-official." Cf. 4.11 ("the gentleman thinks about Virtue, whereas the petty person thinks about physical comfort"); as in 4.9, the point is that the gentlemanly scholar-official is both immune from the allure of externalities (1.16, 4.14, 12.20, 14.30, 15.19) and tireless in his pursuit of the Way (8.7, 9.11, 9.19). This passage can be illustrated by the story in the *Zuo Commentary* of Duke Wen of Jin, who settles in the state of Jin and is provided with a wife and an opulent household, becoming so comfortable that he abandons his original ambition to travel the world. This displeases his followers, and he is eventually reproved by his new wife, "Go! By cherishing my company and the physical comfort you find here, you are in fact ruining your reputation."[2]

14.3 The Master said, "When the state possesses the Way, be audaciously correct in both word and action; when the state lacks the Way, be audaciously correct in action, but let one's speech be conciliatory."

The word translated as "audaciously correct," *wei* 危, means literally "danger from being in a high position" (or, more generally, "dangerous" or "endangered") and is variously glossed by commentators as "strict," "severe" (Bao Xian, He Yan), "lofty/noble" (Zheng Xuan), or "correct" (*Expansive Elegance*). The sense in all of these cases is similar: endangering oneself by stubbornly adhering to "the high ground," as opposed to being "conciliatory" or "accommodating" (*sun* 孫). As Wang Fuzhi observes, "One is conciliatory in speech not out of fear of disaster but because

---

[1] Jiao Xun is making an oblique reference to 6.30, where the "method of Goodness" is described as "being able to take what is near at hand as an analogy."

[2] Duke Xi, Year 23 (636 B.C.E.); Legge 1991d: 187.

actively courting disaster does no good, and is therefore something from which the gentleman refrains. Knowing when to advance and when to retire, when to remain in office and when to resign [*Mencius* 5:B:1], all without departing from the path of rightness—this indeed is the Way of hitting the timely mean." For examples of Confucius being indirect or conciliatory in speech in the face of immoral rulers, see 7.15 and 7.31. Brooks and Brooks remark that an additional point of this passage may be that "the test of not having the Way is . . . the ruler's unwillingness to hear advice. 14.3 implies that candor is crucial to the state, and the ruler its chief enemy" (1998: 119). For the importance of candor for the flourishing of a state, cf. 13.15 and 13.23 and 14.7.

14.4 The Master said, "Those who possess Virtue will inevitably have something to say, whereas those who have something to say do not necessarily possess Virtue. Those who are Good will necessarily display courage, but those who display courage are not necessarily Good."

An observation concerning both the problem of glibness (1.3, 5.5, 11.25, 12.3, 16.4) and the unity of the virtues: a virtue such as courage becomes a vice when not balanced by other virtues (cf. 8.10, 17.23). As Zhu Xi remarks, "One who possesses Virtue harmoniously and effortlessly accumulates it inside, so that eventually it flowers forth on the outside [in the form of words]. On the other hand, those who are able to speak well are sometimes merely glib and loquacious. In his heart, the Good person is not concerned with himself, which means that, when he sees what is right to do, he simply must do it. On the other hand, those who display courage are sometimes merely driven by an overly belligerent physiological disposition."

14.5 Nangong Kuo said to Confucius, "Yi was a skillful archer, and Ao was a powerful naval commander, and yet neither of them met a natural death. Yu and Hou Ji, on the other hand, did nothing but personally tend to the land, and yet they both ended up with possession of the world."

The Master did not answer.

After Nangong Kuo left, the Master sighed, "What a gentlemanly person that man is! How he reveres Virtue!"

Kong Anguo identifies Nangong Kuo as a minister in the state of Lu, an unusually virtuous member of the Three Families, and son of the Meng Yizi mentioned in 2.5; Zhu Xi believes him to be the Nan Rong mentioned in 5.2. Both Yi and Ao were legendary martial heroes of the Xia Dynasty with questionable morals: Yi usurped the throne of one of the kings of the Xia Dynasty, and Ao was the son of one of Yi's ministers. Ao subsequently murdered and dethroned Yi, and was in turn slain and overthrown by one of his own ministers.[3] Yu and Hou Ji, on the other hand, were moral worthies and heroes of civilized arts: Yu tamed the Yellow River and introduced irrigation, receiving the rulership of the world from Shun in return, while Hou Ji ("Lord Millet") is the mythical founder of agriculture and progenitor of the Zhou royal line.[4] The point is that the world is won through moral cultivation and civilization rather

---

[3] For the legend concerning these two figures, see the *Zuo Commentary*, Duke Xiang, Year 4 (568 B.C.E.); Legge 1991d: 424.

[4] See the *Book of Documents* 55 ("Punishments of Lu"; Legge 1991b: 595) for legends of these two figures.

than martial prowess; cf. 8.10, 14.4, and 17.23, where mere martial courage is dismissed as inferior to the balanced moral courage of the gentleman. Zhu Xi suggests that Nangong Kuo meant to compare Confucius to Yu and Ji, and that Confucius remains silent out of modesty: "Probably Kuo brought up Yi and Ao as analogies to the wielders of power in Confucius' time, and Yu and Ji as analogies to Confucius himself, and this is why Confucius did not answer."

14.6 The Master said, "Certainly there are those gentlemen who are not Good, but there has never been a petty person who is Good."

This is a somewhat puzzling passage, and commentators have offered a variety of explanations for how a gentleman could fail to be Good, with most arguing that it is possible for someone to be a gentleman in most respects but still fall short of complete Goodness. The most plausible explanation, though, seems to be that of Huan Maoyong, who explains:

> There are occasions when even a gentleman does things that are not Good, but this does not change the fact that he is a gentleman. Potentially, there are also occasions when a petty person does something that is Good, but this does not change the fact that he is, in the end, still a petty person. Any Goodness displayed by a petty person is temporary and superficial, because his heart remains firmly opposed to Goodness. In this passage, the sage [Confucius] is indicating a method for observing and evaluating other people.

Understood this way—as involving occasional, uncharacteristic behaviors that could potentially deceive an unwary observer—the point of the passage is similar to 2.10 and 4.7, and harmonizes with the concern about appearance and actuality voiced in 12.20, 13.24, 13.26, 15.28, and 17.13. However, this admission that even the gentleman can lapse on occasion contradicts 4.5 ("If the gentleman abandons Goodness, how can he merit the name? The gentleman does not go against Goodness even for the amount of time required to eat a meal").

14.7 The Master said, "If you really care for them, can you then fail to put them to work? If you are really dutiful to him, can you then fail to instruct him?

The first half of this passage concerns the duties of the ruler toward his people: if he genuinely cares for them, he will also make demands of them and urge them on in their work. The second concerns the duties of the minister, who displays his true dutifulness to his lord by remonstrating and instructing when his lord has done something wrong; cf. 13.15, 13.23, and *Mencius* 3:A:4 ("To instruct others in goodness is what it means to be dutiful"). As Mr. Su comments, "Caring for them without putting them to work is the kind of care one shows to livestock; being dutiful without instructing is the kind of dutifulness displayed by a wife or eunuch. Only care that also involves putting them to work can be considered true, profound care, and only dutifulness that also involves instruction can be considered true, great dutifulness."

14.8 The Master said, "In preparing diplomatic orders, Zichan of East Village would have Bi Chen go into the country and draft it, Shi Shu critique and discuss it, the foreign minister Ziyu edit and ornament it, and then finally Zichan himself would mark it with his own unique style."

Zichan was Prime Minister of Zheng, a man much admired by Confucius (5.16 and 14.9). Zheng was a small state surrounded by much more powerful neighbors, but it managed to survive because of the skillful diplomacy of its ministers. The point is thus similar to 4.11 and 14.19: a good ruler or minister is one who understands the character and skills of others, and is able to employ them wisely. As Lu Longqi comments, "This passage uses the example of Zheng's preparation of diplomatic orders in order to illustrate the value of precision and caution when it comes to affairs, as well as the effectiveness of finding the right people and properly employing them." Cf 14.19, where virtuous ministers allow an unworthy ruler to maintain his position.

14.9 Someone asked about Zichan. The Master said, "He was a benevolent man."

They asked about Zixi. The Master replied, "Ah, that man! That man!"

Zichan we have already encountered, and the reason for the Master's judgment seems fairly clear, although some (following *Mencius* 4:B:2) take it as a mild criticism: Zichan was kindly, but not as effective as he could have been. There is a great deal of debate over the identity of Zixi, with a similar lack of clarity about the reason for—and indeed the meaning of—the Master's comment. Some believe him to be the Prince Shen, style-name Zixi, who served as Prime Minister of Chu under King Zhao, and who dissuaded the king from giving Confucius employment. Others argue that he is the Zixi who was a fellow minister of Zichan's in the state of Zheng, and who—though by most accounts worthy—was not quite the equal of Zichan. As for Confucius' remark, most take it as either dismissive or neutral—in the latter case, out of a desire not to be overtly critical.

They asked about Guan Zhong. The Master replied, "Now there was a man. He confiscated the three hundred household city of Ping from the head of the Bo Clan, reducing him to abject poverty, and yet to the end of his days not a single resentful word was uttered against him."

For Guan Zhong, see the commentary to 3.22. The head of the Bo Clan was a minister in the state of Qi, and apparently his fiefdom was confiscated as punishment for an unspecified crime. The most plausible way to understand Confucius' comment is to follow Kong Anguo: Guan Zhong's actions were appropriate and reasonable, and therefore even those who suffered from his decisions could find no reason to blame him. Compare this favorable evaluation of Guan Zhong with 14.16–14.17, and contrast it with 3.22. As for the overall point of the passage, Wang Fuzhi's interpretation seems most plausible:

> With regard to Zichan, Confucius divined his heart on the basis of his actions; with regard to Zixi, he held his tongue, and did not indulge himself in criticism or debate; and with regard to Guan Zhong, he glossed over his crimes and instead highlighted his achievements. All of this illustrates how the sage approves of good qualities and hates faults, seizing upon any positive quality he can find and praising it, while at the same time not giving anyone more than his due, never willing to exaggerate the talents of anyone.

14.10 The Master said, "It is difficult to be poor and still free of resentment, but relatively easy to be rich without being arrogant."

Some commentators read this line together with 14.9, in which case it becomes indirect praise of the head of the Bo Clan, who lived in poverty without resenting the act of justice that deprived him of his estate, and criticism of Guan Zhong, who—as we read in 3.22—allowed his wealth to lead him into excess and ritual improprieties. Others understand it as a separate, independent statement. As He Yan remarks, "Dwelling in poverty is difficult, and enjoying wealth is easy—this is the constant nature of human beings. However, people should work diligently at that which is difficult, and yet not grow careless with regard to that which is easy."

14.11 The Master said, "Meng Gongchuo would make an excellent household manager for the Zhao or Wei, but could not be employed as a minister in Teng or Xue."

Zhao and Wei were powerful noble households in the state of Jin, who eventually (working together with the Han Family) usurped the running of the government, much as the Three Families did in the state of Lu. Teng and Xue were relatively minor, but still independent, states. Meng Gongchuo was a minister in Lu, the head of the Meng Family, and apparently a virtuous (14.12), if not terribly talented, man. The sense seems to be that running even a powerful household is not as challenging as governing a small state, and most commentators see the point of this passage as Confucius' concern about knowing the capabilities of others and employing them accordingly. As Huan Maoyong explains,

> In this remark, Confucius is probably expressing the point that each person has that which they are capable of doing and that which they are incapable of doing, and that when a state employs people, it must do so on the basis of an accurate assessment of their strengths. If even someone as worthy as Gongchuo still has that which he can do and that which he cannot do, we can be sure that this is true of others as well. Confucius' remark is thus meant as a comment on the proper way to employ people—you cannot use them in a manner that conflicts with their talents—rather than as a criticism of Gongchuo.

Alternately, Confucius' intention may be to belittle the Three Families of Lu by unfavorably comparing the talent required to run a noble household with that required to run a legitimate state.

14.12 Zilu asked about the complete person.

The Master said, "Take a person as wise as Zang Wuzhong, as free of desire as Gongchuo, as courageous as Zhuangzi of Bian, and as accomplished in the arts as Ran Qiu, and then acculturate them by means of ritual and music—such a man might be called a complete person."

He continued: "But must a complete person today be exactly like this? When seeing a chance for profit he thinks of what is right; when confronting danger he is ready to take his life into his own hands; when enduring an extended period of hardship, he does not forget what he had professed in more fortunate times—such a man might also be called a complete person."

Zang Wuzhong (grandson of the Zang Wenzhong mentioned in 5.17; cf. 14.14) and Meng Gongchuo (14.11) were both respected officials in Lu, and Zhuangzi was an official in the walled city of Bian, on the eastern border of Lu, who was legendary for his courage. For Ran Qiu as master of the cultural arts, see 6.8. The point here is that only the possession of all of these virtues allows one to merit the description "complete" or "perfect" person (*chengren* 成人), just as the gentleman, who possesses the overarching virtue of Goodness, is often presented as having a number of the lesser virtues in their proper proportions (13.19, 13.27, 14.4, 15.18, 17.6). Confucius' qualification in the second paragraph seems analogous to his characterization of "second-rate" (*ci* 次) scholar-officials in 13.20: in Confucius' corrupted age, it is perhaps too much to ask for true perfection. Some commentators also see this concession to the lowered standards of his age as an encouragement to Zilu, who may have felt intimidated by the likes of former worthies such as Zang Wuzhong and Zhuangzi of Bian.

14.13 The Master asked Gongming Jia about Gongshu Wenzi, saying, "Is it really true that your master did not speak, did not laugh, and did not take?"

Gongming Jia answered, "Whoever told you that was exaggerating. My master only spoke when the time was right, and so people never grew impatient listening to him. He only laughed when he was genuinely full of joy, and so people never tired of hearing him laugh. He only took what was rightfully his, and so people never resented his taking of things."

The Master said, "Was he really that good? Could he really have been that good?"

Gongshu Wenzi is the posthumous title of Gongsun Ba (alternately Gongsun Zhi), a worthy minister in Wei who apparently passed away before Confucius' first visit to that state. Little is known about Gongming Jia, but he was presumably Gongshu Wenzi's disciple or retainer. Gongshu Wenzi clearly had a reputation for virtuous restraint, but what his disciple or retainer is claiming for him is in fact even more impressive. As Huan Maoyong notes, "Not speaking, not laughing, and not taking are all negative restrictions that someone wishing to affect virtue or make a name for themselves could force themselves to adhere to, whereas speaking only when the time is right, laughing only when genuinely full of joy, and taking only what it rightful to take are qualities of the timely sage." Confucius' disbelief probably stems from the fact that Gongming Jia is claiming that his master was a true gentleman, embodying the Way in an *wu-wei* fashion, rather than merely one of the lesser, fastidious men whom Confucius is accustomed to encountering.

14.14 The Master said, "Zang Wuzhong took the walled city of Fang in order to demand from the Duke of Lu that his half-brother Wei be made his successor. Although he said that he was not trying to force his lord's hand, I do not believe it."

Zang Wuzhong, as we saw in 14.12, was a wise minister in Lu. As a result of machinations by the Meng Family, who slandered him to the head of the Ji Family, Zang was forced to flee the state and take refuge in the neighboring state of Zhu. Disturbed that he, as the eldest son in the family, would no longer be able to keep up the sacrifices at the family's ancestral temple in Lu, he sent a message to his half-brothers to approach the Duke of Lu and request that one of them be made his official successor. Simultaneously, he re-entered Lu and took possession of the walled city of Fang, which traditionally belonged to his family. Although he denied it at the time, this was clearly an implicit threat that, if his request were not granted by the Duke, he would continue to hold Fang in open revolt. The Duke acquiesced, and Zang Wei, one of

Zang Wuzhong's half-brothers, was appointed successor.[5] Most commentators take the point of this passage to be that, although clever and wise, Zang Wuzhong was lacking in other moral qualities. A comment attributed to Confucius that concludes the *Zuo Commentary* account of Zang Wuzhong's behavior also implicates the potential danger of a single virtue unbalanced by others, "This is the potential problem with wisdom. You have someone as wise as Zang Wuzhong, and yet he is no longer welcome in Lu, and for good reason. In his actions, he was not submissive, and he did not apply the virtue of understanding (*shu*) in his dealings with others" (Legge 1991d: 504). Confucius' refusal here in 14.14 to accept Zang Wuzhong's own account of his behavior also relates to the theme of judging other people's character: you need to look to their actions, not to their words (cf. 5.10).

14.15 The Master said, "Duke Wen of Jin was crafty, but not correct, whereas Duke Huan of Qi was correct, but not crafty."

Duke Wen reigned as the second of the official hegemons from 636–628 B.C.E., and Duke Huan reigned as the first of the official hegemons from 681–643 B.C.E. (cf. commentary to 3.20 and 14.16). The traditional explanation of Confucius' judgment is that Duke Wen of Jing arrogantly summoned the Zhou king to make a court visit to him and participate in a hunt, in order to successfully show off his own power and enhance his own prestige, whereas Duke Huan dedicated himself to public duty at the expense of his own interests.[6]

14.16 Zilu said, "When Duke Huan had his brother Prince Jiu murdered, Shao Hu died for his master, whereas Guan Zhong did not." He then added, "Does this behavior not fall short of Goodness?"

The Master replied, "It was Guan Zhong's strength that allowed Duke Huan, on many occasions, to harmoniously unite the feudal lords without the use of military force. But as for his Goodness, as for his Goodness . . ."

Both Duke Huan (then merely Prince Xiaobo) and his elder brother, Prince Jiu, had been in exile from Qi, the latter having taken refuge in Lu under the protection of his retainers Shao Hu and Guan Zhong. When Duke Xiang (the older brother of both Jiu and Xiaobo) died, Xiaobo managed to get back to Qi before his brother and seize control of the state. In order to consolidate his position, he then demanded that the Duke of Lu execute his brother and send the two retainers back to Qi. In his grief, and out of a sense of loyalty to his master, Shao Hu refused to return to Qi, and instead killed himself. Guan Zhong, on the other hand, willingly returned, and eventually became the newly-established Duke Huan's prime minister.[7] Zilu clearly disapproves of this behavior, and expects Confucius to share his moral outrage. Beginning with

---

[5] This story is recounted in the *Zuo Commentary*, Duke Xiang, Year 23 (549 B.C.E.); Legge 1991d: 503.

[6] These are the explanations of Zheng Xuan and Ma Rong, followed by Zhu Xi. See the *Annals* and *Zuo Commentary* for Duke Xi, Year 28 (631 B.C.E.), which records the hunting expedition and official reception of the Zhou King in the town of Heyang in Jin, and quotes Confucius as remarking sourly, "A subject summoning his ruler is not something to be emulated" (Legge 1991d: 212).

[7] See the *Zuo Commentary*, Duke Zhuang, Year 9 (684 B.C.E.); Legge 1991d: 84.

Kong Anguo, the standard interpretation of Confucius' final assessment, *ruqiren* 如其仁 (lit. "like his Goodness"), has been to understand it either with an implicit "who" before it ("who could match his Goodness!") or as in the sense of "such was his Goodness!" Such high praise has caused consternation among commentators, considering the negative attitudes expressed toward Guan Zhong in 3.22, as well as the fact that he was serving a hegemon rather than a legitimate king. Zhu Xi follows Kong Anguo, but tries to explain away the contradiction by adding, "probably what he meant is that, although Guan Zhong was not quite a truly Good person, his beneficence extended to all people, and therefore his achievements were Good." A more satisfying way to reconcile 14.16–14.17 with 3.22 is to follow commentators who understand *ruqiren*—like the "Ah! That man! That man!" in 14.9—as a noncommittal "But as for his Goodness, as for his Goodness . . ."

14.17 Zigong asked, "Guan Zhong was not a Good person, was he? When Duke Huan had Prince Jiu murdered, Guan Zhong was not only incapable of dying with his master, he moreover turned around and served his master's murderer as Prime Minister."

The Master replied, "When Guan Zhong served as Duke Huan's Prime Minister, he allowed him to become hegemon over the other feudal lords, uniting and ordering the entire world. To this day, the people continue to enjoy the benefits of his achievements—if it were not for Guan Zhong, we would all be wearing our hair loose and fastening our garments on the left. How could he be expected to emulate the petty fidelity of a common husband or wife, going off to hang himself and die anonymously in some gully or ditch?"

Wearing the hair loose and fastening one's clothes on the left are both barbarian practices. Guan Zhong is credited with helping Qi to unite the Chinese feudal lords, and thereby preventing the Di barbarians from overrunning China. Confucius' point is thus that all Chinese of his age owe Guan Zhong a debt for saving them from having been born as subjects of alien, barbarian masters. The "petty fidelity" of a commoner is perceived as arising from their strict monogamy (a commoner not being able to afford the upkeep of concubines); as Legge puts it, Confucius' retort is essentially, "Do you think Guan Zhong should have considered himself bound to Jiu, as a common man considers himself bound to his wife? And would have had him commit suicide, as common people will do on any slight occasion?" (1991a: 283). This echoes the concern with overly rigid or narrowly understood trustworthiness expressed in 1.13, 13.18, 13.20, and 17.8. There is some debate over whether or not Confucius is entirely excusing Guan Zhong's behavior after the murder of his lord, but in any case it is clear that, in Confucius' view, Guan Zhong's later achievements greatly outweigh any potential initial impropriety.

14.18 Gongshu Wenzi had his household minister Zhuan promoted along with him to the ducal court. When Confucius heard of this, he remarked, "Surely he deserves to be considered 'cultured' (*wen* 文)."

Gongshu Wenzi's posthumous title, *wenzi* 文子, means "cultured master." Qian Dian paraphrases the passage in the *Record of Ritual* that recounts the granting of this title:

Gongshu Wenzi died, and his son Rong, requested that the ruler bestow a posthumous title upon him. The ruler said, "Your honored father participated in the governing of Wei, improving the system of ranks in order to better establish relations with the neighboring states. As a result, the altars to the grain and soil in the state of Wei were not disgraced. Was he not cultured?"[8]

Although in 14.13 Confucius seems slightly dubious about claims that Gongshu Wenzi was a true, wu-wei gentleman, here he appears happy to grant that he is cultured. Read as a companion to 14.13, the subject is the judgment of character: although reluctant to pronounce any of his contemporaries entirely Good, Confucius would still grant them their due.

14.19 The Master remarked that Duke Ling of Wei lacked the Way. Ji Kangzi said, "If that is so, why has he not lost his state?"

The Master replied, "Kong Wenzi manages his diplomatic protocol, Priest Tuo manages his ancestral temples, and Wangsun Jia manages his military affairs. This being the case, how *could* he lose his state?"

We have already encountered Duke Ling, the misguided ruler of Wei addicted to women and military adventures (6.16, 6.28, 13.3, 15.1), as well as the ministers mentioned here: Kong Wenzi in 5.15, Priest Tuo in 6.16, and Wangsun Jia in 3.13. Though capable, none of these ministers were particularly virtuous, which serves to accentuate the importance of choosing ministers wisely: when the talents of ministers are well-matched to their jobs, even ungentlemanly ministers can enable an incompetent ruler to remain in power. Zhu Xi comments, "Although these three men are not necessarily worthies, their talents can still be put to use, and Duke Ling was able to employ them in a manner appropriate to their abilities." Yin Tun adds, "Duke Ling's lack of the Way should have caused him to lose power, but his ability to employ these three men allowed him to still preserve his state. Considering this, how much more could be accomplished by a ruler possessing the Way and employing the worthiest people in the world?" This observation concerning an unworthy ruler's ability to hold onto power may also be intended as a subtle jibe at Ji Kangzi himself.

14.20 The Master said, "If you are shameless in what you propose, you may then find it difficult to put your words into practice."

Here again we have a concern with appearance and actuality: one should not shamelessly exaggerate one's own abilities. Ma Rong takes the passage somewhat differently—"It is difficult to reach a point where you can speak without shame"— commenting, "only when you have the actuality within you can you speak without shame, and accumulating this actuality is difficult to do." The sense, though, is very much the same. For Confucius' concern about action measuring up to speech, cf. 1.14, 2.13, 4.22, 4.24, 12.3, and 14.27.

14.21 When Chen Chengzi assassinated Duke Jian, Confucius ritually bathed himself and then presented himself at the court of Duke Ai, reporting to him, "This Chen Heng has assassinated his lord. I ask that you punish him."

---

[8] The actual passage is more elaborate; see Chapter 4 ("Tan Gong"); Legge 1967, vol. 1: 180–181.

The Duke replied, "Report it to the Three."

Before presenting himself before his lord, a minister must fast and ritually bathe. Confucius' initial comment is a case where different forms of reference matter enough to note: the narrator of this story refers to the new ruler of Qi by his posthumous title Chen Chengzi, but Confucius refers to him by his personal name Heng—i.e., as if he were not a ruler, which of course he has no right to be. This is an example of Confucius' care when it comes to "names." The "Three" referred to by Duke Ai are the heads of the Three Families, who of course wield the real power in Lu—a fact that Duke Ai does not even attempt to conceal.

Confucius said, "Having held rank below the ministers, I did not dare to not report this. Now my lord says, 'Report it to the Three.'" He then went and reported it to the Three, who did not approve his request. Confucius remarked, "Having held rank below the ministers, I did not dare to not report."

Chen Chengzi, personal name Heng, was a minister in Qi who assassinated Duke Jian in 481 B.C.E. and usurped the throne. The account of this event in the *Zuo Commentary* differs somewhat from the version presented here:

> On the day *jiawu*, Chen Heng of Qi murdered his lord Ren at Shuzhou. Confucius fasted for three days and then went to petition his lord to attack Qi. The Duke replied, "Lu has been weaker than Qi for a long time now. How, Sir, do you propose that we attack them?" Confucius replied, "Chen Heng murdered his lord, and has thereby lost the support of half of the population of Qi. This disaffected half of Qi, combined with the masses of Lu, could defeat the remaining half of Qi." The Duke replied, "Go report this to the Ji Family." Confucius declined to do so. Returning from court, he remarked to someone, "Having held rank below the ministers, I did not dare to not speak out."[9]

In the *Zuo Commentary* version, Confucius seems to have some hope of persuading the Duke with his pragmatic argument, and when he fails with the Duke knows better than to try to persuade the Ji Family, who probably admire Chen Heng for having the chutzpah to accomplish something that they themselves have no doubt considered. In the *Analects* version of the story, however, Confucius seems quite clear in advance that Duke Ai will evade his lordly duties and that the Three Familes will rebuff him. The point here seems to be that the rightful duty of a minister is to openly remonstrate with his lord (14.22), and Confucius performs this duty despite knowing that his advice will be ignored—he "knows that what he does is impossible and yet persists anyway" (14.38).

14.22 Zilu asked about serving one's lord.
The Master replied, "Do not deceive him. Oppose him openly."

This is a more general expression of the principle illustrated in 14.21: the duty of the loyal minister is to openly and consistently remind his lord of the demands of rightness (cf. 13.15, 13.23, 14.7). Confucius is contrasting this sort of public, principled opposition with surreptitious factionalism or undermining of one's lord, which is the sort of behavior expected only of the petty person. Cf. 2.14, 4.10.

---

[9] Duke Ai, Year 14 (482 B.C.E.); Legge 1991d: 840.

14.23 The Master said, "The gentleman understands higher things, whereas the petty person understands only the low."

Cf. 4.16 ("The gentleman understands rightness, whereas the petty person understands profit") and 14.35. An alternate rendering of *da* 達 ("understands") might be "attains" or "reaches through to."

14.24 The Master said, "In ancient times scholars learned for their own sake; these days they learn for the sake of others."

Kong Anguo and Huang Kan understand this in terms of the words versus actions dichotomy we have already seen several times. Kong explains, "Those who study for their own sake actually personally put it into practice, whereas those who do it for the sake of others are only able to talk about it." Huang elaborates:

> The ancients learned about those things in which they themselves did not yet excel. Thus, they would study the Way of the Former Kings, desiring thereby to personally put it into practice and perfect themselves, nothing more. People in Confucius' age, on the other hand, did not learn in order to remedy flaws in their own behavior, but rather with the sole purpose of lording it over others and having others praise them as excellent.

Reading this passage along with 4.2, 4.5, 4.9, 4.11–4.12, 4.16, 14.23, and 14.30, a related interpretation is to see the issue as one of motivation: the gentleman learns for the sake of his own improvement and out of love of the Way, whereas the petty person learns in order to acquire an official position and salary. This is how Xunzi understands it; after quoting 14.24, he adds: "The gentleman learns in order to improve himself, whereas the petty person uses learning like a ceremonial offering of birds and calves [i.e., to attract their superior's attention]."[10] Cf. 15.21.

14.25 Qu Boyu sent a messenger to Confucius. Confucius sat down beside him and asked, "How are things with your Master?"

The messenger replied, "My Master wishes to reduce his faults, but has not yet been able to do so."

After the messenger left, the Master said, "Now that is a messenger! That is a messenger!"

Qu Boyu was a virtuous minister in the state of Wei; he appears again in 15.6. He is also mentioned in the *Zuo Commentary* for 558 B.C.E. as a principled minister who leaves a state rather than participate in an uprising against his lord,[11] and must have been significantly older than Confucius. He also appears in the *Zhuangzi* and *Huainanzi*. The former text says that he "Qu Boyu has been going along for sixty years and has changed sixty times, and there has never been a case where he did not start out saying something was right and end up rejecting it as wrong,"[12] and the latter that "Qu Boyu, at age fifty, realized that he had been wrong for forty-nine

---

[10] Chapter 1 ("Encouraging Learning"); Knoblock 1988: 140. Also cf. the comparison of the "learning of the gentleman" and the "learning of the petty person" earlier in the same chapter (Knoblock 1988: 140).

[11] Duke Xiang, Year 14 (558 B.C.E.); Legge 1991d: 465.

[12] Chapter 25 ("Ze Yang"); Watson 1968: 288.

years." Commentators cite this as evidence that Qu Boyu was, indeed, someone who earnestly wished to reduce his faults, but never felt that he was done. Zhu Xi claims that Confucius stayed with Qu Boyu during his time in the state of Wei, and that this is why they remained in touch, but there is no independent evidence to support this. There are probably at least two points to this passage. First of all, Confucius approves of Qu Boyu's noble intentions and realistic evaluation of himself, indications of both an unflagging commitment to further self-improvement (especially impressive at Qu Boyu's age; cf. 8.7) and a commendable degree of modesty (cf. especially 14.20 and 14.27–14.29). The second point relates to the theme of knowing the character of others and properly employing people. Qu Boyu clearly knows how to find a messenger who can "engage in repartee" (13.5) and accurately represent the intentions of his master, while the messenger himself displays an admirable degree of perspicuity. As Huang Kan observes, "In saying, 'But he has not yet been able to do so,' the messenger shows that he has understood the mind of Boyu and is not deceived about his character."

14.26 The Master said, "Do not discuss matters of government policy that do not fall within the scope of your official duties."

Master Zeng added, "The gentleman's thoughts do not go beyond his office"

The first half of this passage is a repeat of 8.14; see that passage for commentary. Master Zeng's gloss may be a traditional saying, as it is also repeated more or less verbatim in the *Book of Changes*, in the "Image" commentary to the Hexagram 52 ("Keeping Still").

14.27 The Master said, "The gentleman is ashamed to have his words exceed his actions."

As Huang Kan explains, "The gentleman is the type of person who pays attention to his words and is careful about his behavior." Cf. 1.14, 2.13, 4.22, 4.24, 12.3, and 14.20.

14.28 The Master said, "The Way of the gentleman is threefold, and yet I have not been able to achieve any aspect of it: 'The Good do not worry, the wise are not confused, and the courageous do not fear.'"

Zigong replied, "[By quoting this saying], the Master has in fact described himself."

The description of the threefold Way of the gentleman here is a repeat of 9.29, and by the time of Book Fourteen may have become a commonly cited maxim in the Confucian school. The point of this more elaborate version seems to be to illustrate the Master's modesty or reluctance to boast, which fits in with the concerns expressed elsewhere in this Book (14.20, 14.27, 14.30) about one's words or reputation exceeding one's actual virtue or ability. The fact that even the Master does not presume to attribute these virtues to himself is probably meant as a warning to others not to be too complacent about their level of moral attainment; as Zhu Xi notes, "The Master here criticizes himself in order to urge on others." Zigong's comment seems tacked on to make it clear that the Master is merely being humble.

14.29 Zigong was given to criticizing others.

The Master remarked sarcastically, "What a worthy man that Zigong must be! As for me, I hardly have the time for this."

Despite the importance of being able to evaluate the character of others that has been stressed throughout this Book, one must not be too eager to pass judgment on others. As we saw immediately in 14.28, even the Master did not presume to declare himself a true gentleman or sage (cf. 7.34), and in that light Zigong's pretension to be an arbiter of virtue becomes even more absurd. This passage might also be compared to other passages where Zigong is criticized by Confucius for being too strict and judgmental with others—i.e., for not moderating his duty-defined demands on others with understanding. The translation follows Zheng Xuan, who reads *fang* 方 as equivalent to *bang* 謗 ("criticize, slander"). This is supported by 15.25 ("When it comes to other people, who should I criticize and who should I praise?"), and is how the passage is understood in the *Record of the Three Kingdoms*:

> Criticism and praise are the source of hatred and love, and the turning point of disaster or prosperity. Therefore, the sage is very careful about them. This is why Confucius said, [quotes 15.25 and 14.29]. If even with the Virtue of a sage Confucius was this reluctant to criticize others, how more reluctant should someone of moderate Virtue be to carelessly criticize and praise?

This is also how the passage is understood by Wu Kangzhai, who remarks, "If day and night I am ceaselessly toiling away at the task of self-examination, where will I find the time to examine others? If I focus my attention on criticizing others, then my efforts with regard to regulating myself will be lax. One cannot but be on guard against this fault!"

14.30 The Master said, "Do not worry that you are not recognized by others; worry rather that you yourself lack ability."

As Wang Kentang comments, "This is because having ability or not is something that lies within one's own control, whereas whether or not one is recognized is under the control of others." Cf. 1.16, 4.14, 15.19, 15.21.

14.31 The Master said, "Not anticipating betrayal, nor expecting untrustworthiness, yet still being the first to perceive it—this is a worthy person indeed."

The gentleman is trusting of others, and expects the best of them. As *Dai's Record* says, "The gentleman does not anticipate badness from others, nor does he suspect others of untrustworthiness." Li Chong sees this open attitude as the key to the gentleman's ability to educate others: "If you perceive an act of untrustworthiness in the beginning and then necessarily expect untrustworthiness in the future, this indicates an impairment of the merit of patient forbearance, and also blocks the road to repentance and change." Nonetheless, the gentleman is not a fool, and is the first to perceive when his trust has been misplaced. The point seems very similar to 6.26 ("the gentleman can be tricked, but not duped").

14.32 Weisheng Mou said to Confucius, "Qiu, what are you trying to accomplish with all this flitting around from perch to perch? Are you not merely showing off your glibness?"

Confucius replied, "I would not presume to be glib; it is just that I am very stubborn (*jigu* 疾固)."

Nothing is known of Weisheng Mou, but he addresses Confucius by his personal name, Qiu, which indicates that he is either very much Confucius' elder, or is deliberately trying to be rude—or possibly both. This is the first of the several encounters between Confucius and primitivist or Daoist-like recluses recorded in the *Analects*; cf. 14.38–14.39, 18.5–18.7. Weisheng Mou, who has presumably withdrawn from public life in disgust, mocks Confucius' travels from state to state in search of an official position as frivolous "flitting from perch to perch," and implies that Confucius' motive is personal vanity. Confucius' reply is quite modest and restrained, considering the shocking nature of the accusation. Bao Xian understands *ji* 疾 as a verb ("to consider to be a fault") and *gu* 固 in the sense of "crudeness," explaining that the point of the Master's reply is that Confucius "was troubled by the crudeness of his age, and wished to put the Way into practice in order to transform it." Cf. *Mencius* 3:B:9, where Mencius similarly defends his debating of rivals as a distasteful necessity if the world is to be saved from disorder. An alternate interpretation of Confucius' reply is provided by Zhu Xi, who takes *gu* as "rigid" or "stubborn" as in the translation, but follows Bao Xian in reading *ji* as a verb. Understood this way, the reply is a criticism of Weisheng Mou: "I am troubled by your rigidity"—i.e., at least I do not sit rigidly at home like yourself and do nothing. This fits with Confucius' criticisms of the overly "fastidious" elsewhere (5.19, 18.8), but, as Chen Tianxiang notes, such tit-for-tat bickering would be out of character for the Master: "Even though Mou is taking advantage of the reverence accorded to an elder in order to speak impudently to him, Confucius would still hold to the etiquette of treating an elder as an elder, and would therefore answer him sincerely, explaining that his itinerate lifestyle is motivated by a concern for the world." The sense in all of these cases, however, is much the same: Confucius is determined to do his best to fulfill his mission as the "bell-clapper of Heaven" (3.24), calling his fallen contemporaries back to the Way—despite his moments of weakness when he feels like throwing in the towel and going off into exile (5.7, 9.14); despite his occasional doubts that Heaven has abandoned him (9.9, 11.9) and that his work is doomed to failure (5.27, 14.38); and despite repeated failures and the mockery of his contemporaries (3.18, 14.35).

14.33 The Master said, "One does not praise a thoroughbred horse for its physical strength, but rather for its character (*de* 德)."

De (normally "Virtue") here has the more archaic sense of general inner character; as Zheng Xuan comments, "*De* here has the sense of balanced excellence." The character of the horse seems to be a metaphor for the inner Virtue of the gentlemanly minister. Jiang Xi explains, "Although the gentleman may have a variety of skills, he should be valued solely for his Virtue." Cf. 3.16.

14.34 Someone asked, "What do you think of the saying, 'Requite injury with kindness (*de* 德)'?"

The Master replied, "With what, then, would one requite kindness? Requite injury with uprightness, and kindness with kindness."

The initial quoted phrase appears in the *Laozi* (Chapter 63)—and Confucius' response to it is certainly anti-Laozian in flavor—but it was likely a traditional saying not necessarily identified with the *Laozi* itself. As He Yan notes, *de* here is used in the more archaic sense of "kindness," and it is possible that 14.33 and 14.34 were paired together because they both use *de* in something other than the standard Confucian sense. The point of 14.34 seems to be that order is brought about through proper discrimination. Each type of behavior has a response that is proper to it: injury should be met with sternness, whereas kindness is to be rewarded with kindness. Failure to discriminate in this way is an invitation to chaos; as Huang Kan notes, "The reason that one does not repay injury with kindness is that, were one to do so, then everyone in the world would begin behaving in an injurious fashion, expecting to be rewarded with kindness. This is the Way of inviting injury." For Confucius, being impartial or just (*gong* 公) means to discriminate properly, giving to each his due.

14.35 The Master sighed, "Alas! No one understands me."

Zigong replied, "How can you say that no one understands you, Master?"

"I am not bitter toward Heaven, nor do I blame others. I study what is below in order to comprehend what is above. If there is anyone who could understand me, perhaps it is Heaven."

Another comment on the Master's failure to find employment or official recognition (cf. 9.13), but the hint of bitterness is then tempered, perhaps in response to the injunction in 14.30 to "not worry that you are not recognized by others, but rather worry that you yourself lack ability." Confucius pursues that which lies within his own control—the study of the Way—and does so for his own self-improvement (14.24), consigning the vagaries of official recognition or attainment of office to fate. Kong Anguo understands that which is "below" as "human affairs," and that which is "above" as "knowing the Heavenly Mandate." Probably what is being described is similar to the progression found in 2.4, where learning and ritual lead to an understanding of Heaven and an wu-wei harmony with the Way of the Ancients. In the end, Confucius thus finds comfort in the thought that, though he is neglected by the rulers of his time, at least Heaven understands him.

14.36 Gongbo Liao submitted an accusation against Zilu to the head of the Ji Family. Zifu Jingbo reported this to Confucius, adding, "That master [i.e., Ji Kangzi] has certainly been led astray by Gongbo Liao, but my influence with him is still sufficient to see to it that Gongbo Liao's corpse is displayed at court or in the marketplace."

The Master said, "Whether or not the Way is to be put into action is a matter of fate. Whether or not the Way is to be discarded is also a matter of fate. What power does Gongbo Liao have to affect fate!"

Zilu was at this time presumably working as steward for the Ji Family. Zifu Jingbo, a minister in the state of Lu—Liu Baonan claims that he was a kinsman of the Meng Family—is claiming that he has enough influence with Ji Kangzi that he can both convince him of Zilu's innocence and see to it that his fellow minister, Gongbo Liao, is punished for his slander. The punishment in such a case of ministerial malfeasance would be public execution, after which, according to Zhou custom, the corpse would be displayed in public for three days. Confucius, sure of his correctness and the correctness of his disciple, sees no need for such machinations. The attitude expressed here is not so much passive fatalism as a surety in one's own rectitude and a confidence that Heaven's will shall be done (cf. 9.5). As Zhang Erqi comments,

That which is certain and cannot be evaded when it comes to the Way of human beings is rightness; that which is original and cannot be disputed when it comes to the Way of Heaven is fate. The fact that poverty, wealth, nobility, baseness, attainment, loss, life, death are all regulated and cannot be forced is the same, whether you are a gentleman or a petty person . . . The gentleman, by means of rightness, makes his peace with fate, and therefore his heart is always calm. The petty person, on the other hand, used cleverness and force in order to struggle against fate, and therefore his heart is always filled with resentment.

Some commentators identify both Gongbo Liao and Zifu Jingbo as disciples of Confucius, but this is unlikely.

14.37 The Master said, "Worthy people go into reclusion because the age itself is disordered; those next in worth withdraw because their state is disordered; next still are those who withdraw because of a discourteous expression on their ruler's face; and finally there are those who will withdraw at a single discourteous word."

This would seem to be another criticism of the excessively fastidious, which would accord with the passages immediately below concerning encounters with principled recluses. Reclusion wins the Master's approval only in extreme situations—when the entire world is disordered—and even then (as we see in 14.38–14.39) it seems that the true gentleman, such as Confucius, will continue to stick it out even in the face of impossible odds. Liu Baonan and Master Cheng argue that the progression described concerns not the moral worth of the person retiring, but rather the level of seriousness of the cause; in support of this interpretation, Liu points to *Mencius* 6:B:14, which enumerates three reasons a gentleman will resign his office and uses the same "next" (*ci* 次) locution. The grammar of 14.37, however, strongly favors the reading reflected in the translation.

The Master said, "Those who did so number seven."

This is an exceedingly cryptic statement that is probably out of place. Most commentators read it together with the statement above ("those who withdrew because the age itself was disordered numbered seven"), and there is some lively debate concerning who exactly these seven might be, but as Zhu Xi concludes, "There is no way to know who the people mentioned might be, and to insist upon trying to identify them in order to substantiate the Master's remark is simply to stretch things too far."

14.38 Zilu spent the night at Stone Gate. The next morning, the gatekeeper asked him, "Where have you come from?"
   Zilu answered, "From the house of Confucius."
   "Isn't he the one who knows that what he does is impossible and yet persists anyway?"

Most commentators believe the Stone Gate to be one of the outer gates of the capital of Lu, and explain that Zilu is returning from having traveled about with the Master in search of employment. The Lu gatekeeper may be a principled recluse,[13] or simply

---

[13] As was mentioned with regard to the border guard at Yi in the commentary to 3.24, disillusioned officials sometimes retired by withdrawing from active life and taking some minor post, such as gatekeeper, that would at least serve to feed their families.

an ordinary functionary, but in any case he shares the view of Weisheng Mou in 14.32 and the recluse in 14.39 that, confronted wherever he goes by indifferent or actively immoral rulers, Confucius should simply give up.

14.39 The Master was playing the stone chimes in the state of Wei.

A man with a wicker basket strapped to his back passed by the door of the Kong Family residence and remarked, "Whoever is playing the chimes like that certainly has something on his mind!" After listening for a moment, he added, "How despicable is this petty stubbornness! If no one understands you, just tend to yourself.

'If the river ford is deep, use the stepping-stones;

If it is shallow, simply raise your hem.'"

The Master [hearing these comments] responded, "Such resoluteness! Who could take issue with that!"

This event is possibly meant to have taken place during Confucius' sojourn in Wei after losing office in Lu (3.24). Confucius' critic is wearing a wicker basket strapped to his back—the sign of a farmer or manual laborer—and yet has an ear for classical music and can quote from the *Odes*. This would indicate that he is no ordinary commoner, but rather a scholar who has gone into reclusion, whether for philosophical or political reasons. Like the figures in 14.32 and 14.38, he is annoyed at Confucius' persistence in the face of an indifferent world, and advises him to simply accord with circumstances—as he himself has presumably done. The final comment of Confucius can be variously rendered. The interpretation adopted in the translation takes it to be sarcastic—recluses like this one are taking the easy way out, and their claim to merely be "according with the times" is mere rationalization; alternately, Yu Yue's understanding of *guo* 果 ("resolute") as *cheng* 誠 ("really, sincerely") makes Confucius' response somewhat softer and more wistful, though still ultimately disapproving: "Ah, truly that would be the easy way to go!" Cf. 8.7, 18.6 and 18.7.

14.40 Zizhang asked, "The *Book of Documents* says, 'Gaozong stayed in his mourning hut, and did not speak for three years.' What does this mean?"

Ritual dictates that, on the death of a parent, a son is to dwell in a crude mourning hut for "three years" (actually two years and one month—i.e., into the third year), clad in rough clothes, eating only plain food, and abstaining from normal pleasures. Gaozong is the posthumous title of the legendary Shang king Wuding, whose traditional dates are 1324–1264 B.C.E. The passage Zizhang quotes is transmitted in slightly different form in the extant *Book of Documents*: "When Gaozong ascended the throne, he took to the mourning shed, and did not speak for three years; afterward, he was still inclined not to speak, but when he did, his words were harmonious";[14] also see the more extended account of Wuding's mourning and silence in the beginning of the "Charge to Yue" chapter of the *Documents*.[15]

The Master replied, "We do not have to confine ourselves to Gaozong—all of the ancients were the same. When their lord passed away, for three years the

---

[14] Chapter 43 ("Against Luxurious Ease"); Legge 1991b: 466.
[15] Chapter 21 ("The Charge to Yue"); Legge 1991b: 248–251.

hundred officials would all see to their own tasks, under the direction of the Prime Minister."

Some commentators, such as Hu Anguo, understand Zizhang's doubt to be how the government could actually function if the new ruler did not perform his functions for three years, and see Confucius' answer as pragmatic: the government continued to function because the Prime Minister took over the supervision of the lesser officials. It is more likely, though, that Zizhang's incredulity is directed toward the length and severity of the mourning period itself, which was apparently viewed as impractical and was no longer being strictly observed in Confucius' time. See 17.21, as well as *Mencius* 3:A:2, where a crown prince of Teng—advised by Mencius to observe the three-year period—is opposed by counselors who claim that the practice has not been observed for generations. Of course, the crown prince ignores his counselors, goes to dwell in a mourning hut and refrains from issuing orders or prohibitions, and as a result wins the widespread admiration of both his officials and his populace. As Huang Kan notes, then, the point of this passage is not merely to put Zizhang's doubts about the *Book of Documents* passage to rest, but also to "serve as a goad to the people of his age." Read together with 14.41, the point is that, if rulers would just observe ritual in the proper fashion, the minor official and common people will be morally transformed and easily governed. As Wang Fuzhi comments,

> During the three-year mourning period, the heir is to dwell in difficult conditions and not engage in governing the state. As a son, if the Son of Heaven can merely give full expression to the heart of the human son, then the great ministers will serve as proper ministers, and will naturally hold fast to the regulations that govern their offices. Only when benevolence and filial piety are on the decline among superiors do we see dutifulness and honesty decrease among inferiors. Therefore, to continue to issue commands and hesitate to hand over the reins of power to one's great ministers when one should be mourning is, in fact, the fastest way to bring about the ruin of noble human relations.

14.41 The Master said, "If those above love ritual, then the common people will be easy to manage."

A general principle to complement 14.40 above. As the *Luxuriant Dew* says,

> In governing a state, there is no greater way to transform it than by reverencing the root. If he can reverence the root, a gentleman's transformative power will be like the spirits, whereas if he cannot reverence the root, he will have no means by which to bring people together. Without the means to bring people together, even harsh laws and heavy punishments will not induce the common people to be obedient.

The "root" mentioned here is, of course, ritual propriety; see 1.2. Cf. 12.17, 13.1, 13.4.

14.42 Zilu asked about the gentleman.
The Master said, "He cultivates himself in order to achieve respectfulness."
"Is that all?"
"He cultivates himself in order to bring peace to others."
"Is that all?"
"He cultivates himself in order to bring peace to all people. Cultivating oneself and thereby bringing peace to all people is something even a Yao or a Shun would find difficult."

Another statement on the importance of ritual propriety—the means by which one cultivates "respectfulness" (*jing* 敬)—for properly ruling the state, with the "gentleman" understood here as the gentleman-as-ruler. Liu Baonan understands "bringing peace to" (*an* 安) in the sense of setting in the proper place, i.e., bringing it about that both ministers and common people stay centered in their role-specific duties. Cf. 13.3, where Zilu is similarly dubious about the power of "rectifying names" to bring about political order, and is accordingly rebuked by Confucius.

14.43 Yuan Rang sat casually, with his legs sprawled out, waiting for Confucius. On seeing him, the Master remarked, "A young man devoid of humility and respect for his elders will grow into an adult who contributes nothing to his community. Growing older and older without the dignity to pass away, he becomes a burden on society." He then rapped him on the shin with his staff.

This rap on the shin with his staff is not intended as corporal punishment, but rather as an indication to Yuan Rang to correct his posture. The proper attitude for receiving a guest is the formal kneeling posture still practiced by the Japanese, sitting on the ankles with the legs folded underneath (10.25). Yuan Rang was apparently sitting in a more comfortable, but shockingly casual, posture: most likely sitting directly on the floor with his legs stretched out or loosely folded in front of him. As in 14.44, this sort of ritual impropriety on the part of a young person is seen by Confucius as boding ill for their future development; cf. 1.2. Some commentators (including Huang Kan and Zhu Xi) see Yuan Rang not as a young acquaintance of Confucius, but rather as an old friend and Daoist free-spirit, no doubt inspired by a *Record of Ritual* account of a rather strange interaction between the two:

There was an old acquaintance of Confucius named Yuan Rang. When his mother died, the Master assisted him in preparing the outer coffin. Yuan then climbed up on the wood and declared, "It has been a long time, indeed, since I have indulged myself in song." He then began singing, "Speckled like a bobcat's head, smooth as the grasped hand of a young maiden!"[16] The Master made as if he did not hear and went away. His followers then asked him, "Could you not, then, have put a stop to it?" The Master said, "I have heard it said that you can never stop treating relatives as relatives, nor treating old friends like old friends."[17]

This *Record of Ritual* story, as well as Huang Kan's characterization of Yuan Rang as a sage "from outside the realm of men," are probably based on stories from the *Zhuangzi* of eccentric Daoist masters singing at the funeral of their friend, or Zhuangzi himself pounding on a tub and singing after the death of his wife,[18] and are therefore likely anachronistic.

14.44 A boy from the Que district came bearing a message to Confucius. Someone asked Confucius about him, saying, "Is this someone who is likely to improve himself?"

---

[16] The lyrics of Yuan Rang's shockingly outlandish song are probably meant to describe the wood out of which the coffin was being made.

[17] Chapter 4 ("Tan Gong"); Legge 1967, vol. 1: 198–199.

[18] For the former story, see Watson 1968: 86–87; for the latter story, 191–192.

According to most commentators, Que was a district of the suburbs just outside one of the gates of Qufu, Confucius' home town. The bearing of messages was a fairly complex ritual task, normally born by adults. Confucius' unnamed interlocutor is impressed by this precocious boy, and expects Confucius to share his admiration.

The Master replied, "I observed him sitting in the presence of adults, and also walking alongside his elders. He is not looking to improve himself, but is just after quick success."

As we read in 13.17, those who "crave speed will never arrive." Brooks and Brooks describe this passage as "another vignette of cultural decline in the young; not a desire to improve oneself by associating with his moral superiors, but an eagerness to get ahead by hanging around the powerful" (1998: 169). In his desire for quick success, this young boy arrogantly flouts the dictates of ritual propriety, which require that boys stand while in the presence of adults, and that juniors walk behind their elders. Again, such a lack of deference to elders and ritual respect in a young person will lead to nothing but trouble. Both 14.43 and 14.44 document disturbing signs of ritual carelessness among the youth of Confucius' age.

BOOK FIFTEEN

Like Book Seventeen, this Book is a lengthy collection of generally short passages without any clear unifying theme.

15.1 Duke Ling of Wei asked Confucius about military formations (*chen* 陳).

Confucius replied, "I know something about the arrangement of ceremonial stands and dishes for ritual offerings, but I have never learned about the arrangement of battalions and divisions."

He left the next day.

Confucius is playing on the word *chen*, which is both a noun referring to military formations and a verb meaning "to arrange" or "set out," often with reference to ritual vessels. The point, of course, is that the true ruler causes his state to prosper by means of Virtue rather than military force. Some commentators read 15.1 and 15.2 as one passage, arguing that the troubles in Chen described in 15.2 occurred after Confucius left Wei because of his conversation with Duke Ling, but there is no compelling reason to read the passages together.

15.2 [When Confucius was besieged] in the state of Chen, all of the provisions were exhausted, and his followers were so weak from hunger that they could not even stand. Upset, Zilu appeared before the Master and said, "Does even the gentleman encounter hardship?"

The Master said, "Of course the gentleman encounters hardship. The difference is that the petty man, encountering hardship, is overwhelmed by it."

As Huang Shisan observes, the point of this passage is that "it is only in adversity that the gentleman reveals himself. 'A fierce blaze or intense fire only adds to the luster of gold'—how true is this proverb!" Besides the oblique reference in 11.2, this is the only appearance of this incident in the *Analects*, but it was a very popular story in later Warring States texts.

15.3 The Master said, "Zigong! Do you take me to be one who has come to understand through learning a wide variety of things?"

Zigong responded, "Yes. Is this not the case?"

"It is not. I bind it all together with a single thread."

An entire book on Confucian hermeneutics could be dedicated solely to a discussion of the various interpretations of this alternate version of 4.15. As mentioned in the commentary to 4.15, many have taken the "single thread" to be an abstract, theoretical principle behind everything the Master teaches and everything that he does. He Yan, for instance, comments:

All of the various roads in the world lead to the same place, and all of the m~ one might have come to the same conclusion. Know the origin of things, and the~ excellences will be mastered. Therefore, it is not necessary to learn a wide vari~ in order to understand the one [underlying principle].

As Jiao Xun notes, however, He Yan's idea of an underlying theoretical uni~ of a neo-Daoist than early Confucian theme, and argues that 4.15 makes it c~ ~at the "single thread" refers to a way of acting in the world: being "dutiful and under-standing (*zhongshu* 忠恕)" or, as Jiao glosses it, "perfecting oneself in order to perfect others." Cf. 15.24, where the "single saying" that can be a guide for one's entire life is identified as sympathetic understanding. Liu Baonan also sees the point of this passage to be emphasizing the importance of actual virtuous conduct rather than theoretical unity:

> The Master has previously said, 'The gentleman is broadly learned with regard to culture" [6.27] and has also described himself as one who "silently comprehends it" [7.2]. Thus, the Master does value understanding it through learning a wide variety of things, and this is why Zigong answers the way he does. However, the Master also says, "There is no one who is my equal when it comes to cultural refinement, but as for actually becoming a gentleman in prac-tice, this is something that I have not yet been able to achieve" [7.33], which shows that conduct or practice is the particular focus of the teaching of the sage. The "Doctrine of the Mean" says, "Broadly learn it, carefully inquire about it, sedulously ponder it, clearly analyze it, and then sincerely put it into practice."[1] Here, "learning, inquiring, pondering, and analyzing" corre-spond to "understanding it through learning a wide variety of things," and "sincerely put it into practice" corresponds to "tying it all together on a single thread" . . . The point is the efficacy of being able to put learning into practice. If one is not able to do this, it is like being a person who can "recite the many odes by heart but, when delegated a governmental task, is unable to carry it out or, when sent out into the field as an envoy, is unable to engage in repartee. No matter how many odes he might have memorized, what good are they to him?" [13.5] When it comes to putting it into practice, nothing more is needed than dutifulness and understanding, and thus this passage and 4.15 can serve to illustrate one another.

15.4 The Master said, "Zilu! Rare are those able to understand Virtue."

One line of interpretation follows Huang Kan is seeing this as a general statement about the moral quality of Confucius' contemporaries, similar in both syntax and theme to 6.29. Alternately, some follow Wang Su in seeing this as a continuation of 15.2, as thus more specifically inspired by Zilu's complaint during the troubles in Chen.

15.5 The Master said, "Is Shun not an example of someone who ruled by means of wu-wei? What did he do? He made himself reverent and took his proper [ritual] position facing south, that is all."

Although the concept of wu-wei, or "effortless action," can be found throughout the *Analects*, this is the only place in the text where the term "wu-wei" appears. There are two distinct lines of interpretation concerning what it would mean to rule by means of wu-wei. One, beginning with He Yan, understands this passage to be referring to what we might be called "institutional wu-wei." Under this interpretation, "wu-wei" is to be understood more in its literal sense of "doing nothing," the point being that, if the ruler can fill his ministerial posts with able people and effectively set the machinery of gov-

---

[1] *Record of Ritual*, Chapter 31; Legge 1967, vol. 2: 318.

ernment in motion, the state will more or less run itself, without any need for action on the part of the ruler himself. As He Yan puts it, "The point is that if you fill your posts with the right people, you can 'do nothing' and yet the state will be governed." This interpretation of 15.5 accords with some of the passages in Book Fourteen that emphasize the importance of employing the right people. Considering the general drift of the *Analects*, however, it is far more likely that ruling by wu-wei refers to ruling by means of Virtue: the ruler morally perfects himself and thereby effortlessly transforms everyone around him. "Wu-wei" in this sense is thus not meant literally ("doing nothing"), the point rather being that one does not force anything or attempt consciously to achieve results—one simply "follows the desires of the heart" (2.4) and everything else falls into place. As Wang Fuzhi explains in his commentary on 15.5,

> Shun's wu-wei is similar to Confucius' not innovating [7.1]: in both cases, the point is that one follows along with the times and thus utilizes them effectively, thereby gradually accumulating one's achievements. "Making oneself reverent" refers to cultivating Virtue within oneself; "taking one's position facing South" refers to allowing one's regulating force to be applied to the common people. All of this refers to the constant Way of the ruler, and cannot really be spoken of as "doing" anything in particular.

This idea of "ruling by not ruling"—concentrating on self-cultivation and inner Virtue and allowing external things to come naturally and noncoercively—has been a constant theme throughout the *Analects*, but cf. especially 1.12, 2.19–2.21, 12.17–12.19, and 13.6. Zhu Xi somewhat bridges the two different interpretations with his observation that "ruling by means of wu-wei refers to the sage accumulating Virtue and thereby transforming the common people, so that there is no need to wait for him to actually do anything in particular . . . Moreover, in this way he also attracts the right people to fill the various offices, which makes it even less likely that one will see traces of the ruler's actions."

15.6 Zizhang asked about getting by in the world (*xing* 行).

Although the basic meaning of *xing* is "conduct," "practice," or "behavior," the context of the passage makes it clear that Zizhang is asking about *successfully* conducting oneself in the world—i.e., making progress, getting ahead, or getting along with others.

The Master replied, "In your speech, be dutiful and trustworthy, and in your conduct be sincere and respectful. In this way, you will always get by in the world, even if you find yourself in some barbarian state. If your words are not dutiful and trustworthy, and your conduct is not sincere and respectful, how can you possibly get along, even in your own region? When standing still, visualize these principles standing by your side; when riding in your carriage, see them resting before you on the crossbar. Only then will you get by in the world."
Zizhang then wrote these words on the end of his sash.

Zhu Xi is probably correct in seeing this as similar to Zizhang's earlier question in 12.20 about being "accomplished"—in both cases, Zizhang asks about a kind of external success in the world, and Confucius then directs his attention inward, toward his own behavior. As Zhu explains, the Master's advice is to "always keep your mind upon dutifulness, trustworthiness, sincerity, and respectfulness, never forgetting them for an instant; wherever you are, imagine them being present with you, as if you could see them. In this way, even if you want to depart from them for a moment, you will be unable to do so." In order to help himself in this task of constant visualization, Zizhang writes the Master's words (or, perhaps, merely the names of the virtues themselves) on the dangling end of his sash so that they will always—and literally—be in his sight.

15.7 The Master said, "How upright was Historian Yu! When the state possessed the Way, he was straight as an arrow, and when the state lacked the Way, he was also straight as an arrow. What a gentleman was Qu Boyu! When the state possessed the Way, he served it; when the state lacked the Way, he was able to roll up his talents and hide them away."

Both of the figures mentioned were ministers in Wei. Historian Yu was famous for his unbending uprightness, illustrated in the story of his death related in many early texts, including a version in the *Exoteric Commentary*. About to expire, he laments to his sons that during his life he has failed to rectify his lord by getting the virtuous Qu Boyu promoted and wicked Mi Zixia demoted, and insists that they give him a humble burial because of this failure. The Duke of Wei comes to the funeral and notices the humble arrangements, and when told the reason for them feels so ashamed that he immediately promotes Qu Boyu and dismisses Mi Zixia. Scribe Yu is thus famous for "having remonstrated with his lord by means of his corpse."[2] There is more commentarial debate concerning the nature of Qu Boyu's achievements. The most plausible way to understand Confucius' description of him is to accept the *Zuo Commentary* report that he resigned his post and left Wei in 559 B.C.E. because of the excesses of Duke Xian, but then returned to serve under Duke Ling, as we have seen in 14.25. Stories in the *Huainanzi*, *Garden of Persuasions*, and *Biographies of Exemplary Women* tell how his virtue and sedulous observance of ritual helped to both morally educate Duke Ling and dissuade other states from attempting to invade Wei. Commentators are generally in agreement that Qu Boyu draws higher praise than Historian Yu because his behavior was more flexible, as befits a gentleman. As Bao Xian remarks, "He was gentle and accommodating, and not recalcitrant with others."

15.8 The Master said, "If someone is open to what you have to say, but you do not speak to them, this is letting the person go to waste; if, however, someone is not open to what you have to say, but you speak to them anyway, this is letting your words go to waste. The wise person does not let people go to waste, but he also does not waste his words."

Part of wisdom is knowing how to adapt one's words to the situation. As Lu Shanji comments, "Both of the faults mentioned have the same root: not knowing others. Knowing others is what the wise person is able to do." Cf. 16.6.

15.9 The Master said, "No scholar-official of noble intention or Good person would ever pursue life at the expense of Goodness, and in fact some may be called upon to give up their lives in order to fulfill Goodness."

As Kong Anguo remarks, the point is that "the scholar-official of noble intention and the Good person do not overly cherish their own lives." An alternate version of Con-

---

[2] Chapter 7.21; Hightower 1952: 245–246.

fucius' statements is found in *Mencius* 3:B:1 and 5:B:7, which recount a story from the *Zuo Commentary* where a gamekeeper risks death by refusing to answer a ritually-improper summons from his lord, and then quote Confucius as remarking, "The scholar-official of noble intention never forgets that he may end up in a roadside ditch, and the courageous scholar-official never forgets that he may lose his head." The idea is that the true devotee of the Confucian Way values it over life itself. This is not to say that such a person is foolhardy or suicidal, merely that, for him, issues of rightness take precedence over self-preservation. As we read in *Mencius* 6:A:10,

> Fish is something that I desire; bear's paw [a rare delicacy] is also something that I desire. If it is not possible to obtain both at the same time, I would give up the fish and take the bear's paw. Life is something that I desire; rightness is also something that I desire. If it is not possible to obtain both at the same time, I would give up life and take rightness. This is because, although life is something that I desire, there are things that I desire more than life. Therefore, life is not something that I seek to preserve at any cost. Death is something that I hate, and yet there are things that I hate even more than death. This is why there are troubles that I do not choose to avoid.

The *Mencius* passage is targeted at the self-preservationist school exemplified by Yang Zhu, and it is possible that 15.9 has a similar target.

15.10 Zigong asked about becoming Good.

The Master said, "Any craftsman who wishes to do his job well must first sharpen his tools. In the same way, when living in a given state, one must serve those ministers who are worthy and befriend those scholar-officials who are Good."

> Most commentators see this passage as concerned with the refinement of native substance. As Huang Kan remarks, "The point is that, despite his talent, a skilled craftsman cannot create a skillful product if his tools are not sharp . . . In the same way, even if a person has worthy talent and fine native substance, when he dwells in a given state his conduct cannot be perfected unless he serves worthy men and befriends those who are Good." For the importance of friends as helpmates in becoming Good, cf. 12.24 and 16.4.

15.11 Yan Hui asked about running a state.

The Master said, "Follow the calendar of the Xia, travel in the carriages of the Shang, and clothe yourself in the ceremonial caps of the Zhou.

> The calendar of the Xia—which was in fact something like a combination calendar and almanac, providing instructions for what to do at various points in the year—began the year in the spring, and was apparently well adapted to the cycles of the seasons and the needs of farmers. The state carriage of the Shang, according to commentators, was stately but relatively unadorned, while the ceremonial cap of the Zhou was elegant and practical; according to Bao Xian, it shielded both the eyes and ears, making it easier to resist distractions and concentrate upon ritual. Both the Shang carriage and Zhou cap thus realized the perfect harmony of form and function without being overly ostentatious. A slightly different interpretation of the carriage and cap is offered by Zhu Xi: the Shang carriage, being an everyday item, exemplified the simplicity of native substance, whereas the Zhou cap, being a special ritual item, represented the flourishing of cultural refinement.

"As for music, listen only to the Shao and Wu. Prohibit the tunes of Zheng, and keep glib people at a distance—for the tunes of Zheng are licentious, and glib people are dangerous."

The Shao and Wu, as we saw in 3.25 and 7.14, represent the best of classical, properly formed music, in contrast to the licentious, seductive popular music of Zheng that was the rage among Confucius' contemporaries. The lyrics of the Zheng music were somewhat racy,[3] and although little is known about the exact nature of the music, commentators assert that it had a simple but catchy beat, was sung by mixed groups of men and women, and gave rise to sexual improprieties—all of which should sound very familiar to concerned parents of any nation or age. As Waley notes,

> Toward classical music, the "music of the former kings" (*Mencius* 1:B:1), ordinary as opposed to serious-minded people had the same feelings as they have towards our own classical music today. "How is it," the Prince of Wei asked Zixia, "that when I sit listening to old music, dressed in my full ceremonial gear, I am all the time in terror of dropping off asleep; whereas when I listen to the tunes of Zheng and Wei, I never feel the least tired?"[4]

Like moralists of our own age, early Confucians were very concerned about the effect of music on people's dispositions, and properly regulating music was seen as a crucial part of ordering the state. Similarly, the quality of a state's music could be used as a diagnostic tool. As the *Record of Ritual* says,

> When an age is disordered, ritual practices become corrupt and music becomes licentious. This is why its tunes are sorrowful without being dignified, ebullient without being peaceful, arrogant and casual in transgressing traditional restraints, recklessly indulgent and forgetting the basics. Such tunes are lax in accommodating vice, and narrow in encouraging selfish desires. They confuse otherwise clear and ordered dispositions, and destroy balanced and harmonious Virtue. This is why the gentleman despises them.[5]

For more on Confucian education and music, cf. 8.8 and 9.15. The tunes of Zheng were seen as counterfeits of true music, just as glib speakers were viewed as counterfeits of genuinely virtuous people. The two are mentioned together because the danger they represent is similar: because of their surface appeal, both can easily lead people astray, and this is why someone wishing to order a state must carefully prevent either one from taking hold. As Kong Anguo remarks, "Both the tunes of Zheng and glib people have the power to move people's hearts, the same sort of power possessed by classical music and worthy men. In the former case, however, this power causes people to fall into licentious disorder and imperils the state, which is why the two things must be gotten rid of and kept at a distance." A very similar point in made in 17.18, where Zheng music and glib people are condemned along with flashy new colors for corrupting traditional standards and leading to disorder.

15.12 The Master said, "A person without concern for what is far away is sure to encounter worries close at hand."

---

[3] Refer to the *Book of Odes*, "Airs of Zheng" (numbers 75–95).

[4] Waley 1989: 250; the citation is from the *Record of Ritual*, Chapter 19 ("Record of Music"); Legge 1967, vol. 2: 116–177. In his response to the prince, Zixia defends the salutary effects of ancient music, condemns the bizarre excesses of the new music, and concludes by reproving the prince for his taste with words that should sound familiar to any curmudgeon fed up with the latest musical fad: "what you just asked about, Sir, was music, but what you happen to like is mere sound."

[5] Chapter 19 ("Record of Music"); Legge 1967, vol. 2: 109.

A note on the importance of forethought. As Huang Kan comments, "In life one should think about that which is gradual and be concerned with that which is distant, in order to guard against things before they happen. In this way, worries and troubles can be kept away."

15.13 The Master said, "I should just give up! I have yet to meet a man who loves Virtue as much as female beauty."

This is a slightly modified repeat of 9.18, with an added note of frustration. See 9.18 for commentary, and cf. 9.24.

15.14 The Master said, "As for Zang Wenzhong, was he not a thief of official positions? He was aware of Liuxia Hui's worthiness, and yet would not have him as a colleague."

We have already seen Zang Wenzhong, formerly a minister in Lu, criticized for his ritual excesses in 5.18. Here he is condemned for having failed to officially recognize Zhan Qin, a virtuous minister in Lu, posthumously known as "Liuxia Hui"—either a single pseudonym (lit. "benevolence under the willow tree"), or a combination of the name of his country estate, Liuxia ("under the willows"), with the posthumous name Hui ("benevolence"). Zang Wenzhong was formerly Minister of Justice in Lu, and was apparently jealous of Liuxia Hui's talents; for more on Liuxia, see 18.2 and 18.8. In the *Zuo Commentary*, Confucius claims that Zang Wenzhong not only failed to recognize Liuxia Hui, but actually demoted him, and this failure is cited there as evidence of Zang's "lack of Goodness."[6] Fan Ziyu comments, "Zang Wenzhong participated in the governing of Lu. If he did not recognize worthiness, this would represent a simple lack of perceptiveness, but to recognize worthiness and then not to raise it up is to actively conceal worthiness. Being unperceptive is a relatively minor crime, but actively concealing worthiness is a serious crime, and this is why Confucius declared that Zang was 'not Good' and moreover called him a 'robber of official position.'"

15.15 The Master said, "Demand much of yourself, but ask little of others, and you will keep resentment at a distance."

A related passage in the *Annals of Lü Buwei* is put in terms of advice for a ruler:

Therefore, the gentleman's demands upon others are determined by the other's abilities, whereas his demands upon himself are determined by the standard of rightness. If your demands upon others are determined by their abilities, they will be easy to satisfy, and if your demands are easy to satisfy, you will win over people. If your demands upon yourself are determined by rightness then it will be difficult for you to do wrong, and if it is difficult for you to do wrong then your conduct will be refined. In this way you can easily take responsibility for the whole world and still have energy to spare. Unworthy people are not this way: they demand rightness from others, and demand from themselves what anyone can attain. When you demand rightness from others, your demands are difficult to meet, and when your demands are difficult to meet you alienate others. When you demand from yourself what anyone can attain, it is easy to do as you wish, and when it is easy to do as you wish, conduct becomes careless. In this way, you become not equal to the great task of ruling the world, and therefore both endangers your own life and bring ruin to the state.[7]

---

[6] Duke Wen, Year 2 (624 B.C.E.); Legge 1991d: 284.

[7] Chapter 19.8 ("The Difficulties of Making Promotions"); Knoblock and Riegel 2000: 505.

As advice for personal self-cultivation, the point is, as Wu Tingdong remarks, that "learning is carried on with regard to oneself only—if you are sincere and strict in regulating yourself, when would you have the time to make demands upon others?" Cf. 4.17, 14.29.

15.16 The Master said, "I have never been able to do anything for a person who is not himself constantly asking, 'What should I do? What should I do?'"

The translation follows Zhu Xi, but the Han commentators read it rather differently, along the lines of, "One might say, 'What can be done? What can be done?', but there is now nothing that I can do." Li Chong, for instance, comments that "one must make plans to deal with problems before they have manifested themselves, and regulate situations before they have become disordered. Therefore, what use is it to wait until one is faced with difficulties and only then say, 'What can be done?'" 15.12 might be cited as support for this interpretation, but it requires reading the text in a somewhat awkward fashion, and Zhu Xi's interpretation is confirmed by an alternate transmission of this passage found in the *Luxuriant Dew*. The point is one that we have seen before: the Master cannot teach someone who is not driven by a need to learn, and he cannot impart the Way to someone who does not, at some level, already love it. This accounts for the frustration expressed above in 15.13: there is nothing the Master can do with someone who loves female beauty more than Virtue. Cf. 5.10 and 7.8.

15.17 The Master said, "People who can spend an entire day together indulging their predilection for petty cleverness, without their conversation ever once touching upon rightness—these are hard cases indeed!"

Here pettiness among a group of people is portrayed as self-reinforcing, a situation we are probably meant to contrast with 15.10, where friendship among the virtuous helps each to "sharpen their tools." As Liu Baonan comments, "this passage is meant as a warning for Confucius' school . . . his point is that a group of people spending the day together should 'cut and polish' [1.15] each other with excellence, rather than delude or lead each other astray with unrighteousness or petty cleverness." Legge observes that there are various ways to take the Master's final statement about these petty people. He Yan takes it to mean that it will be difficult for people like this to succeed: "In the end, they will have achieved nothing." Zhu Xi takes it to mean that such people will meet with difficulties because of their inability to cultivate Virtue. In either case, the sense is quite similar, and the Legge's solution of going with the more literal "hard cases" seems most felicitous; cf. 17.22. Reading this passage with 15.16, we might also remark that this sort of person—entirely unconcerned with matters of rightness—is not the type to ask, "What should I do? What should I do?"

15.18 The Master said, "The gentleman takes rightness as his substance, puts it into practice by means of ritual, gives it expression through modesty, and perfects it by being trustworthy. Now that is a gentleman!"

As in 6.18, the gentleman is portrayed as the balanced product of native substance refined by cultural refinement, with both elements portrayed as crucial. As Xia Xichou observes, "The first level [rightness, substance] is the marrow—without it, one would become one of those types who associates with and participates in the corruption of the village worthy [17.12]. Without the second level [cultural refinement], however, one would possess the fault of excessive bluntness, or would fall into the trap of becoming like the excessively fastidious. This emphasis on both is why the teaching of the sage is comprehensive, balanced, and free of flaws." The focus on rightness also sets up an implicit contrast between the gentleman, who focuses on goods internal to Confucian practice such as rightness, and the petty person, who focuses on externalities. As Wang Yangming remarks, "it is only the gentleman who takes rightness as his substance, in the same way that the petty person takes profit as his substance [4.16]. When one takes profit as one's substance, one loses entirely the fundamentals of character. Then selfish desires take over the heart and become the ruler of the self; the eyes and ears, hands and feet all become the slave of these desires; and all of one's movements, words, and actions are subject only to their command."

15.19 The Master said, "The gentleman is distressed by his own inability, rather than the failure of others to recognize him.

This is almost identical to 14.30; cf. 1.16, 4.14, and 15.21.

15.20 The Master said, "The gentleman is troubled by the possibility that his name will go uncelebrated after his death."

Waley sees this statement as contradicting 15.19, but in fact the two are complementary. Despite Confucius' suspicion of current reputation and his disdain for the judgments of his contemporaries, he did possess a fundamentally optimistic view that virtue *will* eventually be recognized, at least by history. As Gu Yanwu remarks, "The ancients sought posthumous fame, whereas people today are after contemporary fame." For Confucius' belief that he would eventually be vindicated despite his present obscurity, see 14.35. 15.20 also occurs in a *Record of the Historian* account of Confucius where his confidence is seen to waver: "The Master said, 'It's no good, no good! The gentleman is troubled by the possibility that his name will go uncelebrated after his death. My Way is not being put into practice [5.7], so how will I manage to be recognized by later generations?" This account then goes on to explain that the desire for posthumous recognition is what motivated Confucius to compose the *Annals*. The belief that one's true character would be remembered by later generations can thus serve as a spur toward self-cultivation. As Wang Kentang observes:

> The gentleman is not distressed that he will not be famous, but rather that he will lack the substance [that would inspire fame]; he is not distressed by the fact that others fail to recognize him, but rather that he himself has nothing worth recognizing. If we pursue this line of thinking, it becomes clear that, before one passes from this world, one must not cease for an instant to anxiously strive to complete this substance. Therefore, this statement by the Master is intended to encourage people to pursue self-cultivation while there is still time.

Cf. 9.23.

15.21 The Master said, "The gentleman seeks it in himself; the petty person seeks it in others."

This passage is very similar to 14.24. He Yan also links it to 15.15: "The gentleman makes demands upon himself; the petty person makes demands upon others." As Yang Shi observes, 15.19–15.21 seem to constitute a set:

> Although the gentleman is not distressed that others fail to recognize him, he is nonetheless distressed by the possibility that his name will not be celebrated after he dies. Although he

is distressed by the possibility that his name will not be celebrated after he dies, the means by which he seeks [to be worthy of being known] is simply to look within himself and nothing more. The petty person seeks for it in others, and this is why there is no extreme of violating the Way that he will not go to in the pursuit of reward and praise. Although the text of these three passages are not identical, their basic sense is in fact very complementary, and this was no doubt the intention of the editors.

15.22 The Master said, "The gentleman is proud, but not competitive. He is sociable, but not partisan."

For the first half of this statement, cf. 3.7. Kong Anguo connects the second half to 4.10: "Although the gentleman associates with others, he does not conspire with them for personal gain, but rather is simply on the side of what is right." Jiang Xi adds, "The gentleman associates with others by means of the Way. Associating with others, he is inevitably sociable, and this may appear like partisanship. However, he is in fact sociable with others in order to 'cut and polish' himself and perfect his Virtue, rather than to achieve some selfish end." Cf. 2.14.

15.23 The Master said, "The gentleman does not promote someone solely based upon their words, nor does he dismiss words simply on account of the person who uttered them."

The first half of this saying seems to relate to the suspicion of glibness we have seen so many times before; as Bao Xian comments, "Someone who speaks well does not necessarily possess Virtue [14.4], which is why you cannot promote a person based solely upon the basis of their words." There is some debate about the exact sense of the second half. Wang Su interprets it to mean that "one should not ignore excellent words simply because they were uttered by someone devoid of Virtue," whereas Li Chong sees it as an injunction to listen to one's social inferiors: "one should not be ashamed to ask advice of one's inferiors." The latter interpretation is supported by 5.15.

15.24 Zigong asked, "Is there one word that can serve as a guide for one's entire life?"

The Master answered, "Is it not 'understanding' (*shu* 恕)? Do not impose upon others what you yourself do not desire."

This is an alternate version of 4.15, which identifies the "single thread" that unifies the Master's teaching as dutifulness coupled with understanding. It is probable that dutifulness is dropped in 15.24 not only because Zigong asked for "one word," but also because Zigong already possesses dutifulness to a fault, and in fact needs to learn how to moderate it with understanding (cf. 5.4 and 5.12). This passage can also be seen as a continuation of 15.3: the Master actually identifies his "single thread" to Zigong. A passage from the *Exoteric Commentary* clarifies how understanding in the person of the ruler might function:

> The fact that you yourself hate hunger and cold allows you to understand that everyone in the world desires food and clothing. The fact that you yourself hate labor and bitter exertion allows you to understand that everyone in the world desires rest and ease. The fact that you yourself hate poverty and deprivation allows you to understand that everyone in the world desires prosperity and sufficiency. Knowing these three things, the sagely king can order the

world without ever having to descend from his seat. Thus, 'the Way of the gentleman is none other than dutifulness and understanding, that is all' [4.15].[8]

For more on understanding and the "negative Golden Rule," cf. 6.30 and 12.2.

15.25 The Master said, "When it comes to other people, whom have I condemned? Whom have I praised? If I have praised someone, you can be sure it is because they have been put to the test. The common people today are the same people who allowed the Three Dynasties to put the upright Way into practice."

> The "Three Dynasties" refers to the Xia, Shang, and Zhou. There is some debate over how to understand this passage, with Chen Tianxiang, Zhang Zai, and others arguing that the last sentence should be read as a separate passage. In any case, the first half seem related to 14.29, where Confucius obliquely criticizes Zigong for being overly eager to evaluate the character of others; in this sense, 15.25 might be paired with 15.24 as joint warnings to Zigong to be more understanding in his dealings with others. We might also read the first half of the passage together with 15.20: only one's posthumous reputation is accurate, because only after one's life work is complete can one be said to have been "put to the test." The absence of a clear section break in the original text, however, suggests that we should read the last sentence together with the ones that precede it. The best way to make sense of the passage as a whole is to follow the interpretation of Liu Baonan and Bao Shenyan, who see the effect of the ruler upon his people as the "test" of the ruler's character. Liu quotes *Balanced Discourses* in support of his reading:

>> The *History of the Han* says, "Under Yao and Shun, every single person among the common people was worthy of being promoted, whereas under Jie and Zhow every single person was worthy of being punished." [The *Analects* says,] "The common people today are the same people who allowed the Three Dynasties to put the upright Way into practice." The fact that the people under a sagely ruler are one way, and under a bad ruler are another, is due to the effect of moral transformative influence, rather than to differences in inborn nature.

> Thus, the behavior of the common people can be used as a standard for condemnation or praise, because it serves to reflect the moral character of the ruler. An implication of this is that Confucius withholds his praise from the rulers of his time because of the low moral character of his contemporaries. Seeing 15.25 as a criticism of Confucius' age also links it to 15.26.

15.26 The Master said, "I once knew a time when scribes [who did not know how to write a word] would leave the text blank, and those who owned horses [that they could not tame themselves] would lend them to others. Nowadays, there is no one like this."

> The words in brackets have been added to make sense of the passage, in accordance with the interpretation of commentators, who generally follow Bao Xian:

>> In ancient times, when a fine scribe had doubts about how to write a word, he would leave it blank until he had time to consult someone who knew. In the same way, someone who owned horses, but could not manage to adequately tame them, would lend them to others in order to be driven and trained. Confucius says that he himself once knew people like this, but that nowadays there was no one like this left. The point of this remark is to expose the habit of offering dubious explanations [prevalent among his contemporaries].

---

[8]Chapter 3.38; Hightower 1952: 123.

The primary point seems to be that Confucius' contemporaries lack humility, and gloss over their shortcomings (19.8) instead of acknowledging and asking for help in correcting them (1.8, 7.22, 15.30). Huang Kan also sees it as a complaint concerning the desire for fast results, "Confucius here laments the fast-paced disorder of his age . . . in his later years, it was the case that a scribe who did know a word would arbitrarily make something up rather than leave the space blank, and horse owners who were not good trainers were ashamed to admit their lack of ability, insisting upon driving their horses themselves and thereby causing many accidents." These may seem like minor faults, but, as we read in 15.27, "Impatience when it comes to small matters confounds the execution of great plans." Also cf. the beginning of 13.3, where Confucius rebukes Zilu for pretending to knowledge that he does not have.

15.27 The Master said, "Clever words confound Virtue, and impatience when it comes to small matters confounds the execution of great plans."

The suspicion of "clever words" is typical; for the problem of impatience, cf. 13.17 and 14.44, where Confucius complains about his contemporaries' desire for "fast results." "Impatience" (*buren* 不忍) might alternately be rendered "intolerant," which is how Zhu Xi (adding a dash of misogyny and social elitism) takes it: "Clever words confound right and wrong, and listening to them causes a person to lose that to which they should hold fast. Being intolerant when it comes to small matters is the like the love of a wife or the courage of a common person"—i.e., narrowly focused, inflexible, and petty.

15.28 The Master said, "When the multitude hates a person, you must examine them and judge for yourself. The same holds true for someone whom the multitude love."

Again we have the suspicion of public opinion; cf. especially 13.24. As Wang Su comments, "Sometimes one can play to the crowd and please others in a partisan fashion, and sometimes one takes an unpopular stand in opposition to the crowd. This is why both love and hatred must be carefully examined." Yang Shi connects this passage to 4.3: "Only the Good person is able to properly love or despise another. If you accept the love or hate of the masses without examining it, you will sometimes fall victim to selfish distortions." A similar passage in the *Guanzi* is more narrowly focused on the issue of a ruler knowing his underlings:

> If a confused ruler does not examine the achievements of his ministers, he will simply reward those who are praised by the masses. If he does not look carefully into their transgressions, he will simply punish those who are condemned by the masses. In this way, wicked ministers with no achievements will end up being rewarded, and innocent, dutiful ministers will end up being punished.[9]

15.29 The Master said, "Human beings can broaden the Way—it is not the Way that broadens human beings."

As Cai Mo explains, "The Way is silent and without action, and requires human beings in order to be put into practice. Human beings are able to harmonize with the Way— this is why the texts reads: 'Human beings are able to broaden the Way.' The Way does not harmonize with humans—this is why the text reads, 'It is not the Way that broad-

---

[9] Chapter 67 ("Explanation of 'Making the Law Clear'"); Rickett 1998, vol. 2: 162.

ens human beings.'" Liu Baonan similarly argues that the point of this remark is that it is human ability that allows the Way to manifest itself in the world, quoting a line from the *Record of Ritual* that says, "If you are not able to fully realize virtue, the complete Way will not have nowhere to make itself concrete,"[10] as well as a passage from the *History of the Han*:

> When the Way of the Zhou declined with the accession of [the wicked kings] You and Li, it was not that the Way was lost, only that You and Li failed to follow it. With the accession of King Xuan, who focused upon and treasured the Virtue of the Former Kings, that which was stagnant was reinvigorated, and that which was flawed was made complete; the achievements of Kings Wen and Wu were brought back to light, and the Way of the Zhou made its splendid resurgence.

The Way thus is transcendent, in the sense that it continues to exist even when it is not being actively manifested in the world, but it requires human beings to be fully realized.

15.30 The Master said, "To make a mistake and yet to not change your ways—this is what is called truly making a mistake."

Cf. 1.8. An alternate version of this saying attributed to Confucius in the *Exoteric Commentary* reads, "If you make a mistake but then change your ways, it is like never having made a mistake at all."[11]

15.31 The Master said, "I once engaged in thought for an entire day without eating and an entire night without sleeping, but it did no good. It would have been better for me to have spent that time in learning."

Cf. 2.15, which presents thinking and learning as equally important. 15.31, in contrast, stresses the danger of thinking in isolation. Rather than attempt to pointlessly reflect on one's own, the accumulated wisdom of the classics should form the very basis of one's thinking. Thinking outside the context of learning might be compared to randomly banging on a piano in ignorance of the conventions of music: a million monkeys given a million years might produce something, but it is better to start with the classics (cf. 11.25, 17.10). We find a very similar theme in the *Xunzi*, which provides a more succinct version of 15.31, "I once spent the entire day doing nothing but thinking, but this is not as good as even a single moment devoted to learning," and adds:

> I once stood on my tiptoes to look into the distance, but this is not as good as the broad view obtained from climbing a hill. Climbing a hill and waving your arms does not make your arms any longer, but they can be seen from farther away; shouting downwind does not make your voice any louder, but it can be heard more clearly; someone who borrows a carriage and horses does not improve the power of his feet, but he can travel a thousand *li*; someone who borrows a boat and paddle does not thereby become able to swim, but he can cross great rivers. The gentleman by birth is not different from other people—he is simply good at making use of external things.[12]

---

[10] Chapter 32 ("Doctrine of the Mean"); Legge 1967, vol. 2: 323.

[11] Chapter 3.17; Hightower 1954: 94.

[12] Chapter 1 ("Encouraging Learning"); Knoblock 1988: 136.

15.32 The Master said, "The gentleman devotes his thoughts to attaining the Way, not to obtaining food. In the pursuit of agriculture, there is the possibility of starvation; in the pursuit of learning, there is the possibility of salary. The gentleman is concerned about the Way and not about poverty."

"Food" represents external goods in general, the point being that both agriculture and learning are subject to the vagaries of fate. In agriculture, you are likely to end up with food, but fate may bring starvation instead; similarly, learning may lead to official position and salary, but this is by no means guaranteed, and in any case is not the concern of the gentleman. The issue is thus one of motivation: the petty person is focused on external goods, whereas the gentleman cares only for the goods internal to the Confucian Way (cf. 1.14, 4.5, 4.14, 6.11, 7.12, 7.16). Jiang Xi quotes Dong Zhongshu as saying, "Urgently pursuing morality and being constantly concerned about whether or not one is able to transform the common people is the mind of the great person. Urgently pursuing wealth and profit, and being in constant fear that one's coffers will go empty is the mind of the petty person." This passage might also be an oblique jab at the primitivists, who advocated abandoning the relatively risky route of learning and official employment in order to take up a safe, subsistence lifestyle; cf. 13.4.

15.33 The Master said, "If your wisdom reaches it, but your Goodness cannot protect it, then even though you may have attained it, you are sure to eventually lose it. If your wisdom reaches it, and your Goodness is able to protect it, but you cannot manifest it with dignity, then the common people will not be respectful. If your wisdom reaches it, your Goodness is able to protect it, and you can manifest it with dignity, but you do not use ritual to put it into motion, it will never be truly excellent."

The undefined "it" mentioned here may be the Way, although according to early commentators the reference is to official position. Mao Qiling notes similar themes in a passage from the *Book of Changes* ("How does one hold onto an official position? By means of Goodness") and in *Mencius* 4:A:3 ("If the Son of Heaven is not benevolent [*ren*], he will not be able to protect the world; if the feudal lords are not benevolent, they will be unable to protect the altars of the soil and grain"). As an illustration of how someone wise enough to obtain a position can lose it if he lacks other qualities, Liu Baonan quotes the account, cited in 14.14 above, of Zang Wuzhong losing his official post in Lu: "This is the potential problem with wisdom. You have someone as wise as Zang Wuzhong, and yet he is no longer welcome in Lu, and for good reason. In his actions, he was not submissive, and he did not apply the virtue of understanding in his dealings with others." The main theme, then, is that of the gentleman-ruler as "complete person" (14.12), displaying all of the Confucian virtues in a balanced fashion, rather than narrowly possessing merely one or two in isolation. This theme is repeated in the following passage, 15.34.

15.34 The Master said, "The gentleman is incapable of petty cleverness, but he can take on great tasks; the petty person is the opposite."

As Zhang Ping comments, "In order to call someone a 'gentleman,' it is necessary that they have the capacity for great achievements, while it is not at all necessary that they have petty skills . . . we cannot demand comprehensiveness from a gentleman, nor take them to task for minor details of their behavior." The theme here is similar to the claim that "the gentleman is not a vessel" (2.12). Zhu Xi believes the point to be the care with which one must judge others, taking *xiaozhi* 小知 ("petty cleverness") as "knowing [a person's character] from his handling of minor matters." He comments, "The gentleman may not have much to show when it comes to minor tasks, but his talent and Virtue are sufficient for great responsibilities. The petty person, on the other hand, is a shallow, narrow vessel, but this does not preclude the possibility that he may have some specialized talents."

15.35 The Master said, "Goodness is even more vital to the common people than water or fire. I have seen people perish from walking through fire and water, but have never seen anyone perish by walking the path of Goodness."

This is a somewhat mysterious passage, but the point is probably that morality is more important to people than material considerations, and is also more trustworthy, in that things that sustain one physically can turn against one, whereas no harm ever comes from Goodness. As Zhu Xi glosses this passage,

> The common people depend upon water and fire for life, and cannot go without them for even one day. The same is the case with their relationship to Goodness. Water and fire, however, are external things, whereas Goodness is inside the self. Although a lack of water and fire will damage a person's body, a lack of Goodness will cause him to lose his heart-mind, and this is why Goodness is even more vital than water or fire, and why it is even more the case with Goodness that a person cannot go a day without it. When we additionally consider that water and fire are sometimes fatal to people, whereas Goodness has never once killed a person, how much less should we fear Goodness and fail to put it into practice?

Cf. 4.5, 12.7. Li Tong concludes, "This passage is intended by the Master to urge people on toward Goodness, and in this respect is similar to passage that follows."

15.36 The Master said, "When it comes to being Good, defer to no one, not even your teacher."

Deference to elders and teachers is a virtue, but, when it comes to being moral, any hesitation or deference is both unnecessary and harmful. As Zhang Ping comments, "Putting others before oneself, showing no concern for one's physical well-being but caring for things, treading the way of modesty and dwelling in humbleness—these are the means by which one practices Goodness. Acting in this way does not mean that one is not fond of showing deference, it just means that the Way is something with regard to which one does not defer."

15.37 The Master said, "The gentleman is true, but not rigidly trustworthy."

Again we have the concern about petty or rigid trustworthiness (*liang* 諒); for the dangers of excessive or inflexible trustworthiness, cf. 1.13, 13.18, 13.20, and 17.8, and for the importance of flexibility in general, cf. 19.11. As Huang Kan comments, "The gentleman uses discretion to respond to changing circumstances and does not have any single, constant way of doing things. In his handling of affairs he must sometimes bend the rules in order to harmonize with the Way and properly realize principle. Therefore, when the gentleman does something, he is not bound by petty fidelity (*xin*) like those who 'strangle themselves in some gully or ditch.' [14.17]"

15.38 The Master said, "In serving your lord, show respect for the tasks you have been assigned. Do not make the salary you will receive a priority."

The theme here is quite similar to 15.32: the gentleman is focused on his moral duty and the demands of the Way, rather than the prospect of external reward. As Jiang Xi comments, "This remark probably reflects the Master's displeasure over his contemporaries' tendency to serve their lord solely with an eye toward profit and salary." Cf. 6.22, 12.21.

15.39 The Master said, "In education, there are no differences in kind."

It is probably best to read this passage together with 17.2 ("By nature, people are similar; they diverge through practice") and such passages as *Mencius* 3:A:1 and 4:B:32, or the *Xunzi* passage quoted in the commentary to 15.31, which all emphasize that the sages are no different in innate endowment than ordinary people. As Kong Anguo comments, "The point is that there are no differences in kind when it comes to what people bring to the process of education." What distinguishes a sage from an ordinary person is that they are well educated, learn to love the Way, and then work hard at perfecting it. Cf. 7.20 and 7.34, where Confucius denies having any special talents, other than a love for and dedication to the Way. The basic educability of all human beings—even non-Chinese barbarians—has remained a central tenet of Confucianism down to the present day. Notice, however, the contrast with passages such as 16.9. Another grammatically plausible way to render the passage is, "In education there are no distinctions concerning whom is taught," which may be understood as meaning that instruction is open to all, regardless of social class. This would accord with 7.7, as well as a passage from the *Annals of Lü Buwei*: "In offering instruction, a teacher does not challenge a student on the issue of whether he is socially inconsequential or important, noble or humble of birth, rich or poor. Rather, he challenges him as to whether or not he truly seeks the Way. If the person in himself is acceptable, instructing him cannot but be acceptable."[13] Finally, "no distinctions" may refer to the subject matter that is taught, the sense being that instruction is comprehensive in scope rather than specialized, which would accord with passages such as 2.12, 6.13, 9.2, 9.6, 13.4 and 19.7.

15.40 The Master said, "Do not take counsel with those who follow a different Way."

This passage may be intended to pair with 15.39: the only really significant differences are in types of instruction, and one must therefore be careful not to fall under the sway of an improper teaching. This is the interpretation of Zhu Xi and Huang Shisan; the latter notes, "'those who follow a different Way' refers to those heterodox, petty people who harm the [true] Way." Cf. 2.16, 9.30, and 19.4, where Confucius warns against the "crooked ways-teachings" (*xiaodao* 小道) that threaten to "bog down" the aspiring gentleman.

15.41 The Master said, "Words should convey their point, and leave it at that."

As a general statement, this is probably meant as a warning against glibness or cleverness of speech—i.e., allowing the embellishments of cultural refinements to overwhelm the basics of native substance. This is the point of the grammatically very

---

[13] Chapter 4.2 ("Encouraging Learning"); Knoblock and Riegel 2000: 119.

similar 19.14, which concerns ritual behavior rather than speech: "Mourning should fully express grief and then stop at that." As Kong Anguo remarks, "In all things, never allow the substance of the matter to be exceeded. When words convey their point, leave it at that—do not needlessly complicate matters with refined and voluptuous (*wenyan* 文豔) words." Gui Fu notes a parallel passage in the *Book of Etiquette and Ritual* where the context more narrowly concerns the speech of an official envoy: "If one's words are excessive, one comes off as pedantic; if one's words are too few, however, the point [of the mission] is not conveyed. The perfection of meaning is realized when words are just adequate to convey the point."[14]

15.42 The Music Master Mian came to see Confucius.

As mentioned in the commentary to 13.15 above, the post of Music Master was traditionally filled by blind persons in ancient China, both in order to give them a trade in which they could excel and because their sense of hearing was considered more acute that the sighted. Music Master Mian has presumably been brought to Confucius' residence by an assistant, who then leaves him in Confucius' care.

When they came to the steps, the Master said, "Here are the steps." When they reached his seat, the Master said, "Here is your seat." After everyone was seated, the Master informed him as to who was present, saying, "So-and-so is seated here, and So-and-so is seated over there."

When the Music Master left, Zizhang asked, "Is this the way to converse with a Music Master?"

The Master replied, "Yes, this is indeed the way to assist a Music Master."

As Brooks and Brooks note, Zizhang's question is probably inspired by Confucius' "extra solicitude, which seems to sacrifice Confucius' dignity as a host, but which is explained as situationally appropriate" (1998: 135). Reading this as a pair with 15.41, part of the point is no doubt the economy of expression of the Master, who puts aside the normal ritual behavior of a host in order to deftly and respectfully serve as a guide for the blind Music Master, without being overly fussy or condescending. As Xue Xuan comments,

> Observing the Master speaking with the Music Master, we see that his words are casual and relaxed, yet also thoroughly sincere and cordial—truly inspiring in us a rare sort of admiration. Ordinary people know to be respectful when they encounter an important person, but this respectfulness diminishes somewhat when they run into a rival, and often degenerates into nothing more than arrogant casualness when they are dealing with inferiors. The sage, on the other hand, met everyone—superior or inferior, stranger or friend—with the same spirit of sincerity and respect.

Some of the Master's actions here are presented as ritual injunctions in later ritual texts,[15] so an additional point is possibly the Master's effortless accordance with ritual in this particularly complex situation, which is worthy to serve as a model for others. As Zhu Xi remarks, "This passage demonstrates the manner in which the students in the sage's school remarked and carefully reflected upon his every word and gesture."

---

[14] Chapter 18 ("Ritual for Official Visits"); Steele 1917, vol. 1: 233–234.

[15] Cf. the *Record of Ritual*, Ch. 17 ("Smaller Rules of Demeanor"); Legge 1967, vol. 2:80: "When someone who does not have a candle arrives late, they should be informed as to who is present. One should also do the same with blind people."

BOOK SIXTEEN

This is a stylistically somewhat strange Book, and it is here that one begins to find the sort of anomalies—fragmentary passages, unusually long narratives, concern with numbers, Confucius being referred to as "Kongzi" rather than "the Master"— that mark Books Sixteen–Twenty as belonging to the latest stratum of the text.

16.1 The Ji Family was about to attack Zhuanyu.

Zhuanyu was a small vassal state located within the borders of Lu. It was controlled by a minor line of nobility, surnamed Feng, who claimed descent from the legendary sage-king Fu Xi. Kong Anguo speculates that the Ji Family, resenting Zhuangyu's independence and coveting its land, wished to destroy it. As Liu Fenglu notes, there is no record of an attack on Zhuangyu in the *Annals*, which indicates that the attack never occurred—conceivably as a result of the rebuke recorded here dissuading the Ji Family.

Ran Qiu and Zilu came to see Confucius and told him, "The Ji Family is about to take action regarding Zhuanyu."

Confucius replied, "Ran Qiu! Is this not, after all, your fault? Long ago, our former king appointed the rulers of Zhuanyu to preside over the sacrifices to Mount Dongmeng. Moreover, Zhuanyu lies within the boundaries of the state of Lu, and its ruler is a minister dedicated to our altars to the soil and grain. What possible reason could there be to attack him?"

As Kong Anguo explains, both Ran Qiu and Zilu were serving the Ji Family at the time, which is why they came to report this news to Confucius, but Ran Qiu—as the Ji Family steward—was senior to Zilu in their service, and thus particularly implicated in this dubious undertaking. This is why Confucius directs his criticism at Ran Qiu alone. The ruler of Zhuanyu was directly appointed by a Zhou king (King Cheng, according to commentators) to serve the altars of Lu, and thus presented no threat to the state. Of course, the Ji Family is not at all interested in the public good of Lu, only in their own personal power, but Confucius is pointing out their lack of legitimate justification for an attack.

Ran Qiu replied, "Our Master desires it. We two ministers are against it."

Confucius replied, "Ran Qiu! Zhou Ren had a saying, 'He who can display his power should step into the ranks, he who is unable to do so should retire.' Of what use is an assistant who cannot support someone when they are tottering on the brink of disaster, or steady them when they are about to fall? Furthermore, what you have just said is incorrect, for when a tiger or rhinoceros escapes from his cage, or a tortoise shell or piece of jade is ruined in its case, whose fault is it?"

Ran Qiu attempts to foist the responsibility on the Ji Family, but Confucius will not have it. As a minister, it is Ran Qiu's duty to guide his masters and help them to make the right decision; moreover, like someone entrusted with the care of a dangerous or precious object, a minister must take responsibility for the errors committed during his tenure. Zhou Ren was a legendary, wise historian whose sayings also appear in the *Zuo Commentary*.

Ran Qiu said, "Well, Zhuanyu is well-fortified and close to the Ji Family stronghold of Bi. If it is not taken now, it will certainly be a source of anxiety for the Ji Family descendents in later generations."

Confucius replied, "Ran Qiu! The gentleman despises those who, declining to say that they want something, turn around and argue in favor of it."

After failing to foist responsibility on Ji Kangzi, Ran Qiu now tries another tack, attempting to justify Ji Kangzi's plan as mere self-defense. The flimsiness of this argument is immediately apparent, and the Master is further infuriated by Ran Qiu's shameless flip-flopping—first he denies desiring the attack on Zhuanyu, and now he defends it as justified.

"I have heard it said that those who possess a state or noble house are not concerned about whether their people are scarce, but rather about whether their people are content; they are not concerned about poverty, but rather concerned that what wealth they have is fairly distributed.[1] If wealth is fairly distributed, there should be no poverty; if your state or house is in harmony, there should be no scarcity; and if your people are content, there should be no instability. This being the case, if those who are distant will not submit, simply refine your culture and Virtue in order to attract them. Once you have attracted them, you should make them content."

After rebuking Ran Qiu for his lack of scruples, Confucius then discredits his attempted justification of the Ji Family. If the Ji Family were genuinely concerned about Zhuanyu as a potential threat, the proper response would not be a military campaign. Instead, the Ji Family should cultivate their own Virtue in order to bring about the voluntary submission of Zhuanyu.

"Now, you two, Ran Qiu and Zilu, are supposed to be assisting your masters. Yet those who are far away will not submit, and they are unable to attract them; the state is partitioned and crumbling, and they are unable to preserve it; and now you are planning to move with spears and shields against your own countrymen. I am afraid that the source of the Ji Family's troubles lies not in Zhuanyu, but rather within their own chambers."

The point is that Ji Family's troubles are the result of the bad advice they are getting from their own ministers, rather than any external threat. Both Ran Qiu and Zilu are failing shamefully in their duties as ministers, thereby endangering Lu; contrast this situation with that described in 14.19, where the weak and corrupt Duke of Wei enjoys stability and safety because of his able ministers.

---

[1] Transposing two characters that have apparently been misplaced, as is confirmed in the lines that follow, as well as alternate versions of this comment attributed to Confucius in the *Luxuriant Dew* and the *History of the Wei*.

16.2 Confucius said, "When the Way prevails in the world, rituals, music, punitive expeditions, and attacks against foreign powers issue from the Son of Heaven. When the Way does not prevail in the world, these things issue from the feudal lords. When they issue from the feudal lords, it is seldom more than ten generations before the lords lose control of them. When they issue from ministers, it is seldom more than five generations before the ministers lose control of them, and once household ministers seize control of state commands, it is seldom more than three generations before they lose control of them."

This passage may form a pair with 16.1, serving as a bleak assessment of the state of the world when the head of the Ji Family, officially only a minister, can take it upon himself to initiate a military campaign. Many commentators take Confucius' comment here literally, and a great deal of ink has been spilled culling through Chinese historical records, tracing the precise time intervals mentioned in order to document the truth of the Master's claim. Kong Anguo's comment on this passage is representative, if more concise than most:

> After King You of the Zhou was killed by the Quan Rong barbarians, King Ping moved the capital to the east, and this is when the Zhou began to decline. It was beginning in the reign of Duke Yin that the feudal lords began creating new ritual and music, and taking the initiative in launching punitive military expeditions. Ten generations later, during the reign of Duke Zhao, the government of Lu was lost, and Duke Zhao died in Qian Hou. Once Ji Wenzi first took over control of the government, it was five generations later, during the reign of Ji Hengzi, that the Ji Family head was imprisoned by Yang Huo.

Ma Rong then finishes out the account: "Three generations after Yang Huo became the family minister of the Ji Family, he was forced to flee to Qi." It is more likely, however, that the numbers mentioned by Confucius are meant to be taken as expressions of relative magnitude rather than literally, which would explain why they do not match the numbers presented in the actual case-example given in 16.3.

"When the Way prevails in the world, control of the government does not reside with the ministers. When the Way prevails in the world, commoners do not debate matters of government."

The former statement is probably also meant as a criticism of the current situation in Lu, while the latter reflects a traditional ideal of Chinese government that is still very much alive today: political debate among the common people is a sign of disorder, because in a properly run state, the people will be busy and content, and will have no cause to form or express opinions about how the state is being run. Alternately, *yi* 議 ("express opinion, debate") could be taken in a more negative sense ("criticize, critique"), in which case there might be room for positive expressions among the commoners. This is how Huang Kan takes it: "When the lord possesses the Way, sounds of praise will fill the streets, and the sentiments of a harmonious age will prevail. This being so, common people and inferiors will not gather in streets and alleyways to critique and debate the achievements and failures of [those governing] the four quarters of the world."

16.3 Confucius said, "It has been five generations since control of state finances left the Ducal house, and four generations since governmental power fell into in the hands of its ministers. This is why the descendents of the Three Huan are in decline."

The "Three Huan," as mentioned earlier, are the Three Families of Lu, all of whom were descended from the sons of Duke Huan. This passage is probably meant as an actual illustration of the general principle of state decline expressed in 16.2. It is clear in this passage that "generation" (*shi* 世) refers to a reign period (i.e., generation of ruler), which is why five generations of Lu dukes can correspond to four generations of Ji Family ministers. It is unclear whether or not we are to take "generation" in 16.2 in the same sense. As Mr. Su sums up the general import of both 16.2 and 16.3, "Strength is born from stability, and stability comes from having the distinctions between superior and inferior properly established. In Confucius' time, the feudal lords and ministers were both infringing upon the prerogatives of their superiors, and therefore had no way to enforce their commands upon their inferiors. In such a situation, it will not be long before both lords and ministers lose their power."

16.4 Confucius said, "Beneficial types of friendship number three, as do harmful types of friendship. Befriending the upright, those who are true to their word,[2] or those of broad learning—these are the beneficial types of friendship. Befriending clever flatterers, skillful dissemblers, or the smoothly glib—these are the harmful types of friendship."

We see here again the importance of choosing one's friends properly; cf. 1.8, 9.25, 9.30, 12.24, 15.10, 16.5. As Wang Yangming comments,

> In life, it is impossible to go without friends, and when making friends it is unacceptable not to be selective. Befriending those who are upright, true to their word, and broadly learned, you will always get to hear of your own transgressions, learn things that were previously unknown to you, develop your excellences and remedy your faults, open and expand your heart, and every day make further progress in rendering both your Virtue and learning bright and noble. On the other hand, associating with clever flatterers, dissemblers, and the glib will make you dependent upon flattery and constant affirmation; no one will demand excellence of you, and you will grow self-satisfied and complacent; arrogance will develop and you will pursue wrongness, to the point that every day your Virtue and learning will descend further into the depths of immoral crudeness. The benefit and harm provided by friendship are not to be underestimated, and therefore you cannot but be careful in choosing your friends!

16.5 Confucius said, "Beneficial types of joy number three, as do harmful types of joy. Taking joy in regulating yourself through the rites and music,[3] in commending the excellence of others, or in possessing many worthy friends—these are the beneficial types of joy. Taking joy in arrogant behavior, idle amusements, or decadent licentiousness—these are the harmful types of joys."

In this companion passage to 16.4, we see how one's affective responses have significance for moral cultivation: one must learn to take joy in the right sorts of things, because only one who actively takes joy in the Way can genuinely master it (6.20). Both Confucius and Yan Hui seem to have naturally possessed this joy in the Way, but of course the trick is how one can instill this joy in a person who lacks it or, conversely, how one who lacks this joy can go about acquiring it. Cf. 4.6, 5.10, 6.12, 7.30.

---

[2] *Liang* 諒 has had a negative connotation ("rigidly trustworthy") in previous passages (14.18, 15.36), but clearly has a positive sense here.

[3] The Dingzhou text has only "the rites" here.

16.6 Confucius said, "When attending a gentleman, there are three types of errors one may commit. To speak when it is not yet time to speak—this is called being rash. To not speak when it is time to speak—this is called being secretive. To speak without taking into account the countenance of one's lord—this is called being blind."

As Yin Tun observes, the point of this passage is to how to be "timely" in one's speech. Cf. the importance of knowing when to speak up as described in 14.4.

16.7 Confucius said, "The gentleman guards against three things: when he is young, and his blood and vital essence are still unstable, he guards against the temptation of female beauty; when he reaches his prime, and his blood and vital essence have become unyielding, he guards against being contentious; when he reaches old age, and his blood and vital essence have begun to decline, he guards against being acquisitive."

A similar passage in the *Huainanzi* reads, "It is the general nature of human beings that, when young, they are prone to be wild and undisciplined; when in their prime, they are prone to be violent and aggressive; and when old, they are prone to be greedy." Confucius' comment therefore probably reflects common wisdom of the time. This passage is interesting because it is the only place in the *Analects* where human vices are explicitly linked to psycho-physiological factors, and it represents the first evidence we see in the text of the influence of medical theories concerning the blood and vital essence (*xueqi* 血氣) that later had such a large impact on the thought of Mencius, Zhuangzi, and Xunzi. This may be an indication of a relatively late date for this passage. Cf. 9.18, 15.13.

16.8 The Master said, "The gentleman stands in awe of three things: the Mandate of Heaven, great men, and the teachings of the sages. The petty person does not understand the Mandate of Heaven, and thus does not regard it with awe; he shows disrespect to great men, and ridicules the teachings of the sages."

This parallel to 16.7 can perhaps be compared to 2.4, where recognizing or under-standing (*zhi* 知) the Mandate of Heaven is presented as an essential step in comprehending the Way and achieving wu-wei perfection. Two views on how to understand "great men" can be traced back to He Yan and Zheng Xuan, with He Yan arguing that it refers simply to morally great people, such as the sages, and Zheng Xuan arguing that it refers specifically to socio-political superiors. Either interpretation is plausible, but the metaphorical structure of the concept of the "Mandate of Heaven" supports the latter, suggesting a parallel between submitting to fate and showing due deference to a political superior. Things that are beyond the immediate control of the individual (wealth, fame, health, life-span) are metaphorically "commanded" or "mandated" by the Heavenly ruler, and thus the true gentleman—understood in the metaphor as a loyal minister—submits to these "decisions" without anxiety or complaint. The petty person, on the other hand, has no respect for rank, does not know his place, and is always scrambling to get ahead. Cf. 11.19, where the disciple Zigong, who has been engaging in business speculation and trying to get ahead economically, is criticized for "not recognizing fate-Mandate," as well as 12.4 and 12.5.

16.9 Confucius said, "Those who are born understanding it are the best; those who come to understand it through learning are second. Those who find it difficult to understand and yet persist in their studies come next. People who find it difficult to understand but do not even try to learn are the worst of all."

Yan Hui seems to have belonged to the first category (2.9, 5.9, 6.7, 11.4), and Confucius to the second (7.20). In contrast to 15.39, we have here a hierarchy of native ability presented, but the point seems ultimately to be the same: although perhaps more difficult for the less gifted, learning the Way is within the reach of all who are willing to dedicate their life to its pursuit and never give up (cf. 8.7 and 9.11). As Yang Shi observes, "All three of the first categories, although different in terms of native substance, are the same in eventually attaining knowledge. This is why the gentleman values learning, and nothing else. It is only someone who does not learn because he finds it difficult who is ultimately dismissed as inferior."

16.10 Confucius said, "There are nine things upon which a gentleman focuses his attention: when looking, he focuses on seeing clearly; when listening, he focuses on being discerning; in his expression, he focuses on being amiable; in his demeanor, he focuses on being reverent; in his speech, he focuses on being dutiful; in his actions, he focuses on being respectful; when in doubt, he focuses on asking questions; when angry, he focuses on thinking about the potential negative consequences of his anger; and when seeing gain, he focuses upon what is right."

The first line might be more literally rendered, "The gentleman has nine thoughts (*si* 思)," but the point is that there are nine areas with regard to which the gentleman is careful or thoughtful, ranging from the manner in which he holds himself to how he interacts with others.

16.11 Confucius said, "'Seeing goodness, and striving for it urgently, as if never able catch up; seeing badness, and recoiling as if scalded by hot water'—I have seen such people, and have heard such words."

"'Dwelling in seclusion in order to pursue one's aspirations, practicing rightness in order to realize the Way'—I have heard such words, but have yet to see such a person."

The quoted phrases are probably proverbial sayings. The first half of the first saying is similar to 8.17. The second half of the passage may be a critique of the principled recluses we have seen before, and will see again in Book Eighteen: they claim a noble motivation for their actions, but the Master remains dubious. The point, of course, is that words do not always match actions, and therefore one must examine both closely; cf. 5.10.

16.12 "'Duke Jing of Qi had a thousand teams of horses, and yet on the day he died, the people could find no reason to praise him. Bo Yi and Shu Qi starved to death at the foot of Mt. Shouyang, and yet to this day the common people still praise them.'"

Duke Jing (who appears in 12.11) was apparently a stock example of a profligate and arrogantly wealthy ruler. He is contrasted with the stock figures of ascetic morality, Bo Yi and Shu Qi, whom we also encounter in 5.23, 7.15, and 18.8. Huang Kan's commentary here includes an account of their lives that is interesting because it is not drawn from any known extant history, and this must represent a fragment from a now-lost text:

> During his life, Duke Jing had no Virtue but many horses, but when he died both his body and his reputation were lost. This is why the common people could find nothing about him to praise. Bo Yi and Shu Qi were the two sons of Lord Guzhu, the brothers who both declined rulership of the state, and thereupon went to live in reclusion on Mt. Shouyang. When King Wu was going to attack King Zhow, Bo Yi and Shu Qi grabbed the reins of his horses and remonstrating with him, saying, "To be a minister and yet attack your lord—how can this be called dutiful? To lay the corpse out on the ground without a proper burial—how can this be called filial?" The retainers of King Wu wanted to put them to death for these words, but the Grand Duke declared, "These are the sons of Guzhu, the brothers who declined ruler-ship of the state, and the Great King was not able to stop them. They now dwell in reclu-sion on Mt. Shouyang, together displaying rectitude and establishing rightness. Worthy men such as this cannot be put to death." In this way he restrained the retainers. Bo Yi and Shu Qi then returned to Mt. Shouyang, imposing upon themselves the austerity of not eating the millet of the Zhou, but subsisting only upon wild grass and herbs. Later, [a passerby who was out in the wilderness gathering herbs encountered them], and said, "You refuse to eat the millet of the Zhou, but how is it that you are willing to eat the wild grass and herbs of the Zhou?" Upon hearing these words, Bo Yi and Shu Qi immediately stopped eating altogether, and seven days later they were dead.

Duke Jing lived a life of extreme indulgence, while Bo Yi and Shu Qi lived lives of strict asceticism, and yet it is the latter who are remembered and praised to this day. This passage might thus serve as an illustration of 15.20: it is one's posthumous repu-tation that accurately reflects one's character.

"Is this not an example of this?"

The relationship of this final line of 6.12 with the preceding text is a bit unclear. This is a typical locution after a quotation of some sort, which suggests that the story of Duke Jing and Po Yi and Shu Qi has been quoted to illustrate some previously men-tioned principle. What that principle, might be, however, is not entirely clear. Since 16.12 is not introduced by a "Confucius said," Han commentators generally read it together with 6.11, based on the mention of recluses in 6.11 and of Po Yi and Shu Qi here in 16.12. The senses of the two passages do not fit together very well, however, and it is more likely that some introductory text to 16.12, introducing some principle such as "virtuous behavior is more important than wealth," has been lost.

16.13 Ziqin asked Boyu, "Have you acquired any esoteric learning?"

Boyu is Confucius' son, and the disciple Ziqin is curious to see if, because of his special relationship to the Master, he has obtained any sort of esoteric learning not shared with the other disciples.

Boyu replied, "I have not. My father was once standing by himself in the court-yard and, as I hurried by with quickened steps,[4] he asked, 'Have you learned the *Odes*?' I replied, 'Not yet.' He said, 'If you do not learn the *Odes*, you will lack the means to speak.' I then retired and learned the *Odes*.

"On another day, my father was once again standing by himself in the court-yard and, as I hurried by with quickened steps, he asked, 'Have you learned

---

[4] A sign of respect; cf. 10.3.

ritual?"[5] I replied, 'Not yet.' He said, 'If you do not learn ritual, you will lack the means to take your place.' I then retired and learned ritual.

"These two things are what I have been taught."

Ziqin retired and, smiling to himself, remarked "I asked one question and got three answers: I learned about the *Odes*, I learned about ritual, and I learned how the gentleman keeps his son at a distance."

Along with 8.8, this passage serves as one of the clearer expressions of the constitutive function of the Confucian tradition: learning the *Odes* provides one with the resources to speak (cf. 13.5, 17.9–17.10), and learning ritual provides a model for everyday behavior, allowing one to "take one's place" among other adults in society (cf. 2.4, 12.1, 20.3). As Huang Kan notes, "The rites are the root of establishing one's self by means of reverence, frugality, gravity, and respectfulness. With the rites, one can be at ease; without the rites, one will be imperiled." Regarding the principle of "keeping one's son at a distance," Sima Guang remarks, "To 'keep at a distance' refers not to being cold or alienating, but rather to being timely in the way one allows one's son to approach, and always receiving him with ritual propriety. The point is simply that father and son do not consort with one another day and night in an indecently familiar manner." A passage from the *Summary of Discussions* suggests that such formality does not extend to the third generation: "The gentleman keeps his sons at a distance, but is familiar with his grandsons." Boyu's denial that he has received any esoteric instruction accords with the Master's statement in 7.24 that he "hides nothing" from his disciples, as well as the *Analects*'s general eschewal of abstruse concerns in favor of the everyday practicalities of self-cultivation (5.13, 7.21, 7.25).

16.14 With regard to the wife of the lord of a state, the lord refers to her as his "Lady," while the Lady refers to herself as "little child."[6] The people of the state refer to her as "our Lord's Lady," but when abroad refer to her as "Our Orphaned Little Lord."[7] People of other states refer to her as "that Lord's Lady."

This passage is stylistically quite anomalous for the *Analects* and sounds very much like an excerpt from a ritual text such as the *Record of Ritual* that somehow found its way into the *Analects*.[8] This impression is reinforced by the fact that it comes at the end of the Book, a likely location for textual additions. It has thus been dismissed by many modern Chinese and Western scholars as a later interpolation. As Cheng Shude points out, however, the passage seems to have been present in other early versions of the *Analects* besides the extant one, and all of the Han Dynasty commentators treat it as part of the text, explaining it as an attempt on the part of Confucius to correct the ritual improprieties of his contemporaries.

---

[5] Some commentators suggest that *li* 禮 is meant as the title of a text ("the *Rites*"), which would indicate the existence of formal ritual texts—such as the *Record of Ritual*—at the time 16.13 was recorded. This, in turn, would be a sign of a quite late date for this passage.

[6] The term translated as "child" (*tong* 童) usually has a masculine reference, and would usually be rendered "little boy." While it is obvious that referring to oneself as a child is an expression of humility, it is not clear why the wife of a ruler would use this normally masculine term.

[7] "Orphaned One" (*guaren* 寡人) is the ordinary first-person pronoun used by a ruler. Some believe it to refer to the fact that a ruler does not ascend the throne until his father has passed away, but it is more likely a polite expression of humility: "I, this lonely one." It could also be translated less literally as "Deficient One"—i.e., "I, this person deficient in virtue." Cf. *Laozi*, Chapter 39.

[8] Cf. *Record of Ritual*, Chapter 2 ("Summary of the Rules of Propriety"); Legge 1967, vol. 1: 107–108.

BOOK SEVENTEEN

This Book contains a mixture of general observations and historical accounts. 17.1, 17.5, and 17.7 concern Confucius' desire to obtain an official position from which he might affect the world, and the block of sayings from 17.11–17.19 all concern the problem of hypocrisy, the gap between actions and words, and false pretensions to virtue.

17.1 Yang Huo wanted to have an audience with Confucius, but Confucius would not see him. Yang Huo therefore sent Confucius a suckling pig as a gift. Confucius waited until Yang Huo was not at home before going to offer his thanks, but ended up running into Yang Huo on the road.

Yang Huo was a household steward of the Ji Family who was gradually usurping the power of his masters, just as they had usurped it from the Ducal house. Considering Confucius' view of these developments as expressed in 16.2, it is understandable that he is reluctant to associate himself with Yang Huo in any way. There is some commentarial debate concerning the exact nature of the relevant ritual injunction involved in gift-giving, but it is clear that Yang Huo gives Confucius the pig because Confucius will then be ritually obligated to come to his house and give a bow of thanks, and that Confucius attempts to avoid having to actually see Yang Huo by choosing a time when he is not at home, only to have his plan foiled by a chance meeting on the road.

Yang Huo called out to Confucius, "Come! I would like to speak with you." [After Confucius approached him,] he said, "Clutching a treasure to one's bosom, and thereby letting the state go to ruin—could this be called Good?"
   Confucius replied, "No, it could not."
   "Being eager to serve, but repeatedly missing opportunities to do so—could this be called wise?"
   Confucius replied, "No, it could not."
   "The days and months are slipping away, and time is not on our side."
   "Very well," Confucius said. "I will enter official service."

For the metaphor of unused talent or virtue as a hoarded "treasure," see 9.13, where Confucius expresses an eagerness to take his jewel out of hiding and sell it—but only, of course, to the right buyer. It is extremely doubtful that Yang Huo was viewed by Confucius as the right buyer, and most commentators believe Confucius' final statement to be a polite stalling tactic, seeing this exchange as an example of how the Master skillfully and respectfully put off this overbearing usurper. As Zhu Xi explains,

It is not at all that the Master does not wish to enter public service, merely that he does not wish to serve under Yang Huo. Therefore he straightforwardly acknowledges the reasonableness of Yang Huo's remarks in his responses, but does not further engage him in discussion, feigning not to see Yang Huo's real intention. Despite his good intentions, Yang Huo desires that Confucius have an audience with him so that Confucius might be employed to help Yang Huo in bringing disorder to the state of Lu. Therefore, in refusing to have an audience with him, Confucius is manifesting rightness. In going to offer his thanks, he is manifesting ritual propriety. In being sure to wait until Yang is not at home before going to do so, he desires to balance the two demands [those of rightness and ritual propriety]. In encountering him on the road but not attempting to avoid him, he does not go to excessive extremes. In responding to the questions posed to him, he displays a reasonable straightforwardness. In refusing to argue with him to his face, his words are accommodating, while at the same time he does not in any way yield or submit.

17.2 The Master said, "By nature people are similar; they diverge as the result of practice."

Although not a primary concern for Confucius, the topic of human nature (*xing* 性) became a central focus of debate in later Confucianism. Mencius famously declared that "human nature is good (*shan* 善)," and repeatedly defended this claim against his opponents. Xunzi chose human nature as the center of his confrontation with Mencius, famously entitling one of his chapters, "Human Nature Is Bad." The character of human nature was a topic of lively debate throughout pre-Tang Confucian thought, with various positions—it is good; it is bad; it is neutral; it is mixed (some people are born good, others bad)—all being defended as expressions of Confucius' original view. The lack of theoretical consistency in the *Analects* makes it possible to argue for any of these positions. Passages that emphasize the importance of native substance (*zhi* 質) (3.4, 3.8) sometimes seem to imply that at least some people are born with the "stuff" of virtue that merely needs to be refined into full Goodness; passages such as 2.9, 5.9, 11.4, 16.9, and 17.3 imply that some exceptional sages (such as Yan Hui) are born fully good, while 5.10 and 17.3 similarly imply that some are born hopelessly flawed. The general tenor of the *Analects*, however, seems to be summed up fairly well here in 17.2: all people, even non-Chinese barbarians, are born with more or less similar basic stuff, and it is the quality of the tradition into which they are socialized—the consequences of "practice" (*xi* 習)—that really makes the difference.

17.3 The Master said, "Only the very wise and the very stupid do not change."

Some commentators read 17.2–17.3 as a single passage, but the "Master said" locution marks 17.3 as a separate passage. In any case, it is clearly related to 17.2, clarifying that, although people are generally similar by nature, there are exceptions. Commentators are probably correct in reading this passage along with 16.9: the "wisest" are those who are "born understanding it," and the "stupidest" are those "who find it difficult but do not even try to learn." The former do not really need education, whereas the latter either refuse to benefit from it, or are constitutionally unable to do so.

17.4 When the Master went to Wucheng, he heard the sound of stringed instruments and song. Smiling gently, he remarked, "Why use an ox-cleaver to kill a chicken?"

Wucheng was a small city in the south of Lu, whose steward at that time was the disciple Ziyou (cf. 6.14). There are two main interpretations of the Master's remark. The more common is that of Jiang Xi, who comments, "When governing a small city, it is enough to simply make sure that the people's material needs are met and that they are instructed in respectfulness. Teaching them to chant the Way of the Former Kings is like using an ox-cleaver to kill a chicken—it is not really appropriate." Following this interpretation, Waley remarks that the force of Confucius' remark is that Ziyou is effectively "casting pearls before the swine" (1989: 210, n. 2). In Miao Bo's interpretation, on the other hand, it is Ziyou who is the misused instrument: "Ziyou, as steward of this small city, is able to lead the people to take their proper places and bring them joy through stringed music and songs. The Master's comment expresses regret that Ziyou has not gotten the opportunity to lead a thousand-chariot state. Employing Ziyou as steward of Wucheng is like using an ox-cleaver to kill a chicken—his abilities are not being fully utilized."

Ziyou replied, "In the past, Master, I have heard you say, 'If the gentleman learns the Way he will be able to care for others, and if commoners learn the Way they will be easy to manage.'"

[Addressing the disciples who had accompanied him to Wucheng,] the Master said, "Take note, my disciples! What Ziyou says is true. My earlier comment was meant only as a joke."

If Jiang Xi is correct in his interpretation of the Master's initial remark, we may have here an instance of the Master allowing himself to be corrected by a disciple. It is worth contrasting this exchange with 11.25, where Zilu attempts the same trick— taking a saying of Confucius' and using it against him in argument—and is instead sharply rebuked by the Master for being arrogantly clever, or 17.7, where Confucius retorts with a new set of sayings. Under Miao Bo's interpretation, on the other hand, Ziyou has mistakenly understood the Master's initial remark as Jiang Xi does—as a criticism of Ziyou's methods—and the Master modesty declines to correct him, instead offering his apologies.

17.5 Gongshan Furao used the stronghold of Bi to stage a revolt against the Ji Family. He summoned Confucius, and the Master was inclined to go.

Zilu was displeased, and said, "We have nowhere else to go, that is true. But why must we go to the house of Gongshan?"

Traditional historical accounts of Gongshan Furao's revolt differ considerably. The *Zuo Commentary* describes it as occurring in Duke Ding, Year 12 (497 B.C.E.). In this account, Zilu has been made steward of the Ji Family and has convinced the Ji to begin demolishing the family strongholds of the three clans as potential threats against the central government. The attempt to demolish Bi is what leads Gongshan to revolt, and he leads troops in a sneak attack on the Ji Family palace. In this account, far from being summoned by Gongshan, Confucius is portrayed as the Minister of Justice in Lu who sends people to defeat the rebel.[1] The version of the story in the *Record of the Historian* describes the summoning of Confucius, but has Gongshan's revolt occurring in Ding 9 (500 B.C.E.), after Yang Huo's attempted revolt failed and Yang was forced to flee the state. There is probably no way to reconcile the two accounts, but the *Zuo Commentary* version seems more plausible, and also provides a compelling background story: in Ding 5 (504 B.C.E.), Ji Huanzi visited Bi and treated Gongshan with great respect, but one of his retainers was quite rude, sowing the seeds of resentment that flowered three years later, in Ding 8 (501 B.C.E.), when Gongshan joined

---

[1] Legge 1991d: 781.

a group of disaffected ministers supporting Yang Huo in his plan to remove the Three Families from power.

The Master replied, "I have been summoned—how could it be for naught? If I found someone to employ me, could I not establish a new Zhou in the East?"

There is a great deal of debate over how to understand Confucius' response, but the most plausible interpretation holds that Yang Huo's motivation for revolt was mere self-aggrandizement, which is why Confucius refuses his overtures in 17.1. Gongshan Furao, in contrast, wished to overthrow the Three Families in order to strengthen the legitimate Ducal house, which is clearly something that Confucius would find appealing. The state of Lu was located east of the Zhou's original seat of power, so "establishing a new Zhou in the East" refers to re-establishing the Way of the Zhou with Lu as its political center—something that Confucius apparently continued to believe was possible in his lifetime (cf. 6.24). Contrast this apparently rather hopeful passage with the more bitter 17.7.

17.6 Zizhang asked Confucius about Goodness.

Confucius replied, "Someone could be considered Good who is able to, everywhere in the world, put five virtues into practice."

"May I ask what these virtues are?"

"Reverence, magnanimity, trustworthiness, diligence, and kindness. If you are reverent, you will avoid disgrace; if you are magnanimous, you will win the populace; if you are trustworthy, others will put their trust in you; if you are diligent, you will achieve results; and if you are kind, you will have the wherewithal to employ the people."

Here we have another instance of the overarching virtue of Goodness being presented as the harmony of lesser virtues; cf. 13.19, 13.27, and 14.4. There is some commentarial disagreement on how to understand *min* 敏 ("diligence"), with Kong Anguo and others glossing it as *ji* 疾 ("quick to act"), but its usage in 7.20 supports the "diligence" reading.

17.7 Bi Xi summoned Confucius, and the Master was inclined to go.

Bi Xi was the steward of Zhongmou, a city in the state of Jin belonging to Zhao Jianzi, the state's most powerful minister. The *Zuo Commentary* for Duke Ai, Year 5 (491 B.C.E.) says, "In the summer, Zhao Jianzi attacked the state of Wei, and because [of the assistance it had provided to] Fan Zhongxing, he subsequently surrounded Zhongmou."[2] Fan Zhongxing was Zhao Jianzi's enemy, and we must presume that Zhao's wrath was aroused because Bi Xi, although officially supposed to be serving Zhao, was in fact aiding his opponent. This is why Zilu describes Bi Xi as being "in rebellion."

Zilu said, "In the past, Master, I have heard you say, 'The gentleman does not enter into association with someone who treats badly those who are close to him.' Bi Xi is using the city of Zhongmou to stage a rebellion against his superior. How could it be acceptable for you, Master, to go to him?"

---

[2] Legge 1991d: 806.

The Master replied, "Yes, I have said that. But have I not also said, '[A gentleman is] so hard that grinding will not wear him down; so pure that dyeing will not stain him black'? Do you take me to be a bitter gourd, content to merely hang on a string without ever being eaten?"

There are several interpretations of Confucius' remark. Huang Kan reports that some early commentators take *paogua* 匏瓜 ("bitter gourd") to be the name of a star, which hangs in the sky and "cannot be eaten"—i.e., is admired, but brings benefit to no one—and this view is seconded by Jiao Xun and Huang Zhen. Zhu Xi takes it to refer to a gourd, but (misreading He Yan) believes the point to be that a gourd does not need to eat, whereas human beings do, and therefore Confucius must get a job. He Yan's actual interpretation seems best, however: bitter gourds, as opposed to sweet melons, were not eaten, but were rather hollowed out and hung to dry in order to be used as containers. As Mao Qiling explains, "It is probably the case that the usefulness of cultivated vegetables was seen to lie in their edibility, and therefore it was a custom to ridicule something that was useless by calling it a 'bitter gourd,' because bitter gourds are inedible." Confucius' remark is thus a complaint about not being employed (cf. 9.13), and the reference to the hard or white a metaphor for his own incorruptibility: Zilu's misgivings are unjustified, because Confucius can be employed by a less-than-ideal ruler without being led astray. One possible interpretation of Bi Xi's revolt against Zhao Jianzi is that it represented an attempt to break the power of the ministers in Jin and restore the Jin Ducal house to power. Most commentators view Confucius' willingness to answer Bi Xi's summons as similar to his response to Gongshan Furao in 17.5, in that both men, though less than perfectly dutiful or moral, were at least moving in the right direction.

17.8 The Master said, "Zilu! Have you heard about the six [virtuous] words and their six corresponding vices?"

Zilu replied, "I have not."
"Sit! I will tell you about them.

As Kong Anguo explains, "Zilu had stood up to answer the Master [as required by ritual], and therefore the Master tells him to take his seat again."

"Loving Goodness without balancing it with a love for learning will result in the vice of foolishness. Loving wisdom without balancing it with a love for learning will result in the vice of deviance. Loving trustworthiness without balancing it with a love for learning will result in the vice of harmful rigidity. Loving uprightness without balancing it with a love for learning will result in the vice of intolerance. Loving courage without balancing it with a love for learning will result in the vice of unruliness. Loving resoluteness without balancing it with a love for learning will result in the vice of willfulness."

The "six words" are the six virtues named, each paired with an attendant vice (*bi* 蔽; lit. "obscuration"). Learning is presented as a force able to restrain or regulate the inherent emotional "stuff" of human beings, which would tend toward excess if left to develop on its own; cf. 8.2, where the restraining force is ritual. The discipline provided by training in traditional cultural forms allows one to reshape one's native substance and hit on the mean of virtue (cf. 1.12). This description of the "six virtuous words" and their attendant vices is reminiscent of Aristotle's discussion of the virtues and their excesses and deficiencies. Aristotle describes his virtues as the mean (*mesotes*) point between two extremes: truthfulness or straightforwardness, for instance, is the mean between the vice of excess (boastfulness) and the vice of deficiency (self-deprecation).[3] Although Confucius discusses his virtues in pairs (the virtue and its excess when not restrained by the rites or learning) rather than triads (the virtues and its excess and deficiency), the basic conceptual structure of the "mean"—in Chinese, *zhong* 中, or "the center of an archery target"—is very similar, based as it is on the metaphor of a physical continuum with extreme ends or edges and a desirable mid-point. For more on the mean in the *Analects*, cf. 6.29, 13.21, 20.1.

17.9 The Master said, "Little Ones, why do none of you learn the *Odes*? The *Odes* can be a source of inspiration and a basis for evaluation; they can help you to come together with others, as well as to properly express complaints. In the home, they teach you about how to serve your father, and in public life they teach you about how to serve your lord. They also broadly acquaint you with the names of various birds, beasts, plants, and trees."

For the *Odes* as a source of inspiration, cf. 8.8, and as a resource for interpersonal communication, cf. 13.5. This passage fleshes out Confucius' comment in 16.13 to his son, Boyu, that "unless you learn the *Odes*, you will be unable to speak." As Zhu Xi comments,

> The *Odes* stimulate the mind and inspire the ambition, and examining them allows one to understand success and failure. They express harmony without getting carried away, and express complaint without falling into anger. With regard to the Way of human relationships, there are none which are not contained in the *Odes*; these two [i.e., serving one's father and one's lord] are cited because they are the most important. Moreover, the remainder of the *Odes* is able to serve as a broad resource for a knowledge of things in the world.

The *Odes* play a broad role in fostering in the individual the ability to speak and inter-act socially, providing the student with everything from quotations and turns-of-phrase useful in social situations to exemplary models of the most important role-specific duties. Seen in this light, the Master's rebuke of Boyu in 17.10 is quite understandable.

17.10 The Master said to Boyu, "Have you mastered the *Odes* from the 'South of Zhou' and the 'South of Shao'? A man who has not mastered the 'South of Zhou' and the 'South of Shao' is like someone standing with his face to the wall, is he not?"

The "South of Zhou" and "South of Shao" are the first two sections of the "Airs of the States" portion of the *Book of Odes*, and here probably stand in for the *Odes* as a whole. The sense of this passage is thus similar to 16.13 and 17.9: without the knowledge pro-vided by the *Odes*, one will lack the means to think clearly or associate with others. Some commentators believe that it is merely these two sections of the *Odes* that Confucius has in mind, but the sense is in any case much the same. As Liu Baonan remarks,

> It seems to me that these two sections of the *Odes* are entirely concerned with the Way of husbands and wives, which in turn is the first step in kingly moral transformation. Thus, the

---

[3] *Nicomachean Ethics* 1127a–b.

gentleman, in reflecting upon himself, must first cultivate it inside. Only then can he use it to discipline his wife, extend it to his brothers, and finally rely upon it to manage the state. The *History of the Han* says, "Once the Way of the household is cultivated, the principle of the world is obtained." This is exactly what I mean. Is it not also possible that, at the time this dialogue occurred, Boyu was establishing his household, and the Master therefore particularly singled out the "South of Zhou" and "South of Shao" in order to instruct him?

17.11 The Master said, "When we say, 'the rites, the rites,' are we speaking merely of jade and silk? When we say, 'music, music,' are we speaking merely of bells and drums?"

Reading this passage together with 3.3 and 3.12, one point could be that, just as true music requires not merely instruments, but also sensitive musicians to play them, so true ritual requires not merely traditional paraphernalia, but also emotionally committed, sensitive practitioners. Most commentators, however, understand the message as concerning the confusion of means and ends among Confucius' contemporaries. As Wang Bi comments,

> The governing principle of ritual is respect; jade and silk are merely the means for expressing and adorning respect. The governing principle of music is harmony; bells and drums are merely the tools with which music is made. In Confucius' age, that which went by the name of "ritual" emphasized gifts and offerings at the expense of respect, and that which went by the name of "music" failed to harmonize with the Ya and Song, despite its profusion of bells and drums. Therefore Confucius is here attempting to rectify the meanings of these words.

Understood this way, this passage may serve as another example of the "rectification of names" that Confucius held to be so important (cf. 6.25, 12.11, 13.3).

17.12 The Master said, "To assume a severe expression while being weak inside—is this not, to take an analogy from the common classes, like breaking into a home in order to commit burglary?"

"Lower classes" is a rendering of *xiaoren* 小人 (elsewhere: "petty person"), here used in its socio-economic sense in order to make the point that, while poverty-struck commoners commit transgressions in order to steal physical objects, the "petty people" among the aristocratic and educated classes—who, being well-off materially, have no need to literally commit burglary—steal metaphorically, the object of their "burglary" being a good reputation or worldly renown. This idea of hypocrisy as metaphorical thievery—to "lack the substance but steal the name," as Zhu Xi puts it—also features in 17.13.

17.13 The Master said, "The village worthy is the thief of virtue."

Probably the best commentary on this passage is *Mencius* 7:B:37, where Mencius quotes 17.13, and then is asked for further explanation by the disciple Wan Zhang:

> "What sort of person is this, who is referred to as a 'village worthy'?"
> "He is the type of person who says, 'Why be so grandly ambitious?' His words have nothing to do with his actions, and his actions have nothing to do with his words. Such a person then goes on to declare, 'The ancients, the ancients, why were they so standoffish and cold? When

you are born in an age, you should accommodate yourself to it. As long as you do so skill-fully, this is acceptable.' Someone who, in this way, tries to surreptitiously curry favor with his contemporaries—this is the 'village worthy.'"

"If everyone in a village praises a man as being worthy, and nowhere can you find someone who does not consider him worthy, what did Confucius mean by calling such a person a 'thief of Virtue'?"

"Those who try to censure him can find no basis; those who try to criticize him can find no faults. He follows along with all the vulgar trends and harmonizes with the sordid age. Dwelling in this way he seems dutiful and trustworthy; acting in this way, he seems honest and pure. The multitude are all pleased with him—he is pleased with himself as well—and yet you cannot enter with him into the Way of Yao and Shun. This is why he is called the 'thief of Virtue.' Confucius said, 'I despise that which seems to be but in fact is not. I despise weeds, for fear they will be mistaken for domesticated sprouts. I despise glibness, for fear it will be mistaken for rightness. I despise cleverness of speech, for fear it will be mistaken for trustworthiness. I despise the tunes of Zheng, for fear they will be mistaken for true music. I despise the color purple, for fear it will be mistaken for vermillion [17.18]. I despise the village worthy, for fear that he will be mistaken for one who truly possesses Virtue.'"

The village worthy is one who carefully observes all of the outward practices dictated by convention and so attains a measure of social respect, but who lacks the inward commitment to the Way that characterizes the true Confucian gentleman. Confucius refers to him as the "thief of Virtue" because from the outside he *seems* to be a gen-tleman laying a false claim to Virtue. By serving as counterfeit models of virtue for the common people, the village worthy is in effect a false prophet, not only blocking the development of true virtue in himself but also leading others astray. This is why Confucius despises him. Cf. 12.20, 13.24, 15.28, and especially 17.18.

17.14 The Master said, "To hear something on the road, and then repeat it everywhere you go, is to throw Virtue away."

The early commentators take this "something" that is heard as some valuable teach-ing that one learns about "on the road" (i.e., through hearsay, informal instruction, etc.), and then goes about repeating, without actually ever fully examining it or putting it into practice. As Huang Kan explains,

> Mere rote-learning is not sufficient to make one a teacher of others. In order to teach others, one must first be able to 'both keep past teachings alive and understand the present' [2.11], and one must examine what one has learned in detail and practice it for a long time. Only then is one ready to repeat and transmit teachings to others. If, instead, one hears something on the road, and then turns around and repeats it to someone else, a great deal of nonsense and foolishness will inevitably be the result.

Jiang Xi adds, "In Confucius' age, even those who were formally engaged in study did not learn for their own sake [14.24]—how much less so those who 'heard about it on the road'! The more you pursue superficialities, the more profoundly Virtue is wasted." On this understanding, this passage is a critique of hypocritical or unqualified teach-ers, which fits 17.14 into the series of sayings from 17.11–17.19. An alternate inter-pretation is presented by Wang Fuzhi, who sees this passage as a critique of those who circulate unsubstantiated gossip—nothing that you hear should be passed on until you have personally substantiated its truthfulness.

17.15 The Master said, "Is it really possible to work alongside one of these common fellows in serving your lord? Before such a person has obtained an official position, all that concerns him is getting one; once he has gotten one, all that concerns him is hanging onto it. And if he is concerned about hanging onto it, there are no extremes to which he will not go."

Confucius' concern seems to be that petty people, who study only for the sake of salary (8.12) and care nothing for the Way, may be led to all sorts of excesses in order to hang onto a profitable, secure source of income—what modern Chinese call the "iron rice bowl." Another potential concern is the fact that such selfish people contribute nothing to the public good. As a passage in the *History of the Han* complains before quoting 17.15, "Consider the great ministers who are to be found in court nowadays: with regard to their superiors, they are unable to correct them, and with regard to their inferiors, they do nothing to improve the lot of the common people. They are all so much dead weight, feeding at the public trough without contributing anything."

17.16 The Master said, "In ancient times, people had three type of faults, which have perhaps since disappeared. In ancient times, those who were wild were at least forthright; nowadays, they are simply deviant. In ancient times, those who were proud were at least principled; nowadays, they are simply belligerent and easily provoked. In ancient times, those who were stupid were at least upright; nowadays, they are simply devious."

Compare this complaint to 8.16: even in their faults, the ancients were superior to the people of Confucius' age. Zhu Xi claims that the difference is due to a decline in the common people's "endowment of vital energy" (*qibing* 氣稟), but this is explicitly contradicted by passages such as 17.2 ("by nature people are similar; they diverge as the result of practice") and 15.25, which points out that the common people of Confucius' age are the same that the rulers of the Three Dynasties used to "put the upright Way into practice." As Wang Fuzhi observes, "[The common people of Confucius' age] are made the way they are by the effects of instructive transformation . . . the Master's point is merely to lament the progressive decline of the customs of his age, and the fact that the customs and practices of the common people have gradually diverged from those of the ancients."

17.17 The Master said, "A clever tongue and fine appearance are rarely signs of Goodness."

This is a repeat of 1.3, possibly included here by the editor(s) because it fits in so well with the passages that surround it. Refer to 1.3 for commentary, and also cf. 5.5, 11.25, 12.3, 16.4, and especially 15.11, where the danger presented by "glib people" is compared to the derangement of morals brought about by the music of Zheng, a sentiment repeated in 17.18.

17.18 The Master said, "I hate that purple has usurped the place of vermillion, that the tunes of Zheng have been confused with classical music, and that the clever of tongue have undermined both state and family."

Vermillion—the color of the Zhou—was the traditional and proper color for ceremonial clothing, and purple a mixed, more "modern," and increasingly popular variant;

cf. 10.6 and *Mencius* 7:B:37, quoted in the commentary to 17.13. A passage in the *Hanfeizi* tells how purple was popularized by Duke Huan of Qi (685–643 B.C.E.), who started a craze for purple garments among his people by wearing purple himself, apparently because he possessed a stock of purple garments he had to unload and wished to create a profitable market for them. "Duke Huan of Qi was fond of wearing purple." the *Hanfeizi* says. "The people of Qi esteemed it as well, and were willing to exchange five plain garments for a single purple one."[4] The target of Confucius' scorn is thus perhaps the first recorded marketing fad in history. For the political trouble caused by both the Zheng music and the clever of tongue, see 15.11. The danger represented by all of these phenomena—purple, the tunes of Zheng, clever speakers—derives from the fact that, as Liu Baonan concludes, "they seem to be the real thing, but in fact are not."

17.19 The Master sighed, "Would that I did not have to speak!"

Zigong said, "If the Master did not speak, then how would we little ones receive guidance from you?"

The Master replied, "What does Heaven ever say? Yet the four seasons are put in motion by it, and the myriad creatures receive their life from it. What does Heaven ever say?"

> Reading this passage together with the ones that precede it, the theme is related to the suspicion of glibness and hypocrisy: whenever there is speech, there is the danger of a discrepancy between speech and action, which is why Confucius elsewhere has been led to declare that "the Good person is sparing of speech" (12.3) and "reticence is close to Goodness" (13.27). We see here again the metaphor of Heaven as ruler: Heaven governs the natural world in an effortless fashion, without having to issue orders, and the counterpart to Heaven in the social world is the sage-king of old, someone like Shun, "who ruled by means of wu-wei" (15.5). We have already seen the analogy between the wu-wei manner of ordering the human world and the spontaneous harmony effected by Heaven in the natural realm in 2.1, where one who rules by means of virtue is compared to the Pole Star. Like the natural world, then, a properly ordered human society functions silently, inevitably and unselfconsciously. Confucius' somewhat exasperated remark here is therefore inspired by the contrast between the natural, silent, and true order that prevailed in ancient times and the garrulous, self-righteous, hypocritical disorder that characterizes his own age.

17.20 Ru Bei [sent a messenger expressing his] wish to have an audience with Confucius, but Confucius declined, saying that he was ill. As soon as the messenger went out the door, however, Confucius picked up his zither and sang, making sure that the messenger could hear him.

> Not much is known about Ru Bei except a couple passing references in early ritual texts, although he was apparently a person from Lu. A passage from the *Exoteric Commentary* quoted in the *Imperial Readings* records a saying attributed to Zilu: "I have heard from the Master that a scholar-official seeking an audience or a woman seeking a marriage without using a proper go-between—this is not the behavior of a gentle-

---

[4] Chapter 32 ("Outer Congeries of Sayings, The Upper Left Series"); Liao 1959, vol. 2: 53–54.

man." It seems most likely that Ru Bei's error is seeking to obtain an audience with Confucius in a ritually inappropriate manner. Zhu Xi, relying on an account in the *Record of Ritual* that describes Ru Bei seeking ritual instruction from Confucius,[5] believes him to be a disciple who has no need of a go-between, but who has committed some unspecified crime. In any case, at least one point of this passage seems to be to illustrate the method of delivering an elegant, devastating insult—as in our culture, sickness was the standard pretext in early China for polite demurrals, but here Confucius wishes to make it eminently clear that his stated pretext is just that. As Simon Leys observes, "Polite insult maybe be more prudent, but it is also the supreme form of insult; it appears here that Confucius was also a great master of this subtle art" (1997: 203). Commentators generally see the purpose of this insult to be to inspire Ru Bei to reflect deeply on his own behavior and reform himself.

17.21 Zai Wo asked about the three-year mourning period, saying, "Surely one year is long enough. If the gentleman refrains from practicing ritual for three years, the rites will surely fall into ruin; if he refrains from music for three years, this will surely be disastrous for music. After the lapse of a year the old grain has been used up, while the new grain has ripened, and the four different types of tinder have all been drilled in order to rekindle the fire. One year is surely long enough."

There is some evidence from early texts, such as the *Book of Odes*, that a three-year mourning period (usually understood as *into* the third year—i.e., twenty-five months) for one's parents had at least some currency. As we have already seen in 14.40, however, this three-year period was viewed as impractical by many of Confucius' contemporaries, and we mentioned the claim of official in Teng, recorded in *Mencius* 3:A:2, that such was not even the practice of the ancients. Both of these arguments against the three-year period were later raised and pursued in detail by Mozi.[6] Here Zai Wo appears as a critic of the practice from within Confucius' own school, repeating Zizhang's implicit criticism in 14.40 that three years is impractical and counterproductive, and then adding a novel cosmological twist: if people want to model their behavior on Heaven, the one-year Heavenly cycle should be their standard. Ma Rong explains that the "rekindling of the fire" mentioned by Zai Wo refers to a ritual of renewal whereby, at the beginning of each season, a new ceremonial fire was lit from the wood of a tree appropriate to that season. After the passage of four seasons, the cycle was complete, and thus—Zai Wo claims—should one's mourning for one's parents' death also come to an end. This concern with cosmology marks this passage as rather late. This rather persuasive argument of Zai Wo's may also be an illustration of the eloquence attributed to him in 11.3, although such facility with words is, of course, a mixed blessing (at best) in Confucius' eyes, no doubt partly because it allows one to rationalize one's own immorality (cf. 11.25).

The Master asked, "Would you feel comfortable then eating your sweet rice and wearing your brocade gowns?"
    "I would."

---

[5] Chapter 21 ("Miscellaneous Records"); Legge 1967, vol. 2: 166–167.
[6] See especially Chapter 25 ("Simplicity in Funerals"); Mei 1929: 123–134.

The Master replied, "Well, if you would feel comfortable doing so, then by all means you should do it. When the gentleman is in mourning, he gets no pleasure from eating sweet foods, finds no joy in listening to music, and feels no comfort in his place of dwelling. This is why he gives up these things. But if you would feel comfortable doing them, then by all means you should!"

> While mourning his parents, a son is restricted to ordinary millet to eat—rice being an unusual luxury in northern China of this time—and rough hemp for clothing, and is to refrain from such pleasures as music or sex. He is also to dwell in a specially built mourning hut rather than his ordinary chambers. Refer to the commentary for 14.40.

After Zai Wo left, the Master remarked, "This shows how lacking in Goodness this Zai Wo is! A child is completely dependent upon the care of his parents for the first three years of his life—this is why the three-year mourning period is the common practice throughout the world. Did Zai Wo not receive three years of care from his parents?"

> Kong Anguo understands this judgment of "not Good" to signify that Zai Wo "lacks a feeling of benevolence (*ren'en* 仁恩) toward his parents"; such an understanding of *ren* as a kind of feeling (compassion, empathy) would also mark this passage as rather late (cf. 12.22). Miao Bo, however, argues for a more standard *Analects* understanding of *ren* as general moral excellence cultivated by means of ritual: Zai Wo's failure is not one of feeling, but rather of ritual propriety. What is certainly new here, in any case, is defense of a ritual standard in terms of an essential characteristic of human biology: the fact that an infant is helpless at birth and is completely dependent upon his or her parents for the first three years of life. The implication is that the length of the mourning period is not an arbitrary cultural artifact, but is rather grounded in the very nature of human experience. This sort of direct link between Confucian practice and human nature is rarely postulated in the *Analects*, but later becomes one of the major elements in the thought of Mencius.

17.22 The Master said, "Spending the entire day filling himself with food, never once exercising his mind—someone like this is a hard case indeed! Do we not have the games Bo and Yi? Even playing these games would be better than doing nothing."

> For the locution "hard case," cf. the similar statement in 15.17. Bo 簿 probably refers to the ancient boardgame of *liubo* 六簿, which was also used for divination. Yi is identified by most commentators as the traditional boardgame now called *weiqi* 圍棊 in modern Chinese, but better known to Westerners by the Japanese pronunciation *go*. This passage may be paired with 17.21 because of the laziness of Zai Wo; cf. 5.10. As Li Tong notes, "It is not that the sage is teaching people to play Bo and Yi; his statement is rather meant as an expression of his extreme disapproval of not applying one's mind at all."

17.23 Zilu asked, "Does the gentleman admire courage?"

The Master said, "The gentleman admires rightness above all. A gentleman who possessed courage but lacked a sense of rightness would create political dis-

order, while a common person who possessed courage but lacked a sense
ness would become a bandit."

"Gentleman" and "common person" are here meant in terms of social rank, as in
17.12 and 17.25. The general point is that virtues must be balanced by one another:
an individual virtue like courage, possessed in isolation, is potentially dangerous (cf.
8.10). More particularly, some commentators suggest that Zilu has been singled out
for this teaching because courage uninformed by other virtues, such as wisdom, was
his particular fault (cf. 5.7, 7.11, 11.3, 11.22). For the more general idea of virtues
unbalanced by traditional restraints turning into vices, see 17.9.

17.24 Zigong asked, "Does the gentleman also have those whom
he despises?"

The Master replied, "Yes, he does. He despises those who proclaim the faults
of others; those who, occupying an inferior position, slander their superiors; those
who are courageous but lack ritual; and those who are resolute and daring, but
overly stubborn."

As Zhu Xi observes, the concern here seems to be a lack of balance in one's
personal qualities: "Proclaiming the faults of others indicates that one lacks a
sense of compassion or tolerance; being an inferior and slandering one's superiors indicates that one lacks a dutiful and respectful heart; being courageous without ritual propriety leads to political disorder [17.25], while being resolute and yet
stubborn leads to arbitrary and rash behavior. This is why the Master despises these
qualities."

"Do you, Zigong, also have those whom you despise?"

Zigong said, "I despise those who parrot others' ideas and mistake this for
wisdom; those who mistake insubordination for courage; and those who mistake
the malicious exposing of other's private affairs for uprightness."

The emphasis in Zigong's response seems to be on semblances of virtue; cf. especially
17.13 and 17.17–17.18.

17.25 The Master said, "Women and servants are particularly hard to manage:
if you are too familiar with them, they grow insolent, but if you are too distant
they grow resentful."

This is an infamously misogynous passage that some later commentators have sought
to soften. The use of the word *yang* 養 ("manage," "care for," "raise") suggests the
context of aristocratic household management, which is why *xiaoren* 小人 is best translated in its more concrete social sense of "servants" or lower class people. Some claim
that, considering this household management context, "women" (*nuzi* 女子) is meant
only to refer to slave women or female servants. Such women were certainly still being
kept in aristocratic households in Confucius' age, but so were male slaves and servants, which means that even under this interpretation we have the problem of why
women in particular are being singled out. In the *Zuo Commentary* we read, "Female
attractive power (*nude* 女德) is infinite, and there is no end to the resentment of

women."[7] Du Yu's commentary on this passage paraphrases 17.25: "The disposition of women is such that if one is familiar with them they do not know when to stop or when is enough, whereas if one is distant with them their resentment knows no bounds." The danger of "female power" is a constant theme in traditional texts from the earliest times, usually manifesting itself in two ways: more generally, as a force analogous to alcohol that intoxicates men and leads them into immorality, and more specifically in the form of the deleterious influence of concubines or dissolute wives who hold the ear of the ruler and thereby lead the state into moral and political ruin.[8] We have already seen examples of the former sense in 9.18 and 15.13, and the latter in the person of the infamous Nanzi of Wei in 6.28. With this in mind, the sense of 17.25 is probably one that would not seem particularly strange to a man in Victorian Europe: considering their potentially dangerous sexual power and inability to control themselves, household women (i.e., wives and concubines), like servants, need to be managed firmly, but with respect, if they are to remain obedient and not overstep their proper roles.

17.26 The Master said, "If, having reached the age of forty, you still find your-self despised by others, you will remain despised until the end of your days."

The point here seems similar to 9.23 ("once a man reaches the age of forty or fifty without having acquired a degree of learning, we can conclude from this fact alone that he is not worthy of being held in awe"), especially if we take 9.23's *wen* 聞 ("learning") as "reputation." There is a tension between this statement and passages such as 12.20 and 13.24, where public opinion is viewed with suspicion, but perhaps the point here is, as Zhu Xi suggests, merely "to urge people to improve themselves and make good their faults before it is too late." An alternate interpretation is advanced by Yu Yue, who believes this to be a lament by Confucius concerning himself: "Since I am already forty years old and yet still despised by others [i.e., not employed], I will remain this way until the end of my days." Understood this way, the sentiment here would be similar to 5.7 and 9.9.

---

[7] Duke Xi, Year 24 (635 B.C.E.); Legge 1991d: 192.

[8] This is the context of the *Zuo Commentary* passage previously quoted.

BOOK EIGHTEEN

This Book consists primarily of accounts of historical figures and encounters between Confucius and contemporary recluses—both primitivists who reject society altogether, and principled recluses disgusted with the present age. The main themes seem to be of timeliness and balance: both the ancients and Confucius knew how to respond to the age, and they are contrasted with rigid, overly purist recluses, who in clinging to virtue and avoiding the complexities of negotiating their contemporary world, lose some of their humanity. Confucius' remark in 18.8 serves to sum up the theme of all of the recluse-encounter passages (14.32, 14.38–14.39, 18.5–18.7): "I am different from all of them in that I have no preconceived idea concerning what is permissible and what is not." We also see Confucius' rather tragic sense of mission: he knows that his efforts are probably doomed to failure, but cannot but try to do something. The passages from 18.8–18.11 are fragmentary and textually corrupt in various ways, and seem to have been somewhat arbitrarily inserted into the end of the Book, possibly grouped together because 18.8–18.9 and 18.11 contain lists of proper names.

18.1 The Master of Wei left his side, the Master of Ji became his slave, and Bi Gan remonstrating with him and was therefore put to death. Confucius said, "In them, the Shang had three Good men."

The "him" referred to here is the evil king Zhow, the last ruler of the Shang Dynasty; both Wei and Ji were semi-independent states within the Shang realm. There is some discrepancy in the historical accounts concerning the relationship of the Master of Wei to King Zhow, although all agree that the Master of Wei was the eldest son of the Shang ruler, and the future King Zhow the youngest. All accounts agree that the Master of Ji and Bi Gan were uncles of King Zhow. According to a long account provided by Huang Kan, all three of these figures were appalled by the behavior of the notoriously cruel and immoral King Zhow, but their responses varied because of their situations. The Master of Wei, as the eldest son of the former Shang ruler, felt his first responsibility to be assuring the continuity of the family ancestral sacrifices, and therefore he fled in order to devote himself to the care of the clan's ancestral temple. The Master of Ji, the elder of the two uncles and a senior official, realized that things were hopeless after repeated attempts to remonstrate with King Zhow. Death was not an option for him because his important official status might render him useful in the future, so he feigned madness in order to divert Zhow's wrath, allowing himself to be enslaved. Bi Gan, the younger uncle and a minor official, was unburdened by familial or official responsibilities, and therefore felt himself free to follow his conscience and forthrightly denounce the King. The general lesson provided by their examples, Huang Kan concludes, is this:

Their motivation for what they did was Goodness—a concern for the age and a willingness to abandon their own lives in order to be of use. Although their courses of action were different, all three were similarly motivated by a concern for the age and for the common people, and if they all could have changed places, each would have been able to do as the other had done . . . Each responded with perfect appropriateness to the situation, all of them serving as model ministers worthy of being emulated, and this is why they are praised as Good.

Bi Gan also serves for Confucians as the stock figure exemplifying the lesson that the gentleman may end up in ditch as a result of his devotion to rightness (15.9); cf. stories of him in *Mencius* 2:A:1 and 4:A:6.

18.2 When Liuxia Hui was serving as Captain of the Guard, he was dismissed three times. People said to him, "Sir, is this not grounds for simply leaving?"

He replied, "If I serve others by means of the upright Way, where can I go and not end up being dismissed three times? If, instead, I were to serve others in a crooked, accommodating manner, what need would I have to leave my home state?"

The post held by Liuxia Hui—literally "Leader of the Scholar-Officials" (*shishi* 士師)—was a minor one in the Ministry of Justice, apparently something like a public prosecutor or judicial magistrate; cf. 19.19. This passage is probably paired with 18.1 because of the analogy between Bi Gan and Liuxia Hui: neither is burdened by particularly heavy family or official duties, and thus both are free to openly follow the "upright Way" regardless of the consequences—although these consequences were much more severe in Bi Gan's case. Also cf. 15.14 and 18.8.

18.3 With regard to how he should treat Confucius, Duke Jing of Qi said, "I cannot treat him as I would the head of the Ji Family; I shall treat him at a level somewhere between that of the head of the Ji Family and the head of the Meng Family." On a later occasion, he remarked, "I am too old, I will not be able to employ him." Confucius then left the state of Qi.

Zhu Xi is probably correct in thinking that neither of these statements by Duke Jing were made in Confucius' presence, but rather reached him indirectly. The version of this encounter found in the *Record of the Historian* (which records it as occurring in 515 B.C.E.) has the other ministers in Qi reacting with anger and jealousy to the exalted treatment accorded Confucius, which then contributes to Duke Jing's reluctance to actually employ him. In any case, the point is probably Confucius' sense of "timeliness" (*shi* 時)—knowing when to stay and when to go. As Jiang Xi remarks, "The unicorn cannot be caught by a jackal, and the phoenix cannot be attacked by a hawk. That which the Master presented to others was inevitably the correct Way, and thus Duke Jing was unable to put him to use, excusing himself on account of age. If he could harmonize with a ruler, the Master would go see them; if he became estranged from them, he would leave. This illustrates the principle that the sage is not inflexible." Incidentally, it is highly unlikely that any ruler of the time could have even remotely conceived of treating Confucius as if he were the equal of the head of the Ji Family, so this exaggerated portrayal of Confucius' importance marks this as a later passage. As Waley observes, "The Confucius who ranked above the head of the Meng family is already well on the way towards apotheosis" (1989: 218, n. 4).

18.4 The people of Qi sent a gift of female entertainers. Ji Huanzi accepted them [on behalf of the Duke of Lu], and court was not held for several days. Confucius thereupon left the state of Lu.

Despite Ji Huanzi's position as *de facto* ruler of Lu, it is unlikely that he would receive an official gift from another state; Kong Anguo is no doubt correct in explaining that Ji Huanzi's role was to allow the Duke of Lu[1] to accept the gift, and perhaps to enjoy it along with him. Alternate versions of this event are recorded in the *Record of the Historian* and the *Hanfeizi*; the latter is more concise:

> Confucius was serving in the government of Lu, which concerned Duke Jing of Qi.[2] Li Qie said to the Duke, "Why does my lord not invite Confucius to come to Qi with a large salary and high position? Then send Duke Ai some dancing girls in order to flatter him and make him feel honored. As long as the novelty of his pleasure in them lasts, he will certainly neglect the affairs of state, and this will in turn inevitably cause Confucius to remonstrate with him. Once Confucius remonstrates with him, he will no doubt find himself slighted and cold-shouldered in Lu." Duke Jing said this was an excellent idea, and thereupon ordered Li Qie to send Duke Ai a gift of six dancing girls. Duke Ai was greatly pleased by them, and as a result neglected affairs of state. Confucius remonstrated with him and was not heeded, and thereupon left the state to go to Chu.[3]

The account here in 18.4 says nothing of remonstration, but rather implies that Confucius simply left in disgust. As Bao Xian remarks, "Seeing pleasures of the flesh so exalted in his state, and a court so lacking in ritual propriety, how could the Master abide it?" Cf. 15.1, where Confucius leaves in disgust after being asked about military affairs by Duke Ling of Wei.

18.5 Jieyu, the Madman of Chu, passed by Confucius singing a song:

> "Oh phoenix! Oh phoenix!
> Why has your Virtue so declined?
> What is past is beyond remonstration,
> But the future can still be pursued.
> Give it up! Give it up!

Those who participate in government these days court nothing but danger."
 Confucius descended from his carriage and wished to speak with him, but Jieyu scurried away and avoided him. Therefore Confucius did not get to speak with him.

Jieyu's song rhymes in the original Chinese. There are many stories about Jieyu in Warring States and Han texts, including an alternate, slightly more elaborate version

---

[1] Kong Anguo believes this Duke to have been Duke Ding, whereas the *Hanfeizi* account cited below claims that it was Duke Ai.

[2] The Duke is worried that Confucius' sagely advice will allow the state of Lu to become stronger and challenge the power of Qi.

[3] Chapter 31 ("Inner Congeries of Sayings, Lower Series"); Liao 1959, vol. 2: 21–22. A *Record of Ritual* account agrees with the *Hanfeizi* that this incident caused Confucius to leave Lu for Chu, but an alternate version in the *Family Sayings* says that Confucius went instead to Wei. Again, the idea of Confucius serving in the highest levels of government and striking fear in the hearts of neighboring rulers is the product of the later cult of Confucius, rather than a reflection of any kind of historical fact.

of this encounter between him and Confucius recorded in the *Zhuangzi*.[4] The *Biographies of High-Minded Scholar-Officials* describes him as a primitivist self-preservationist, who "was fond of nourishing his nature, and personally ploughed the fields in order to make a living. During the time of King Zhao of Chu, he saw that the government of Chu would not last, and therefore he feigned madness in order to avoid public service. For this reason he was known among his contemporaries as 'the Madman of Chu.'" In his song, he makes a flattering comparison between Confucius and the phoenix, whose arrival is an auspicious omen (9.9), but, as Huang Kan notes, "the phoenix waits until the appearance of a sagely ruler before it shows itself, whereas now Confucius is traveling about, meeting with rejection everywhere he goes. This is why Jieyu says that the phoenix's Virtue has declined." The basic message of the song is very similar to the advice given by recluses in 14.38–14.39 and 18.6–18.7 below: considering that Confucius has met with no success in the political realm, he should just stop trying. Although many Western translators and some traditional commentators see this series from 18.5–18.7 as "the subversive product of the Daoist imagination" (Leys 1997: 206) intended to mock Confucius that somehow infiltrated the *Analects*, the point of these passages (as in 14.38–14.39) is in fact to vindicate Confucius by presenting his way as more noble, though more difficult, than the way of these social drop-outs.[5] As Wang Fuzhi observes, "In the world, there are rightful duties that simply cannot be evaded, and yet these recluses focus on nothing but keeping their hands from getting dirty . . . This is why, every time that they mock Confucius, he responds with honest concern for them, and desires to speak with them in order to broaden their minds. This illustrates how Confucius was the supreme educator."

18.6 Confucius passed Chang Ju and Jie Ni, who were yoked together pulling a plow through a field. He sent Zilu to ask them where the ford was to be found.

Confucius and his entourage were apparently attempting to cross a nearby river, but this passage is probably also to be read allegorically: the "ford" is the way out of the "great flood" of chaos mentioned below. The use of self-consciously primitive technology by these two figures (most plows were ox-drawn by this time), as well as their knowledge of Confucius' identity revealed below, makes it clear that they—like the farmer/music critic in 14.39—are no ordinary commoners, but rather educated, primitivist recluses who have deliberately rejected society and culture. Like many of the figures in the *Zhuangzi*, their names appear to be allegorical (*changju* 長沮 means "Standing Tall in the Marsh" and *jieni* 桀溺 "Prominent in the Mud"); the appearance of this literary technique and the complex narrative quality of this passage mark it as quite late.

Chang Ju inquired, "That fellow holding the reins there—who is he?"
    Zilu answered, "That is Confucius."

---

[4] Chapter 4 ("In the World of Men"); Watson 1968: 66–67.

[5] It is also rather absurd to think that overtly anti-Confucian passages could somehow have been "snuck into" the *Analects* by philosophical rivals. As Brooks and Brooks remark, "We can see the Daoists sneaking up to Confucian headquarters in the dead of night. We can see them jimmying open a window. We can see them taking the *Analects* manuscript out of its drawer in the office desk. We can see them writing anti-Confucian anecdotes in it. We can hear them chortling as they vanish into the night. What we *can't* see is the scene next morning, where [the editor of the *Analects*] comes in, opens the book, finds the Daoist stories, scratches his head, mumbles, 'Well, yeah; I guess I *must* have,' and calls the students in to memorize them" (1998: 183).

"Do you mean Confucius of Lu?"

"The same."

"Then *he* should know where the ford is."

As Ma Rong explains, this comment is apparently meant as a jab at Confucius' itinerant ways: "The point is that, since Confucius travels about so much, he should know himself where the ford is."

Zilu then asked Jie Ni.

Jie Ni also replied with a question: "Who are you?"

"I am Zilu."

"The disciple of Confucius of Lu?"

"Yes."

"The whole world is as if engulfed in a great flood, and who can change it? Given this, instead of following a scholar who merely avoids the bad people [of this age], wouldn't it be better for you to follow scholars like us, who avoid the age itself?" He then proceeded to cover up his seeds with dirt and did not pause again.

Zilu returned and reported this conversation to Confucius. The Master was lost in thought for a moment, and then remarked, "A person cannot flock together with the birds and the beasts. If I do not associate with the followers of men, then with whom would I associate? If the Way were realized in the world, then I would not need to change anything."

This characterization of these recluses as "living like the birds and beasts" sums up the Confucian criticism of the primitivist-Laozian project: rightful social duties and the elaborations of culture are part of any properly human life, and to abandon these to lead a solitary, primitive lifestyle is to abandon one's humanity. Confucius' compassion for the suffering of the world is such that he cannot take what he views as the easy way out—simply withdrawing from society and living the life of a noble, unsullied recluse—although his mission as the "bell-clapper of Heaven" (3.24) is grueling and fraught with difficulties and frustrations. At least two stories in the *Zhuangzi* are apparently inspired by this passage. In Chapter 6, Confucius is portrayed somewhat sympathetically as one "punished by Heaven," who admires the wild and free Daoist masters but is fated to act in the conventional world, whereas in Chapter 20 the Daoists get the last say, and Confucius is portrayed as finally abandoning the social world and going to dwell as a recluse among the birds and beasts.[6]

18.7 Zilu was traveling with Confucius, but had fallen behind. He encountered an old man carrying a wicker basket suspended from his staff. Zilu asked, "Have you seen my Master?"

The old man answered,

> "'Won't soil his dainty hands
> Can't tell millet from corn.'
> Who, then, might your master be?"

He then planted his staff in the ground and began weeding.

[Not knowing how to reply], Zilu simply remained standing with his hands clasped as a sign of respect.

---

[6] For the former, see Watson 1968: 87, and the latter Watson 1968: 214.

The old man's comment is a rhyming verse in the Chinese—an indication that again we are not dealing with an ordinary, illiterate farmer. Its target is both Zilu and Confucius: in his scholar-official dress and with his unsoiled hands, Zilu is clearly not suited to manual labor in the fields. The farmer is gently mocking both Zilu's uselessness and the sort of education that produced it. Zilu does not respond to this rather rude remark, probably out of respect for the old farmer's age, and his quiet, dignified demeanor apparently wins the old man over.

The old man subsequently invited Zilu back to his house to stay the night. After killing a chicken and preparing some millet for Zilu to eat, he presented his two sons to him. The next day, Zilu caught up to Confucius and told him what had happened.

"He must be a scholar recluse," the Master said. He sent Zilu back to the old farmer's house to meet with him again, but by the time Zilu got there the man had already disappeared. Zilu then remarked, "To avoid public service is to be without a sense of what is right. Proper relations between elders and juniors cannot be discarded—how, then, can one discard the rightness that obtains between ruler and minister? To do so is to wish to keep one's hands from getting dirty at the expense of throwing the great social order into chaos. The gentleman takes office in order to do what is right, even though he already knows that the Way will not be realized."

Commentators believe that Zilu's final remarks are delivered to the old farmer's two sons, presumably to be passed on when he returns. The point is that the old recluse clearly recognizes the first set of relationships (between elders and juniors) in requiting Zilu's formal hand clasping—an expression of respect by a younger man for an elder—by providing Zilu with proper hospitality and formally presenting his sons, but he ignores the second (between ruler and minister) by living in reclusion and avoiding any sort of official contact. Cf. the account of a similar encounter between Confucius, Zilu, and a recluse in the *Zhuangzi*.[7]

18.8 Those men who went into seclusion include Bo Yi, Shu Qi, Yu Zhong, Yi Yi, Zhu Zhang, Liuxia Hui, and Shao Lian.

These men were all famous recluses who withdrew from public service on moral grounds. The version of the *Analects* on which Zheng Xuan based his commentary apparently mentioned only five people here, dropping Yi Yi and Zhu Zhang. In any case, Zhu Zhang is dropped in the elaboration below, which suggests that the name has crept in by mistake.

The Master said, "Unwilling to lower their aspirations or bring disgrace upon their persons—such were Bo Yi and Shu Qi."

For Bo Yi and Shu Qi, see the commentary to 5.23, 7.15, and 16.12.

Of Liuxia Hui and Shao Lian he said, "Although they lowered their aspirations and brought disgrace upon their persons, at least their speech was in accord with their status and their actions were in accord with their thoughts."

---

[7] Chapter 12 ("Ze Yang"); Watson 1968, 285–286.

For Liuxia Hui, see 15.14 and 18.2. Little is known about Shao Lian besides a mention in the *Record of Ritual*, where he and an older brother are described as Eastern barbarians who are, nonetheless, very sincere and conscientious mourners.[8]

Of Yu Zhong and Yi Yi he said, "Living in seclusion and freely speaking their minds, their persons remained pure and their resignations from office were well-considered."

Nothing certain is known about either of these figures. Zhu Xi identifies Yu Zhong as Zhong Yong, the brother of the Great Uncle mentioned in 8.1 (see the commentary to 8.1 for both Zhong Yong and the Great Uncle). Qing scholars such as Huan Maoyong, however, argue fairly convincingly against this identification.

He concluded, "I, however, am different from all of them in that I have no preconceived notions of what is permissible and what is not."

As Ma Rong comments, "The Master did not necessarily have to enter service, nor did he necessarily have to withdraw from service—he is 'merely on the side of what is right [4.10].'" This sums up what separates a true gentleman such as Confucius from the merely pure or fastidious: he is the "timely sage" (*Mencius* 5:B:1), and thus is able to respond flexibly to the demands of the situation. Cf. especially 10.27.

18.9 Senior Music Master Zhi went to Qi; Conductor for the Second Course[9] Gan went to Chu; Conductor for Third Course Liao went to Cai; Conductor for the Fourth Course Que went to Qin; the large drum player Fangshu went to live on the banks of the Yellow River; the hand-drum player Wu went to live on the banks of the Han River; and Junior Music Master Yang and stone-chime player Xiang went to live on the coast.

Music Master Zhi appeared in 8.15, and, according to the *Family Sayings*, stone-chime player Xiang once gave zither lessons to Confucius. Nothing is known concerning the other musicians mentioned. Most commentators take this passage as a description of the exodus that followed the final decline of the court music in Lu during the reign of Duke Ai. "During the reign of Duke Ai," Kong Anguo explains, "Ritual was ruined and music collapsed, and therefore all of the musicians in Lu left." Some commentators attempt to link this passage to 18.4, identifying the straw that broke the camel's back as Duke Ai's acceptance of dancing girls from Qi (who presumably performed to something along the lines of the licentious music of Zheng), but more probably the exodus of the musicians is simply presented here as one more symptom of the general moral decline in Lu. As Ames and Rosemont remark, "It is difficult to keep good music and bad government together" (1998: 269, n. 325).

18.10 The Duke of Zhou said to the Duke of Lu, "The gentleman does not neglect his relatives, nor does he cause his great ministers to be angry about not being properly employed. Therefore, he does not dismiss someone who has been

---

[8] Chapter 21 ("Miscellaneous Records"); Legge 1967, vol. 2: 153–154.

[9] An official title, referring to the conductor who was in charge of the music played during the state banquets.

long in his service, unless they commit a grave offense, and he does not demand everything from any one person."

> The "Duke of Lu" mentioned here is presumably Boqin, the son of the Duke of Zhou, who was given Lu as his fief. Most commentators understand this passage as advice occasioned by the enfeofment of the young Duke. Like the passages that surround it, it seems to be a random, traditional saying preserved in Lu that somehow found its way into the end of Book Eighteen. Han Yu, however, believes it to be something deliberately cited by Confucius as a warning to Duke Ai to be more careful in his employment of people. For the injunction against "demanding perfection from one person," cf. 13.25.

18.11 The Zhou had eight [worthy] scholar-officials: the Eldest-Sons Da and Kuo, the Second-Sons Tu and Hu, the Third-Sons Ye and Xia, and the Youngest-Sons Sui and Gua.

> According to commentators, these eight were four sets of twins born to the same mother during the reign of King Cheng (according to Zheng Xuan) or King Xuan (according to Ma Rong and Liu Xiang). Each twin's name rhymes with that of his brother in archaic Chinese pronunciation. The unusualness of a single woman giving birth to four sets of twins, all of whom grew into moral worthies, is apparently what makes this noteworthy, and some commentators further understand this profusion of great men from one family as intended to illustrate the greatness of the Zhou. Like some of the other passages, 18.11 seems to be a random bit of lore that somehow found its way into the end of this Book.

BOOK NINETEEN

This Book consists entirely of sayings from the disciples, many of which are summaries or elaborations of themes already seen in earlier Books. A number of uncharacteristic features emerge in this Book, especially in the second half, and this is probably indicative of a fairly late date. For instance, in 19.22–19.25 Confucius is referred to by the style-name Zhongni 仲尼 ("Second-Son Ni"), a first for the Analects, *although this practice is common in later—especially non-Confucian—texts. Similarly, in passages 19.23–19.25 we see the beginnings of the myth of Confucius' mysterious, transcendent character that became the basis of Confucius' deification in the Han Dynasty.*

19.1 Zizhang said, "To submit to fate when confronted with danger, to think of rightness when presented with an opportunity for gain, to focus on respectfulness when offering sacrifices, and to concentrate upon your grief when in mourning—these are the qualities that make a scholar-official acceptable."

Most commentators understand this to be a summary of the minimum qualities that are necessary to make one an acceptable scholar-official—the word "acceptable" (*ke* 可) giving the impression that even more is ideally expected. For accepting one's fate in the face of danger, cf. 14.12; for rightness and gain, cf. 14.12, 16.10; for respectfulness in sacrifice, cf. 3.12; and for grief in mourning, cf. 3.4, 19.14.

19.2 Zizhang said, "If you are not grand in the manner you hold onto Virtue, or sincere in your trust in the Way, how can you be said to possess anything? How can you be said to lack anything?"

As Kong Anguo comments, "The point is that, without these qualities, one is not even worthy of being valued or slighted." Liu Baonan sees this as a critique of "those contemporaries of Zizhang who were content with petty achievements or confused by heterodox doctrines"—such people are dismissed as not even worth discussing. Cf. 13.20.

19.3 The disciples of Zixia asked Zizhang about social relations.

Zizhang said, "What does Zixia have to say about this?"

They responded, "Zixia says, 'Associate with those who are acceptable, and reject those who are unacceptable.'"

Zizhang said, "This is different from what I have learned. The gentleman treats the worthy people with reverence, and is tolerant of the masses; he praises excellence, but takes pity on those who are incapable. If I am truly a great worthy, what will I not tolerate in my dealings with others? If I am, in fact, unworthy, then people will reject me—what need is there for me to reject them?"

Interpreters of this passage break down roughly into two main camps: the "complementary" camp, which believes that both maxims are correct in their own context, and the "opposite excesses" camp, which believe that both maxims are incorrect expressions of the two disciples' idiosyncratic natures. Both Bao Xian and Zheng Xuan belong to the first camp, arguing that the two maxims simply relate to different spheres of social interactions. As Bao Xian puts it, "Zixia's maxim is appropriate for relations with friends, whereas Zizhang's maxim is appropriate for relations with the masses." In support of this interpretation, we might cite 1.8, 9.25, and 16.4–16.5 as instances where the Master advocated choosiness in picking one's friends, and 1.5–1.6 for the idea of a ruler extending benevolent caring to the common people. Huang Shisan also sees the two maxims as complementary, although he believes they relate to different phases in the process of education rather than different social spheres: Zixia's maxim is appropriate for beginning students, who need to be very careful about what influences they subject themselves to, whereas Zizhang's maxim reflects the magnanimous attitude of the perfected sage. In the second camp are commentators such as Luan Zhao, who remarks,

> If you are too tolerant then you will win over the masses, but will also be indiscriminate in your friendships; if you are too choosy then you will harmonize with very few people, and will end up personally isolated. Here we see clearly how each of the maxims is inspired by the two disciples' one-sided natures, and that neither of them measures up to the broad, inclusive scale of the Master.

Zhu Xi agrees with Luan Zhao, remarking that one must avoid the excesses of both disciples: it is necessary to be careful in choosing one's friends, but one must also avoid becoming overly narrow-minded. Huan Maoyong also sees the two maxims as expressions of the disciples' own flaws, with Zixia "not going far enough" and Zizhang going "too far."

19.4 Zixia said, "Although the byways no doubt have their own interesting sights to see, one who wishes to reach a distant destination fears becoming mired. This is why the gentleman does not take the byways."

Although He Yan and Zheng Xuan take "byways" (*xiaodao* 小道—lit. "minor ways") to refer to heterodox doctrines (cf. 2.16), Zhu Xi is probably correct in understanding it to refer to minor, specialized talents "such as agriculture, gardening, medicine, or divination." Such specialized skills are not bad in themselves, but they distract one from the overall task of self-cultivation (the "distant destination" of moral perfection), and are not worthy of the gentleman; cf. 2.12, 9.2, 9.6, 9.7, 13.4, and 19.7. 19.4 is paraphrased in a passage from the *History of the Han*, where the "great Way" of the gentleman is presented more narrowly as the study of the classics: "The Five Classics were assembled by the sage, and there is nothing among the myriad things in the world that is not completely recorded therein. Petty disputations ruin rightness, and byways will not bring one through to one's destination, which is why one who wishes to reach a distant destination fears becoming mired. None of these minor things are worth one's attention."

19.5 Zixia said, "Being aware every day of what he still lacks, and after a month's time not forgetting what he is already capable of—a person like this can be said to love learning."

Huang Kan observes that "this is intended to urge people on in their learning," and compares it to 2.11, which he understands in the sense of "keeping what one has previously learned in one's mind in order to understand new things." Being aware of what one still lacks is a motivation to learn more, and retaining what one has already learned prevents backsliding. Cf. 1.15 and 19.6.

19.6 Zixia said, "Learning broadly and firmly retaining what one has learned, being incisive in one's questioning and able to reflect upon what is near at hand—Goodness is to be found in this."

Here the combination of learning and personal reflection is presented as one of the keys to attaining Goodness; cf. 2.15 and 2.18.

19.7 Zixia said, "The various artisans dwell in their workshops in order to perfect their crafts, just as the gentleman learns in order to reach the end of his Way."

Jiang Xi is probably correct in thinking that part of the point here is that learning is something that one needs to acquire through hard work: "A craftsman is certainly not born skillful. He must spend time in his workshop in order to broaden his knowledge, and as his knowledge broadens, his skill is perfected. Similarly, the gentleman is not able to intuitively comprehend everything he needs to know—he must learn in order to broaden his thinking, and as his thinking is broadened, his Way will become perfected." Zixia is likening the practice of the gentleman to more mundane craft practices (cf. other craft metaphors for self-cultivation in 1.15, 3.8, 5.10, 15.10), but with the clear implication (especially after 19.4) that the way of the gentleman is the higher and more inclusive path.

19.8 Zixia said, "When a petty person commits a transgression, he is sure to gloss it over."

The translation follows Kong Anguo and Huang Kan in taking *wen* 文 as a verb (*wenshi* 文飾; "to gloss over"). Kong's explanation is that the petty person "glosses over his transgressions, and does not divulge the real situation." Huang Kan elaborates:

> When the gentleman commits a transgression, it is because of an error in his behavior, not because he deliberately chose to act that way. Therefore, when he is made aware of his transgression, he corrects it [1.8, 7.22]. When a petty person commits a transgression, however, he does so consciously and deliberately, and therefore wishes to gloss it over, being unwilling to admit that he has done something wrong.

An alternate way to read this passage—not as well supported by the grammar—would be to take *wen* as a noun: "When a petty person commits an error-transgression, it is sure to be on the side of cultural refinement." This is how *wen* is understood in a similar passage in the *Record of the Historian*: "When the gentleman commits a transgression, it can be excused on the basis of native substance; when a petty person commits a transgression, it can be excused on the basis of cultural refinement." In this case, the point would be that a gentleman is sometimes led to excessive but sincere actions by his "untrimmed" native substance (5.22), whereas a petty person's errors tend to involve hypocrisy or insincerity.

19.9 Zixia said, "The gentleman has three aspects: when you gaze upon him from afar, he appears grave and imposing; once you approach him, he appears mild and welcoming; and when you listen to his words, he appears strict and serious."

These different aspects are probably various manifestations of the same inner disposition, merely appearing to be different from the outside. As He Yan comments: "The gentleman straightens himself internally by means of respectfulness, and rectifies himself externally by means of rightness. His words are correct and he embodies straightness, his Virtuous manner revealing itself naturally. Although people might say that he possesses different aspects, the gentleman does not in fact really change." Cf. the description of Confucius in 7.38.

19.10 Zixia said, "The gentleman imposes labors upon his people only after earning their trust. If he does so before having earned their trust, they will think him cruel. The gentleman remonstrates with [his ruler][1] only after earning his trust. If he does so before having earned his trust, his ruler will think him insolent."

Regarding the first injunction, cf. 12.7. As Zhu Xi observes, the point of this passage is that "both in serving superiors and employing inferiors, one must first be sincere in intention and enjoy the other's confidence before one can act."

19.11 Zixia said, "As long as one does not transgress the bounds when it comes to important Virtues, it is permissible to cross the line here and there when it comes to minor Virtues."

An illustration of this principle is found in a story from the *Exoteric Commentary*, where it is put into the mouth of Confucius:

> When Confucius encountered Cheng Muzi in the region of Yan, he lowered the canopy of his carriage and talked with him for the rest of the day. After some time, he turned to Zilu and said, "Make up fourteen bundles of silk and present them to the gentleman." Zilu replied, "I have heard from the Master that scholar-officials do not receive one another when on the road"[2] Confucius said, "As long as one does not transgress the bounds when it comes to important Virtues, it is permissible to cross the line here and there when it comes to minor Virtues."[3]

For similar themes in the *Analects*, cf. 9.3 and 15.37. An alternate interpretation is offered by Kong Anguo and Huang Kan, who take the passage to be referring to two levels of people, along the lines of "Those with great Virtue do not transgress the bounds; when it comes to people of small Virtue, crossing the line here and there is acceptable." This reading is supported by a comment attributed to Confucius in the *Xunzi*: "Correct when it comes to important regulations, but occasionally crossing the line here and there when it comes to minor regulations—such is the middling gentleman (*zhongjun* 中君)."[4] The interpretation adopted in the translation seems preferable, however, having more support in the *Analects* itself.

19.12 Ziyou said, "Among the disciples of Zixia, the younger ones are fairly competent when it comes to tasks such as mopping and sweeping, answering

---

[1] The received text does not mention the ruler, but the context of remonstration seems to require that we add it, and the fact that alternate transmissions of this passage in the *History of the Later Han* and other texts do explicitly include "his ruler" suggest that these words have dropped out of the received text.

[2] I.e., without observing the formalities of presenting an introduction and being ritually received.

[3] Chapter 2.16; Hightower 1952: 54–55.

[4] Chapter 9 ("On the Regulations of the King"); Knoblock 1990: 97.

summons, and entering and retiring from formal company, but these are all superficialities.[5] They are completely at a loss when it comes to mastering the basics. Why is this?"

When Zixia heard of this, he remarked, "Alas! Ziyou seems to have missed the point. Whose disciples will be the first to be taught the Way of the gentleman, and then in the end grow tired of it? It is like the grass and the trees: you make distinctions between them according to their kind. The Way of the gentleman, how can it be slandered so? Starting at the beginning and working through to the end—surely this describes none other than the sage!"

Ziyou is criticizing Zixia for making his younger disciples practice minor ritual tasks instead of teaching them about the "important" issues, but what he fails to understand is only someone who starts at the beginning of the Way of the gentleman can truly walk it to its end. This means that the teacher must distinguish between the "grass" (the younger students at the beginning of the path) and the "trees" (the more mature students capable of advanced work), and target his instruction accordingly—forcing students to learn things of which they are not yet capable lead only to exhaustion. As Bao Xian notes, "Zixia's point is that those who are taught the Way too early will inevitably be the first to grow tired, and therefore he starts his disciples off with minor tasks, and only later instructs them in great matters." A further import of the metaphor is that the manner with which one comports oneself with regard to small matters is connected organically to how one will develop in the end; therefore, one cannot neglect the "roots," nor can one rush the process. As Huang Kan remarks, "Because the great Way of the gentleman is so profound, the only way to study it broadly is in stages." For the "root" metaphor, cf. 1.2 and 3.4, and for the importance of the details of daily behavior in judging and cultivating one's character, cf. 2.10. An alternate reading of the final line is, "Possessing both the beginning and the end [at the same time]—surely only the sage is like this!" Under this interpretation, the point is that, while most people have to proceed in a step-wise fashion, there are rare sages who possess it all at birth.

19.13 Zixia said, "One who excels in his official position should then devote himself to learning. One who excels in learning should then devote himself to official service."

Following Ma Rong's gloss of *you* 優 ("to excel"; cf. 14.11) as "having energy to spare" (i.e, being "overqualified") this passage might alternately be rendered, "One with energy to spare after fulfilling his official responsibilities should devote it to learning. One with energy to spare after learning should devote it to official service." In the first sense, the point would seem to be that learning is required for an excellent official to be truly excellent, in the same way that official service should be the natural outgrowth of excellence in learning the Confucian Way. In the second sense, part of the point is that, as Zhu Xi remarks, "a public official who attempts to engage in learning without having the energy to spare will fall into the error of turning his back on the public good in order to pursue his private interests, and a student who has energy to spare but does not enter public service cannot avoid the charge of cherishing his own self to the point that he forgets about others."

---

[5] Lit. "the branches" (*mo* 末), contrasted with the "basics"—lit., the "root" (*ben* 本).

19.14 Ziyou said, "Mourning should fully express grief and then stop at that."

Reading this passage together with 3.4 and 15.41, this is a warning against allowing cultural refinement to overwhelm native substance. Kong Anguo and Huang Kan read it rather differently, however, seeing it as a warning against allowing oneself to be overwhelmed by grief to the point of personal harm. As Huang Kan puts it, "Although mourning rituals are based upon the emotion of grief, the filial son cannot allow excessive grief to harm his health." Cf. 19.17.

19.15 Ziyou said, "It is difficult to measure up to my friend Zizhang, but even so he is still not Good."

Bao Xian comments, "The point is that Zizhang's countenance and mastery of etiquette is difficult to equal." Zhu Xi reads *wei* 為 as a full verb rather than a copula, giving the reading, "My friend Zizhang does what is difficult to do," adding the gloss, "Zizhang's conduct is exceedingly noble, but he is lacking when it comes to sincerity, substance, and genuine concern." Commentators are here relying upon 11.16 (where Zizhang is described as "overshooting the mark") and 11.18 (where he is described as being "prone to excess"), as well as 19.16.

19.16 Master Zeng said, "How full of himself Zizhang is! It is hard to be Good in the company of such a person as this."

A passage in the *Xunzi* provides a similar assessment of Zizhang's character, as reflected in his later followers: "Their caps are bent and twisted, their robes floating and billowing; they glide along as if they were an Yu and march about as if they were a Shun—such are the base *ru* of the school of Zizhang."[6] As Fan Ziyu comments, "Zizhang had more than enough on the outside, but he was insufficient on the inside, and therefore none of the disciples were willing to grant that he was Good. The Master said that 'strong-willed, decisive, unaffected, and reticent—these qualities are close to Goodness' [13.27], showing his preference for having more than enough on the inside while being insufficient on the outside, which in his view was almost enough to make one Good."

19.17 Master Zeng said, "I have heard from the Master that, even when a person has not yet been able to exert himself to the fullest, he will necessarily do so when it comes to mourning his own parents."

A similar passage in the *Mencius* reads, "When mourning one's own parents, one must certainly exert oneself to the utmost" (3:A:2). The genuine and powerful grief one experiences on the death of a parent assures that the cultural forms of mourning will be fully supported by emotional substance, even in otherwise insincere people.

19.18 Master Zeng said, "I have heard from the Master that, while it is possible to match the filial piety of Meng Zhuangzi in most respects, it is difficult to match the way he refrained from changing the ministers or governmental policies of his father."

---

[6]Chapter 6 ("Contra Twelve Philosophers"); Knoblock 1988: 229.

Meng Zhuangzi was a minister in Lu, member of the Meng Family and son of Meng Xianzi. Meng Xianzi died in 554 B.C.E., and Meng Zhuangzi died only four years later. Most commentators point out that Meng Zhuangzi's achievement is only impressive if we understand that the ministers and policies of his father were less than ideal. As Ma Rong comments, "This passage refers to the fact that, during the mourning period [of three years], Meng Zhuangzi could not bear to change the ministers or governmental policies of his father, even though they were not good." There is some independent evidence for the undesirability of Meng Xianzi's administration in the *Zuo Commentary* and the *History of the Jin*, the latter of which observes that "Meng Xianzi's contentious ministers numbered five." For the principle of leaving the ways of one's father unchanged as an expression of filial piety, see 1.11 and 4.20.

19.19 When the Meng Family appointed Yang Fu to be their Captain of the Guard, he went to ask Master Zeng for advice. Master Zeng said, "It has been a long time since those above lost the Way, and so the people lack guidance. When you uncover the truth in a criminal case, proceed with sorrow and compassion. Do not be pleased with yourself."

Yang Fu was apparently a disciple of Master Zeng. Ma Rong's comment on this passage reads: "The fact that the common people have become scattered and confused, aimlessly drifting about and getting into trouble with the law, is all the doing of their superiors—it is not the fault of the people. It is thus appropriate to feel sorrow and pity, rather than to take joy that one is able to discover the truth in criminal cases." Li Ao believes the injunction to be against taking joy in actively punishing the people, but the sense is much the same in either case: the level of morality among the common people is a direct reflection of the virtue of their leaders, and thus the key to eliminating crime is to reform the virtue of the people above (cf. especially 12.17–12.19). For the long-standing state of affairs whereby those above lost the Way and therefore brought confusion to the people, cf. 3.24. A more elaborate and evocative version of Master Zeng's advice is found in *Discourses on Salt and Iron*:

> Master Zeng said, "For a long time those above have lost the Way and the common people have been confused. If you discover the truth in a criminal case, do not take joy in your own abilities, but rather feel sorrow and pity. Not to feel pain at how the people have fallen into disorder, but rather to be proud about one's own ability to capture a criminal, is to be like a hunter who takes joy in seeing birds or beasts struggling in his nets and snares."

19.20 Zigong said, "Zhow's wickedness was really not as extreme as they say. This is why the gentleman hates to dwell in low places, because all the badness in the world gathers there."

Zhow, of course, is the famously evil last king of the Shang Dynasty (18.1), whose name—usually paired with the equally evil last king of the Xia, King Jie—became a byword for immorality. Liu Baonan takes the final *e* 惡 ("badness") in the sense of "bad reputation" (*e'ming* 惡名), seeing the point of the passage to be that Zhow was not the extreme monster that history has made him out to be, but that by "taking the low ground" he set himself up to become a symbol of badness. In support of this interpretation, he cites several passages from early histories that paraphrase 19.20 in describing the development of a bad reputation, as well as a passage from the *Liezi* that observes that "all of the praise in the world has gathered around the names of Shun, Yu, the Duke of Zhou, and Confucius, whereas all of the ill repute (*e*) has gathered around the names of Jie and Zhow."[7] This interpretation is adopted by Zhu Xi, who remarks,

> Low-lying ground in a landscape is a place where water gathers. This serves as a metaphor for the fact that, when a person is actually corrupt or base, they will become a gathering place for bad reputation. In making this comment, Zigong's intention is to encourage people to be constantly cautious and on guard with regard to themselves, never allowing themselves to fall into a bad place for even a moment. This is not to say that Zhow was originally innocent, or that there is no basis at all for his bad reputation.

An alternate interpretation is presented by Cai Mo and Huang Kan, who take *e* in the sense of "bad people" (*e'ren* 惡人), understanding the point to be that Zhow's personal immorality attracted other immoral people to him, resulting in a synergistically bad effect far beyond the individual badness of any of the people involved. A passage from the *Zuo Commentary* can be cited in support of this interpretation: "Formerly, when King Wu was enumerating the crimes of Zhow to the feudal lords, he said, 'Zhow served as host for all of the vagabonds and miscreants in the world, and they flocked to him like schools of fish in the deep.'"[8] This interpretation is also supported by passages in the *Analects* that emphasize the care with which one must choose one's company (1.8, 4.1, 16.4–16.5).

19.21 Zigong said, "A gentleman's errors are like an eclipse of the sun or the moon: when he errs, everyone notices it, but when he makes amends, everyone looks up to him."

Huang Kan's interpretation of this metaphor seems apt:

> An eclipse of the sun or the moon is not the result of deliberate action on the part of the sun or moon; in the same way, a gentleman's transgression is not intentional . . . Everyone sees an eclipse of the sun or moon, in the same way that everyone sees the transgression of the gentleman, because he does not attempt to conceal it . . . When an eclipse of the sun or moon passes, darkness is transformed into light, and everyone in the world together cranes their neck to gaze upon it. In the same way, the Virtue of the gentleman is not permanently sullied by prior transgressions.

Cf. the importance of "making emends" (*gai* 改) when one has erred (1.8, 7.22), as well as the repetition of 19.21 in *Mencius* 2:B:9.

19.22 Gongsun Chao of Wei asked Zigong, "From whom did Confucius acquire his learning?"

Zigong replied, "The Way of Kings Wen and Wu has not yet fallen to the ground—it still exists in people. Those who are worthy understand its greater aspects, while those who are unworthy understand its lesser aspects. There is no one who does not have the Way of Wen and Wu within them. From whom did the Master *not* acquire his learning? And what need was there for him to have a formal teacher?"

---

[7] Chapter 7 ("Yang Zhu"); Graham 1990: 150.

[8] Duke Zhao, Year 7 (534 B.C.E.); Legge 1991d: 616.

Gongsun Chao was a minister in Wei. The point of Zigong's response, Liu Baonan explains, is that the Way of the ancient Zhou kings was still preserved in the cultural practices of Confucius' age:

> The Master's learning followed the Zhou in all respects. As we read in the "Doctrine of the Mean," "Confucius reverenced and transmitted [the Way of] Yao and Shun, and modeled himself on the cultural brilliance of Wen and Wu"[9] . . . The transmission of the great Way began with Yao and Shun and reached the Zhou of Confucius' age, grandly embodied in their ritual and musical institutions. This is why Confucius declared that "Now that King Wen is gone, is not culture now invested here in me?" [9.5] . . . Worthy people recognize the greatness of its Heavenly provenance and its ability to order the human world, whereas the unworthy notice only the minor details of its artifacts and regulations. This is the manner in which the Way of Wen and Wu was still preserved, and the Master engaged in the editing and organizing of texts, as well as the praising and cultivating of practices, in order to create manifest cultural forms that could be recognized and known by others. Histories tell us that the Master questioned Laozi about ritual, inquired about music from Chang Hong, asked Master Tan about ministerial posts, and studied the zither with Music Master Xiang. If a person had something good to say or something good to demonstrate, the Master found him worthy to emulate, and therefore everyone served as his teacher. Is this not indeed what is referred to as accumulating great achievements?

For the evidence of Zhou cultural forms still present in the Lu of Confucius' time, cf. 3.9 and 6.24, and for his practice of always learning from others, cf. 3.15, 7.22, 7.32.

19.23 Shusun Wushu remarked to his ministers at court, "Zigong is an even greater worthy than Confucius." Zifu Jingbo reported this to Zigong.

> Shusun Wushu was a high minister in the state of Lu, a member of the Shu Family. Zifu Jingbo was one of lower ministers in his court; cf. 14.36 for his friendly attitude toward Confucius.

Zigong replied, "Let us use the analogy of a residence surrounded by a wall. The walls around my residence are only shoulder-high, so people can look over them and see the beauty of the chambers and apartments within. The walls of the Master's residence, on the other hand, are fifteen feet high. This means that, unless one is able to enter through the gate, one cannot see the fineness of the ancestral temples or the luxuriousness of the various offices. Those who have been able to enter through the gate are rather few, so it is not at all surprising that your master spoke as he did."

> We see here the beginning of the myth of Confucius as a mysteriously transcendent and incomprehensibly profound being that became the basis of his deification in the Han. Zigong was one of the more successful of Confucius' disciples, eventually serving as a high minister in the states of both Lu and Wei—a much higher position than Confucius ever obtained—which is probably why he is singled out for praise by third parties here and in 19.25.

19.24 Shusun Wushu was disparaging Confucius.

Zigong said, "It is pointless, Confucius cannot be disparaged. The worthiness of other people is like a hill or mound, in that one can still climb to the top of

---

[9] Chapter 31 of the *Record of Ritual*; see Legge 1967, vol. 2: 326.

it. Confucius is like the sun and the moon—it is impossible to surmount him. Even if a person wished to cut himself off from their radiance, what harm could he do to the sun and the moon? All this would serve to show is that such a person did not know his limits."

A comment on this passage by Jiao Yuanxi makes it clear how far 19.24 has come from the earlier ideal of Confucius as an ordinary man, someone who simply loved the ancients and worked hard at learning:

> Hills and mounds can be created by piling up earth, and although they may be of different heights, none of them are entirely cut off from the ground. This is why they can serve as metaphors for what can be achieved by means of learning and exertion.[10] The sun and the moon are formed by and obtain their radiance from Heaven, and are therefore metaphors for that which cannot be obtained by means of human effort.

By equating Confucius with the sun and the moon, 19.24 makes him into a transcendent being, qualitatively different from other people. Contrast this especially with 7.20, 7.33, and 9.8.

19.25 Chen Ziqin said to Zigong, "You show reverence to Confucius, but how could he be more worthy than you?"

Ziqin, who also appears in 1.10 and 16.13, was a disciple of Confucius.

Zigong replied, "A gentleman can be judged wise or unwise on the basis of a single comment—this is why one cannot fail to be careful in one's speech. One cannot equal the Master anymore than one can climb a stairway to the heavens. Had the Master acquired control of a state or noble family, then, as they say: 'When he raised them up, they would stand; when he led them forward they would advance; when he comforted them they would come; and when he moved them they would become harmonious.' His birth was glorious and his death was universally mourned. How could anyone equal him?"

In later myth, Confucius is often referred to as the "throneless ruler," the idea being that, if only he had been given a position of authority, he would have re-established the universal peace and order of the early Zhou. 19.25 represents what is probably the earliest statement of this idea. Liu Baonan points out a similar passage in the *Xunzi*:

> Zaofu was the most skilled charioteer in the world, and yet without horses and a chariot he would have no way to display his abilities. Yi was the most skillful archer in the world, and yet without a bow and arrow he would have no way to display his achievements. A great *ru* is skilled at harmonizing and unifying the world, and yet without a domain of one hundred square *li*, he has no way to display his achievements.[11]

Liu adds, "The master never managed to be employed in a powerful position, and therefore no one in his age recognized his sageliness, and some even went so far as to disparage him."

---

[10] See 9.19 for piling up earth as a metaphor for self-cultivation.

[11] Chapter 8 ("The Teachings of the Ru"); Knoblock 1990: 78.

BOOK TWENTY

This Book consists of only three passages, of which the first two are exceptionally long. The first passage, 20.1, apparently stood alone as a Book by itself in the Ancient text version of the Analects, *and it is a rather mixed bag. The first half appears to be a collection of fragments from the* Book of Documents, *and the only way to extract any kind of sense from it is to see it as a chronological account of how each of the various ancient dynasties got their starts; the second half is more stylistically typical of the* Analects, *and appears to be a comment on the first half. Passages 20.2–20.3 are more coherent than 20.1, and reinforce themes found earlier in the text. Book Twenty as a whole strikes one as a somewhat random collection of passages that, for whatever reason, were not fitted into other Books.*

20.1 Yao said, "Oh, you Shun! The orderly succession of Heaven now rests upon your shoulders. Hold faithfully to the mean. If those within the Four Seas should fall into hardship and poverty, Heaven's emoluments will be cut off from you forever."

The occasion of this remark is Yao's passing on of the throne to Shun. This address of Yao's does not appear in Chapter 1 ("The Canon of Yao") of the current *Book of Documents*, but pieces of it can be found in the probably spurious Chapter 3 ("The Counsels of the Great Yu"), where they are presented as Shun's words to Yu. The translation of the second half of the passage follows Zhu Xi, who understands it as a warning to Shun: if Shun should fail to care for and protect the people, Heaven's favor will be withdrawn from him. Bao Xian takes it somewhat differently: "If you can faithfully hold to the mean, you will be able to exhaustively extend [your rule] throughout the Four Seas, and Heaven's emoluments will last forever." Huang Kan follows Bao Xian, elaborating: "If Shun is able to internally hold fast to the Way of the correct mean, then his Virtuous instructive influence will externally cover the Four Seas, so that everyone will submit and be transformed, and there will be nowhere that this influence does not reach." Zhu Xi's reading seems preferable, however, better fitting the context in which these lines appear in the received version of the *Documents*, and allowing a less forced reading of the text.

Shun charged Yu with the same words.

Here we have the transition from Shun's rule to first founder of the Xia Dynasty, Yu. When Shun passed the throne on, he made the same pronouncement that Yao had made to him.

[Tang] said, "I, your little child Lü, dare to offer up a black bull in sacrifice, and make so bold as to plainly declare to you, my Most August Sovereign Lord, that I do not dare to pardon those who have committed offenses. Your servant, Lord, conceals nothing; examine my actions with your mind, oh Lord. If I should personally commit an offense, let not the punishment be visited upon the inhabitants of the myriad regions; if the inhabitants of the myriad regions commit offenses, let the punishment be visited upon me personally."

The personal name Lü in this declaration marks it as the words of Tang, the supposed founder of the Shang Dynasty, who—unlike Yu and Shun before him—had to take his throne by force of arms. Again, the passage does not correspond exactly to anything in the received *Documents*, but fragments of it are scattered throughout Chapter 12 ("The Announcement of Tang"). Kong Anguo believes this to be the declaration made by Tang to Heaven before he launched his punitive attack on the last of the Xia kings, the infamous Jie. Although the color of the Shang was to be white, Kong explains that Tang offers a black bull—black being the color of the Xia—because he does not yet dare to alter the Xia rituals. Understood this way, this declaration serves as Tang's excuse for having to resort to force, the point being that, in attacking the Xia, he is merely doing Heaven's will, serving as the instrument of Heaven's wrath in punishing the evil Jie. The request, "examine my actions with your mind, oh Lord" (lit. "let the review-inspection lie in the Lord's mind"), is a declaration of sincerity: Tang has nothing to hide, and his motivations are pure.

The Zhou were generously endowed, rich in excellent men.

We have now moved on to the transition to the Zhou. The translation follows He Yan in reading this first sentence together with 8.20: the Zhou had ten worthy ministers. It might alternately be rendered, "The Zhou gave generous gifts, and excellent men were enriched thereby," presumably referring to the enfeofment of those who aided in the Zhou conquest of the Shang. This latter reading is supported by a fragment, "[King Wu] gave generous gifts to all within the Four Seas, and the myriad people joyfully submitted," in the received *Book of Documents*.[1]

[King Wu said,] "Though I may have many close kinsmen, it is better to employ Good men. If any of the Hundred Clans commit a transgression, let the punishment be visited upon me alone."

The quoted words are presumed by most commentators to be the words of King Wu after he had conquered the Shang, and they are in fact attributed to him in an alternate version of this account found in the *Mozi*.[2] The first half of King Wu's statement appears in the received version of the *Documents*,[3] and Kong Anguo's interpretation of it is as follows: "King Wu would punish even a close relative who was not dutiful or worthy—his punishment of prince of Guan and the prince of Cai are examples of this.[4] By 'Good men' he means people like the Master of Ji and Master of Wei.[5] If they came, he would employ them." An alternate rendering of this line is suggested in a commentary to the *Documents* falsely attributed to Kong Anguo—"the point is

---

[1] Chapter 31 ("The Successful Completion of the War"); Legge 1991a: 316.

[2] Chapter 15 ("Impartial Caring"); Mei 1929: 86.

[3] Chapter 28 ("The Great Declaration, Part II"); Legge 1991a: 292.

[4] Two members of the Zhou royal house who were punished by the Duke of Zhou; see the *Book of Documents*, Chapter 17 ("The Charge to Zhong of Cai"); Legge 1991a: 487.

[5] Worthy ministers who attempted to reform the evil King Zhow; cf. 18.1.

that, although King Zhow has many close relatives around him, they are not the equal of the many Good men of the Zhou family"—and this reading is adopted by Zhu Xi.

He was scrupulous about weights and measures, carefully examined models and regulations, restored neglected official posts, and the administration of the four quarters was thereby carried out.

In the *History of the Han*, this section is presented as an injunction from the mouth of Confucius, rather than a description of the actual behavior of King Wu. In the absence of a marker such as, "The Master said," however, it seems best to take it and the following sections as accounts of King Wu's rule.

He restored destroyed states, re-established interrupted lines of succession, raised lost people back into prominence, and the hearts and minds of all the people in the world turned to him.

According to the *Exoteric Commentary*,[6] "restoring destroyed states" refers to returning land to the blameless descendents of those whose states were confiscated for wrongdoing, and "re-establishing severed lines of succession" refers to allowing worthy individuals from side-branches of a family to take over the succession, rather than allowing a line to die out. "Lost people" probably refers to virtuous men who had gone into reclusion to avoid immoral rulers.

He gave weight to the people, food, mourning, and sacrifice.

As Kong Anguo comments, "The common people are important because they are the basis of the state; food is important because it is the livelihood of the people. Mourning is important because it is the means by which one gives full expression to grief, and sacrifice is important because it is the means by which one fully expresses respect."

Generous, he won over the masses. Trustworthy, the people put their faith in him. Diligent, he was successful. Just, [the people] were pleased.

Kong Anguo concludes, "This sums up the means by which the two Lords and three Kings established order, and is recorded in order to serve as a message to later generations."

20.2 Zizhang asked Confucius, "What must a person be like before he can be employed in government service?"
The Master replied, "He must respect the five virtues, and get rid of the four vices. Then he can be employed in government service."

For a similar enumeration of virtues and vices, cf. 17.8.

Zizhang asked, "What are the five virtues?"
The Master replied, "The gentleman is benevolent without being wasteful, imposes labor upon the people without incurring their resentment, desires without being covetous, is grand without being arrogant, and is awe-inspiring without being severe."

---

[6] Chapter 8.17; Hightower 1952: 270.

For "grand without being arrogant," cf. 13.6, and for "awe-inspiring without being severe," cf. 7.38.

Zizhang asked, "What does it mean to be benevolent but not wasteful?"

The Master replied, "Benefiting the people based on an understanding of what is truly beneficial to them—is this not 'benevolent without being wasteful'? Imposing labor upon the people only at the rights times and on the right projects—who will resent it?[7] Desiring Goodness and attaining it—what is there left to covet? Whether he is dealing with a few or with many, with the great or with the humble, the gentleman does not dare to be casual—is this not 'grand without being arrogant'? The gentleman straightens his robe and cap, adopts a respectful gaze, and is so dignified in appearance that people look upon him with awe— is this not 'awe-inspiring without being severe?'"

Zizhang asked, "What are the four vices?"

The Master replied, "Executing the people without having instructed them— this is cruelty. Expecting perfection without having warned people when they are about to make a mistake—this is oppressive. Demanding punctuality without having yourself issued proclamations in a timely fashion—this is to be a pest. Being consistently stingy when it comes to disbursing funds and rewarding people—this is officious."

We see here the consistent theme that those in power have a responsibility to the common people: superiors cannot expect the people below them to be good if they themselves are not good, and cannot make unreasonable demands and expect them to be satisfied.

20.3 Confucius said, "One who does not understand fate lacks the means to become a gentleman. One who does not understand ritual lacks the means to take his place. One who does not understand words lacks the means to evaluate others."

Ming 命 here probably refers to "fate" rather than the "Mandate of Heaven" (cf. 2.4), although of course the two concepts are related. Kong Anguo remarks, "Fate refers to the allotment of success and failure." Huang Kan elaborates,

When it comes to those things in life that are subject to fate, whether or not one receives them is up to Heaven, therefore one must understand fate. If one does not understand fate and tries to forcibly pursue those things that are subject to it, one will not be able to perfect the Virtue that will allow one to become a gentleman.

Similar observations about fate are found in the *Mencius*. 7:A:1 reads, "Preserving one's heart-mind and nourishing one's nature are the mean by which to serve Heaven. Considering with equanimity an untimely death or long life, and cultivating oneself in order to simply await what comes—these are the means by which to establish fate." In 7:A:3, the issue of fate is linked to the distinction between internal and external concerns:

---

[7] Cf. 1.5 and the injunction to "employ the common people only at the proper times." The reference is to public works and military levies, which should not be onerous or interfere with the cycle of agricultural work.

"Pursue them, and you will get them; let go and you will lose them."[8] This refers to situation where pursuing it helps one to get it, because the search lies within oneself. "Pursuing it requires a technique; whether or not you actually get it is a matter of fate." This refers to a situation where pursuing it does not help one to get it, because the search lies outside oneself.

The point is that the aspiring gentleman needs to focus his energy on the internal goods of the Confucian practice, the attainment of which is within his control, instead of wasting his time pursuing such externalities as wealth or fame; cf. 4.14, 11.18, 12.5, 15.32. With regard to ritual, the aspiring gentleman must understand it because it is the means by which he becomes socialized, and therefore a true human being (16.13). As Huang Kan observes, "Ritual governs reverence, dignity, temperance, and respectfulness, and thus is the root of establishing oneself. A person who does not understand ritual lacks the means to establish himself in the world." Zhu Xi adds, putting it more vividly, "A person who does not understand ritual has no idea where to focus his eyes and ears, and has no place to put his hands and feet." Finally, with regard to understanding words, most commentators take this to refer to an ability to judge other's characters from their utterances. As Liu Baonan remarks, "Words are the voice of the heart. Words can be either right or wrong, and therefore if one is able to listen and distinguish between the two types of words, one will also be able to know the rightness or wrongness of the speaker."

---

[8] A quotation from *Mencius* 6:A:6, where the reference is to the Confucian virtues—the proper object of pursuit for a Confucian gentleman.

ROMANIZATION

There are several systems of romanization used to represent Chinese pronunciation. Pinyin 拼音, created by the mainland Chinese government, has recently become the standard in the field, and is used throughout this Book. Below is a table that provides conversions to the older, but still not uncommon, Wade-Giles system.

Pinyin	Wade-Giles
b	p
c	ts'/tz'
ch	ch'
d	t
g	k
ian	ien
j	ch
k	k'
ong	ung
p	p'
q	ch'
r	j
si	ssu/szu
t	t'
x	hs
you	yu
yu	yü
z	ts/tz
zh	ch
zhi	chih
zi	tzu

APPENDIX 1:
GLOSSARY OF TERMS

Below is a list of terms appearing in the text of the *Analects*, the commentary, or the appendices that may be unfamiliar to readers, at least with regard to their significance in the Confucian context. Certain terms from the *Analects* itself (e.g., Goodness, the gentleman) appear so often in the text that providing passage references would not be helpful; for other terms, reference is made to passages that shed light on their meanings.

Benevolence (*hui* 惠). A virtue particularly important when it comes to superiors' actions toward those in their charge, or the behavior of parents toward their children. Also the translation of *ren* 仁 ("Goodness") in post-*Analects* texts. 4.11, 5.16, 14.9, 17.5, 20.2.

Cheng-Zhu 程朱 School. A school of neo-Confucianism named after Cheng Yi 程颐 (1033–1107) and Zhu Xi 朱熹 (1130–1200), sometimes alternately referred to as the "learning of principle" (*lixue* 理學) or "rationalist" school. See the entry on Zhu Xi in Appendix 4 for more details.

Courage, courageous (*yong* 勇). A virtue inherited from the Zhou martial ideal of the gentleman, but subordinated in the Confucian context to more important virtues such as wisdom or rightness. The disciple Zilu, a former warrior, often serves as an example of the danger of impetuous courage uninformed by other virtues (5.7, 11.13; cf. 7.11, 8.10, 17.23), and we might contrast him with figures who are presented as displaying modest, genuine courage (6.15). In its proper place, however, courage is an important quality of the gentleman, allowing him to pursue the moral Way without fear (9.29, 14.28).

Culture, cultural refinement (*wen* 文). Literally referring to writing, *wen* often serves in the *Analects* as a general term pertaining to the sort of acculturation—training in ritual, the classics, music, etc.—acquired by someone following the Confucian Way (6.27, 9.5). In this respect, it is often portrayed metaphorically as a kind of adornment or refinement of the "native substance" (*zhi* 質) an uneducated person brings to the process of acculturation. It is often emphasized that cultural refinement requires a suitable substrate of native substance, as in 3.8, where *wen* is compared to cosmetics applied to a beautiful face, but ultimately a proper balance between the two must be struck (6.18, 12.8). Sometimes *wen* is also used in the more narrow sense of a set of specific practices like those later formalized as the so-called "six arts" of ritual, music, archery, charioteering, calligraphy, and mathematics, in which any gentleman was trained (see 1.6; similar to the sense of *yi* 藝, "arts," in 7.6).

Daoism, Daoist (*daojia* 道家). Literally the "School of the Way," this is a term retrospectively applied to thinkers such as the author(s) of the *Laozi*, the *Zhuangzi*, and the *Liezi*, who were viewed as emphasizing common themes, including an opposition to the Confucian project of acculturation and an emphasis on naturalness. See Graham 1989: 170–172 for more on the term "Daoism" and its referents.

Duke (*gong* 公).   Title held by those families given fiefs by the Zhou kings, and who, in the traditional feudal system, were answerable only to the king himself.

Dutifulness, dutiful (*zhong* 忠).   Dutifulness is the virtue of fulfilling one's role-specific obligations, and is often linked to political duties (especially of a subordinate toward his superior) and to ritual obligations. Although *zhong* is often translated as "loyalty," "dutifulness" is preferable because the ultimate focus is on one's ritually-prescribed duties rather than loyalty to any particular person. Indeed *zhong* involves opposing a ruler who is acting improperly (13.15, 13.23, 14.7). Examples of dutiful behavior are found in 5.19 and 14.21, descriptions of the restrictions placed upon one's behavior by the demands of duty are found in 8.14 and 14.26. For its relationship to the virtue of "understanding," see 4.15.

Fate (*ming* 命).   Also see "Mandate." In the sense of "fate," *ming* refers to the whole range of circumstances that are both external to the Confucian practice itself and beyond the control of human beings. Even when used in the sense of "fate," *ming* continues to preserve its connection to Heaven and the metaphor of "mandating" or "commanding": fate is what is mandated by Heaven, the normative standard of the universe. It is therefore not only pointless, but also morally wrong, to struggle against it. The proper attitude of the gentleman is to accept what fate brings and focus his attention on things actually within his control, such as self-cultivation. See 6.10, 7.3, 7.19, 11.18, 12.4–12.5, 14.36, 19.1, and 20.3.

Filial piety, filial (*xiao* 孝).   The virtue of being a dutiful and respectful son or daughter, considered by Confucius to be the key to other virtues developed later in life. See especially 1.2, 2.5, 2.7–2.8, and 19.18. For an observation on the debt owed to parents, see 17.21.

Gentleman (*junzi* 君子).   Meaning literally "son of a lord," *junzi* referred in Western Zhou times to a member of the warrior aristocracy. In Confucius' hands, it comes to refer to anyone capable of becoming a kind of moral aristocrat: an exemplar of ritually-correct behavior, ethical courage, and noble sentiment—in short, a possessor of Goodness.

Glibness, glib (*ning* 佞).   Glibness is a negative quality that is attacked throughout the text. The original Zhou meaning of *ning* was something like "attractive or noble in speech," but in giving it the negative sense of "glibness," Confucius portrays *ning* as the false, external counterfeit of true, inner "Goodness" (see especially 1.3). This is no doubt the sentiment behind such passages as 12.3 ("The Good person is sparing of speech") and 13.27 ("reticence is close to Goodness"), as well as Confucius' general suspicion of language and outward show. See especially 5.5, 11.25, 12.3, 15.11, and 16.4.

Goodness, Good (*ren* 仁).   In the *Analects*, Goodness refers to the highest of Confucian virtues. In pre-Confucian texts such as the *Book of Odes*, *ren* was an adjective referring to the appearance of a handsome, strong, aristocratic man, and the term is cognate with the word meaning "human being" (*ren* 人). In this context, *ren* would thus perhaps be best rendered as "manly." One of Confucius' innovations was to transform this aristocratic, martial ideal into an ethical one: *ren* in the *Analects* refers to a *moral*, rather than physical or martial ideal. In post-*Analects* texts, it has the more specific sense of empathy or kindness between human beings—especially for a ruler toward his subjects—and in such contexts is therefore usually translated as "benevolence." Although we see hints of this later usage in the *Analects* (12.22, 17.21), it is much more commonly used there in the more general sense of "Goodness," the overarching virtue of being a perfected human being, which includes such qualities as empathetic understanding (*shu* 恕) or benevolence (*hui* 惠).

Heaven (*tian* 天). The tribal god of the Zhou, who is deliberately conflated in Zhou writings with the Shang's god, the Lord on High. Early graphic forms of *tian* seem to picture a massive, striding, anthropomorphic figure, who is from the earliest times associated with the sky. Hence "Heaven" is a fairly good rendering of *tian*, as long as the reader keeps in mind that "Heaven" refers to an anthropomorphic figure—someone who can be communicated with, angered, or pleased—rather than a physical place. From Zhou times on, Heaven is viewed as the source of normativity in the universe, the all-powerful Being who, when pleased with proper ritual conduct, charges its representative on earth with the Mandate to rule, as well as the power of virtue that made realizing the Mandate possible. Heaven is also viewed as responsible for everything beyond the control of human beings (things relegated to "fate") and—in Confucius' view—for revealing to human beings the set of cultural practices and texts collectively known as "the Way."

Hermeneutics, hermeneutical. Referring to interpretation or the theory of interpretation, from the name Hermes, Greek messenger of the gods.

Hegemon (*ba* 霸). Alternately translated as "Lord Protector," this was a position officially recognized by the Zhou kings in 681 B.C.E., when Duke Huan of Qi was appointed first hegemon to unite the Chinese states in defense against barbarian invasion. Although theoretical merely regents of the Zhou king, the hegemons in fact ruled independently, and the post itself represented an important erosion in the authority of the Zhou kings. See Rosen 1976 for more.

Learning (*xue* 學). The common alternate translation of this term is "study," which gives it too much theoretical flavor. Although "learning" generally does focus upon classical texts, its point is the actual practice of emulating and internalizing of ideal models of behavior and speech exemplified in these works. In addition, the scope of learning extends beyond textual study, and includes observing and benefiting from the behavior of others (7.22, 19.22). The role of classical texts, such as the *Book of Odes*, is not only to give one the language to express oneself (16.13, 17.9), but the accumulated wisdom of the ancients that they represent is to form the very basis of one's thinking (*si* 思). See especially 1.1, 1.7, 5.28, 6.3, 16.13, 17.8, and 19.5–19.7.

Legalism, Legalist (*fajia* 法家). More accurately, though awkwardly, referred to as the "School of Statecraft," this is a retrospective term for a group of thinkers, such as Hanfeizi or Shen Buhai, who emphasized the importance of impartial, amoral techniques for state management, including a strong emphasis on punishment and reward.

Li 里. Unit of measurement, equal to approximately one-third of an English mile.

Lord on High (*shangdi* 上帝). The Lord on High seems originally to have been a non-human god who gradually came to be viewed as the first human ancestor of the Shang people, and—by virtue of seniority—the most powerful of the ancestor spirits. The Lord on High and the other ancestor spirits of the Shang were viewed as dwelling in a kind of netherworld somewhere above the human realm (hence the Lord "on High"). From this vantage point they continued to monitor the behavior of their descendents, receive sacrificial offerings from them, hear questions and requests, and control all of the phenomena seen as lying beyond human control, such as weather, health and sickness, success or failure in battle.

Lu-Wang 陸王 School. A school of neo-Confucianism named after Lu Deming 陸德明 (1139–1193) and Wang Yangming 王陽明 (1472–1529), sometimes alternately referred to as the "study of the mind" (*xinxue* 心學), or "idealist" school. See the entry on Wang Yangming in Appendix 4 for more details.

Mandate (*ming* 命).   Also see "fate." *Ming* refers literally to a command issued by a political superior to an inferior or a decree issued by a ruler. In a metaphorical and religious sense, it refers to Heaven's command to his proxy on earth, the king, to rule the human world. In Shang and Zhou times, the Lord on High or Heaven was believed to grant the Mandate to rule the world to the ruler who maintained ritual correctness. Zhou texts claim that the Shang lost the Mandate because of gross ritual improprieties and general immorality, which motivated the Lord on High/Heaven to withdraw the Mandate from the Shang and give it to the Zhou. Since the holder of the Mandate was believed to also receive virtue from Heaven as a sign of its favor, he would be able to rule by means of wu-wei. 2.4, 16.8.

Material force (*qi* 氣).   Refer to the entry "Neo-Confucianism."

Mysterious Learning (*xuanxue* 玄學).   Refers loosely to a syncretic movement that flourished in the Wei-Jin Period (220–420), related to the so-called "Pure Talk" (*qingtan* 清談) movement (the two movements are sometimes subsumed under the rubric "neo-Daoism") It focused metaphysically on the concept of "non-being" (*wu* 無), seen as the mysterious progenitor of the entire phenomenal world; politically on the concept of effortless action or wu-wei as a means of rulership; and personally on the importance of attaining "emptiness" (*xu* 虛) and living in a free and easy manner, unconstrained by social norms. Although much of the metaphysics was drawn from Daoism, this movement also drew heavily upon Confucian social and political thought, and many of its advocates — the most prominent being Wang Bi, He Yan, and Guo Xiang — wrote commentaries on the Confucian classics.

Native substance (*zhi* 質).   Native substance refers to the moral "stuff" that a person brings to the process of acculturation, probably consisting of both inborn qualities and characteristics developed in early childhood. Although Confucius felt that a balance between native substance and cultural refinement was ideal (6.18, 12.8), his dislike for hypocrisy at times caused him to place more emphasis on the importance of native substance (3.3, 3.4, 5.10, 5.22).

Neo-Confucianism (*lixue* 理學).   Collective term for the various schools of Confucianism that arose during the Song and Ming dynasties as a conscious reaction against the dominance of Buddhism in the Tang. They saw their task to be eliminating the "alien" influence of Buddhism and the antisocial influence of Daoism, and thereby bringing China back to the original teachings of Confucius. Despite this professed mission, modern scholars have noted that the various schools of neo-Confucianism — despite their differences — generally share a set of characteristics that distinguish them from "classical" Confucianism. To begin with, neo-Confucians believe that Mencius was the true follower of Confucius and that Mencius' view that "human nature is good" was shared by Confucius, and that this is a view that must be embraced by any orthodox Confucian. As noted in the entry on the *Mencius* in Appendix 5, this is by no means an accurate portrayal of pre-Qin Confucian thought and probably stems from a desire (though probably unconscious) to accord with the Chinese Buddhist teaching that all human beings possess a pure Buddha-nature. In addition, neo-Confucians understand the nature of Mencius' claim in what might be characterized as a Buddhist sense; whereas Mencius believes that human beings are born *potentially* good, neo-Confucians understand his claim to mean that human beings are born with goodness already complete somewhere within them, which means that it only needs to be uncovered in some fashion. They also pick up from Han syncretic Confucianism and Chinese Buddhism a strongly metaphysical slant, evinced most obviously in their use of a dichotomy between "principle" (*li* 理) and "material force" (*qi* 氣). Principle, identical to the Way, is perfectly good and contains all of the ordering structure of the universe. The second term, *qi*, means something like "vital essence"—the animating force in all living things—in pre-Qin writings, but by the Han came to refer, in philosophical writings, to the dynamic and yet tangible material "stuff" that makes up the visible universe (hence "material force"). Generally, this material force is understood to be structured by principle, although there is a great deal of controversy among neo-Confucians about the precise relationship between the two (or even if they are ultimately distinct or identical). These "neo-Confucian" philosophical assumptions are shared by virtually all of the commentators from the Song to the Ming Dynasties quoted in our translation, as well as many of the Qing scholars, although in the Qing some effort was made to approach *Analects* interpretation in a more historically responsible manner.

Primitivism, primitivist. A retrospective term referring in particular to the followers of Shen Nong 神農 ("The Divine Farmer"), a group of "levelers" who believed that stratified societies, vocational specialization, and advanced technology should be abandoned as unnatural, and that everyone—from ruler down to common person—should work together in the fields. The primitivists are often associated with the Daoists, and indeed one of the primary Daoist texts, the *Laozi*, features many primitivist themes. For an encounter between some followers of Shen Nong and Mencius, see *Mencius* 3:A:4, and for more on primitivism and its influence on early Chinese thought, see Graham 1989: 64–74.

Principle (*li* 理). Refer to the entry "Neo-Confucianism."

Purity, pure (*qing* 清). A minor virtue having to do with refraining from unworthy behavior or avoiding disgrace, generally discussed in the text with regard to its being taken to an inflexible extreme, as in 5.19, 14.1, 18.8.

Rightness, right, righteous (*yi* 義). This term generally refers to a kind of cultivated sense of what is right and morally proper (4.10, 4.16, 5.16, 15.18, 17.23, 19.1), although at times it has the more specific sense of "rightful duty" in a political context, as in 18.7.

Ritual, ritual propriety (*li* 禮). A set of traditional religious and moral practices, which in the Confucian context were believed to have been revealed to the Zhou kings by Heaven. The scope of ritual is quite broad, encompassing not only sacrificial offerings to the spirits, but also aspects of one's daily lives that we might be tempted to label as "etiquette," such as the manner in which one dresses, takes one's meal, approaches one's ministers, etc. (see especially Book Ten). By submitting to and internalizing ritual forms, an aspiring gentleman is able to restrain improper inborn tendencies (8.2, 12.1), acquire the means to "take his place" (*li* 立) among other adults in society (2.4, 8.8, 16.13, 20.3), and thereby win the favor of Heaven. Ritually-acquired virtue is also portrayed as the only proper way to rule the world (3.11, 12.11, 14.41).

Ru 儒. This term, which later came to mean "Confucian," appears only once in the *Analects* (6.13), and referred in Confucius' time to a class of specialists concerned with transmitting and preserving the traditional rituals and texts of the Zhou dynasty. Confucius was probably a *ru*, although he sought to distance himself from *ru* who pursued cultural training solely in order to obtain official positions, social prestige, and salary.

Scholar-official (*shi* 士). The lowest of the three classes of public office holders, this term originally referred to an aristocratic warrior, but had, by the time of Confucius, come to refer to a class of people who filled the middle and lower ranks of state governments, primarily in civil posts. Like Confucius, it seems that a subset of these scholar-officials were also *ru* 儒.

Thinking (*si* 思).   This term might also be rendered as "concentration" and refers to focusing one's attention on a subject or the attempt to process or reflect upon information that one has learned. While learning takes place within a certain structured context, it involves more than simply the passive absorption of knowledge; learning (what one hears from teachers and reads in the classics) and thinking (how one processes and integrates this knowledge) must be properly balanced (2.15, 15.31). Indeed, the ideal student must come to the project possessed by an inchoate need for what learning is able to provide and a passion for acquiring it (7.8, 9.31).

Trustworthiness, trustworthy (*xin* 信).   In certain contexts, this term is also rendered as "true to one's word." A minor, but nonetheless useful, virtue that unfortunately—like purity or uprightness—can easily be taken too far by those who are not virtuous in other ways. For trustworthiness in the positive sense, see especially 2.22 and 16.4. For the problems of excessive trustworthiness (sometimes rendered "petty fidelity"), see 13.18, 13.20, 14.17, 15.37, and 17.8. Also refer to the contrast of trustworthiness and rightness in 1.13.

Understanding (*shu* 恕).   The character itself is made up of components meaning "comparing" (*ru* 如) and "heart-mind" (*xin* 心), and is defined in the *Analects* in terms of what might be called a "negative" version of the Golden Rule: "Do not impose on others what you yourself do not desire" (15.24; cf. 5.12). It might thus be rendered as "understanding," in the sense of an ability to show sympathy, through putting oneself imaginatively in another's place or "being able to take what is near at hand as an analogy" (6.30). In 4.15, coupled with dutifulness (*zhong* 忠), it is described as the "single thread" tying together all that Confucius taught, and in 15.24 it is described as the "single teaching which can be a guide to conduct throughout one's life." "Understanding" seem to refer to an intuitive ability to amend or suspend the dictates of dutifulness—or to apply them flexibly—when holding to them rigidly would involve "imposing on others what you yourself do not desire," and the ability to combine role-specific properness with some sort of context-sensitivity is an essential aspect of the overall virtue of Goodness.

Uprightness, straightness (*zhi* 直).   Refers to a kind of moral rectitude (6.19, 18.2), and also has the sense of "forthright"—i.e., not being shy about informing others of their faults—and in this sense represents the opposite of obsequiousness (see esp. 15.7, 16.4). It is normally a desirable virtue, but—like trustworthiness—can easily turn into the vice of intolerance, rudeness, or excessive rigidity when not possessed by a true gentleman (5.24, 13.18, 17.8).

Virtue (*de* 德).   "Virtue" works as a rendering for this term because it refers to moral worthiness ("virtue" in the more common sense) as well as the particular "power" residing in a person or thing—the original sense of the Latin *virtus*, still preserved in modern English in such expressions as, "by virtue of his great intelligence, he was able to solve the problem." Virtue in the early Shang context referred to a kind of attractive, charismatic power residing in a ruler who had won the endorsement of the ancestral spirits. This power could be perceived by others, serving as a visible mark of the spirits' favor, and its attractive qualities allowed the ruler to both acquire and retain supporters. This sense of Virtue was inherited by the Zhou, who saw it as a gift from Heaven for proper ritual conduct, and by Confucius, although for Confucius it was no longer the sole prerogative of the ruling class: *anyone* who genuinely embraced the Way could obtain Virtue from Heaven. In both Western Zhou texts and the *Analects*, however, it is the power of Virtue to attract people in a noncoercive, almost magical way that allows a moral ruler to govern by means of wu-wei or "effortless action." See especially 2.1, 4.25, 7.23, 12.19, 14.42, and 15.5.

(The) Way (*dao* 道).   Referring literally to a physical path or road, *dao* also refers to a "way" of doing things, and in the *Analects* refers to *the* Way: that is, the unique moral path that should be walked by any true human being (6.17), endorsed by Heaven and revealed to the early sage-kings. More concretely, this "Way" is manifested in the ritual practices, music, and literature passed down from the Golden Age of the Western Zhou.

Wisdom, wise (*zhi* 智, 知).   An important virtue that seems to involve a cognitive understanding of the Way, as well as an ability to accurately perceive situations and judge the character of others. See especially 2.17, 5.7, 6.22–6.23, 14.14, 14.28, 15.8, and 15.33.

Wu-wei 無為.   Meaning literally "no-doing" or "non-doing," wu-wei serves as both individual spiritual ideal and political ideal for Confucius. It might be best translated as "effortless action," because it refers not to what is or is not being done, but to the *manner* in which something is done. An action is wu-wei if it is spontaneous, unselfconscious, and perfectly efficacious. The state of wu-wei represents a perfect harmony between one's inner dispositions and external movements—and thus is perceived by the subject to be "effortless" and free of strain—as well as a state of harmony between the individual and Heaven, which means that a person in the state of wu-wei also possesses Virtue. In the political realm, wu-wei refers to ruling by means of Virtue. Wu-wei is therefore an effortless form of rulership whereby the ruler merely makes himself correct and thereby wins the spontaneous fealty of everyone in the world. For wu-wei as personal ideal, see especially 2.4, most of Book 10, and 14.13; as political ideal, see especially 2.1, 2.21, 8.18–8.19, 12.19, 13.6, 15.5, and 17.19.

APPENDIX 2:
DISCIPLES OF CONFUCIUS

The following list of disciples is confined to those who appear in the *Analects* itself, and the accounts omit most of the later traditions about the disciples of Confucius that were developed in such Han texts as the *Family Sayings* and the "Biographies of Disciples of Confucius" chapter of the *Record of the Historian*, the historical accuracy of which is not certain. Since many of Confucius' sayings seem to be tailored to the needs of the disciple receiving the teaching, it is helpful to have some sense of each disciple's character. For this purpose, a finding-list of passages in which each disciple appears is provided. Italics in the finding list refer to commentary rather than main text.

Boniu 伯牛.　Style-name of Ran Geng 冉耕. He was a native of Lu, was known for virtuous conduct, and died young of a terrible disease, possibly leprosy. 6.10, 11.3.

Bo Yu 伯魚.　Style-name of Kong Li 孔鯉, son of Confucius, who died relatively young. 11.8, 16.13, 17.10.

Fan Chi 樊遲.　Common name for Fan Xu 樊須, style-name Zichi 子遲, native of Qi 齊. The fact that he is repeatedly warned against acquisitiveness (6.22, 12.21) is understood by some commentators to imply that greed was his particular flaw. 2.5, 6.22, 12.21, 12.22, 13.4, 13.19.

Jilu 季路.　Very little is known about this disciple, except for the fact that he was known for his administrative skill. 11.3.

Lao 牢.　Style-name Zikai 子開, sometimes identified with a figure named Qinzhang 琴張, otherwise unknown. 9.7.

Master You 有子.　Respectful form of address for You Ruo 有弱, style-name You 有, a native of Lu. His honorific title indicates that he was the head of his own school of disciples after Confucius' death. 1.2, 1.12, 1.13, 2.21, 12.9.

Master Zeng 曾子.　Respectful form of address for Zeng Shen 曾參, style-name Ziyu 子輿, native of Lu and son of Zeng Dian 曾點 (style-name Zengxi 曾皙), who in turn was probably one of Confucius' earliest disciples. Master Zeng was known particularly for his filial piety, and authorship of both the "Great Learning" chapter of the *Record of Ritual* and the *Classic of Filial Piety* were later attributed to him. As his honorific title indicates, he became the head of his own school after Confucius' death, and the *History of the Han* records the existence of a book—no longer extant—recording his teachings. His grandson Zisi 子思 was supposedly the teacher of Mencius, thus—in the eyes of Song neo-Confucians, at least—assuring the direct orthodox transmission of Confucius' teachings to Mencius. 1.4, 1.9, *2.12*, 4.15, 8.3, 8.4, 8.5, 8.6, 8.7, 11.8, *11.23*, 11.26, *12.5*, 12.24, 14.26, *17.11*, 19.16, 19.17, 19.18, 19.19.

Nan Rong 南容.　"Nan Rong" is usually identified as the style-name of the disciple Nangong Tao 南宮韜 of Lu. Because of his integrity, Confucius gives his niece to him in marriage in 5.2 (cf. 11.6). Zhu Xi believes him to be the same person as the otherwise unknown Nangong Kuo 南宮适 in 14.5.

Qidiao Kai 漆彫開. Style-name Zikai 子開 or Ziruo 子若, alternately known as Qidiao Qi 漆彫啟 (his original personal name *qi* 啟 became taboo during the reign of Emperor Jing of the Han, and was replaced by the synonym *kai* 開). He was an important disciple of Confucius who later founded his own sub-school of Confucianism. The *History of the Han* attributes to him a book of 13 chapters, the *Qidiaozi* 漆彫子, which is no longer extant. The *Family Sayings of Confucius* describes him as being a student of the *Book of History* who was not inclined to take public office. 5.6.

Ran Qiu 冉求. Style-name Ziyou 子有, also known as Ran You 冉有, a native of Lu. Ran Qiu was skilled in statecraft, administration, and the cultural arts, but is harshly criticized by the Master for his behavior as steward for the Ji Family of Lu, and for not being sufficiently eager when it came to self-cultivation. *2.12*, 3.6, 5.8, 5.22, 6.4, 6.8, 6.12, 7.15, 11.3, 11.13, 11.17, 11.22, 11.24, 11.26, 13.9, 13.14, *13.23*, 14.12, 16.1, 20.2.

Shen Cheng 申棖. Style-name Zhou 周, reportedly from Lu, although Brooks and Brooks speculate—based on his surname—that he may have been from a family of refugees from the small state of Shen, south of Lu, which was conquered by Chu in 688 B.C.E. (1998: 24). Very little is known about him and appears in only one passage where we learn that he is full of desires and therefore not resolute. 5.11.

Sima Niu 司馬牛. Style-name Ziniu 子牛, proper name Sima Geng 司馬耕. He has traditionally been identified with a figure of the same name who appears in the *Zuo Commentary*, Duke Ai 14 (483 B.C.E.),[1] the youngest brother of a prominent military family in the state of Song. His older brothers included the Song military minister, Huan Tui 桓魋,[2] who threatened Confucius' life in 7.23, and who planned and executed an unsuccessful revolt against the rightful lord of Song in 483 B.C.E. Another of Niu's older brothers, Xiang Chao 向巢, was also a military official (Minister of the Left) in Song. Xiang Chao was apparently a somewhat arrogant and self-aggrandizing man, who was forced to flee the state after Huan Tui's attempted revolt. If commentators are correct that Sima Niu's conversation with Confucius in 12.4 occurred before Huan Tui's revolt, it probably took place in Song, while Sima Niu was still holding office. The Sima Niu of the *Zuo Commentary* resigned his official post in disgust after the flight of his two older brothers and emigrated in 483 B.C.E., apparently ending up in Lu, where he presumably had the conversation with Zixia recorded in 12.5. Some later commentators reject this identification of the disciple Ziniu with the figure Sima Niu in the *Zuo Commentary*, but this identification goes back to the Han dynasty and seems to make sense of the passages in which this disciple appears. 12.3–12.5.

Wuma Qi 巫馬旗. Common name for Wuman Shi 巫馬施, style-name Ziqi 子旗, native of Chen and apparently a disciple of Confucius. 7.31.

Yan Hui 顏回. Style-name Ziyuan 子淵, also known as Yan Yuan 顏淵. Native of Lu, born into poverty, and the Master's most gifted disciple. Tragically, he died at a young age (there is some debate about how young), a loss that affected Confucius profoundly. *1.1*, 2.9, *4.2*, 5.9, 5.26, 6.3, 6.7, 6.11, 7.11, 8.5, 9.11, 9.20, 9.21, *11.2*, 11.3, 11.4, 11.7, 11.8, 11.9, 11.10, 11.11, 11.19, 11.23, 12.1, 15.11, *16.5*, *16.9*, *16.11*.

---

[1] Legge 1991d: 839–840.

[2] The family's ordinary surname was Xiang 向, but as descendents of Duke Huan 桓 they were also allowed to use this surname, and the military title of *sima* 司馬 (Master of the Horse) had been in the family so long that it was also used by them at times as a surname.

Yuan Si 原思.   Common name of Yuan Xian 原憲, style-name: 子思. Little is said about this disciple in the *Analects* other than the report in 6.5 that he was appointed steward and wished to decline his official salary, and the account of his question about shame in 14.1, but it is apparent that he was one of the excessively "pure" or "fastidious" men of whom Confucius disapproved. Later legends arose documenting his austerities and harsh reclusive lifestyle, and he apparently had his own quite substantial line of disciples, despite the dismissive treatment in the *Analects*. 6.5, *13.21*, 14.1.

Zai Wo 宰我.   Common name of Zai Yu 宰予, style-name Ziwo 子我. Employed by Duke Ai of Lu as a ritual specialist, but criticized by Confucius for his laziness and lack of Goodness. 3.21, 5.10, 6.26, 11.3, 17.21.

Zengxi 曾皙.   Style-name of Zeng Dian 曾點, father of Master Zeng and one of the senior disciples of Confucius, presented in a very favorable light in his sole appearance in the text. *11.23*, 11.26.

Zhonggong 仲弓.   Style-name of Ran Yong 冉雍. He was a native of Lu, of humble background, and is consistently praised by the Master. 5.5, 6.1–6.2, 6.6, 11.3, 11.13, 12.2, 13.2.

Zigao 子羔.   Style-name of Gao Chai 高柴, a man from either Wei (according to Zheng Xuan) or Qi (according to the *Family Sayings*). Described by Confucius as "simpleminded" in 11.18. His only other appearance in the *Analects* is in 11.25, where Zilu suggests him as a potential magistrate of the Ji Family stronghold of Bi.

Zigong 子貢.   Style-name of Duanmu Ci 端木賜. Important disciple of the Master, featured prominently in Book 19, but criticized in other parts of the text for his inflexibility and overspecialization. 1.10, *1.15*, 2.12, 2.13, 3.17, 5.4, 5.9, 5.12, 5.15, 6.8, 6.30, 7.15, 9.6, 9.13, *10.13*, *11.2*, 11.3, 11.13, 11.16, 11.19, 12.7, 12.8, 12.23, 13.20, 13.24, 14.17, 14.28, 14.29, 14.35, 15.3, 15.10, 15.24, *17.11*, 17.19, 17.24, 19.20, 19.21, 19.22, 19.23, 19.24, 19.25.

Zihua 子華.   Style-name of Gongxi Chi 公西赤, also known as Gongxi Hua 公西華, a native of Lu. Apparently skilled at ritual tasks, and employed at some point by the Three Families of Lu. 5.8, 6.4, 11.22, 11.26.

Zijian 子賤.   Style-name of Fu Buqi 宓不齊 of Lu, who became governor of Shanfu 單父. 5.3.

Zilu 子路.   Style-name of Zhong You 仲由, native of Lu and one of Confucius' earliest disciples. Zilu was a former warrior and was admired by Confucius for his courage, but seems to lack other virtues (such as good judgment) that would balance out his courage. As the Master predicted in 11.13, Zilu eventually died a violent death during a civil war in Lu. 2.12, 2.17, 5.7, 5.8, 5.14, 5.26, 6.8, 6.28, 7.11, 7.19, 7.35, 9.12, 9.27, 10.27, *11.2*, 11.12, *11.13*, 11.15, 11.18, 11.22, 11.24, 11.25, 11.26, 12.12, 13.1, 13.3, *13.21*, 13.28, 14.12, 14.16, 14.22, 14.35, 14.38, 14.42, 15.2, 15.4, 16.1, *17.1*, 17.5, 17.7, 17.8, 17.23, 18.6, 18.7, *19.11*.

Ziqin 子禽.   Style-name of Chen Kang 陳亢, native of Chen. In 19.25, he appears insufficiently awed by Confucius' accomplishments. 1.10, 16.13, 19.25.

Zixia 子夏.   Style-name of Bu Shang 卜商, a native of Wei. Zixia was particularly known for his learning, cultural refinement, and quick grasp of the Master's teachings, and is credited in later traditions with the transmission of many classical texts. He is sometimes criticized by Confucius for being too cautious. He apparently became the head of his own school after Confucius' death since Book Nineteen of the *Analects* is dominated by his sayings. 1.7, 2.8, 3.8, 6.13, 11.3, 11.16, *11.25*, 12.5, 12.22, 13.17, *15.11*, Book 15 n.13, 19.3–19.13.

Ziyou 子游. Style-name of Yan You 言游, also known as Yan Yan 言偃. Little is known about this disciple, other than the fact that he served as steward of a city in Lu (6.14), and was praised by the master for his mastery of the arts in 11.3. 2.7, 4.26, 6.14, 11.3, 17.4, 19.12, 19.14–19.15.

Zizhang 子張. Style-name of Zhuangsun Shi 顓孫師, a native of Chen. Zizhang was skilled at ritual, but apparently prone to excess and overly concerned with externalities. His later followers come in for criticism from Xunzi (*19.16*) for being ostentatious and superficial. 2.18, 2.23, 2.24, 5.19, 11.16, 11.18, 11.20, 12.6, 12.10, 12.14, 12.20, 14.40, 15.6, 15.42, 17.6, 19.1–19.3, 19.15–19.16, 20.2.

APPENDIX 3:
HISTORICAL PERSONAGES

This appendix provides an index and short description of historical personages mentioned in the *Analects* or in the commentary, other than disciples of Confucius (covered in Appendix 2) or authors of important early texts (covered in Appendix 5). Minor historical figures who are only mentioned once in the commentary are not included, and italics indicate that the reference is to the passage commentary.

Ancient Duke Danfu 古公亶甫. Father of the Great Uncle and Great King, grandfather of King Wen. *8.1.*

Ao 羿. Legendary Xia Dynasty naval commander of questionable morals, son of a murderer and usurper, who was in turn was murdered by one of his own ministers; known for feats of strength, such as handling warships. *7.21, 14.5.*

Bi Chen 裨諶. Minister in the state of Zheng under Prime Minister Zichan, who sought out the solitude of the countryside when given the task of drafting important state documents. *14.8.*

Bi Gan 比干. Uncle and minister of evil King Zhow, with whom he bravely remonstrated, incurring King Zhow's wrath and eventually being executed. Paragon minister and exemplar of the virtues of dutifulness and uprightness. *18.1.*

Bi Xi 佛肸. Steward of Zhongmou 中牟, a city in state of Jin 晉. *17.7.*

Bo Yi 伯夷 and Shu Qi 叔齊. Semi-legendary figures said to have lived at the end of the Shang Dynasty. They were both princes in the Shang state of Guzhu 孤竹, sons of the ruler Mo Yi 墨台. When their father died, each ceded to the other, neither wishing to take the throne over his brother, with the result that the throne remained vacant. When the Shang fell to the Zhou, they went into voluntary exile and reportedly starved themselves to death, refusing out of loyalty to their former king to eat the grain of the Zhou. Their names are thus bywords for rectitude, dutifulness, and purity. *5.23, 7.15, 15.40, 16.12, 18.8.* Cf. the legends about Bo Yi in *Mencius* 2:A:2, 2:A:9, 5:B:1, 6:B:6, 7:B:15.

Chang Ju 長沮. Primitivist recluse. *18.6.*

Cheng Chengzi 陳成子. Personal name Heng 恒, minister of Qi who murdered Duke Jian of Qi in 481 B.C.E. and usurped the throne. *14.21.*

Chen Wenzi 陳文子. Minister in state of Qi. *5.19, 13.21.*

Chen (Xizi) Qi 陳 (僖子) 乞. Evil minister in the state of Qi, who took over the running of the state from the rightful lord, Duke Jing, during the Duke's lifetime, and then assassinated the Duke's appointed heir and usurped the throne. *12.11.*

Conductor for the Fourth-course Que 缺.

Conductor for the Second Course Gan 干.

Conductor for the Third Course Liao 繚.

All three were conductors who emigrated from the state of Lu. 18.9.

Count Qin 伯禽. Son of the Duke of Zhou, who was originally given the state of Lu as his fief. *6.24*, 18.10.

Cuizi 崔子. Minister in state of Qi, said to have assassinated Lord Zhuang 莊 of Qi in 548 B.C.E. 5.19.

Duke Ai 哀 (of Lu) (r. 494–469 B.C.E.). One of the nominal rulers of Lu during Confucius' lifetime, although Lu was in fact controlled by the Ji Family. 2.19, 3.21, 6.3, *8.14*, *11.7*, 11.25, 12.9, *13.7*, 14.21, 18.4, *18.9*.

Duke Chu 出 of Wei. Title adopted by Duke Ling's grandson, Zhe 輒, when he assumed the throne in 493 B.C.E. 7.15, 13.3, *13.7*.

Duke Ding 定 (of Lu) (r. 508–495 B.C.E.). One of the nominal rulers of Lu during Confucius' lifetime, although Lu was in fact controlled by the Ji Family. 3.19, 13.15, *16.3*.

Duke Huan 桓 (of Lu) (r. 710–693 B.C.E.). One of the former Dukes of Lu, ancestor of the so-called "Three Families" of Lu. *16.3*.

Duke Huan of Qi 齊桓公. Personal name Xiaobo 小白, he seized power after the death of his father, eliminated his elder brother as a competitor for the throne, and then reigned as the first of the official hegemons or Lord Protectors (*ba* 霸) from 681–643 B.C.E., with the clever and able Guan Zhong as his Prime Minister. 3.22, 14.15–14.17, *17.18*.

Duke Jian 簡 (of Qi). Murdered by Chen Chengzi in 481 B.C.E. 14.21.

Duke Jing 景 of Qi (r. 547–490 B.C.E.). In Duke Zhao, Year 25 (516 B.C.E.) Confucius arrived in Qi to find that Duke Jing, near the end of his reign, was in dire straights. His nominal minister, Chen Qi, had usurped control of the state, and the Duke's plan to pass over his eldest son for the succession had set off contention among his sons. In the end, he failed to clearly establish a successor, and thereby set the stage for Cheng Chengzi assassinating Duke Jing's successor, Duke Jian, and usurping control of the state. *8.14*, 12.11, *13.5*, 16.12, 18.3, *18.4*.

Duke Ling 靈 of Wei 衛. A weak ruler, with a fondness for women and violence, who was able to hold onto power during his lifetime with the aid of able ministers, but whose misjudgment set off a power struggle in Wei after his death. He was the father of Prince Kuai Kui 蒯聵, grandfather of the future Duke Chu 出 of Wei, and his consort was the notorious Nanzi 南子. *6.16*, *13.3*, 14.19, 15.1, *15.7*, *16.1*.

Duke of She 葉公. Personal name Zigao 子高, lord of the walled city of She, located in the state of Chu 楚, and minister to the Chu king. 7.19, 13.16, 13.18.

Duke of Zhou 周公. Brother of King Wu, who, after King Wu's death, served as regent for his son, the future King Cheng 成, until King Cheng was old enough to take office. A paragon of dutifulness and virtue, and particular hero of Confucius'. *3.10*, *6.24*, 7.5, 8.11, *11.12*, 11.17, *13.7*, 18.10, 19.20.

Duke Wen of Jin 晉文公. Second of the official hegemons, ruled 636–628 B.C.E. He maintained an opulent household, and was judged by Confucius to have been "crafty but not correct." 3.17, *14.2*, 14.15, *16.3*.

Duke Xuan 宣 (of Lu). Doubled the traditional ten percent tithe on agricultural production in 593 B.C.E. *12.9*, *16.3*.

Eldest-Sons Da 達 and Kuo 适. Virtuous Zhou ministers. 18.11.

Fangshu 方叔.   Drummer who emigrated from the state of Lu. 18.9.

Fu Xi 伏羲.   Legendary sage, supposed creator of the Chinese writing system and the hexagrams of the *Book of Changes*. 9.9, 16.1.

Gao Yao 皋陶.   A famously virtuous minister, raised up by the Sage-king Shun. 6.9, 12.22, *13.18*.

Gaozong 高宗.   Posthumous title of the legendary Shang king Wuding 武丁, who reigned from 1324–1264 B.C.E. 14.40.

Gongbo Liao 公伯寮.   Minister to the Ji Family of Lu who slandered the disciple Zilu. 14.36.

Gongming Jia 公明賈.   Disciple or retainer of Gongshu Wenzi. 14.13.

Gongshan Furao 公山弗擾.   Also known as Gongshan Funiu 公山弗狃, style-name Zixie 子洩. From the stronghold city of Bi, he staged a revolt against the Ji Family. 17.5.

Gongshu Wenzi 公叔文子.   The posthumous title of Gongsun Ba 公孫拔 (alternately Gongsun Zhi 公孫枝), a worthy minister in Wei who apparently passed away before Confucius' first visit to that state. 14.13, 14.18.

Gongsun Chao 公孫朝.   Minister in the state of Wei. 19.22.

Gongye Chang 公冶長.   The identity of Gongye Chang is not clear. Although he is identified by the *Record of the Historian* as a man from Qi, Kong Anguo and others describe him as a disciple of Confucius from Lu. Confucius gave him his daughter in marriage, despite the fact that he had been convicted of a crime. His name later became associated with a variety of legends attributing him with the ability to understand the language of birds and other animals, including an amusing story that describes him being falsely accused of murder because he overheard a group of birds discussing the location of the body of a murder victim. He is freed only after having demonstrated his supernatural abilities to his jailor (286). 5.1.

Great Duke (*taigong* 太公).   The head of the Jiang 姜 clan, the Zhou's primary allies in the conquest of the Shang. He and his descendents were given the state of Qi 齊 as their fief. 6.24, *16.12*.

The Great King (*taiwang* 太王).   One of the three sons of Ancient Duke Danfu and father of King Wen. *8.1*, *16.12*.

The Great Uncle (*taibo* 太伯).   One of the three sons of Ancient Duke Danfu, older brother of the Great King, who ceded his right of succession to the Great King because he knew this was the wish of his father. *7.31*, *8.1*, *18.8*.

Guan Zhong 管仲.   Clever and able Prime Minister to Duke Huan of Qi in the seventh century B.C.E., who enabled the Duke to become the first of the official hegemons or Lord Protectors (*ba* 霸). In helping bring about an alliance of Chinese states under his Duke, he performed an invaluable service by enabling China to defend itself against invading barbarians. Confucius admired his skill and achievements, but had doubts about his moral worthiness. 3.22, 14.9, *14.10*, 14.16, 14.17.

Historian Yu 史魚.   A somewhat inflexible man known for his uprightness. 15.7.

Hou Ji 候姬 ("Lord Millet").   Legendary inventor of agriculture and progenitor of the Zhou royal line. 14.5.

Huan Tui 桓魋.   Huan Tui was a military leader in the state of Song who apparently wished to do Confucius harm. According to an account in the *Record of the Historian*, while in Song Confucius and his disciples were one day practicing ritual beneath a large tree when Huan Tui, in an attempt to kill Confucius, cut the tree down. This event apparently occurred around 493 B.C.E. *7.23, 12.4.*

Jieyu 接輿. The "madman of Chu." 18.5.

Ji Huanzi 季桓子. One of the heads of the Ji Family of Lu. *16.2, 16.3, 17.5,* 18.4.

Ji Kangzi 季康子. One of the heads of the Ji Family of Lu. 2.5, 2.20, 6.8, 10.16, 11.7, *11.17,* 12.17, 12.18, 12.19, 14.19, *16.1.*

Ji Pingzi 季平子. One of the heads of the Ji Family of Lu. *3.21, 16.3.*

Ji Wenzi 季文子 (d. 568 B.C.). The first head of the Ji Family to wield real power in Lu. 5.20, *13.21, 16.2, 16.3.*

Ji Zicheng 棘子成. Minister of Wei. 12.8.

Ji Ziran 季子然. Younger brother of Ji Kangzi. 11.24.

Junior Music Master Yang 少師陽. Musician who emigrated from Lu. 18.9.

King Jie 桀. Evil last king of the Xia Dynasty. 19.20, *20.1.*

King Tang 湯. Personal name Lü 履, supposed founder of Shang Dynasty. 12.22, 20.1.

King Wen 文 ("Cultured King"). Remained loyal to the evil King Zhow, last ruler of the Shang Dynasty, hoping to reform him through virtuous example. His son, King Wu, finally revolted against King Zhow, establishing the Zhou Dynasty, taking for himself the title "Martial King," and posthumously declaring his father to be the "Cultured King." *3.20, 5.21, 8.20, 9.5, 13.7, 15.29, 19.22.*

King Wu 武 ("Martial King") r. 1122–1115 B.C.E. Militarily defeated the evil Zhow, who showed himself incapable of reform, to found the Zhou Dynasty. *3.16, 3.25,* 8.20, *15.29, 16.12, 19.20,* 19.22, 20.1.

King Zhow 紂. The decadent and evil last king of the Shang Dynasty, who was finally overthrown by King Wu. *3.25, 16.12, 18.1,* 19.20, 20.1.

Kong Wenzi 孔文子. Kong Wenzi ("Cultured Master Kong") is the postumous title of Kong Yu 孔圉, referred to as Zhongshu Yu 仲叔圉 in 14.19, minister in the state of Wei (d. ca. 480 B.C.E.). Despite his flattering posthumous title, Kong was a rather unvirtuous person, known for disloyalty and dissoluteness. 5.15, 14.19, 15.1.

Kuai Kui 蒯聵. In 496 B.C.E. Prince Kuai Kui, son of Duke Ling of Wei, made a failed attempt upon the life of Duke Ling's infamous consort Nanzi and was forced to flee the country, abandoning his right to succession. In the summer of 493 B.C.E. Duke Ling died, and—over the protests of Nanzi—his grandson Zhe 輒, son of Kuai Kui, was made ruler and given the title of Duke Chu 出 of Wei. Kuai Kui, living in exile in the state of Jin, subsequently repented of his former decision and began maneuvering to have himself installed as ruler of Wei. Kuai Kui's efforts were vigorously resisted by his son, now Duke Chu, who fought to hold onto power. *7.15, 11.13, 13.3.*

Lin Fang 林放. A man of Lu, about whom little is known except that he shared Confucius' concern about the decline of ritual in his state. 3.4, 3.6.

Liuxia Hui 柳下惠. A virtuous minister in Lu, clan-name Zhan 展, personal name Huo 獲, and style-name Qin 禽 or Ji 季. He was posthumously known as Liuxia Hui, which may represent a single pseudonym (lit. "benevolence under the willow tree"), or (according to Zheng Xuan) a combination of the name of his country estate, Liuxia ("under the willows"), with the posthumous name Hui ("benevolence"). 15.14, *15.40*, 18.2, 18.8.

Meng Jingzi 孟敬子.   Member of the Meng Family of Lu, minister and son of Meng Wubo. 8.4.

Meng Wubo 孟武伯.   Member of the Meng Family of Lu, son of Meng Yizi and minister of Lu. 2.6, 5.8.

Meng Yizi 孟懿子.   Head of the Meng Family and minister in state of Lu. 2.5, 2.6.

Meng Zhifan 孟之反.   Style-name of Meng Zhice 孟之側, a Minister of Lu whose forces were routed by the state of Qi in a battle outside the Lu capital in 485 B.C.E. He courageously stayed in the rear to defend his forces during their retreat, but modestly deprecated his behavior. 6.15.

Min Zijian 閔子騫.   Style-name of Min Sun 閔損, a figure renown for his filiality. Several early texts have stories concerning the filiality of Min Zijian, which differ regarding some details but which all present a respectful son dealing selflessly with a classically evil stepmother. 6.9, 11.3, 11.5, 11.13, 11.14.

Music Master Mian 師冕.   Blind Music Master who visited Confucius. 15.42.

Music Master Zhi 師摯.   State conductor in Lu. 8.15, 18.9.

Nangong Kuo 南宮适.   14.5. Kong Anguo identifies Nangong Kuo as a minister in the state of Lu, an unusually virtuous member of the Three Families, and son of the Meng Yizi mentioned in 2.5; Zhu Xi believes him to be the Nan Rong mentioned in 5.2.

Nanzi 南子.   Notoriously corrupt and lascivious consort of Duke Ling. 6.28, *7.15*, *13.3*.

Ning Wuzi 甯武子 (7th c. B.C.E.).   Ning Wuzi is the posthumous name of Ning Yu 甯俞, a minister in the state of Wei, who served during the reign of Duke Cheng 成 of Wei (who ascended the throne in 633 B.C.E.). His father, Ning Zhuangzi 甯莊子, served under the previous lord of Wei, Duke Wen 文, and Ning Wuzi apparently inherited the office from him. 5.21.

Old Peng 老彭.   Somewhat mysterious figure, perhaps a great worthy of Yin Dynasty; fond of transmitting ancient tales. 7.1.

Priest Tuo 祝鮀.   Glib minister of Wei. 6.16, 14.19.

Prince Jing of Wei 衛公子荊.   Minister of Wei, scion of the Ducal house, praised for his lack of acquisitiveness and his financial restraint. 13.8.

Prince Jiu 公子糾.   Exiled from Qi with younger brother, Prince Xiaobo 小白—the future Duke Huan of Qi—and then murdered by him. 14.16, 14.17.

Qu Boyu 蘧伯玉.   Minister in state of Wei, known for his virtue. 14.25, 15.7.

Ru Bei 孺悲.   Not much is known about Ru Bei except a couple of passing references in early ritual texts, although he was apparently a person from Lu, and is said to have sought an audience with Confucius in a ritually-inappropriate manner. 17.20.

Second-Sons Tu and Hu 仲突仲忽.   Virtuous Zhou ministers. 18.11.

Shao Hu 召忽.   Retainer of Prince Jiu of Qi, who killed himself rather than betray Prince Jiu. 14.16, *14.17*.

Shao Lian 少連. Famous recluse who withdrew from public service on moral grounds. 18.8.

Shi Shu 世叔. Given-name Youji 遊吉, referred to in the *Zuo Commentary* as Zi Taishu 子太叔. Minister in the state of Zheng under Prime Minister Zichan. 14.8.

(Sage-king) Shun 舜. One of the great early sage-kings, and a paragon of virtue in the eyes of Confucius. *3.25, 6.26, 6.30, 8.18, 8.20, 13.18, 14.42, 15.5, 17.13, 17.19, 19.16, 19.20, 19.22, 20.1.*

Song Chao 宋朝. A handsome aristocrat from Song who became a minister in Wei. 6.16.

Tantai Mieming 澹臺滅明. A virtuous, dutiful senior official who served under Ziyou in the city of Wu-cheng 武城 in the state of Lu. The *Record of the Historian* lists him as a disciple of Confucius, style-name Ziyu 子羽, thirty-nine years junior to the Master. Some scholars have argued that Tantai Mieming is simply an alternate name for the disciple Master Zeng, who is also described as being from Wu-cheng. See Brooks and Brooks 1999: 280 for an argument that "Tantai Mieming" is merely a pun upon Master Zeng's name Zeng Shen 曾參. 6.14.

Third-Sons Ye and Xia 叔夜叔夏. Virtuous Zhou ministers. 18.11.

Upright Gong 直躬. A man from Chu who reported his father for stealing a sheep; became a stock figure in early texts for uprightness or trustworthiness taken to an excessive extreme. 13.18.

Wangsun Jia 王孫賈. A military minister in Wei, portrayed in 3.13 as the real wielder of power in Wei. 3.13, 14.19.

Weisheng Gao 微生高. Many commentators believe that the Weisheng Gao mentioned in 5.24, identified as a man from Lu, is the same person as the Wei Sheng 尾生 mentioned in many early texts (*wei* 微 and *wei* 尾 being somewhat interchangeable) as an example of trustworthiness taken to an excessive extreme. *1.13, 5.24, 13.18.*

Weisheng Mou 微生畝. Nothing is known of Weisheng Mou, but in 14.32 he addresses Confucius by his personal name, Qiu 丘, which indicates that he is either very much Confucius' elder, or is deliberately trying to be rude—or possibly both. Probably a principled recluse. 14.32.

Wu 武. Hand-drummer who emigrated from the state of Lu. 18.9.

Xiang 襄. Stone-chime player who emigrated from the state of Lu. 18.9.

Yan Lu 顏路. Father of the disciple Yan Hui. 11.8.

Yan Pingzhong 晏平仲. Posthumous name of Yan Ying 晏嬰, a virtuous minister in the state of Qi and contemporary of Confucius, in whose name the *Annals of Master Yan* was compiled. 5.17.

Yang Fu 陽膚. Disciple of Master Zeng, appointed police magistrate by the head of the Meng Family. 19.19.

Yang Huo 陽貨. Alternately known as Yang Hu 陽虎, a family minister of the Ji Family who physically resembled Confucius. *9.5, 16.2, 17.1.*

Yang Zhu 陽朱. Famous self-preservationist and recluse, who left no writings of his own, but whose views on individualism, avoiding public service and living out one's natural lifespan are recorded in the *Mencius* and other early texts. See Graham 1989: 53–64 on "Yangism." *2.16, 15.9.*

Yao 堯.   Legendary, virtuous early sage-king, predecessor of Shun. 3.25, 6.30, 8.19, 14.42, *19.22*, 20.1.

Yi 羿.   Legendary archer and prince during the Xia Dynasty, who overthrew one of the Xia kings and usurped his place. 14.5, *19.25*.

Yi Yi 夷逸.   Famous recluse who withdrew from public service on moral grounds. 18.8.

Yi Yin 伊尹.   A famously virtuous minister raised up by Tang. 12.22, *15.40*.

Youngest-Sons Sui and Gua 季隨季騧.   Virtuous Zhou ministers. 18.11.

Yu 禹.   Legendary founder of the Xia Dynasty, most famous for taming the Yellow River and thereby saving China from its periodic floods. 8.18, 8.21, 14.5, *19.16*, 20.1.

Yuan Rang 原壤.   An overly casual acquaintance of Confucius. 14.43.

Yu Zhong 虞仲.   Famous recluse who withdrew from public service on moral grounds. 18.8.

Zang Wei 臧為.   Half-brother of Zang Wuzhong, appointed successor to the Duke of Lu at Zang Wuzhong's urging. 14.14.

Zang Wenzhong 臧文仲.   Zang Wenzhong is the posthumous title of the Lu minister Zang Sunchen 臧孫辰, who apparently was known by his contemporaries as a man of wisdom, but who was repeatedly criticized by Confucius. 5.18, 15.14.

Zang Wuzhong 臧武仲.   Grandson of Zang Wengzhong, a wise, but not entirely scrupulous, minister in Lu. 12.18, 14.12, 14.14.

Zhou Ren 周任.   A legendary, wise historian. 16.1.

Zhuan 僎.   Household minister of Gongshu Wenzi. 14.18.

Zhuangzi of Bian 卞莊子.   Official in the walled city of Bian, on the eastern border of Lu, legendary for his courage. 14.12

Zhu Zhang 朱張.   Famous recluse who withdrew from public service on moral grounds. 18.8.

Zichan 子產.   The style-name of Gong-sun Qiao 公孫僑, a minister in the state of Zheng 鄭, renowned for his virtue and praised by Confucius. 5.16, 14.8, 14.9.

Zifu Jingbo 子服景伯.   Minister in state of Lu, friendly to Confucius. 14.36.

Zisang Bozi 子桑伯子.   There is some debate concerning the actual identity of Zisang Bozi. Zhu Xi says only that he is a person from Lu, but early commentators identify him as a minister from the state of Qin, or identify him with the easy-going Daoist sage Master Sang-hu 桑乎 (雽) mentioned several times in the *Zhuangzi* and/or the casual Zisang Bozi who is visited by Confucius in a story from the *Garden of Persuasions*. 6.2.

Ziwen 子文.   First took office as *lingyin* 令尹 in the state of Chu in 663 B.C.E. The title of *lingyin* (translated as "Prime Minister"), which was used only in Chu, probably referred originally to a military commander, but "by the seventh century had assumed the function of prime minister, in charge of both civil and military administration" (Blakeley 1999: 56). Ziwen was renown for his integrity and devotion to the state. 5.19.

Ziyu 子羽.   Style-name of Gong Sunhui 公孫揮, knowledgeable and eloquent foreign minister in Zheng under Prime Minister Zichan. 14.8.

Zuoqiu Ming 左丘明. There is some controversy over the identity of Zuoqiu Ming, but the *Record of the Historian* and other Han texts describe him as the Grand Historian of Lu who later authored the *Zuo Commentary* in order to make Confucius' intention in writing the *Annals* clear. Some scholars argue that the Zuoqiu Ming mentioned in 5.25 (possessing the double-surname Zuoqiu) should be distinguished from the author of the *Zuo Commentary* (who has only the single surname), but others argue that the *-qiu* 丘 suffix could have been dropped for reasons of simplicity of reference or because the word *qiu*—Confucius' personal name—became tabooed among Confucian schools after the Master's death. Zhu Xi and other later scholars came to doubt this whole tradition, believing that Zuoqiu Ming was simply a famous worthy who lived before Confucius' lifetime. 5.25.

APPENDIX 4:
TRADITIONAL CHINESE
COMMENTATORS CITED

Short biographical notes for each of the commentators cited are included below. Only the briefest of information is provided for minor commentators mentioned only once or twice, most space being reserved for major, frequently cited commentators. Western-style dates are provided when available; otherwise simply the dynastic period is indicated. For more extensive notes, as well as an explanation of sources, see the Reference Edition of this translation (www.hackettpublishing.com).

Bao Shenyan 包慎言.   Qing Dynasty. Bao's works include studies of the *Gongyang Commentary* and other early classics.

Bao Xian 包咸 (c. 6 B.C.E.–65).   Han Dynasty. A high official and scholar who moved in imperial circles, Bao was trained in the Lu version of the *Analects*, and taught this version of the text to the Han prince.

Cai Mo 蔡謨 (281–356).   Jin Dynasty. Cai was a successful general and high civil official, known for both his strategic acumen and broad scholarly knowledge. His commentary to the *Analects* is quoted in Huang Kan's sub-commentary.

Chao Yuezhi 晁說之 (1059–1129).   Song Dynasty. Scholar, official, and admirer of Sima Guang, Chao was an avid student of the Confucian classics, although he advised taking a critical stance toward them because of what he saw as Buddhist, Daoist, and Legalist interpolations. In his later years, he developed a strong personal and scholarly interest in Buddhism. His commentary to the *Analects* is cited in Zhu Xi's *Collected Line-by-Line Commentary to the Four Books*.

Chen Houfu 陳厚甫.   Qing Dynasty. Quoted in *The Reading Notes of Mr. Dongshu* (*dongshu dushuji* 東塾讀書記) by the Qing philologist and classicist Chen Feng 陳澧 (1810–1882), otherwise unknown.

Chen Tianxiang 陳天祥 (1230–1316).   Yuan Dynasty. Scholar, official, and general.

[Master] Cheng 程子.   Refer to the entry for Cheng Yi.

Cheng Hao 程顥 (1032–1085).   Older brother of Cheng Yi (the two are collectively referred to as the "Cheng brothers"), he shared many of his metaphysical and ethical views, although his youthful interest in Daoism and Buddhism, as well as his greater emphasis on intuition and internalism, has led some scholars to see in his thought an anticipation of certain aspects of the Lu-Wang school.

Cheng Yaotian 程瑤田 (1725–1814).   Qing Dynasty. A renowned scholar of the Confucian classics who served in the office of "Teacher of the *Analects*" (*jiaolun* 教論), and was also an accomplished musician, poet, astronomer, and mathematician. He was a careful student of the classics and the commentarial tradition, affirmed that the main content of the teachings of the disciples of Confucius consisted of returning to the practice of governing and cultivating one's own self, and was opposed to metaphysical, neo-Confucian interpretations of Confucius' theory of human nature. In his youth, he was a friend and fellow-student of Dai Zhen's.

Cheng Yi 程頤 (1033–1107). The younger brother of Cheng Hao, both of whom studied for a year with Zhou Dunyi and had intellectual ties to Zhang Zai. Cheng is credited with setting the intellectual tone for what would become the Cheng-Zhu school, transmitting his teachings through his disciple Yang Shi to Yang's disciple Li Tong, who in turn was the teacher of Zhu Xi. Cheng Yi and his older brother were instrumental in making "principle" the central focus of neo-Confucian thought, with Cheng Yi coining the famous saying, "Principle is one, but its manifestations are many." His emphasis on correcting the mind through study and rectification of one's dress and demeanor can be seen as giving the Cheng-Zhu school its characteristic externalist bent. It is presumed that most of the commentary to the *Analects* attributed to "Master Cheng" in Zhu Xi's *Collected Line-by-Line Commentary to the Four Books* refers to Cheng Yi, although which brother is being quoted is difficult to establish for certain.

Dai Zhen 戴震 (1724–1777). Qing Dynasty. Renowned classicist, official, and philosopher, he played an important part in compiling the massive survey of the imperial library, *Complete Collection of the Four Treasuries* (*siku quansu* 四庫全書), commissioned by the imperial court. He was known for studies in phonology and his efforts to build on the work of earlier "Han school" scholars who wished, by means of phonological and etymological rigor, to purify classical exegesis of the influence of Song neo-Confucian metaphysics. He is most famous, however, for his philosophical attacks on Song neo-Confucianism and his own rationalistic, pragmatic philosophical position, which posited a monism of material force that evolved and underwent changes in accordance with regular laws—a kind of principle embedded in material force—that could be elucidated through objective, rigorous study of the physical world, the classics, and history.

Du Yu 杜預 (222–284). Jin Dynasty. A scholar of the classics, official, and general.

Fan Ning 范甯 (339–401). Jin Dynasty. Blocked from public service early in his life because of a powerful enemy of his family, he eventually rose to high office after this person's death, only to be eventually relieved of his duties as the result of a financial scandal. Fan disapproved of what he saw as his contemporaries' tendency to disregard both rituals and laws, and since he attributed this decline of morals to the flourishing of the "Mysterious Learning" school associated with Wang Bi and He Yan, he was a frequent critic of these two scholars.

Fan Ziyu 范祖禹 (1041–1098). Song Dynasty. Official, philosopher, and historian, Fan was a member of the Hanlin Academy,[1] prominent participant in the compilation of official histories, and lecturer to the emperor. He studied with the Cheng brothers, and his thought and writings—especially his commentary to the *Analects*, cited in Zhu Xi's *Collected Line-by-Line Commentary to the Four Books*—was very much derived from them. He was politically conservative and particularly known philosophically for his emphasis on the importance of sincerity (*cheng* 誠) for both personal self-cultivation and political order. Although he believed sincerity was part of inborn human nature, he thought that

---

[1] The Hanlin Academy was an elite imperial academic institution founded by the Emperor Xuan Zong (r. 712–756) in the Tang.

most people had to struggle to regain it, and advocated as the primary method for doing so the Confucian practice of "dutifulness and understanding." In this respect, Fan was a vociferous opponent of Daoism, arguing that, by de-emphasizing the importance of the Confucian virtues and moral self-cultivation, it led human beings into chaos and confusion.

Fu Guang 輔廣.　Song Dynasty. Fu was a minor office holder and devoted disciple of Zhu Xi, whose association with the politically unpopular Zhu eventually forced him to retire to his native town in the south and open a scholarly academy. He was strongly critical of the government for overly burdening the people with regulations and taxes, and differed somewhat from Zhu in emphasizing that economic prosperity was a worthy goal, as long as it were pursued within the limits set by rightness.

Ge Yinliang 葛寅亮.　Ming Dynasty.

Gu Yanwu 顧炎武 (1613–1682).　Ming-Qing Dynasty. As an influential historian, geographer, classicist, and philosopher, and staunch Ming loyalist, Gu adamantly refused to serve the Manchu Qing Dynasty. He attributed the fall of the Ming to the spiritual and intellectual weakness engendered in Chinese elites by the empty metaphysical speculation of Song neo-Confucianism. He advocated an approach to the classics based on historical accuracy, philological evidence, and inductive methods drawing on the broad accumulation of data, and also urged scholars to eschew Song commentaries on the classics for the less metaphysically elaborate and presumably more historically accurate Han commentaries, such as those of Zheng Xuan. He can be considered one of the founding figures of the Qing "evidential" or philological approach to classical studies that is now the standard in the field.

Gui Fu 桂馥 (1736–1805).　Qing Dynasty. Philologist and classicist, Gui is particularly known for his work on early dictionaries such as the *Explaining Words* and his work on reconstructing archaic pronunciations.

Guo Xiang 郭象 (c. 252–c. 312).　Jin Dynasty. Renown official and "Mysterious Learning" thinker, Guo is famous for his annotated edition of the *Zhuangzi*, but passages from his otherwise lost *Commentary to the Analects* (*lunyu zhu* 論語注) are quoted in Huang Kan.

Han Yu 韓愈 (768–824).　Tang Dynasty. Often identified as the forerunner of neo-Confucianism, Han Yu is best known for his attacks on Daoism and Buddhism (personally quite costly for him at the time), which he believed to be disruptive of natural human relations; his focus on human nature as a topic of inquiry, and his theory of the "three grades" of human nature; his insistence of the importance of "correct transmission" of Confucian doctrines, and his placement of Mencius in this orthodox lineage; and his citations from the *Book of Changes* and "Great Learning" and "Doctrine of the Mean" chapters of the *Record of Ritual*, which helped to put these works at the center of later neo-Confucian metaphysics.

He Yan 何晏 (c.190–249).　Three Kingdoms Period. Together with Wang Bi, He Yan is traditionally cited as the founder of the so-called "Mysterious Learning" school. He was a rather prominent figure, grandson of a great general of the Eastern Han Dynasty, and adopted son of the famous Cao Cao 曹操, who attempted—but failed—to unify China after the collapse of the Han. He Yan was renown both for his intellect and physical beauty, married a princess, and eventually entered the ranks of the nobility as Marquis-consort. He was killed in 249, after the failure of the Cao Shuang 曹爽 revolt in which he participated. He was a student of Daoism and the *Book of Changes*, and is often described as interpreting the *Analects* through the lens of such "Daoist" concepts as "nothingness" (*wu* 無) and "emptiness" (*xu* 虛). He is traditionally credited with editing *Collected Explications of the Analects* (*lunyu jijie* 論語集解)—one of our main sources for otherwise lost Han Dynasty commentaries—although this attribution has been disputed by some modern scholars.

Hong Xingzu 洪興祖 (1090–1155).　Avid scholar of the classics and conscientious official, Hong was very devoted to the ideal of applying "benevolent government" to the common people. His commentary to the *Analects* is cited in Zhu Xi's *Collected Line-by-Line Commentary to the Four Books*.

Hu Anguo 胡安國 (1074–1138).　Classicist and philosopher, he was a close associate of Xie Liangzuo, Yang Shi, and You Zuo, and considered Cheng Yi to be his intellectual inspiration. Hu emphasized the importance of hard work in self-cultivation, which he saw as being based on dutifulness and trustworthiness, the extension of knowledge, and personal respectfulness. His commentary to the *Analects* is cited in Zhu Xi's *Collected Line-by-Line Commentary to the Four Books*.

Hu Bingwen 胡炳文 (1250–1333).　Yuan Dynasty. Hu was a devotee of the Cheng-Zhu school of neo-Confucianism, wrote a commentary to the *Annals*, and was the author of *Comprehending the Four Books* (*sishu tong* 四書通), from which his *Analects* commentary is cited.

Huan Maoyong 宦懋庸.　Qing Dynasty.

Huang Gan 黃榦 (1152–1221).　Song Dynasty. Student and son-in-law of Zhu Xi, Huang was dedicated to the transmission of the "orthodox" Cheng-Zhu school of interpretation.

Huang Kan 皇侃 (488–545).　Northern and Southern Dynasties Period. Huang Kan had scholarly inclinations from a very early age, and studied the classics under a famous Confucian scholar as a young man, specializing in the early ritual texts, the *Classic of Filial Piety*, and the *Analects*. He was also a practicing Buddhist and created a variety of intellectual and practical links between Buddhism, Daoism, and Confucianism. He was the author of the *Sub-commentary to the Meaning of the Analects* (*lunyu yishu* 論語義疏), based upon He Yan's commentary, which was lost in China, but then rediscovered in Japan in the 18th century. This eclectic sub-commentary (*shu* 疏) contains Huang's own comments, as well as the comments of more traditional Confucian scholars, Daoist thinkers, and Buddhist monks.

Huang Peifang 黃培芳 (1779–1859).　Qing Dynasty. Scholar, essayist, and poet, one of the "Three Masters of Verse" in Guangdong Province.

Huang Shisan 黃式三 (1789–1862).　Qing Dynasty. A scholar broadly versed in the classics, particularly early ritual texts and the thought of Zheng Xuan, Huang shared the general Qing distaste for metaphysical speculation. He believed that the world consisted of material force alone, in which principle was embedded, and felt that any attempt to discuss principle or the Way outside of the context of the physical world would lead to nonsense. He also opposed Zhu Xi's distinction between human "moral nature" and "material nature," arguing that there is no human nature apart from the physical body and its needs. He similarly dismissed the common neo-Confucian conception—shared by both the Cheng-Zhu and Lu-Wang schools, and ultimately derived from Buddhism—that human desires are inherently evil, believing that it is only desires that have not been corrected and regulated by ritual and other cultural standards that are problematic. In this respect, he differed from the idealism of the Lu-Wang school in arguing that ritual and other standards are tools that are both external to human nature and essential for properly shaping it.

Huang Zhen 黃震 (1212–1280).   Song Dynasty. A fourth-generation disciple of Zhu Xi, Huang was a stanch defender of the Cheng-Zhu orthodoxy in the waning years of the Song Dynasty, although he had his own strong opinions on how to understand the tradition. One of his primary complaints against his contemporaries was their focus on theory rather than practice, and he forcibly argued for understanding principle as something immanent in everyday human affairs, rather than an object of abstract speculation. He also deplored his contemporaries' obsession with the subject of human nature, arguing that Confucius' only statement on the topic, 17.2, was all that needed to be said, and that proper Confucians should focus their attention upon the influence of practice rather than nature.

Jia Changchao 賈昌朝 (998–1065).   Song Dynasty. Jia held a variety of academic and administrative posts, including Lecturer at the Imperial Clan Palace and Attendant to the Emperor, and had many contacts among the eunuchs and other members of the imperial court.

Jiang Xi 江熙.   Jin Dynasty. Generally characterized as a Daoist-inclined scholar, Jiang compiled *Collected Commentaries on the Analects* (*lunyu jijie* 論語集解), no longer extant, portions of which are quoted in Huang Kan.

Jiao Hong 焦竑 (1540–1620).   Ming Dynasty. Jiao was a prominent scholar of the classics who was first placed in the Palace Examination of 1589, and who was subsequently appointed to high academic posts at the imperial court. He believed that Buddhism and Confucianism were fundamentally reconcilable, devoting much of his scholarly effort to demonstrating parallels between the Buddhist canon and Confucian classics. He argued that the Buddhist sutras served as the best commentaries on the *Analects* and the *Mencius*. His syncretism also embraced the Daoist classics, for which he authored several commentaries.

Jiao Xun 焦循 (1763–1820).   Qing Dynasty. Classicist, mathematician, and drama critic. Unsuccessful in his official examinations, Jiao retired to his studio and devoted his life to writing and study, acquiring broad expertise in the entire classical canon. He was particularly devoted to the *Mencius* and *Book of Changes*, analyzing the latter in terms of mathematical theory, and believing that the *Changes* could in turn be used to explicate the other classics. Philosophically, he believed that the Way or principle was inseparable from material force, representing the pattern of the movement of material force. He was also a fatalist, believing that fate, in the form of the cyclic movement of material force, could not be altered. He also opposed the Cheng-Zhu rejection of desire as inherently bad, believing that true benevolence consisted of regulating and harmonizing human desires so that they could be properly satisfied.

Jiao Yuanxi 焦袁熹 (1661–1736).   Qing Dynasty. A classicist who held the post of Lecturer on the *Analects* at a regional academy, Jiao was a specialist in the study of the *Annals* and a close associate of Lu Longqi.

Jin Lüxiang 金履祥 (1232–1303).   Song-Yuan Dynasty. Jin was a classicist and neo-Confucian thinker in the Cheng-Zhu school. He held some minor academic posts early in his life, but then went into retirement after the fall of the Song and dedicated himself to textual studies and writing. An accomplished scholar of the *Book of Odes* and *Book of Documents*, he interpreted these and other early texts in such a way that their message would be consistent with that of the Cheng-Zhu branch of neo-Confucianism.

Kong Anguo 孔安國 (156–74 B.C.E.).   Han Dynasty. An 11th generation descendent of Confucius, Kong held a variety of important posts, including Governor of Linhuai, although he died at a young age. Little is known about his thought. Kong's commentary to the *Analects* is cited from the *Collected Explications of the Analects*, although many scholars believe that the commentary attributed to him is, in fact, a forgery.

Kong Yingda 孔穎達 (574–648). Tang Dynasty. Famous classicist and educator, Kong was a broadly learned prodigy called to the imperial court at an early age. His *Corrected Meaning of the Five Classics* (*wujing zhengyi* 五經正義), published in 653, immediately became a standard of classical scholarship, and he also collaborated on the writing of the *History of the Sui*.

Li Ao 李翱 (fl. 798). Tang Dynasty. Student or friend of Han Yu, and along with him one of the forerunners of the neo-Confucian movement. See the entry on Han Yu.

Li Chong 李充. Jin Dynasty. Scholar, official, and "Mysterious Learning" thinker, reputedly fond of Legalist thought in his youth. Passages from his otherwise lost collected commentary to the *Analects* are cited in Huang Kan.

Li Guangdi 李光地 (1642–1718). Qing Dynasty. A prominent neo-Confucian of the Cheng-Zhu school, editor of the *Collected Works of Zhu Xi*, and famous "defender of the orthodoxy." Li held a variety of academic and administrative posts, and eventually became a confidant of the Kangxi 康熙 Emperor, having a considerable influence on the emperor's political philosophy. No doubt one of the most appealing aspects of his thought for the emperor was his argument that Zhu Xi's thought could be understood as supporting imperial authority, with reverence for one's political superiors serving as an important method of self-cultivation, banishing selfish thoughts and freeing one from heterodox doctrines. Philosophically, he largely held to orthodox Cheng-Zhu line, although he somewhat softened Zhu's emphasis on the priority of principle over material force, sometimes suggesting that principle and material force were merely different aspects of the same thing.

Li Tong 李侗 (1093–1163). Song Dynasty. Neo-Confucian thinker, twice-removed student of the Cheng brothers and teacher of Zhu Xi, among other important figures. He generally followed Cheng Yi in his metaphysics, but particularly emphasized the importance of "quiet sitting" in the process of self-cultivation, which he felt was the most effective method for eliminating human desires and other external pollutants that obscure one's originally pure moral nature. His commentary to the *Analects* is cited in Zhu Xi's *Collected Line-by-Line Commentary to the Four Books*.

Li Wei 李威 (dates uncertain, fl. 1770–1790). Qing Dynasty. Li held a variety of administrative posts in Guangdong Province before eventually settling in his native Fujian Province and serving as Lecturer. In his later years, he became a devotee of the Lu-Wang school, convinced that the Cheng-Zhu practice of "investigating things" led only to the accumulation of fragmented, useless knowledge, and that the best method of study was practical experience.

Liu Baonan 劉寶楠 (1791–1855). Qing Dynasty. Both a successful administrator and classical scholar, Liu dedicated the scholarly activities of the latter part of his life to putting together a state-of-the-art critical edition of the *Analects*. Because he considered both Huang Kan and Xing Bing's commentarial editions to be full of errors, he used He Yan's *Collected Explication of the Analects* as his basis, adding other Han commentaries, selected Song commentaries and sub-commentaries, and the best products of Qing philology and textual history. Because of the demands of his administrative duties, Liu passed away before the fruit of these labors, the *Correct Meaning of the* Analects (*lunyu zhengyi* 論語正義), could be finished, but this work was completed by his son. The gov-

erning hermeneutical strategy of this work was to "let the classics explain the classics"—
in other words, to use other classical Confucian texts in order to elucidate the meaning
of the *Analects*, in order to avoid importing anachronistic philosophical baggage.

Liu Fenglu 劉逢祿 (1776–1829).   Qing Dynasty. Liu was a classicist and expert in the
Gongyang Commentary, which he argued was more authoritative than the *Zuo Commentary*. In his interpretation of the classics, he emphasized grasping the general sense
rather than focusing on textual minutia, but also insisted upon historical and philological accuracy. Liu was an influential commentator and textual critic who published works
on many of the classics, and his range of research interests was particularly broad.

Liu Kai 劉開 (1784–1824).   Qing Dynasty. Scholar and poet.

Liu Xiang 劉向 (c. 77–6 B.C.E.).   Han Dynasty. A descendant of the younger brother of
Liu Bang 劉邦, founder of the Han Dynasty, he was a fairly influential intellectual and
writer, interested in the occult and a master of the Confucian canon.

Lu Longqi 陸隴其 (1630–1692).   Qing Dynasty. Important scholar and official, known
for his incorruptibility and concern for the well being of the common people. Lu was
also an impassioned defender of the Cheng-Zhu orthodoxy, declaring that "the teaching
of Zhu Xi is the door to Confucius and Mencius; trying to study Confucius and Mencius
without going through Zhu Xi would be like trying to enter a room without going through
the door." The belief behind this sentiment was that the message of Confucius and
Mencius had been lost in the intervening centuries, and only recovered again by the Song
neo-Confucians. Lu was also highly critical of the Lu-Wang school, because in his view
their radical internalism—essentially a form of Chan-Zen Buddhism in Confucian garb—
was fundamentally opposed to the proper Confucian concern with "things and affairs" in
the outside world.

Lu Shanji 鹿善繼 (1575–1636).   Ming Dynasty.

Luan Zhao 欒肇.   Jin Dynasty. There is no biography of Luan Zhao in the *History
of the Jin*, but Lu Deming describes him as a man from the Tai Shan region of China
who held office under the Jin. His *Explaining Doubtful Points of the Analects* (*lunyu shiyi*
論語釋疑) is no longer extant, but large portions of it are preserved in Huang Kan's
sub-commentary.

Ma Rong 馬融 (77–166).   Han Dynasty. A classicist and thinker in his own right, Ma
adhered to the "Yin-Yang" cosmology of his time, which held that certain patterns in the
Heavenly realm were mirrored in the human realm, with the two realms influencing one
another through a kind of analogical resonance. For instance, if the emperor manifested
obedience in his own person, this would help the seasons to follow their proper course;
similarly, disruptions in the natural order of things would manifest themselves in social
and political disorder. Ma was a famous commentator and teacher of the classics in his
own age, and produced a number of outstanding students, including Zheng Xuan.
Although an adherent to the so-called "Ancient text" school,[2] he often employed New
Text readings when appropriate, and thereby helped to blur the line between the two
school's approaches to the classics. He was also somewhat eclectic philosophically;
although a Confucian, he had an interest in Daoist texts such as the *Laozi* and *Zhuangzi*.

---

[2] The "Ancient text" school was devoted to the set of texts written with archaic versions of Chinese
characters that began to be discovered in the Han Dynasty, especially in the first c. B.C.E., whereas
the "New text" school believed these texts to be spurious and preferred to use the received versions
of the classics, written with contemporary-style Chinese characters.

This interest in Daoism, as well as his somewhat free and easy personal manner, is thought to have had an influence on the later "pure talk" movement that eschewed ritual standards and conventional morality. His commentary to the *Analects* is cited in He Yan's *Collected Explications of the Analects*.

Mao Qiling 毛奇齡 (1623–1716).   Ming-Qing Dynasty. Well-known classicist, philosopher, and writer. Mao briefly went into reclusion after the fall of the Ming, but then reentered public life, enticed by the special national examination held in 1679 by the Qing to lure reclusive Ming-loyalists back into public service. He was one of only fifty people to pass the exam and was subsequently assigned to the Hanlin Academy, where one of his duties was to help compile the official *History of the Ming*. Mao was a man of wide talents, famous for his poetry as well as his extensive mastery of the classics. He was also fond of controversy and debate, and took a special interest in refuting the views of previous scholars when it came to textual analysis of the classics. A follower of the Lu-Wang school, he believed that this school represented the true legacy of Confucius, and expended much intellectual effort in demonstrating how the entire Confucian canon could be reconciled with the teachings of the "learning of the mind." In his view, self-cultivation consisted of nothing more than recovering one's original mind. He reaffirmed Wang Yangming's doctrine of the unity of knowledge and action, and emphasized the pernicious influence of human desires—the primary barrier to one seeking to recover the original mind. Mao also acknowledged the parallels between Lu-Wang neo-Confucianism and Chinese Buddhism, but believed that neo-Confucianism differed from Buddhism in its emphasis on putting the original mind to work in the social world.

Miao Bo 繆播.   Jin Dynasty. Official and scholar, known for his keen intellect and debating skills. His commentary is no longer extant, but is partially preserved in Huang Kan's sub-commentary.

Miao Xie 繆協.   Jin Dynasty. Little is known about this figure, other than that he authored a short text called *Explaining the Analects* (*lunyu shuo* 論語説) that is no longer extant, but that is partially preserved in Huang Kan's sub-commentary.

Qian Daxin 錢大昕 (1728–1804).   Qing Dynasty. Classicist and historian, member of the Hanlin Academy. He was an extremely learned scholar whose exceptionally broad research interests—ancient phonology, metallurgy, calendrics, geography, genealogies—earned him the title of "the Greatest Confucian of the Age." Qian argued that the point of the classics was to learn how to practice morality, and that the best way to understand the classics was through historical and philological rigor.

Qian Dian 錢坫 (1744–1806).   Qing Dynasty. A classicist and famous calligrapher, Qian was a phonetics and geography specialist, and spent thirty years of his life writing a massive commentary to the *Record of the Historian*.

Sima Guang 司馬光 (1019–1086).   Song Dynasty. Famous historian, politician, political theorist, philosopher, and member of the Hanlin Academy. In his writings, he emphasized the importance of ritual, believing it to be the key to both realizing one's own nature and ordering the state.

Su Shi 蘇軾 (1039–1101).   Song Dynasty. Famous writer and thinker, he is best known philosophically for his belief that Confucianism, Daoism, and Buddhism were essentially one teaching, although the content of his thought often has a particularly Buddhist flavor.

Mr. Su 蘇氏.   The "Mr. Su" cited in Zhu Xi's *Collected Line-by-Line Commentary to the Four Books* may be Su Shi (above), his brother Su Che 蘇轍 (1039–1112), a classicist and writer, or Su Xun 蘇洵 (1009–1066), writer, philosopher, and the father of Su Shi and Su Che. Su Xun was particularly known for his view that human nature is bad and requires the restraining influence of ritual in order to become orderly.

Sun Chuo 孫綽 (320–377). Jin Dynasty. A scholar and writer, he held a variety of posts in the imperial court. As a young man, he was fascinated with Daoism, and eventually became a devotee of the Mysterious Learning school. Sun was of the opinion that Confucianism, Daoism, and Buddhism were all ultimately the same teaching, with Buddhism and Daoism teaching the "inner" aspects of the Way and Confucianism focusing upon it "outer" application in the world. Sun also believed that human nature is originally pure, but then is "agitated" by contact with the world and the arousal of human desires. His commentary to the *Analects* was lost sometime after the Tang Dynasty, but is partially preserved in Huang Kan's sub-commentary.

Sun Qifeng 孫奇逢 (1585–1675). Ming-Qing Dynasty. Neo-Confucian thinker, educator, and classicist. After the fall of the Ming, he retired from public life, dedicating his life to education and scholarship. He was one of the main figures in an early Qing movement to reconcile the Cheng-Zhu and Lu-Wang schools, arguing that Wang Yangming's cultivation of "innate knowledge" and Zhu Xi's "investigation of things" are basically the same thing. Sun felt that too much energy had been wasted in sectarian disputes, and that both the Lu-Wang and Cheng-Zhu schools "took truth alone as their guiding value, the realization of Heavenly principle as their main goal, and real-life usefulness and the maintenance of proper social relations as their practical effect." Like many Ming-Qing neo-Confucians, Sun was also critical of empty metaphysical speculation concerning principle and human nature, arguing that personal practice and real-world results should be the focus of study. His later years were focused on classical study, where his emphasis was the potential application of the classics to one's life, rather than philological or textual details.

Wang Bi 王弼 (226–249). Famous "Mysterious Learning" thinker, scholar, and official, Wang is best known for his annotated edition of the *Laozi*, the basis of the received version of the text and oldest extant commentary upon it. Philosophically, he is best known for his emphasis on "non-being" (*wu* 無) and principle, both referents to a kind of transcendent, fundamental reality that Wang believed was the basis of the phenomenal world. His commentary to the *Analects* is cited in Huang Kan.

Wang Fuzhi 王夫之 (1619–1692). Ming-Qing Dynasty. A scholar and Ming Dynasty loyalist, the thirty-three year-old Wang led a small force in ill-fated resistance against Qing forces when they invaded his native Hunan Province. After his defeat, he went into retirement rather than serve the new Qing Dynasty, and devoted the rest of his life to scholarship. He is sometimes described as a "materialist" for opposing the Cheng-Zhu school dichotomy of principle and material force, as well as the monism of principle advocated by the Lu-Wang school, with the claim that only material force exists in the world, and that principle is nothing more than patterns of this material force. Wang is also famous for his view of history, which was fairly radical at the time: he saw history as a progressive rather than cyclic, and felt that patterns from the past cannot necessarily be used to govern the present. Wang was also extremely critical of the influence of Daoist and Buddhist metaphysics on Confucianism, and in his exegesis of the Confucian classics attempted to recover what he saw as their essentially practical, this-worldly emphasis. In this desire to purge *Analects* interpretation of Song and Ming neo-Confucian metaphysics, in many ways, Wang anticipated in the more historically sophisticated approach of later Qing Dynasty scholars.

Wang Kentang 王肯堂. Ming Dynasty. Scholar, official, and physician.

Wang Niansun 王念孫 **(1744–1832).**   Qing Dynasty. Classicist, scholar, and official, known in his youth for precociousness, he published a variety of respected works on geography and river control that grew out of his official duties in the Department of Waterways. A student of Dai Zhen's, he was also known for his work on phonetics and etymology. He is best known for work on annotating and emending Warring States and Han texts, his work on the dictionary *Expansive Elegance*, and his works on archaic phonetics.

Wang Shu 王恕 **(1416–1508).**   Ming Dynasty. Wang spent most of his life serving in various high offices, and was renown as a virtuous and effective minister. Many of the people he promoted during his official career went on to become prominent figures as well. In his later years, he retired to devote himself to writing and the study of the classics. He was a somewhat independent thinker, difficult to classify in terms of any of the existing schools of thought. He shared the basic neo-Confucian suspicion of human desires, believing that they are fundamentally incompatible with Heavenly principle, and celebrated Mencius's focus on exhausting one's heart-mind in order to know human nature and Heaven, thereby foreshadowing Wang Yangming's emphasis upon the "learning of the mind." He also anticipated Wang Yangming in emphasizing the essential unity of knowledge and action, with action being the natural unfolding of any sort of true knowledge, as well as in his assertion that the purpose of learning is realized in words and actions, rather than empty speculation.

Wang Su 王肅 **(c. 195–256).**   Han-Three Kingdoms Period. Wang held a series of prominent official positions in his lifetime and had access to the inner imperial circles of the Wei Dynasty. He was also an accomplished scholar and wrote commentaries on all of the major Confucian classics, many of which were explicitly targeted at what Wang viewed as the misleading commentaries of Zheng Xuan. Wang saw the first task of the commentator to be textual verification and the accurate glossing of terms, and with regard to *Analects* commentary felt that Ma Rong was much more responsible than Zheng Xuan in this respect. His own commentary to the *Analects* is cited in He Yan's *Collected Explications of the Analects*. Some later scholars have also attributed to Wang Su authorship of the *Family Conversations of Confucius*.

Wang Yangming 王陽明 **(1472–1529).**   Ming Dynasty. Famous neo-Confucian thinker, follower of the teachings of Lu Deming 陸德明 (1139–1193), and founding figure in the Lu-Wang 陸王 "learning of the mind" (*xinxue* 心學), or "idealist" school of neo-Confucianism. Like Lu Deming, Wang was a vocal critic of Zhu Xi and the Cheng-Zhu brand of neo-Confucianism, arguing that their concern with "study and inquiry" and the gradual accumulation of knowledge led to a pedantic, disjointed, overly theoretical grasp of Confucianism. Unlike Zhu Xi, Wang was a man of action in addition to being a scholar, serving as a high official as well as a general responsible for putting down uprisings in the south of China, and was a popular and charismatic teacher. He is most famous for his claim that there is nothing in the world but principle, which is identical to the human mind—that is, observable phenomena are not the result of the interactions of material objects composed of material force, but are rather emanations of the mind. This means that Zhu Xi's dualism of principle and material force is incorrect, and Zhu's program of acquiring knowledge through the "investigation of things" is therefore doomed to failure, since there are no things in the world to investigate. All necessary moral knowledge is already in the mind in the form of principle, which means that the task of self-cultivation consists of nothing more than activating this "innate knowledge" through the elimination of selfish desires, achieving a sincere "unity of knowledge and action" where innate knowledge is instantly and spontaneously translated into action in the world. Although Wang's extreme internalism seems rather foreign to the *Analects*, his claim that

Confucius was more concerned with action than theoretical study is basically sound, and served as an important corrective to the teachings of the Cheng-Zhu school.

Wang Yinzhi 王引之 (1766–1834).   Qing Dynasty. Official and scholar, eldest son of Wang Niansun. He was a member of the Hanlin Academy and noted philologist, best known for his systematic studies of ancient Chinese grammatical particles and critical emendations of glosses of the classics. He also collaborated with his father on a variety of projects, including a study of ancient dictionaries and reference works on names of figures in the Spring and Autumn, Warring States, and Qin periods.

Wei Guan 衛瓘 (220–291).   Jin Dynasty. A high official and author of *Collected Commentaries on the Analects* (*lunyu jizhu* 論語集注), portions of which are preserved in Huang Kan.

Wu Jiabin 吳嘉賓 (1802–1864).   Qing Dynasty. A classicist with "Han School" tendencies, in that he was inclined to eschew the Song commentaries and approach the classics directly, attempting to derive their meaning from context and common sense. He is particularly known for his work on the *Record of Ritual*.

Wu Tingdong 吳廷棟 (1793–1873).   Qing Dynasty. Classicist and official, he was particularly interested in the study of Song neo-Confucianism and the relationship between Buddhism and Confucianism. In his view, the primary fault of Buddhism was that it focused on the abstract at the expense of the practical. In this respect, he felt that the Cheng-Zhu school should be viewed as the orthodox line of Confucianism, because of its emphasis on study and rightness in human relations, and he criticized the internalism of the Lu-Wang school as leading to moral relativism.

Xia Xichou 夏錫疇 (1732–1798).   Qing Dynasty. A scholar in the Cheng-Zhu tradition, he believed that this school of neo-Confucianism represented the orthodox transmission of the spirit of Confucius.

Xie Liangzuo 謝良佐 (1050–1103).   Song Dynasty. One of the four renown disciples of the Cheng brothers, he believed that principle was an unavoidable, inexorable law of the universe, governing everything in the world as well as the human mind, and that in order to comprehend this principle—originally "one body" with the human mind—it was necessary to eliminate the influence of external forces, such as desire or greed. His focus on the mind, as well as the influence of Chan-Zen Buddhism on his thought, caused Zhu Xi to compare him to Lu Deming. His commentary to the *Analects* is cited in Zhu Xi's *Collected Line-by-Line Commentary to the Four Books*.

Xing Bing 邢昺 (931–1010).   Tang-Song Dynasty. Xing held a variety of important academic posts during his lifetime and was a prominent member of the Hanlin Academy. Together with other scholars, he prepared critical editions of most of the major Confucian classics, including the *Analects*. He is often described as a pivotal figure in the shift from "Han Dynasty learning" to Song neo-Confucianism. For instance, he opposed the then popular view of Dong Zhongshu that differences in moral and intellectual worth could be attributed to three different grades of human nature, arguing instead that all people are equally endowed at birth with the same, unsullied nature, and that differences then arise in response to subsequent agitation of this nature by external things.

Xue Xuan 薛瑄 (1389–1464).   Ming Dynasty. A prominent neo-Confucian scholar and member of the Cheng-Zhu school. He continued the Cheng-Zhu emphasis on the importance of learning, although he slightly modified the orthodox metaphysics by suggesting that since principle resides in material force, it is impossible to know which should be given priority.

Yang Liang 楊倞 (fl. 818). Tang Dynasty. Minor office holder and was otherwise unknown except for his commentary to the *Xunzi*.

Yang Shi 楊時 (1053–1135). Song Dynasty. Philosopher, scholar, and official, one of the four renown disciples of the Cheng brothers. He particularly followed Cheng Hao in his thought, emphasizing that all of principle is contained within the self, and often in his writings seeking to blur the distinction between the inner self and outside things. He followed the Chengs in seeing the "investigation of things" as the key to recovering principle, but tended to emphasize the importance of internal recognition over external acquisition of knowledge. In this respect, his views anticipate certain themes in the Lu-Wang school. He was also somewhat influenced by Daoist ideals. His commentary to the *Analects* is cited in Zhu Xi's *Collected Line-by-Line Commentary to the Four Books*.

Yin Tun 尹焞 (1070–1142). Scholar and official, and devoted disciple of Cheng Yi, whom he followed quite closely in his ethics and metaphysics. His commentary to the *Analects* is cited in Zhu Xi's *Collected Line-by-Line Commentary to the Four Books*.

You Zuo 游酢 (1053–1123). Song Dynasty. Philosopher, scholar, and official, one of the four renowned disciples of the Cheng brothers. Although a member of the Cheng school, You was also heavily influenced by Buddhist thought, and believed that Buddhism and Confucianism were fundamentally compatible. He was also a devotee of the *Book of Changes*, believing that it contained within it all of the principles of the world. His commentary to the *Analects* is cited in Zhu Xi's *Collected Line-by-Line Commentary to the Four Books*.

Yu Yue 俞樾 (1821–1906). Qing Dynasty. One of the most prominent figures in Qing philology and textual studies, Yu was a member of the Hanlin Academy and served in a variety of academic posts before retiring from official life and devoting himself full time to classical studies. He believed that the most important techniques in rendering the classics readable for contemporary readers were restoring original word and sentence orders (sometimes altered in transmission), establishing the proper senses of individual words, and—most importantly—being more aware of the use of "phonetic loan words." Phonetic loan words are Chinese characters that are used with the intended sense of another word with a different graphic form but similar pronunciation; especially in pre-Qin texts, before the Chinese written language was standardized, this phenomenon was quite common. Yu believed that many of the difficulties encountered in reading the classics were due to a failure to recognize the use of loan characters—an often quite challenging task, requiring an intimate knowledge of ancient Chinese phonology—and in his commentaries, he often raises the possibility of this phenomenon to suggest alternate readings. Yu's analyses of the classics are widely admired for their philological acumen, and he has had a large influence on both Chinese and foreign students of the Chinese classics, particularly in Japan.

Zhai Hao 翟灝 (1736–1788). Qing Dynasty. A scholar and professor, Zhai was widely versed in the classical canon, particularly specializing in the Four Books. His commentaries are carefully considered and nonpartisan, drawing on both Han and Song commentaries in formulating his opinions.

Zhang Erqi 張爾岐 (1612–1699). Qing Dynasty.

Zhang Ping 張憑. Jin Dynasty. Official and scholar, whose commentary to the *Analects* is cited in Huang Kan's sub-commentary.

Zhang Shi 張栻 (1133–1180).   Song Dynasty. Famous scholar and thinker. Although Zhang followed Cheng Yi's thought in most ways, he also emphasized the importance of the mind and is seen as some as a transitional figure between the Cheng-Zhu and Lu-Wang schools of neo-Confucianism. Ethically, he believed that, because of the deleterious influence of human desires, making a proper distinction between rightness and profit-benefit was crucial to the individual's moral development. His commentary to the *Analects* is cited in Zhu Xi's *Collected Line-by-Line Commentary to the Four Books*.

Zhang Zai 張載 (1020–1077).   Famous early neo-Confucian thinker. Like Zhou Dunyi, he drew upon the *Book of Changes* to give Confucianism a metaphysical framework, borrowing from that text the concept of the Great Ultimate (*taiji* 太極) to describe the source of the phenomenal world. Zhang advocated a kind of monism of material force, arguing that the various things in the universe are simply different aspects of material force, the evolution of which is guided by principle. His idea that the universe is one, although its manifestations are many, had a huge influence on later neo-Confucian thought, and informed his understanding of benevolence (*ren* 仁) as a kind of universal love. He was the uncle and teacher of the Cheng brothers, and his commentary to the *Analects* is cited in Zhu Xi's *Collected Line-by-Line Commentary to the Four Books*.

Zhao Qi 趙岐 (c. 108–201). Han Dynasty.   A classicist whose particular specialties were the *Analects* and the *Mencius*, Zhao believed that the *Analects* was the key to all the classics and traditional culture, and that the *Mencius* was modeled upon the *Analects*. He is best known for his commentary to the *Mencius*—the oldest extant commentary to that work—as well as editing the *Mencius* down by discarding four "outer" chapters he considered to be extraneous.

Zhao You 趙佑 (1729–1800).   Qing Dynasty. Scholar and official.

Zheng Ruxie 鄭汝諧.   Song Dynasty. Scholar and official, who also authored a commentary to the *Book of Changes*.

Zheng Xuan 鄭玄 (127–200).   Famous classicist and commentator. As a commentator to the *Analects*, Zheng focused upon glossing archaic characters and explaining the text in terms other classics. His *Mr. Zheng's Commentary to the Analects* (*lunyu zhengshi zhu* 論語鄭氏注) was extremely important and influential up through the Tang Dynasty, officially recognized by the imperial court and the subject of national university chairs, but was suddenly lost sometime between the late Tang and early Song Dynasty. Parts of it were preserved in other works, and this is the source of the Zheng Xuan comments cited in Cheng Shude and reproduced in our work.

Mr. Zhou 周氏.   Han Dynasty. Author of a commentary to the *Analects* quoted in He Yan's *Collected Explications of the Analects*, and about whom nothing else is known.

Zhou Dunyi 周敦頤 (1017–1073).   Song Dynasty. Traditionally considered to be the founder of neo-Confucianism, Zhou was a syncretic Confucian thinker who set the tone for later neo-Confucianism by giving Confucianism a cosmological grounding, deriving the idea of a transcendent unity to the cosmos from Chinese Buddhism and the *Book of Changes*. The Cheng brothers visited and studied with him for a year, and in later genealogies, he is identified as the founder of the Cheng Yi-derived line of transmission.

Zhousheng Lie 周生烈 (fl. 230).   Three Kingdoms Period. Scholar and official, whose commentary to the *Analects* is no longer extant, but preserved in part in He Yan's *Collected Explications of the Analects*.

Zhu Xi 朱熹 (1130–1200).   It is probably not an exaggeration to say that Zhu Xi is the most influential thinker in Chinese history after Confucius. A third-generation student of Cheng Yi (through Yang Shi and Li Tong), Zhu Xi avoided public office for most of his adult life, preferring to devote himself to scholarship. He established a school of neo-Confucian thought—later known as the Cheng-Zhu 程朱, "learning of principle" (*lixue* 理學), or "rationalist" school   that remained the dominant orthodoxy throughout the Chinese cultural sphere into the twentieth century, and which continues to inform the beliefs of many contemporary neo-Confucians. One salient feature of the Cheng-Zhu school is a dualism with regard to principle and material force. Principle is identical to the Way, perfectly good, and prior to material force. It requires material force to manifest itself in the world, however, at which point it immediately becomes contaminated by this contact, in the same way that clean water is fouled when flowing in a dirty channel. The clean water is not changed in its essence, however—being merely mixed with a something alien to it—and thus can be returned to its originally pure state if this contaminant is somehow removed or settled out. This dualism with regard to principle and material force corresponds to a dualism with regard to human nature: although all human beings possess a "moral nature" that is identical to principle, as soon as they take on physical form, this original nature becomes contaminated with material force, resulting in the mixed "material nature" with which we are burdened at birth. Desires, which are essentially bad, spring from this corrupt material nature. The task of self-cultivation, then, is to attempt to gradually purify the material nature and recover the original moral nature. Meditation is helpful in this respect, since it helps to calm the material force, but since our own nature is already hopelessly corrupted, outside help is essential. This help comes in the form of one's teacher, who is able to guide one in the process of the "investigation of things" (*gewu* 格物). A term from the "Great Learning" chapter of the *Record of Ritual*, the "investigation of things" for Zhu consisted of the cumulative and extensive study of physical things in the world and—more importantly—the texts of the Confucian tradition, which collectively contain within them all of the elements of original principle. By means of a lifetime of intensive study, the student could gradually piece together again the elements of original principle that are obscured in him, and thereby come to clear away the obscurations of material force and eventually manifest the original moral nature in his own person. Like all neo-Confucians, then, Zhu Xi accepted the Mencian theory that human nature is good, but not in the radically subjective sense of Wang Yangming: although originally good, we lose this goodness immediately upon birth, and therefore need to rely upon external training and study to recover it. With this essentially externalist bent, Zhu's views seem to correspond more closely with that of the original Confucius than those of Wang Yangming. One of Zhu's most enduring contributions to Chinese intellectual life was his editing of the *Analects*, the *Mencius*, and the "Great Learning" and "Doctrine of the Mean" chapters of the *Record of Ritual* to form the so-called "Four Books," which eventually became the basis of the civil service examination from 1313–1905, and which were therefore studied and memorized—along with Zhu's commentary to them—by all educated Chinese during this period and beyond. Zhu's commentary to the *Analects* still dominates the way the text is understood in both Asia and the West, and although in many places he understands Confucius through the lens of anachronistic, neo-Confucian concepts, the enduring influence of his commentary stems in no small part from its eloquence, brilliance, and frequently profound insight.

Zhu Zhongdu 褚仲都.   Northern and Southern Dynasties. In a biography of Zhu's son in the *History of the Liang*, Zhu is described as a specialist in the *Book of Changes*, an historian-official, and an expert in the Five Classics. His *Analects* commentary exists only in isolated quotations in Huang Kan's work.

APPENDIX 5:
TRADITIONAL CHINESE TEXTS

The following are brief descriptions of the traditional Chinese texts mentioned in the translation or commentaries. The standard English-language reference book on this topic is Loewe 1993, which contains essays on early Chinese texts by top scholars in the field; most of the entries are simply summaries of these essays—with added elaboration in cases where more about the philosophical positions expressed in the text is necessary—and the reader is referred to Loewe 1993 for more details. Certain texts are cited in the translation by abbreviated titles, indicated in parens.

Annals (chunqiu 春秋). Literally, "The Spring and Autumn," the *Annals* is a very terse historical record of the state of Lu from 722–481 B.C.E., noting in bare outline the internal affairs of Lu, diplomatic meetings, wars, and the occurrences of natural disasters. Traditionally it was attributed to Confucius, but modern scholars doubt that Confucius authored the text, although it is very possible that he knew it as something like its current form. (Anne Cheng in Loewe 1993: 67–76.)

Annals of Lü Buwei (lüshi chunqiu 呂氏春秋). Something like an encyclopedia of late Warring States knowledge, this book was composed sometime around 239 B.C.E. under the patronage of Lü Beiwei 呂不韋, a high minister in the state of Qin 秦 who committed suicide in 235 B.C.E. It is very well organized topically for a text of the period, and is generally regarded as a "syncretic" text, combining Confucian, Mohist, and Daoist material. Knoblock and Riegel 2000 provide a complete English translation. (Carson and Loewe in Loewe 1993: 324–330.)

Annals of Master Yan (yanzi chunqiu 晏子春秋). This book is a collection of speeches and descriptions of virtuous behavior of Yan Ying 晏嬰, a minister of Qi mentioned in *Analects* 5.12, the *Mozi*, and the *Zuo Commentary*. The *Record of the Historian* says that he died around 500 B.C.E., and although it is unlikely that any portion of the text was actually composed by Yan Ying, it is possible that disciples assembled parts of the text not long after his death. The text apparently existed in some form by the early Han, although some scholars have argued that our received text is a later forgery. (Stephen Durrant in Loewe 1993: 483–489.)

Balanced Discourses (lunheng 論衡). Written by Wang Chong (c. 27–100), this text "is concerned with a variety of questions raised in philosophy, history, literature and natural science . . . and may be regarded as an encyclopedic collection of the claims and beliefs of Chinese religion, thought, and folklore" (Pokora and Loewe, in Loewe 1993: 309). It was probably completed around 70–80. (Pokora and Loewe in Loewe 1993: 309–313.)

Bamboo Annals (zhushu jinian 竹書紀年). A chronicle discovered in a tomb in c. 281, covering a period from the time of the mythical Yellow Emperor up until the year 299 B.C.E. It is difficult to know exactly what the relationship is between our extant versions of the text—a "modern text" portion assembled sometime during the Jin Dynasty, and an "ancient text" portion assembled from early commentaries and other sources—and the original document found in the tomb of the King of Wei, which had been sealed in 299 B.C.E., but portions of the received text seem to be of genuinely ancient provenance. (David Nivison in Loewe 1993: 39–47.)

Biographies of High-Minded Scholar-Officials (*gaoshizhuan* 高士傳). A Jin Dynasty text attributed to Huang Fumi 皇甫謐, which was probably added to by later scholars.

Book of Changes (*yijing* 易經). The core portion of this text, sometimes separately referred to as the *Zhou Changes* (*zhouyi* 周易), is a cryptic divination manual of probably quite ancient provenance, organized around sixty-four "hexagrams" composed of a series of either solid or broken lines. Guidance was sought by randomly generating a hexagram out of a series of broken and solid lines, and then reading the statements attached to the hexagram. This earliest stratum probably reached its final form in the late Western Zhou. Appended to this earliest stratum are various commentaries that expand on its cryptic utterances, clarifying the judgments or offering moral observations. These commentaries date from various periods, but it is the opinion of Edward Shaughnessy that they "attained their present form in the mid-third to early second century" B.C.E. (in Loewe 1993: 221). Traditionally, the *Zhou Changes* was attributed to the legendary sage-king Fu Xi, King Wen, and the Duke of Zhou, and the commentaries attributed to Confucius himself, but these claims have been doubted in China from at least the Song, and are now entirely dismissed by both Chinese and Western scholars. The standard English translation is Wilhelm and Baynes 1950, and readers are also referred to Shaughnessy's translation of a version of the text, differing somewhat from the received text and dated to 168 B.C.E., discovered in a tomb in 1973. (Shaughnessy in Loewe 1993: 216–233.)

Book of Documents (*shujing* 書經 or *shangshu* 尚書). Covering a period from the ancient sage-kings through the Zhou Dynasty, this book consists primarily of pronouncements of kings or ministers. The earliest portions of it represent the oldest writings in China's traditional literature, but at least half of the received text was forged in the early fourth century. The debate concerning the likely dates of individual chapters and passages is quite complex; interested readers are referred to Shaughnessy's discussion in Loewe 1993: 376–389, and the works cited therein, for details. For an English translation, refer to Legge 1991b or Karlgren 1950a.

Book of Etiquette and Ritual (*yili* 儀禮). Known by a variety of names in the Han, this text consists primarily of ritual regulations for "scholar-officials" (*shi* 士), the lowest level of the aristocracy. Scholars today reject the traditional claim that the Duke of Zhou compiled this and other early ritual texts. Although some version of this text existed prior to the burning of the books by the First Emperor of Qin, it is unclear how much of the received text consists of pre-Han material. William Boltz's conclusion is that "it seems reasonable to accept as likely the supposition that the extant (*Book of Etiquette and Ritual*) is in origin part of a larger corpus of similar ceremonial and ritual texts dating from pre-Han times, perhaps as early as the time of Confucius; that much of this was lost by the Han; and that some may have come to be preserved in the text known today as the *Record of Ritual*" (Loewe 1993: 237). A full English translation is available in Steele 1917. (Boltz in Loewe 1993: 234–243.)

Book of Odes (*shijing* 詩經). Our primary textual source, along with the *Book of Documents*, for pre-Confucian Zhou culture, the *Odes* is a collection of 305 poems that date from c. 1000–600 B.C.E. The content is varied, ranging from intimate lyrical expressions of longing for a lover gone off to war to solemn state hymns. Although the *Odes* was traditionally said to have been edited by Confucius—who supposedly chose from thousands of poems, selecting only those that were morally and artistically superior—there is no reason to think that Confucius had any role in its compilation. In fact, large sections of it consist of rather racy folk poetry whose content later provided an interpretative challenge to Confucian moralists, who were committed to seeing the *Odes* as the expression of ancient sage-poets. Their response was to interpret problematic *Odes* metaphorically: the desire of an amorous poetess for an illicit rendezvous in the woods, for instance, became the yearning of a loyal minister for his lord. Reference to the *Odes* in the translation and commentary are to the so-called "Mao number"—that is, their number in the now-standard edition compiled by Mao Gong 毛公 in the early Han. For translations, refer to Legge 1991c, Karlgren 1950b, and Waley 1960. (Loewe in Loewe 1993: 415–423.)

Classic of Filial Piety (***xiaojing*** 孝經).   A short text on the virtue of filial piety, consisting of conversations between Confucius and Master Zeng. It was traditionally attributed to either Confucius or Master Zeng, and it is not implausible to think that Master Zeng or his disciples compiled at least portions of it. In any case, William Boltz points out that sizeable portions of the text are cited in the *Annals of Lü Buwei*, which means that something like our extant version must have been circulating prior to 239 B.C.E. (Boltz in Loewe 1993: 141–153.)

Dai's Great Record of Ritual (***"Dai's Record"***) (***dadai liji*** 大戴禮記).   A miscellaneous collection of passages from various pre-Han and Former Han sources, traditionally attributed to the ritualist Dai De 戴德 (first c. B.C.E.), but probably assembled sometime after second century C.E. (Jeffrey Riegel in Loewe 1993: 456–459.)

Discourses on Salt and Iron (***yantielun*** 鹽鐵論).   An account of a court debate ordered by an imperial edict in 81 B.C.E., ostensibly concerning the imperial monopoly on salt and iron, but in fact ranging over a wide variety of topics. It was most likely completed during the reign of Emperor Xuan 宣 (74–49 B.C.E.). (Loewe in Loewe 1993: 477–482.)

Discourses on the Mean (***zhonglun*** 中論).   A philosophical text written by Xu Gan 徐幹 (171–218), covering a variety of topics (politics, ethics, calendrics, ritual) from a primarily Confucian perspective. (John Makeham in Loewe 1993: 88–93.)

Exoteric Commentary on the Han School of the Book of Odes (***"Exoteric Commentary"***) (***hanshi waizhuan*** 韓氏外傳).   The title of this text is somewhat misleading, as it is not properly a commentary on the *Book of Odes* itself, but rather an eclectic collection of anecdotes and moral and practical advice, each vignette capped with a quotation from the *Book of Odes*—the purpose of the stories seemingly to be to illustrate the practical use of the *Odes* cited. The text draws on a variety of Warring States sources, and is attributed to Han Ying 韓嬰, a Former Han scholar whose dates are c. 200–120 B.C.E., although it has almost certainly been corrupted in transmission. For an English translation, see Hightower 1952. (Hightower in Loewe 1993: 125–128.)

Expansive Elegance (***guangya*** 廣雅).   A dictionary compiled by Zhang Yi 張揖 during the Three Kingdoms period.

Explaining Words (***shuowen jiezi*** 說文解字).   The first comprehensive dictionary of Chinese, this text was compiled by Xu Shen 許慎 (c.55–c.149) and completed in 100. (Boltz in Loewe 1993: 429–442.)

Family Sayings of Confucius (***"Family Sayings"***) (***kongzi jiayu*** 孔子家語).   A collection of ancient lore concerning Confucius' teachings and life, most of which consists of pre-Han and early Han materials probably handed down by Confucius' disciples and meant to supplement the *Analects,* although there are also some third century portions added by the editor of the received version, Wang Su 王肅 (195–256). (R.P. Kramers in Loewe 1993: 258–262.)

Garden of Persuasions (shuoyuan 説苑). A collection of stories and political admonitions collected from earlier materials, assembled by Liu Xiang 劉向 (79–8 B.C.E.) and presented to the emperor in 17 B.C.E. (David Knechtes in Loewe 1993: 443–445.)

Gongyang Commentary (gongyang zhuan 公羊傳). One of the three major extant commentaries on the *Annals,* traditionally said to have originated with the disciple Zixia and passed down for several generations until recorded by Mr. Gongyang in the Former Han. Modern scholars believe that the Gongyang already existed in written form in the late Warring States, however, although it was lost during the Qin and reconstituted in the early Han. (Anne Cheng in Loewe 1993: 68.)

Guanzi 管子. Traditionally attributed to Guan Zhong (see Appendix 3), this massive syncretic text contains discussions on government policy (often from a Legalist perspective), self-cultivation and meditation techniques, economic theory, and a wide variety of other topics. It was compiled in its present form by Liu Xiang 劉向 (79–8 B.C.E.) in c. 26 B.C.E. from earlier materials, some of which may date to the fifth century B.C.E. An English translation is available in Rickett 1985. (Rickett in Loewe 1993: 244–251.)

Guliang Commentary (guliang zhuan 穀粱傳). One of the three major extant commentaries on the *Annals,* the *Guliang Commentary* is partially based on the *Gongyang Commentary,* and is therefore probably of somewhat later origin. (Anne Cheng in Loewe 1993: 68.)

Hanfeizi 韓非子. One of the primary texts of the so-called "Legalist" or statecraft movement, most this text is probably from the hand of Hanfeizi (c. 280–c.233 B.C.E.), a prince in royal line of the minor state of Han 韓. It consists of a series of fairly tightly arguments on particular topics, organizing and synthesizing many of the ideas of earlier Legalists such as Shang Yang 商鞅, Shen Dao 慎到, and Shen Buhai 申不害. Hanfeizi was a student of Xunzi's and, along with his fellow student Li Si 李斯, served as an advisor to the future First Emperor of Qin, who eventually unified China by implementing certain Legalist policies. Hanfeizi was betrayed by Li Si, who was jealous of his influence, and forced to commit suicide in c. 233 B.C.E. A full English translation is found in Liao 1959. (Jean Levi in Loewe 1993: 115–124.)

The Hidden Meaning of the Analects (lunyu yinyi 論語隱義). The *History of the Sui* notes the existence of this text along with a commentary, both described as lost, and attributes the text (probably falsely) to Guo Xiang. Some extant fragments are recorded in the *Imperial Readings.*

History of the Han (hanshu 漢書). Often later referred to as the *History of the Former Han (qianhanshu 前漢書),* this official history of the Former or Western Han Dynasty was compiled by Ban Gu 班固 (32–92). (A.F.P. Hulsewé in Loewe 1993: 129–136.)

History of the Jin (jinshu 晉書). Official dynastic history, completed during the Tang Dynasty.

History of the Later Han (houhanshu 後漢書). Official dynastic history, compiled around 430.

History of the Sui (suishu 隋書). Official dynastic history, completed during the Tang Dynasty.

History of the Wei (weishu 魏書). Official dynastic history, compiled in 554.

Huainanzi 淮南子.   An eclectic collection of essays stemming from scholarly debates at the court of Liu An 劉安 (c. 179–122 B.C.E.), king of Huainan, sometime before 139 B.C.E. These essays cover a wide variety of topics and represent many schools of thought, and include a large number of citations from pre-Han texts. It was probably assembled by scholars at Liu An's court, possibly edited together by Liu An himself, and presented to the Han emperor in 139 B.C.E. (Charles Le Blanc in Loewe 1993: 189–195.)

Imperial Readings of the Taiping Period ("*Imperial Readings*") (*taiping yulan* 太平御覽).   An encyclopedia of extracts from dynastic histories and classical works for the emperor's edification, compiled in 983 by an imperial commission. It often preserves variations of passages found in extant versions of texts, as well as additional passages that apparently dropped out of extant versions.

Laozi 老子.   Also known as the *Classic of the Way and Virtue* (*daodejing* 道德經), this is probably the earliest of the so-called "Daoist" texts, and has traditionally been attributed to an ancient sage named Laozi (lit. "The Old Master"). Most likely, however, it was compiled by an editor or group of editors of a somewhat primitivist bent sometime in the early Warring States period. One of its primary themes is an opposition to learning, cultural knowledge, and morality—all of which are dismissed as "unnatural" and therefore contrary to the Way—and many of these critiques seemed aimed directly at the teachings of the *Analects*. There has been a great deal of debate about the dating of the *Laozi* relative to other Warring States texts, but internal evidence suggests that it is roughly contemporaneous with the *Analects*, and that it pre-dates other Warring States texts such as the *Mencius*, *Zhuangzi*, and *Xunzi*. There are an extraordinary number of English translations of the *Laozi* in circulation; the reader is referred particularly to Lau 1963 and Ivanhoe 2002. (See Boltz in Loewe 1993: 269–292.)

Liezi 列子.   Usually classified as a "Daoist" text, and traditionally attributed to a certain Lie Yukou 列禦寇, said to have lived around 400 B.C.E. There is a fair amount of debate concerning the dating and authenticity of this text, but most probably it is a mixture of materials ranging from pre-Qin times to as late as the 4th century. A full translation is available in Graham 1990. (T.H. Barrett in Loewe 1993: 298–308.)

Luxuriant Dew of the Annals (*chunqiu fanlu* 春秋繁露).   Attributed to Dong Zhongshu 董仲舒 (c. 179–c. 104 B.C.E.), a scholar at the Han imperial court, this text describes the ethical and political principles to be gleaned from the *Annals*, as understood through the *Gongyang Commentary* and further interpreted in terms of the cosmological theories of the time. Although there are concerns about the authenticity of the received text, there is good reason to believe that the majority of it is authentic. (Davidson and Loewe in Loewe 1993: 77–87.)

Mencius 孟子.   The record of the writings of a self-proclaimed follower of Confucius, Mengzi 孟子 (late fourth c. B.C.E.), better known in the West through the latinization "Mencius." The authenticity of the received text is not generally doubted, although the first commentator to the text, Zhao Qi 趙岐 (d. 201), apparently excised four "outer" chapters of an original eleven-chapter text because he considered them extraneous. Mencius saw it as his task to defend the vision of Confucius against the variety of rival schools of thought that had sprung up in the Warring States, including the Mohist, Yangists, and Primitivists. In doing so, he modified Confucius' original vision in many ways, although he himself believed that he was merely developing theme already implicit in the *Analects*. Mencius is most famous for his claim that "human nature is good," by which he meant that human beings have a natural tendency to develop the Confucian virtues, and that ritual training and learning of the classics merely function to nourish and gently guide this inborn *telos*. This theory of human nature was intended both as a critique of Mohism, which Mencius believed tried to force people to behave in unnatural ways, and as a refutation of the Laozian-Primitivist critique of Confucianism as being unnatural. Xunzi and others later criticized Mencius for having distorted Confucius' original vision, but the Song Dynasty neo-Confucians elevated him to the status of Confucius' true successor, a status he enjoys in China to this day. The best full English translation remains Lau 1970. (See D.C. Lau in Loewe 1993: 331–335.)

Mozi 墨子. This text is the record of the teachings of the Mohist school, the earliest rivals of Confucius, which was founded by Mozi in the late fifth century B.C.E. and died out by the 2nd c. B.C.E. The Mohists are best known for their belief that what is moral or "right" (*yi* 義) can be determined by calculating what is the most materially beneficial or profitable (*li* 利), which in turn is measured in terms of the wealth, population, and order of the state. They felt that many of the trappings of Confucian culture—such as ritual, music, funeral practices, etc.—failed this measure of rightness, and thus should be abandoned as immoral and wasteful. They also criticized the Confucian celebration of filial piety, arguing that "impartial caring" (*jian'ai* 兼愛) was preferable to Confucian nepotism; although they acknowledged that people naturally tended to favor their family and friends, they believed that this and other undesirable tendencies in human beings could be overcome through rational argumentation and a strict system of reward and punishment. A translation of most of the text is available in Mei 1980. (See Graham in Loewe 1993: 336–341.)

New Arrangement (xinxu 新序). A collection of moralistic tales, traditionally attributed to Liu Xiang 劉向 (79–8 B.C.E.), but apparently a selection of passages from earlier Warring States and Han texts merely edited together ("newly arranged") by him. (Knechtges in Loewe 1993: 154–157.)

Record of Ritual (liji 禮記). A compilation of ritual injunctions and anecdotes, without any clear organizing principle, the dating of which has always been somewhat controversial. Although some scholars have argued that the entire text was a product of the Later Han, the discovery in 1993 of a bamboo version of Chapter 34 ("Black Gown") in a tomb that was closed in 278 B.C.E. proves that at least portions of the text date to the Warring States period (see Jingmen Municipal Museum 1998). A full English translation is available in Legge 1967. (See Riegel in Loewe 1993: 293–297.)

Record of the Historian (shiji 史記). A history of China from mythical antiquity down to the late second century B.C.E., traditionally said to have been begun by the Grand Historian Sima Tan 司馬談 (d. 100 B.C.E.) and continued and finished by his son and successor in office, Sima Qian 司馬遷 (c. 145–c. 86 B.C.E.), although the latter is usually mentioned as the sole author. Additional chapters were apparently added after Sima Qian's death, and scholars suspected certain chapters as being later reconstructions. Almost all of the text has been translated into various European languages, but no complete English translation exists. (Hulsewé in Loewe 1993: 405–414.)

Record of the Three Kingdoms (sanguozhi 三國志). A history of the Three Kingdoms Period, compiled by Chen Shou 陳壽 (233–297).

Summary of Discussions in the White Tiger Hall ("Summary of Discussions") (baihutong 白虎通). Consisting primarily of questions and answers concerning the classics, this text is supposedly a summary complied by the historian Ban Gu 班固 (32–92) of a meeting in a place called White Tiger Hall. Called by imperial decree in 79, and attended by leading ministers and scholars, the purpose of the meeting was to settle controversial issues concerning the interpretation of the classics. Later scholars have questioned the authenticity of the received text, but no doubt at least portions of it consist of Ban Gu's original report, and the text as a whole probably reached its present form no later than the third century. (Loewe in Loewe 1993: 347–356.)

Xunzi 荀子. Traditionally attributed to "Master Xun," Xun Qing 荀卿 of Zhao 趙, an official in the state of Qi and Chu, philosopher and self-proclaimed follower of Confucius, and teacher of Li Si and Hanfeizi. His dates are uncertain, but he seemed to have died at an advanced age a decade or two before the end of the Warring States period. There are doubts about the authenticity of portions of the received text, several chapters of which probably represent writings of disciples of Xunzi. Xunzi is most well known for his claim that "human nature is bad," directly targeted at Mencius, and intended to correct what he saw as Mencius's lack of emphasis on the importance of cultural forms, teachers, and hard work in the process of self-cultivation. In Xunzi's view, Mencius's claim that human nature tends toward morality naturally is a concession to the Daoists and betrayal of Confucius' original vision, which was that human nature had to arduously be reshaped over the course of a lifetime in order to become moral. Although Mencius eclipsed Xunzi's influence after Mencius was made part of the official canon in the Song, Xunzi is receiving increasing attention from modern scholars. A full, annotated English translation of the text is available in Knoblock 1988, 1990, and 1994. (Loewe in Loewe 1993: 178–188.)

Yan Family Explications (*yanshi jiaxun* 顏氏家訓). A collection of political and moral maxims and observations, as well as explanations of the classics, written in the Sui by Yan Zhitui 顏之推 (531–c. 591).

Zhou Ritual (*zhouli* 周禮). This text purports to be a record of the governmental system of the royal state of Zhou. It apparently did not exist before the Former Han, but it likely is made up of largely pre-Han material. (Boltz in Loewe 1993: 24–32.)

Zhuangzi 莊子. Traditionally attributed to "Master Zhuang," who lived in the 4th century B.C.E., this "Daoist" text has long been recognized as a composite work, although the seven so-called "Inner Chapters" are probably the work of a single author sometime in the 4th century B.C.E. Much of the text is devoted to criticism of both the Confucians and Mohists for their conceptual rigidity and artificiality, which prevents them from accessing natural, Heavenly forces within themselves and therefore living long, satisfying, and healthy lives. A complete translation is available in Watson 1968, and a more philosophically oriented translation of the "Inner Chapters" in Graham 2001. (Harold Roth in Loewe 1993: 56–66.)

Zither Song (*qincao* 琴操). A Han Dynasty musical text attributed to the writer and scholar Cai Yong 蔡邕 (132–192).

Zuo Commentary (*zuo zhuan* 左傳). By far the longest of the three commentaries on the *Annals*, it also provides the most historical detail. The traditional account is that it was authored by the Zuo Qiuming 左丘明 mentioned in *Analects* 5.25 as a commentary on the *Annals*, but this has long been challenged because the *Zuo* does not always match the *Annals*: it covers a longer period of time, and there is often "commentary" with no corresponding text, or text lacking commentary. There is a great deal of controversy concerning the authenticity and origin of the *Zuo*, but conceivably it represents an independent historical text covering the Spring and Autumn period that was then cut up and supplemented in order to serve as a commentary to the *Annals*. Possible dates that have been proposed by modern scholars range from the fifth century B.C.E. to the first century B.C.E. A full English translation is provided by Legge 1991d. (Anne Cheng in Loewe 1993: 69–71).

BIBLIOGRAPHY

For a more extensive annotated bibliography, including a survey of secondary scholarship on the *Analects*, please refer to the Reference Edition of this translation (www.hackettpublishing.com)

Other Important English Translations of the Analects

Ames, Roger and Rosemont, Henry. 1998. *The Analects of Confucius: A Philosophical Translation*. New York: Ballantine Books. (Includes the Chinese text, extensive introduction and bibliography, and notes upon the Dingzhou fragments of the *Analects*; follows a rather untraditional interpretation of the text.)

Brooks, E. Bruce and Brooks, A. Taeko. 1998. *The Original Analects: Sayings of Confucius and His Successors*. New York: Columbia University Press. (Follows the Brooks' radical reorganization of the text and includes the Brooks' own commentary on individual passages; the translation is at times awkward, but is perhaps the most precise and scholarly one available in English.)

Dawson, Raymond. 1993. *Confucius: The Analects*. Oxford: Oxford University Press. (Very solid, traditionally oriented translation, but with little annotation.)

Huang, Chichung. 1997. *The Analects of Confucius*. New York: Oxford University Press. (One of the few translations to provide some traditional commentary and alternate readings of passages [in the form of footnotes]. Also seems to be based on Cheng Shude's edition of the text; often follows the Han commentators, but sometimes adopts Zhu Xi's readings, all without attribution.)

Lau, D.C. 1992. *Confucius: The Analects*. New York: Penguin Books. (The classic and most commonly read translation, originally published in 1979; generally follows Zhu Xi's interpretation without attribution. Second edition [published by Chinese University of Hong Kong in 2001] includes Chinese text.)

Legge, James. 1991a. *Confucian Analects*. Taipei: SMC Publishing. (Reprint of Legge's classic translation, originally published in 1893; includes Legge's own helpful commentary and some citations from traditional commentators, especially Zhu Xi.)

Leys, Simon (a.k.a. Pierre Ryckmans). 1997. *The Analects of Confucius*. New York: W.W. Norton & Company. (An elaborated version of Ryckmans's 1987 French translation of the *Analects* [published by Gallimard], with additional notes aimed at the English-language reader. Very fresh and original in style, although occasionally at the expense of literalness; helpful, though sometimes somewhat idiosyncratic, annotation.)

Soothill, William. 1910. *The Analects of Confucius*. Yokohama: Fukuin Printing Company. (Contains extensive comments from the translator, as well as Zhu Xi's commentary more or less in its entirety [in both Chinese and English].)

277

Waley, Arthur. 1989. *The Analects of Confucius*. New York: Vintage Books. (Originally published in 1938, this is perhaps the most smooth and literary of *Analects* translations, with excellent notes; generally eschews Zhu Xi and follows the pre-Tang commentators.)

Translations of Other Early Chinese Texts Cited in Commentary and Appendices

Graham, A.C. 1990. *The Book of Lieh-tzu: A Classic of Tao*. New York: Columbia University Press. (Translation of the *Liezi*.)

Hightower, James. 1952. *Han Shih Wai Chuan: Han Ying's Illustrations of the Didactic Applications of the* Classic of Songs. Cambridge, MA: Harvard University Press. (Translation of the *Exoteric Commentary*.)

Ivanhoe, P.J. 2002. *The Daodejing of Laozi*. New York: Seven Bridges Press.

Karlgren, Bernhard. 1950a. *The Book of Documents*. Göteborg: Elanders.

——. 1950b. *The Book of Odes*. Stockholm: Museum of Far Eastern Antiquities.

Knoblock, John. 1988–1994. *Xunzi: A Translation and Study of the Complete Works*. 3 vols. Stanford: Stanford University Press. (1988: vol. 1; 1990: vol. 2; 1994: vol. 3.)

Knoblock, John and Riegel, Jeffrey. 2000. *The Annals of Lü Buwei*. Stanford, CA: Stanford University Press.

Lau, D.C. 1963. *Lao-tzu: Tao Te Ching*. New York: Penguin. (Translation of the *Laozi*.)

——. 1970. *Mencius*. New York: Penguin.

Legge, James. 1967. *Li Chi: Book of Rites*. 2 vols. New York: University Books. (Translation of the *Record of Ritual*, originally published in 1885.)

——. 1991b. *The Shoo King (The Chinese Classics, vol. III)*. Taipei: SMC Publishing. (Translation of the *Book of Documents*, originally published in 1865.)

——. 1991c. *The She King (The Chinese Classics, vol. IV)*. Taipei: SMC Publishing. (Translation of the *Book of Odes*, originally published in 1871.)

——. 1991d. *The Ch'un Ts'ew with the Tso Chuen (The Chinese Classics, vol. V)*. Taipei: SMC Publishing. (Translation of the *Annals* and *Zuo Commentary*, originally published in 1872.)

Liao, W.K. 1959. *The Complete Works of Han Fei tzu: A Classic of Chinese Political Science*. 2 vols. London: A. Probsthian.

Mei, Yi-Pao. 1980. *The Works of Motze*. Taipei: Wen chih ch'u pan shê. (Translation of the *Mozi*.)

O'Hara, Albert. 1981. *The Position of Women in Early China According to the Lie nu chuan*. Westport, CT: Hyperion Press. (Translation of *Biographies of Exemplary Women*.)

Rickett, Allyn. 1985. *Guanzi: Political, Economic, and Philosophical Essays from Early China*. 2 vols. Princeton, NJ: Princeton University Press.

Shaughnessy, Edward. 1996. *I Ching: The Classic of Changes*. New York: Ballantine. (Translation of a version of the *Book of Changes* unearthed in 1973.)

Waley, Arthur. 1960. *The Book of Songs*. New York: Grove Press. (Translation of the *Book of Odes*.)

Watson, Burton. 1968. *The Complete Works of Chuang Tzu*. New York: Columbia University Press. (Translation of the *Zhuangzi*.)

Wilhelm, Richard and Baynes, Cary. 1950. *The I Ching or Book of Changes*. Princeton, NJ: Bollingen.

Brief Selection of Secondary Scholarship

Dawson, Raymond. 1981. *Confucius*. New York: Hill and Wang. (Short introduction to Confucius, the *Analects*, and Confucianism in Chinese culture.)

Fung Yu-lan. 1952. *A History of Chinese Philosophy*. 2 vols. Princeton, NJ: Princeton University Press. (Standard account of history of Chinese thought, from earliest times up to the 20th century.)

Graham, A.C. 1989. *Disputers of the Tao: Philosophical Argument in Ancient China*. LaSalle, Il: Open Court. (An excellent general introduction to early Chinese thought, with a chapter devoted to Confucius.)

Ivanhoe, P.J. 2000. *Confucian Moral Self Cultivation*, Second Edition. Indianapolis: Hackett Publishing Company. (Excellent short, clear introduction to the thought of Confucius, Mencius, Xunzi, Zhu Xi, Wang Yangming, and Dai Zhen.)

Loewe, Michael., ed. 1993. *Early Chinese Texts: A Bibliographical Guide*. Berkeley, CA: Institute of East Asian Studies. (Standard reference work for early Chinese texts.)

Loewe, Michael and Shaughnessy, Edward, eds. 1999. *The Cambridge History of Ancient China: From the Origins of Civilization to 221 B.C.* Cambridge: University of Cambridge Press. (Collection of essays on early Chinese history up until the Qin unification.)

Munro, Donald. 1969. *The Concept of Man in Early China*. Stanford, CA: Stanford University Press. (Discussion of early Chinese conceptions of the self.)

Schaberg, David. 2001. "'Sell it! Sell it!' Recent Translations of *Lunyu*." *Chinese Literature: Essays, Articles, Reviews* 23: 115–39. (Comparative reviews of Ames and Rosemont, Lau, Dawson, Leys, Huang, Hinton, and Brooks and Brooks.)

Schwartz, Benjamin. 1985. *The World of Thought in Ancient China*. Cambridge: Harvard University Press. (Classic introduction to early Chinese thought, with a chapter devoted to Confucius.)

Van Norden, Bryan, ed. 2002. *Confucius and the* Analects: *New Essays*. New York: Oxford University Press. (Wide-ranging anthology on various aspects of the *Analects*.)

2a. Justice is Confucius being a virtous gentleman. (2.3)(7.3)(8.1)
(12.19)(14.42)(15.5) The educated and enlightened will disagree
on what is justice. Therefore, they will differ in making
rules. But b/c it's a democratic debate they will have
to come to a compromise that addresses everyones
needs The ignorent and enlighted will have to come up
with some common ground in order to live a more
peaceful life. Or like socrates puts it the enlighted will
have more power of the ignorant people.

- True wisdom is when one knows they don't know everything
this is why Secrets thinks people ignorant. (108)

* A just society has laws everyone must follow, regardless
of class. Within this society you take part in the
job that makes you happy and do not envy others.

Confucius idea on Justice
- Yes Confucian ideals have to do with respecting the ansectore
and not controlling each other but rather allowing
people to learn and educate each other.

- While in the Republic the guardians are seen as the
smartest and therefor determine everything that will
happen to the producers. Confucius claims that people must
be educated (2.17)(6.22) while Plato states that only
guardians need education. (401-404) The guardians are
able to determine everyones role in the society & whether
or not they belong with the producers or as guardians.
Yes Confucius would say ungentlemenly.

3. Socrates anger (375c, 411c) Confucius (2.18, 6.3, 8.13)
* Confucius would claim that having emotions like grief
  and anger is not good b/c it would distract people
  from being more righteous.
* Plato is afraid of emotions he believes that you must
  control others emotions that is why he put restrictions
  on music and other things. He fears it will make
  society more dangerous.
* Confucius would disagree with anger and be okay
  with grief. Confucius heavily believes in the importance
  of filial piety which has to do with respecting so having
  emotions are not seen as poorly but rather should relate
  to good and making society a better place. (387b)
* However Confucius would believe that education is important
  therefore poetry is. Socretry is against the innovation of
  poetry. Socrates does not want poetry to cause rebellion.
  New poetry is not allowed to producers b/c know one ones
  how they'll react.
* 590c Socrates says people should be lied to that they are
  assigned to each job in the class. (400 protects education to
                    (rulers.)